AMERICA
AT WAR

AMERICA AT WAR

Concise Histories of U.S. Military Conflicts
from Lexington to Afghanistan

TERENCE T. FINN

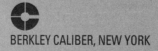

BERKLEY CALIBER, NEW YORK

THE BERKLEY PUBLISHING GROUP
Published by the Penguin Group
Penguin Group (USA) LLC
375 Hudson Street, New York, New York 10014, USA

USA • Canada • UK • Ireland • Australia • New Zealand • India • South Africa • China

penguin.com

A Penguin Random House Company

This book is an original publication of The Berkley Publishing Group.

Library of Congress Cataloging-in-Publication Data

Finn, Terence T.
America at war : concise histories of U.S. military conflicts from Lexington to Afghanistan /
Terence T. Finn.
p. cm.
ISBN 978-0-425-26858-2
1. United States—History, Military.   I. Title.
E181.F48   2014
355.00973—dc23
2013032320

PUBLISHING HISTORY
Berkley Caliber trade paperback edition / January 2014

PRINTED IN THE UNITED STATES OF AMERICA

10 9 8 7 6 5 4 3 2 1

Cover design by Jason Gill.
Interior maps by Eureka Cartography, Berkeley, CA.
Interior text design by Laura K. Corless.
Title page art © iStockphoto.com/pixhook.

To JMP, with my love

Running a war seems to consist in making plans and then ensuring that all those destined to carry it out don't quarrel with each other instead of the enemy.

—FIELD MARSHAL LORD ALANBROOKE
War Diaries 1939–1945

Yet the experiences of these masses will have taught the United States for the future that the business of war cannot be learnt in a few months, and that in a crisis lack of this experience costs streams of blood.

—FIELD MARSHAL VON HINDENBURG
The Great War

War, moreover, displays as do few other undertakings the grim and the great in human nature. It produces death and destruction while generating innovation in organization, technology, ethics, and law. It unleashes cruelty and exposes cowardice while inspiring camaraderie and courage. It produces regimentation, obedience, and a concentration on self-preservation even as it cultivates leadership, instills a sense of duty, and honors principles worth dying for.

—PETER BERKOWITZ
The Wall Street Journal

CONTENTS

FOREWORD

War is a nasty business. As one who has seen combat in several wars, I can say that with certainty. Yet despite the death and destruction it brings—even when fought for worthwhile reasons—war has been a constant in mankind's journey through time.

Certainly that is true in America's case. The history of the United States reveals armed conflict to be a significant presence, a theme throughout. Indeed, our country was established by musket and cannon. In 1776 men died so that a new and free nation might come to be. Let's remember that before George Washington became president of the United States, he was commander of the Continental Army, a general leading troops into battle.

Like all generals that followed, Washington understood that commanding an army in the field was in part a management job. Soldiers had to be recruited, trained, and equipped, and then deployed. A plan of battle needed to be devised, then executed, and invariably adjusted, during all of which time supplies had to flow continuously to the troops. Of course, setbacks had to be endured, and once victory had been achieved, the troops had to be kept productively occupied. Moreover, throughout the campaign, allies needed to be accommodated and political leaders informed such that they remained confident of success. None of this was, or is, easy. What's remarkable is that over time the United States has had extremely capable field commanders. Some are well known. Ulysses S. Grant and George Patton come to mind. Others less so. Daniel Morgan, George Meade, and

William Simpson are three who led Americans into battle without becoming household names.

If one wishes to understand American history, knowledge of our country's military past is essential. *America at War* provides such knowledge. Well researched and remarkably complete, the book tells what happened and why in the twelve major wars the United States has fought. I believe this book should be essential reading for students of U.S. history and for military officers around the world.

Throughout our nation's history there have been memorable moments on the fields of battle: Winfield Scott's assault on Mexican troops at the Convent of San Mateo, Joshua Chamberlain's bayonet charge down Little Round Top in 1863, the Americans at Utah and Omaha Beaches in 1944, the U.S. Air Cavalry at the Ia Drang Valley in Vietnam, and the Thunder Run of American armored units through Baghdad in 2003. All of these, and more, receive proper attention in Terence Finn's book.

The author also gives appropriate attention to my sister services, the U.S. Navy and the United States Air Force. His book covers the rich heritage of naval combat in the War of 1812, notes the little-noticed contribution of American sailors in the First World War, emphasizes the victories at sea in the second great war, and, appropriately, makes mention of the navy's contributions to the Coalition's success in removing Saddam Hussein's troops from Kuwait in 1991.

America at War also describes the role the air force has played in combat around the world. Noteworthy in my mind, and Finn's, are the clashes of F-86s against MiG-15s in the skies above the Yalu River during the Korean War, usually resulting in American victories. Noteworthy too—if less successful—were the F-105 strikes against targets in and around Hanoi during the Vietnam War.

I realize I've not mentioned the United States Marines, so let me simply say that they are a magnificent combat organization and that their exploits receive due mention in *America at War*. Their role in the march to Baghdad during the Iraq War is one truly memorable example of their skill as warriors.

Of course, despite a preponderance of success, Americans in battle on occasion have fared poorly. Here too Finn points out the results, and appropriately so. He mentions the failure at Queenstown Heights in 1812, Hooker's dismal showing at Chancellorsville, and others, including what must rank as the worst performance of any American field army: the rout of U.S. forces in Korea by the Chinese in 1950.

Then too there are moments in our military history that can be deemed obscure, worthy of mention if only to reveal the scope and depth of combat American style. The author mentions several in *America at War*. My two favorites are: (1) the use by the navy of a single fourteen-inch battleship gun mounted on a railroad car to serve well inland as heavy artillery during World War I, and (2) the amphibious landings in Southern France— Operation Dragoon—by the U.S. Seventh Army just two months after the Allied invasion of Normandy in June of 1944. These episodes, and others like them, are rarely recalled, yet they too are part of our military heritage.

Educators today often lament the lack of knowledge of history among Americans, particularly young Americans. They, teachers and scholars, want our citizens to be more aware of the individuals and events that comprise the American experience. In politics, economics, diplomacy, art, and science the study of America's past is an intellectually rewarding endeavor, relevant to understanding where our country is today and where it might be headed. I would add that part of the past that needs also to be examined is the story of America's fighting men and women. A good place to start would be this admirable work.

General Barry R. McCaffrey, U.S. Army (Ret.)
Alexandria, Virginia
June 1, 2013

PREFACE

Not surprisingly, American history is multidimensional. There is diplomatic history, literary history, political history, economic history, and so on. There is also military history, a subset that, in fact, receives considerable attention in the publishing world. While scholars of the military arts produce solid works, popular histories tend to focus on specific battles (such as Gettysburg) or certain campaigns (such as the one in Normandy in 1944) or individual wars (such as the War of 1812). What seems to be missing are books that cover in one volume the major wars the United States has fought.

Hence, this book.

By providing brief narrative accounts of these conflicts, this book's goal is to enable the reader to understand what happened in each war and why the battles at such places as Saratoga, Antietam, Manila Bay, and Midway were pivotal events in the history of the United States. These battles, as well as others, affected the outcome of conflicts which, in turn, shaped the political and economic landscape America confronted once the shooting ceased. The outcomes and the circumstances by which they came about matter—not just because the world became a different place. The outcomes also matter because the violence inherent in warfare results in the loss of life, often in great numbers.

In recounting events that occurred, each chapter in this book speaks to death and destruction. In some cases, casualties from a battle can only be approximate. In other cases the number can be precisely stated. In both instances, the calculations too easily become simply statistics. The reckoning of each individual lost represents a human being who, had he or she survived, might have brought hope, kindness, love, or security to those left behind.

Most certainly war is a human tragedy. Yet, given its frequency, war appears to be part and parcel of the American journey. Sometimes, despite the killing, armed conflict is conducted for a noble or worthwhile purpose, with results that make the world a safer or more just place in which to live. This author would contend that most of the wars engaged in by the United States seem to fit in this category.

The book has twelve chapters. Why these wars and not others? The twelve were selected because they met the following criteria: (1) the war needed to be large in scale, involve substantial combat, and engage a considerable portion of U.S. armed forces; (2) the enemy needed to be a sovereign state (here, Afghanistan is perhaps the exception); (3) the war had to involve the United States of America when constituted as a nation; and (4) the outcome, whether the United States won or lost, had to be significant in terms of influencing America's future.

Employing these criteria, the 1898 war with Spain makes the list. So does the First World War and the war in Vietnam. The Cold War, the French and Indian War, and the incursion into Panama do not. By these criteria, starting in 1775, the United States has gone to war twelve times.

The book provides a brief, easy-to-read account of each of the twelve wars. The chapters may serve to refresh one's awareness of what happened or may offer an introduction to the conflict. In either case, the hope is to provide the reader who may or may not be familiar with American history with an understanding of what took place on those occasions when the United States went to war.

To assist the reader, maps drawn by Stace Wright of Eureka Cartography are provided at the beginning of each chapter. Given that war has a geographic dimension, the maps are included in order to help the reader follow the flow of events.

The accounts of the wars related in this book are neither revisionist in character nor radically new in interpretation. Rather, they are consistent with traditional scholarship, providing narratives with which most historians would concur. If standard fare, the accounts nevertheless hopefully convey much of the drama that unfolded once U.S. citizens answered their country's call to arms.

Should the reader seek more knowledge about and greater insight into the conflicts described herein, a list of "Selected Readings" is provided. Organized by chapter, these additional works are worth examining. All are recommended. Together they form the research on which this book is based.

Producing *America at War* required more than a manuscript. Essential to the endeavor were the considerable talents of my Berkley Publishing Group editor, Natalee Rosenstein, and editorial assistant, Robin Barletta. For their patience and hard work I am most grateful. The artistic contributions of Jason Gill (cover) and Laura K. Corless (interior design) speak for themselves. This book would not be complete without the maps expertly created by Stace Wright of Eureka Cartography. Nor would it read as well were it not for the skill of Marla Handelman. For his counsel and support, I thank my friend Richard Kalter. My agent, Robert G. Diforio, who like several of the generals in the narratives that follow, is an expert in his craft. I am indeed appreciative for his guidance and tenacity.

The origin of *America at War* lies with my novel *To Begin Again*. That story takes place during the Korean War. It is about a university professor who, recalled to the air force in 1951, goes to Korea, where he flies F-86 Sabre jets in combat high above the Yalu River. In order to provide context with which to better understand and appreciate the events recounted in the novel, the book begins with a summary of the war. As she read and typed the piece into her computer, my wife, Joyce Purcell, concluded that the summary was most helpful. She then suggested a book containing similar narratives that covered all the major wars fought by the United States. Such a book, she said, might well be read by those who do not study history but have a genuine interest in reading a concise account of one or more of America's wars from 1775 to the present. Her suggestion—as well as her editing skills and encouragement—caused this book to be written.

1

INDEPENDENCE

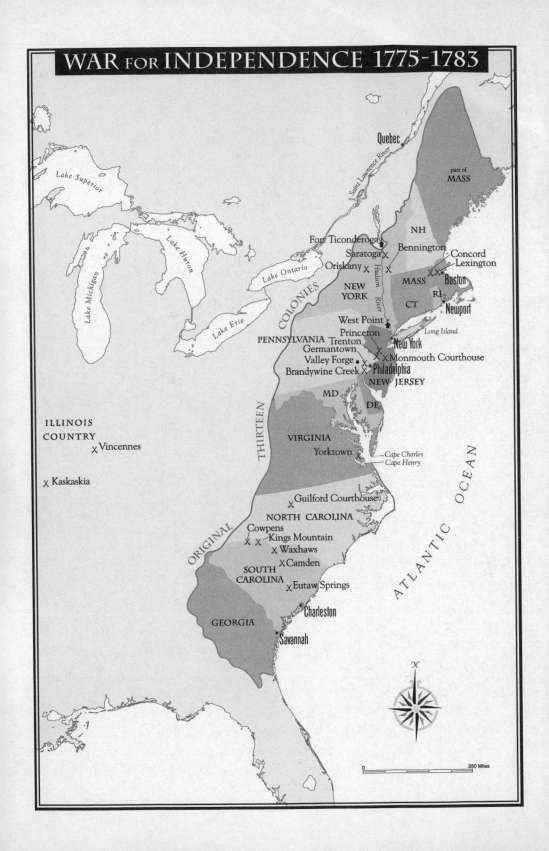

WAR FOR INDEPENDENCE 1775-1783

Lake Superior

Lake Michigan

Lake Huron

Lake Erie

Lake Ontario

Saint Lawrence River

Quebec

part of
MASS

NH

Fort Ticonderoga

Bennington

Concord
Lexington

Saratoga

Oriskany

MASS

Boston

Hudson River

NEW
YORK

CT

RI

Newport

THIRTEEN COLONIES

West Point

Long Island

Princeton

PENNSYLVANIA

Trenton

New York

Germantown

Monmouth Courthouse

Valley Forge

Brandywine Creek

Philadelphia

NEW JERSEY

MD

DE

ILLINOIS
COUNTRY

Vincennes

VIRGINIA

Yorktown

Cape Charles
Cape Henry

Kaskaskia

ATLANTIC OCEAN

Guilford Courthouse

ORIGINAL

NORTH CAROLINA

Cowpens

Kings Mountain

Waxhaws

Camden

SOUTH
CAROLINA

Eutaw Springs

Charleston

GEORGIA

Savannah

0   250 Miles

1775–1783

Of the sixteen thousand residents in Boston in 1775 many were loyal to the Crown. However, many were not, and of these, more than a few had—in word and deed—committed acts of violence against British officials. Tensions in the city were high, and by April, Boston was a tinderbox ready to explode. So too was the countryside.

Lieutenant General Thomas Gage was the commander in chief of the British army in America and also, in response to the dumping of tea in Boston Harbor, military governor of Massachusetts. He had already acted. In September 1774 Gage had sent troops to Somerville to retrieve cannons and gunpowder belonging to the king. Now he dispatched a large force to Concord, a village eighteen miles outside of Boston. Its mission was to seize arms stored there by the colonists. By doing so the general hoped to demonstrate British resolve and douse the flames of rebellion.

His troops marched first to Lexington, where, on the village green, a small number of Americans had assembled, armed, as were the British soldiers, with muskets. Shots were exchanged—who fired the first shot is unknown—and eight of the Americans were killed. Ten were wounded. The rest, all local "Minutemen," fled. The British then proceeded to Concord, where, on a wooden bridge north of the town, American resistance was more vigorous. The result was numerous casualties, on both sides. In response the British troops retreated to Boston, harassed along the way by Americans hiding behind trees and fences. Once safely back, the troops—

Gage had sent seven hundred men—counted the cost: 247 British soldiers had been killed or wounded.

Events then proceeded quickly. Connecticut, New Hampshire, and Rhode Island sent militia to aid their Massachusetts brethren. Hence Boston soon became surrounded by well over twelve thousand colonial soldiers. Gage received five thousand additional troops, including three generals destined to play key roles in the coming wars: William Howe, Henry Clinton, and John Burgoyne. The Continental Congress adopted the New England militia as the Continental army and directed Pennsylvania, Maryland, and Virginia to send soldiers to Boston, which they did. And, to link the Southern colonies to what had been a New England rebellion, the Congress on June 15, 1775, appointed a Virginia aristocrat with limited military experience as commander in chief of all American forces. His name was George Washington.

On July 3, Washington took command of the newly established Continental army, in a field in Cambridge not far from Harvard College. But already a fierce battle had taken place.

On the night of June 16, 1775, the New Englanders fortified Breed's Hill on the Charlestown peninsula, across from Boston proper. The next day Gage attacked. His strategy was not subtle. He ordered a direct assault up the hill. Gage, Howe, and Clinton wanted to show the rebels the unstoppable might of Britain's regular army. They did so though the first two attacks were repulsed. The third succeeded in part because the Americans ran short of ammunition. Toward the end of the battle, fighting occurred on Bunker Hill, elevated land to the north. By nightfall, the British controlled the peninsula. But they had paid a steep price: 27 of their officers had been killed, with 63 wounded. Casualties among ordinary soldiers were staggering: 226 killed and 828 wounded. The Americans—all their troops were New England militia—had more than 400 killed or wounded. Despite the outcome, the rebels claimed victory. They had met the best England could throw at them and done well. And in a scenario that would be replayed again and again, they had lived to fight another day.

The shots fired at Lexington, Concord, and Breed's Hill were significant. They marked the beginning of an eight-year conflict from which a new nation would emerge, but only after the ground had absorbed much British, German, Canadian, French, and American blood.

How had it come to this? How had the Americans arrived at the point of such opposition to British rule that muskets and bayonets had become the vehicles of dissent? After all, the colonists under George III had enjoyed a good life. The thirteen Atlantic coastal colonies were economically prosperous. They were, essentially, self-governing. They enjoyed privileged access to Britain's mercantile system. On the high seas their ships were safeguarded by the Royal Navy. On land, the king's army, in defeating the French and their Native American allies, had removed external threats. And in the matter of taxation, the Americans paid considerably less in taxes per capita than their fellow subjects in England.

Yet the colonists revolted, or at least a large number of them did. Why? Essentially, they objected to British interference in their lives. In communities established to secure religious freedom, they resented one form of worship being sanctioned by the state. In a society that traditionally distrusted standing armies, they disliked the presence of soldiers in their homes and towns. In colonies where land was available to any free and enterprising man, they objected to a Royal Decree ("the Proclamation Line") that, in setting the inland boundaries of the colonies, forbade settlers from moving west beyond the Appalachian mountains into lands reserved for Native Americans. And regarding London's insistence on taxing the colonists, they opposed revenue-raising measures in which they had no say.

Boston was not the only battleground in 1775. In late fall the Americans invaded Canada. In doing so, they hoped to forestall British attacks from the north, spread mischief among the French-speaking inhabitants, and if possible, annex their northern neighbor as the fourteenth colony. The invasion itself was two-pronged. One force, led by Generals Philip Schuyler and Richard Montgomery, proceeded via Lake Champlain and Montreal. Another, with Benedict Arnold in command, trekked through the Maine woods. Their joint objective was Quebec, for whoever held that city controlled Canada. Unfortunately for the Americans winter had arrived by the time they reached Quebec. The invaders were woefully short of food, clothing, military supplies, and men, many of whom had deserted or died.

Moreover, French citizens remained loyal to Britain, and the king's commander, Sir Guy Carleton, was more than equal to his task.

On the last day of December 1775, Montgomery and Arnold—an ill Schuyler having returned to New York—led a desperate, nighttime attack on the city. It failed. Quebec, and therefore Canada, remained in British hands. Montgomery was killed and Arnold, with his ragtag force, departed, thoroughly dispirited and decisively defeated.

By the spring of 1776 Gage had been recalled and Howe was now commander of British forces in Boston. These numbered approximately eight thousand men. Washington, laying siege to the city, had almost twice as many. What he did not have, and needed, were cannons. Until Colonel Henry Knox, later his commander of artillery, went to Fort Ticonderoga, located at the northern end of Lake George, and, in a remarkable feat, dragged fifty-eight cannons three hundred miles through the mountains to Boston. Washington placed these on Dorchester Heights, overlooking the city. Howe's position became vulnerable and he evacuated Boston on March 17. The Americans legitimately could claim a major victory.

Four months later, on July 4, they declared their independence. The day before the Americans signed their historic document, the British, determined to restore the Crown's authority, landed thirty thousand troops on Staten Island in New York. Conveyed in 170 ships, the force—under the command of William Howe—constituted the largest military expedition England had ever sent abroad. Included among the soldiers were several regiments of German mercenaries.

Expecting an attack on New York, Washington had brought his army south. He occupied the city, some twenty-five thousand people living mostly at the tip of Manhattan, and fortified Brooklyn Heights across the East River on Long Island, where, as on Dorchester Heights, artillery could be decisive.

Howe struck on August 22, 1776. He landed troops in Brooklyn and, in a major battle, defeated his opponents, inflicting well over one thousand casualties and taking an equal number of prisoners, while losing only four hundred men. Washington, however, avoided capture. With his remaining forces he retreated to Manhattan, skillfully executing a nighttime crossing of the river that separates the two islands.

Urged to follow up on this victory quickly, Howe hesitated. He waited until September 13 before attacking again. This time British troops crossed the East River and landed at Kips Bay (at the site of the present 34th Street). They soon controlled Manhattan, save one fort. A month later Howe sent them across Long Island Sound to Throgs Neck, where, in late October, a fierce battle took place at White Plains. Who won is debatable, but regardless, the British turned south and in mid-November captured the remaining fort on Manhattan. Its loss was catastrophic for the Americans, who had more than two thousand men killed or taken prisoner while handing over vast amounts of supplies to the English. Afterward, Washington, who had been outgeneraled by Howe, moved the remnants of his army north, crossing the Hudson River at Peekskill, and then retreated south into New Jersey. Late in the year, pursued by the British, he crossed the Delaware River into Pennsylvania, with his army and the Continental cause close to collapse.

Howe was knighted for his successful campaign in New York. As the weather turned cold, he established a series of outposts in New Jersey to keep an eye on Washington. Confident he could end the rebellion in the spring, Sir William and his army settled into comfortable winter quarters in Manhattan.

Encamped by the Delaware, Washington's army lacked shelter, food, and clothing, and it soon would lack men as many enlistments were due to expire the first day of January. Bleak as the situation was, it was made worse by the winter weather that brought snow to the land and ice to the river.

Most generals would have given up or tried simply to survive. Not George Washington. He devised an offensive operation daring in the extreme. Three columns of troops would cross the river at night and attack British outposts, and they would do so the day after Christmas, when the enemy, Hessian mercenaries, could be expected to be resting after an evening of revelry.

On Christmas Day 1776, the Continental army moved out. Two of the columns failed to cross a Delaware River that was clogged with chunks of ice. But, thanks to Colonel John Glover's Marblehead, Massachusetts, men—who had transported Washington and his men across the East River in the retreat from Brooklyn—and to Washington himself, the main column, some twenty-five hundred troops, made the crossing. They then marched eight miles in the bitter cold, many without shoes, to the town of Trenton, where fourteen hundred Hessian soldiers were stationed. Washington attacked, and in less than ninety minutes, he crushed the Germans. They suffered 22 dead, 98 wounded, and had 918 men taken prisoner. The Americans had fewer than 10 killed or wounded.

Howe responded to this unexpected setback by dispatching Charles, Lord Cornwallis, to deal with Washington. With five thousand British soldiers, Cornwallis marched south from New York and cornered his opponent near Trenton, leaving a rearguard at Princeton. On January 2, his position established to his satisfaction, Cornwallis waited until morning, when he hoped and expected to finish off Washington and his little army.

But, once again, George Washington did not stay put. Unbeknownst to the British, he slipped away at night and in the morning surprised those redcoats left behind at Princeton. The result was a battle the Continental army clearly won, small in scale perhaps, but a victory nonetheless.

In less than ten days, at a time of year when armies traditionally did not campaign, Washington in two bold strokes rescued the Continental cause. What had become a failing enterprise was revitalized. The successes at Trenton and Princeton embarrassed the British, gave hope to the American army, and restored faith in Washington's leadership. But most important of all, the victories meant that the war for independence, if not yet won, most certainly had not been lost.

By the spring General Howe was ready to renew the war. He chose to target Philadelphia, with forty thousand inhabitants the largest city in the colonies, and the de facto capital of the Americans. Choosing to travel by sea rather than marching through New Jersey, he and his eighteen thousand men sailed from New York and in August disembarked at the northern tip of the Chesapeake Bay, some forty miles from the Pennsylvania city. Roughly halfway between lay Brandywine Creek. There, Washington moved his troops into position to defend Philadelphia, and the two armies met. The Continental army fought well, but Howe's generalship and the redcoats' skill were evident. The British prevailed.

Washington retired in good order and encamped northwest of the city.

Howe placed his troops nearby, in Germantown, and directed Cornwallis, with four thousand soldiers, to occupy the city, which he did, entering Philadelphia on September 26, 1777. Lord Charles and his men were warmly welcomed. Philadelphia may have hosted the Continental Congress (which fled to York), but its citizens, at least many of them, were loyalists at heart.

Once again, Washington rallied his men, and to Howe's surprise, they attacked the British troops stationed in Germantown. The battle took place on October 4. Washington's plan was complicated and confusion reigned, with, at one point, Continental soldiers firing on one another. The British rallied and, in the end, won the battle. The Americans had about one thousand men killed or wounded; the British half that number.

By the end of 1777 the two principal cities in America, New York and Philadelphia, were under British control. The Continental army had been beaten at both Brandywine and Germantown. And many Americans, from Georgia to New Hampshire, had remained loyal to the king. Thus Howe had reason to be pleased. But he was not. Sir William knew that up north, near Albany, disaster had struck: an entire British army had surrendered to the rebels.

John Burgoyne was a playwright, a member of parliament, and a man who enjoyed London society. He was also a major general in the British army. Lord George Germain was a politician, retired soldier, and a favorite of the king's who served in government as secretary of state for the American colonies. In this latter capacity he in essence directed the British war effort. Early in 1777, Burgoyne proposed to Germain a plan that would strike hard at the rebels and lead, he believed, to a successful conclusion of the war.

Burgoyne proposed that he lead an army south from Canada into New York. A smaller force would attack from the west, traveling east across the Mohawk Valley. At the same time Howe in Manhattan would launch a major attack up the Hudson. The three forces would converge at Albany and destroy the rebels. The resulting victory would isolate the New England colonies, enabling His Majesty's troops to deal separately and methodically with the other provinces. Moreover, when they saw a large British force achieve success in battle, those Americans still loyal to the king would rise in support, while those on the fence would swing to the British side.

The plan was not without merit, and it gained Germain's approval. Unfortunately for the British and for Burgoyne, its execution was to be flawed. An earlier attack from Canada in 1776 had failed due to winter weather and Benedict Arnold's vigorous defense at Valcour Island. Nevertheless, Burgoyne, promoted to lieutenant general, was confident his expedition would succeed.

In June 1777 his army began to move. It was composed of approximately seven thousand men and consisted of British regulars, German mercenaries, Canadian militia, and three hundred Native Americans, the latter to serve as scouts. Its artillery numbered 138 field pieces, and its excessively large number of supply wagons, according to one historian, carried "numerous ladies of high and low estate."

At first the expedition went well. The British secured Fort Ticonderoga in July and later defeated a small rebel force at Hubbardton. Then everything turned sour. Burgoyne chose to proceed through the forests rather than by water, causing a delay that gave the Americans time to react. Supplies began to run low. The Native American scouts proved unreliable. The force coming from the west was stopped in battles at Oriskany and Fort Stanwix. An effort by the Germans to secure much needed food and horses was crushed near Bennington. And, incredibly, Germain did not order Howe to march north to Albany (Sir William proceeded south to Philadelphia). So Burgoyne and his depleted force were left to fight alone.

During the War for Independence, American forces operated in three areas or departments. Washington commanded the main army and waged war primarily in Pennsylvania, New Jersey, and lower New York. A Northern Department and a separate Northern army carried on the fight in New England and upstate New York. The Southern Department operated in Virginia, the Carolinas, and Georgia. Although Washington was the Continental army's commander in chief, he did not appoint general officers. Congress did. It did so often with political parameters, as each colony demanded its share of brigadiers and major generals.

To command the Northern Department Congress first appointed Philip Schuyler, who, on his return from Canada, creditably organized Northern forces. In actual command of the Northern army was Major General Horatio Gates, ably assisted by Benedict Arnold, Benjamin Lincoln, and Daniel Morgan. Much was expected of Gates, the Continental army's first adjutant general. He did not disappoint. When Burgoyne finally arrived in the vicinity of Albany, Gates positioned his army to fight. In September the first battle took place at Freeman's Farm. The outcome was a draw with both sides sustaining substantial losses. The second battle occurred early in October at Bemis Heights, where, in large part due to Arnold's leadership, the British were defeated. Burgoyne then retreated toward Saratoga, where, surrounded by an army far larger than his and running out of supplies, he surrendered on October 17, 1777.

The capitulation by Burgoyne and his army had an effect far greater than simply the removal of a British army from the field, significant though that was. Freeman's Farm and Bemis Heights provided the French the opportunity to convince themselves that aiding the Americans would be advantageous to King Louis. As a monarchy France had little reason to support a revolt against a king. But assisting those who were fighting a traditional enemy, in this case, Great Britain, had much to recommend it.

So, early in 1778, the American colonies and the Kingdom of France signed a treaty under which the latter would provide the former with money, arms, and soldiers. Already, France surreptitiously had sent over the first two (as had the Dutch). Now soldiers came as well. In July 1780 four thousand well-trained, well-equipped French troops under the command of the Comte de Rochambeau arrived in America, disembarking at Newport, Rhode Island. One of the first steps taken by Rochambeau was to place his forces under the command of George Washington. Just as important to the American cause was the financial support France provided. During most of the conflict, the Continental Congress and its armies had little money. Moreover, the currency the Congress issued declined in value so that, more often than not, American generals in command lacked funds to pay their troops or purchase supplies. French money rectified this.

French assistance also was rendered on the high seas. France contributed to the military equation something the Americans neither had nor could have. That was a fleet capable of challenging the Royal Navy.

Three times a French fleet sailed to America. In July 1778, warships flying the fleur-de-lis appeared off New York and Newport. But their efforts were of little consequence and in November they departed. A year later a large naval force, in company with American infantry, attacked the British-held city of Savannah. The attack failed and many French sailors and marines were killed. So, again, the ships departed. The third expedition, a fleet under the command of the Comte de Grasse, entered the Chesapeake in 1781. Its efforts—to be explained later—would prove decisive.

Though it was small, the Americans did possess a navy. In October 1775, the Continental Congress approved the outfitting of several small warships, and one month later in Philadelphia, John Adams drafted "Rules for the Regulation of the Navy of the United Colonies." Earlier, George Washington had secured his own collection of vessels that attacked British supply ships. By 1777, when his "fleet" disbanded, the general's naval force had captured fifty-five prizes.

Late in 1775, the Congress authorized the construction of thirteen frigates (requiring that they be built in seven different colonies) and appointed the first officers of the Continental navy. Of the five first lieutenants so designated, the most senior was a Scotsman named John Paul Jones.

These frigates, and later additional vessels, achieved several successes. In 1776, for example, the Continental brig *Andrew Doria*, under the command of Captain Nicholas Biddle, took ten British ships during a four-month voyage. In 1777, Captain Lambert Wickes's brig *Reprisal* captured five prizes off the coasts of Spain and France. And, in 1778 John Paul Jones, now a captain, took the sloop *Ranger* to England, raiding its west coast and causing great alarm though little damage. Sixteen months later he engaged a British man-of-war that was escorting a convoy of forty-one ships. The ensuing battle was long and bloody. The result was a victory for Jones, who gained immense fame. However, the convoy escaped, and the British commander, having put up a spirited defense, was knighted by George III.

Yet, overall, despite these successes, the Continental navy did not accomplish much. During the years 1775–1783 its defeats far exceeded its victories. For example, of those thirteen frigates authorized in 1775, only seven got to sea and all were lost.

Where the Americans achieved considerable maritime success was with privateers. These were privately owned armed vessels. Because they sailed under official commissions issued by the colonial governments, they were not considered pirates. Privateers were a fact of life in the eighteenth and nineteenth centuries, and their employment was widespread. Most European nations sponsored them, and in France their captains often became national heroes.

Given that the American colonies were coastal entities, they had substantial maritime capabilities. Their citizens could build ships, raise crews, and sail the oceans. As privateers made large profits from successful cruises—they kept what they captured—incentives to sponsor and sail in such vessels were great. Hence, throughout the War for Independence, large numbers of American privateers, especially from New England, were active in Atlantic and Caribbean waters, hunting for unescorted British ships.

These privateers—there were some 440 of them by 1781—caused significant damage to England's vast maritime enterprise. How many British ships the American privateers captured is in dispute; the number lies somewhere between two hundred and four hundred. However, the cost to the Americans was not negligible. Sailors captured by the Royal Navy—and there were many—were imprisoned in hulks, rotting ships from which masts and guns had been removed. These were moored in British-controlled harbors. Conditions aboard the hulks were dreadful and many prisoners failed to survive.

Of course men died on land as well. The causes of death were many: disease, malnutrition, weather, medical ignorance, and British gunfire. All but the last were in evidence at Valley Forge, a nondescript piece of real estate twenty miles northwest of Philadelphia where, after the Battle of Germantown, Washington and his army spent the terrible winter of 1777–1778. Conditions in the American camp were dreadful. At times men ate their shoes. More than twenty-two hundred men did not survive. Beyond the loss of life the tragedy was that many of the supplies needed had been obtained but not delivered. Clothes, for example, were stored in a warehouse in Lancaster, Pennsylvania. What had occurred was the collapse of the army's supply system. Washington therefore appointed a new quartermaster general, Nathanael Greene, who, prior to his military service, had been a successful businessman. Greene spent the next two years improving the supply corps, which at one time employed more than three thousand men engaged in securing the means to clothe, house, and transport American soldiers.

Washington made another appointment that would change things for the better. In February 1778, there had appeared at Valley Forge a Prussian officer by the name of Friedrich Wilhelm Ludolf Gerhard Augustin von Steuben. Washington made him the officer in charge of training, and von Steuben, who knew his trade, built the Continental army into a highly professional force. In May Congress rewarded him with the rank of major general and made von Steuben the army's inspector general.

During the War for Independence the Continental Congress gave commissions to numerous Europeans who, like the Prussian drill master, had come to aid the American cause. Many, however, were dilettantes and contributed little. But a few made major contributions: Casimir Pulaski, a Pole, was a fearless cavalry leader. Johann deKalb was a senior commander in the South. And George Washington's favorite, the Marquis de Lafayette, a major general like von Steuben, commanded American troops in Rhode Island, New York, New Jersey, and Virginia.

By the spring of 1778 Washington and his much improved army were still at Valley Forge. But the British, who also had not moved, had made a major change. General Howe had resigned and returned to England. Sir William believed military success in the colonies required an additional thirty-five thousand troops, which he knew would not be forthcoming. So he declared the war unwinnable and departed. Lord Germain then had to find a new commander. He selected Sir Henry Clinton. A senior officer known to be personally brave yet prone to caution, Clinton had served as Howe's second-in-command. His military record was sound, despite having played a major role two years before in an unsuccessful effort to seize Charleston. So on March 21, 1778, Henry Clinton took control of the British army in America.

Almost immediately he was directed by Germain to send some of his troops to the West Indies and to Florida. With his army reduced in size Clinton decided to concentrate his forces in New York, evacuating Philadelphia on June 18. Washington promptly occupied the city and proceeded to pursue Clinton, who had left by land rather than by sea.

General Washington was looking for a fight, and at Monmouth Court House in New Jersey he found one. The Continental army attacked the British on June 28, and in a fierce engagement, both sides lost approximately 350 men. Clinton and his army survived and soon reached New York. Washington, aware that a decisive victory could have been achieved but wasn't, took solace in the solid performance of his von Steuben–trained regulars.

Too weak in numbers to challenge Clinton in New York, Washington dispatched part of his force to Rhode Island. There, under the command of Major General John Sullivan, they were to conduct a joint operation with French troops against British-held Newport. The French soldiers had been transported in ships commanded by the Comte d'Estaing. However, the arrival of a British fleet caused the French admiral to withdraw. A storm then damaged his vessels, and seeking repairs, he sailed away. Sullivan subsequently attacked on his own, but failed to dislodge the British.

He had greater success against Native Americans. In 1779 Washington asked Sullivan to lead an expedition into western Pennsylvania and New York, where Native Americans, in addition to siding with the British, had themselves conducted savage attacks on white settlers. Sullivan accepted the assignment and, with four thousand soldiers, set out to punish the Indians. This he accomplished. Villages were destroyed, food was seized and warriors killed, in part as retaliation for the massacres the Native Americans had committed at Wilkes-Barre and Cherry Hill. The enemy— and that is what Washington considered them to be—was dealt a serious blow.

Throughout the war state militia, Continental regulars, and ordinary farmers battled Native Americans in the colonies' Western frontiers. There was much bloodletting, and savagery was in evidence on both sides. The outcome was predictable. The resources of the Native Americans, both human and material, were substantially depleted.

One campaign in the West did not center around the native population. In 1778 and 1779 the Virginian George Rogers Clark led a small band of militia into what is now Illinois, Indiana, and Kentucky. His goal was to capture British outposts at Kaskaskia and Vincennes, which, after enduring much hardship, he did. Though small in size, Clark's victories were significant when four years later in Paris the boundaries of a new nation were drawn.

During 1779 three events of note took place: one at sea, one on land, and one far from the thirteen colonies. In June, in Madrid, Spain declared war against England, further enlarging the conflict. Britain, thereafter, had to fight two European powers in addition to contesting the American colonies. In September, French and American troops failed to seize Savannah, losing more than eight hundred men in the attempt, including Count Pulaski. In October, John Paul Jones, aboard the *Bonhomme Richard*, made himself legendary when in the middle of a bloody sea fight he responded to the British captain's call to surrender by proclaiming, "I have not yet begun to fight."

The battle at Monmouth Court House was the last major engagement in the North. Thereafter the focus of the conflict, from today's perspective, shifted to the South, except for one historic occurrence. That was the defection to the British of Benedict Arnold, one of the Americans' better known senior commanders. Totally unexpected, Arnold's action sent shock waves throughout the rebel cause. People everywhere were in disbelief. Why did he do it? The answer seems to be that he was in debt and angry over a perceived lack of recognition. He also may have thought the British were going to win. They rewarded him both with money and a commission in His Majesty's army. He then took command of loyalist troops and raided communities in Virginia, including Richmond. Arnold, of course, achieved immortality, but not of the kind he sought.

The year 1780 saw the fortunes of the Americans again become extremely low. Few battles had been won. Supplies for the armies were insufficient. The Continental currency was worthless. There were mutinies in Washington's army. Moreover, the winter of 1779–1780 was terrible, worse than at Valley Forge the previous year. And Arnold's treason took place that summer. But two battles in the South were of even greater impact, suggesting to the British that at last victory was within reach.

In May 1780 Major General Benjamin Lincoln surrendered Charleston to a large force led by Sir Henry Clinton, who had sailed from New York to South Carolina. The British wanted the town as a base of operations in the South, an area they expected to be supportive of the Crown. Lincoln lost not only the town, he also turned over five thousand men, practically the entire army of the Southern Department. To make matters worse a company of Virginia militia moving north after the surrender were cornered at Waxhaw, close to the border with North Carolina. After a brief fight, the Americans asked for quarter—that is, they surrendered. Quarter, however, was denied. Banastre Tarleton, the British commander, had his men kill all of the rebels.

The Waxhaw Massacre reflected the brutality of the war in the South, where the conflict was as much a civil war among Americans as it was a conflict against the British. Tarleton's men were American loyalists.

Another engagement in the South exemplifies this internal aspect of the conflict. At King's Mountain in western Carolina a British officer, Patrick Ferguson, and his nine hundred men found themselves surrounded and outnumbered by an American force of backwoodsmen. When the October battle concluded, Ferguson and two hundred of his men were dead. Many others were wounded and seven hundred were prisoners. Notably, except for Ferguson and a few of his officers, everyone who participated in the battle were Americans. No British redcoats were there.

The second event in 1780 favorable to the king's cause occurred at Camden, South Carolina, in mid-August. Two months before, the Continental Congress had appointed Horatio Gates in command of the army in the South. Much was expected of this hero of Saratoga. Gates, confident to a fault, rushed into battle. The result was a crushing defeat, with the American general scampering three miles to personal safety. Gates thus destroyed his reputation as well as his army.

With Gates in disgrace, a new commander of the Southern Department was needed. The choice lay with the Congress in Philadelphia, and it selected Washington's quartermaster general, Nathanael Greene. A better selection could not have been made. Somehow Greene rebuilt the army and then engaged the British in several battles. That he won none of these did not matter. He fought well, kept his army intact, and wore down the enemy. They were now commanded by Lord Cornwallis, Clinton having returned to New York.

Nathanael Greene rode into Charlotte, North Carolina, then a town of some twenty houses and two main streets, late in December 1780. The army he commanded numbered approximately fifteen hundred men. About one-third of these were reliable Continentals, the rest militia. One of his first steps was to divide his force in two, an action contrary to standard military doctrine. He remained in command of one element. The other he gave to Daniel Morgan.

Morgan was a rugged frontiersman who had fought well at Quebec and Saratoga. Now a brigadier general, he took his small force to western Carolina, to a spot where stray cows often assembled. Chasing him was Banastre Tarleton. Morgan devised unconventional tactics, placing his militia troops in the front line with his Continentals well to the rear. This was risky as militia in the past had run from bayonet-equipped redcoats. Morgan asked his militiamen to fire but twice and then retire. He placed a few sharpshooters among them and awaited Tarleton's arrival. He expected Tarleton to attack, suffer some initial losses, then, smelling victory, rush after the retreating militia headlong into the volleys of Morgan's Continental regulars. Essentially, that is what happened. The American victory at Cowpens—it took place on January 19, 1781—cost Morgan twelve dead and sixty wounded. In defeat Tarleton had thirty-nine officers killed, more than twice that number of men slain, and some six hundred soldiers taken prisoner. It could have been worse. Morgan forbade his men to take "Tarleton's quarter" as some wished to do.

Morgan's victory at Cowpens is considered a minor military classic. His plan took advantage of the enemy's likely behavior and negated the weakness of his own troops. Its execution was near perfect and its impact, if not decisive, was significant. Its effect was to raise the flagging morale of those in America striving for independence, and conversely, it damped the enthusiasm of those contemplating support for the Crown. As importantly, Cowpens meant that Cornwallis's small army was smaller still.

Regardless, the British general held firm to his goal, which was to bring Greene into battle, defeat his forces, and thereby secure for the Crown the three most southern colonies. However, Cornwallis faced several problems: he was short of supplies, the local population was providing less assistance than expected, and Greene was devilishly difficult to engage.

They met finally at Guilford Courthouse in North Carolina, on March 15, 1781. By then Greene's forces actually outnumbered those of Cornwallis. Showing the courage typical of British redcoats, the English attacked. At one point the outcome looked to favor the Americans. But Cornwallis trained his artillery on where the battle was most fierce, killing both the enemy and some of his own men. This proved decisive. The British carried the day and Greene retired, though in good order. Nathanael Greene would fight again, at Hobkirk's Hill and Eutaw Springs. There, once more, the king's soldiers would win, but Greene and his army would survive. The British would hold the field of battle but little else.

Cornwallis meanwhile had gone north into Virginia, contrary to orders from General Clinton. He reasoned that his little army—once thirty-five hundred, now reduced to one thousand—could not succeed in the Carolinas. So in April 1781 he chose to rendezvous with the British troops in Virginia, hoping with a larger force to draw the Americans into a major battle. If he could win it, and he expected to, he could put an end to the rebellion. Once in Virginia he needed to be able to be supplied from the sea. To encamp, Cornwallis chose the town of York, a small community on a river that fed into the Chesapeake Bay.

In Newport, Rochambeau learned that a French fleet would arrive off the Chesapeake in August. He and Washington, who was keeping an eye on the British in New York, conceived a bold plan. Together, they would march south to the York peninsula and lay siege to Cornwallis. If the French fleet could hold off the Royal Navy, Cornwallis would be trapped.

On June 10, 1781, the first French troops left Newport. They and four thousand others would meet up with Washington's army and march 756 miles, arriving at Williamsburg in September. The combined French-American force was large. It numbered about eighteen thousand men, far more than that of Cornwallis.

At first Cornwallis was not alarmed. True, he had his back to the sea, but his army would be reinforced and, if need be, evacuated by the navy.

Did not Britain rule the waves? Had not the Royal Navy defeated French fleets whenever they met?

Two points of land, both in Virginia, define the entrance to the Chesapeake Bay. They are Cape Charles to the north and Cape Henry to the south. The distance between them is small, approximately fourteen miles. On September 5, 1781, a naval engagement occurred offshore. Known as the Battle of the Capes, it receives scant attention in history books. Yet it ranks among the most important in history. On that day, the French fleet, still under the command of the Comte François Joseph Paul de Grasse, battled British ships commanded by Admiral Sir Thomas Graves. Graves was no Horatio Nelson. After two and a half hours of exchanging gunfire, he withdrew, sailing back to New York. Cornwallis was left to fend for himself.

There was not much the British general could do. Laying siege to York, French and American cannons bombarded the town. The town was soon wrecked, British casualties were growing in number, and (typically) supplies were short. Both the French and the Americans had men killed and wounded, but the outcome was never in doubt. On October 17 Cornwallis proposed a cessation of hostilities. Two days later the British marched out of town and threw down their muskets. More than seven thousand men surrendered. Like Burgoyne before him, Cornwallis had lost an entire army.

"Oh God! It is all over," exclaimed Frederick Lord North upon learning of the events at York. Lord North was the king's principal minister, in whose government Germain served. His remark was not far from the truth, as nearly everyone in Britain and America realized that Cornwallis's surrender signaled the end of the war. By late 1781 the fighting was essentially over, despite the king still having thirty thousand redcoats in the colonies. Lord North's government collapsed in November and peace negotiations began thereafter in Paris. The American side was led by Benjamin Franklin. However, these negotiations took a considerable amount of time, during which the armies in America kept careful watch on each other. Finally, in September 1783, a peace treaty, now called the Treaty of Paris, was signed. In it Britain recognized the United States as an independent nation, no longer subject to the Crown's authority. The war was over.

Why did Britain lose?

She was, after all, a major European power, economically strong and mostly victorious in past military engagements. Yet she failed to quell the rebellion in America. Why did she fail? Several factors help explain the defeat.

At the top of the list is the fact that the British army was too small. Its paper strength was 48,647 men, although the actual number was far fewer. The number of men under arms was insufficient to meet the army's obligations, which ranged beyond America, to Gibraltar, the West Indies, Canada, Ireland, India, and the home counties. Even with the addition of thirty thousand German mercenaries, the British lacked the necessary manpower. Nor was the army alone in its difficulty. The Royal Navy too was consistently short of sailors (hence the device of impressment to man the ships). The problem was fundamental. With a population of only some nine million, England simply could not field the military forces it required.

Moreover, once France entered the conflict, Britain had to focus its attention on her traditional cross-channel rival. After Saratoga, the American war, for the British, became a secondary concern. What was happening in the waters between France and England and in the Caribbean was of greater concern. Take 1779, for example, when a large combined French and Spanish fleet sailed up the Channel intent on invasion. Or, the year before, when the Royal Navy had to fight a major battle with the French off the French island of Ushant. Or, in 1780, when the British outpost at Gibraltar came under siege. All this occurred during the War for Independence. Of course, the British had their revenge. In 1781, soon after Yorktown, the Royal Navy crushed the fleet of Admiral de Grasse at the Battle of the Saints in the West Indies. Britain would continue to rule the waves, just not on the Chesapeake.

For the British, the war in America was not a popular one, and the country was far from united in regard to the conflict. Whig opposition to the war was substantial. For example, in February 1781, before Cornwallis's surrender, a motion in parliament to keep soldiers at home rather than send them to America was defeated but garnered 165 votes. Ordinary people also were against the war. In April 1779, recruits of the 71st Highlanders mutinied when ordered to America. They were willing to fight the French and the Spaniards, but not the Americans. Throughout Britain many felt either that the colonists had been denied the rights Englishmen enjoyed or that they weren't worth the cost in blood and treasury.

No explanation for Britain's defeat can exclude the commanders entrusted with the conduct of the war. In particular, three generals bear responsibility for the outcome. All were senior officers in the army and not without talents. Yet they proved inadequate to the task assigned them. Sir William Howe was the first. True, he won several battles, but he hesitated when he should have been more aggressive, defeating the Continental army but never—as he could have—destroying it. Then there was his replacement, General Clinton. He too chose not to wage a vigorous war, preferring to lament his own situation, which he usually saw as a predicament. Moreover, had Henry Clinton possessed a shred of strategic initiative, he would have, on his own, ventured north to aid Burgoyne. However, no single individual possesses greater responsibility for Britain's defeat in the American war than Lieutenant General John Burgoyne. The expedition in 1777 from Canada was his plan, and he executed it very poorly. Of course, Germain should have sent definitive orders to Clinton in New York City, but the fiasco at Saratoga was of Burgoyne's own doing.

Taken together, Generals Howe, Clinton, and Burgoyne could have produced different results, but they did not. Yet in accounting for Britain's defeat, one other senior officer requires mention. That would be Sir Thomas Graves, whose command of his ships at the Battle of the Capes gives new meaning to the adjective "lackluster." Had Graves handled his fleet more vigorously, as later admirals of the Royal Navy would handle theirs, the outcome of Cornwallis's campaign in Virginia would have been different. So, as much as anyone, Thomas Graves joins John Burgoyne and the others as men responsible for the loss of the American colonies.

Why did the Americans win?

After all, the thirteen colonies had limited resources, lacked seasoned military commanders, and were saddled with a Congress that was at best half-effective. Moreover, the population, mostly farmers and merchants, was divided as to which side should triumph. Yet the Americans managed not only to engage the British for eight years but also to win. They defeated a first-class military power. How were they able to do this? The explanation lies beyond the reasons given above for Britain's defeat. Something else accounts for the outcome.

First and foremost the Americans won because France came to their aid. The French provided arms and supplies. They provided soldiers, and perhaps more important, they provided money. More than once, the French rescued the Americans when the latter's treasury was depleted. One example from 1781 reveals the importance of French financial assistance. When Washington planned to march south with Rochambeau to trap Cornwallis, he had no money to pay his troops, who therefore were reluctant to move. The French commander gave him the funds and the army marched to Virginia. No fact is more important to understanding the American victory in the War for Independence than the largesse of the French.

There is a second reason why the rebel Americans triumphed. It is a simple one: George Washington was the commander in chief of the Continental army. He was a remarkable individual, deserving of his reputation. Personally brave, he was a man of impeccable integrity whose commanding presence was felt by all. That he lost more battles than he won matters not. He won when he had to, and as important, he held the army together under the most difficult of circumstances. To put down the rebellion, the British needed to eliminate Washington and his army. George Washington made sure he and his troops survived, and in doing so, he brought victory to the Continental army and to the cause for which it fought.

Of course, Washington was not the only American general. There were others, and several were successful, which is surprising given the lack of command experience these men possessed. The senior British officers all had experience in the field. These men did not. Yet at Bennington, Saratoga, Cowpens, and other battles, American field commanders performed admirably. One such general stands out. He is Nathanael Greene, whose campaign in the South was masterful. That the thirteen colonies, lacking much of a military tradition, could produce such men is rather remarkable.

One final factor helps explain why the Americans won. From 1775 to 1783 there were in the colonies a sufficient number of men able and willing to fight for something they believed in. Whether in the Continental army or the state militia, men—ordinary men—felt compelled to endure hardship and risk life to expel the British from land they considered their own. To be sure, American victory in the War for Independence required French assistance and the services of George Washington and his fellow officers. But without men from New Hampshire, Maryland, the Carolinas, and the other colonies, men who left their families with musket in hand, men who believed in independence, the war that gave birth to a new nation would not have been won.

2

1812

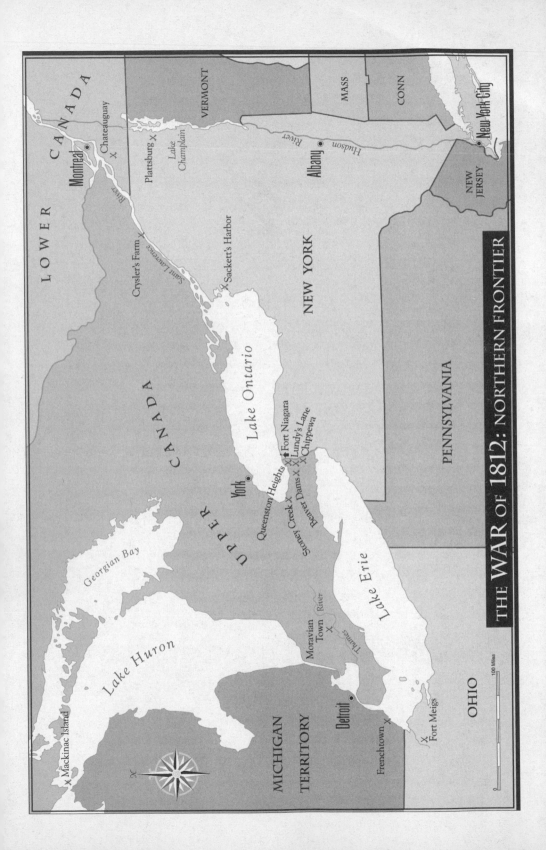

THE WAR OF 1812: NORTHERN FRONTIER

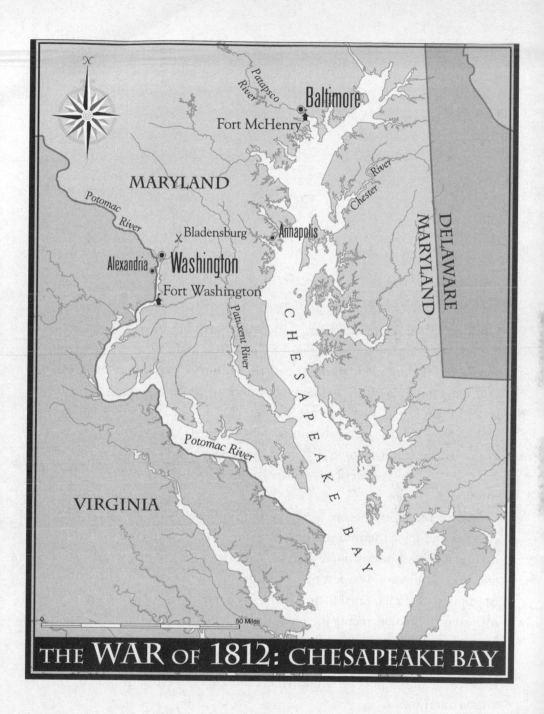

THE WAR OF 1812: CHESAPEAKE BAY

1812–1815

On June 1, 1812, James Madison, America's fourth president, sought from Congress a declaration of war against Great Britain. In his message to the legislature the president summarized the country's grievances. Madison said England unlawfully kidnapped American seamen, forcing them to serve in the Royal Navy. He complained that English trade regulations violated the rights of neutrals and thereby harmed American commerce. He noted the insulting tone of British diplomacy. And he implied that in reference to Native Americans on the frontier, British actions were full of mischief.

All of Madison's points were valid. The Royal Navy did seize U.S. citizens and force them to serve on British warships. England's "Orders-in-Council" did discriminate against American merchants, whose ships comprised the second largest merchant fleet in the world. Moreover, British diplomats often treated their American counterparts with disdain. And ministers in London, seeing the possibility of a Native American federation to serve both as a buffer state for Canada and a wall against further westward expansion of the United States, frequently were scheming with native tribes to stem the flow of white Americans eager to settle in the Northwestern territories.

Madison got what he sought, signing the declaration on June 18. But the vote was hardly unanimous. In the House of Representatives not a single Federalist voted in the affirmative, the vote being seventy-nine to forty-nine. In the upper chamber thirteen senators opposed war, six fewer than the number supporting the president. Differences were regional. War hawks in the South and West wanted to fight. People in New England felt otherwise. The region's well-being depended on trade, which they knew would be crippled. So strong was New England's opposition to the war that initially Massachusetts and Connecticut did not send militia to meet their state's military quota. And farmers in New York and Vermont, and in what is now Maine, traded with their Canadian neighbors throughout the conflict. One key customer was the British army, whose troops in Spain and Portugal depended on American grain.

In 1812 Britain was at war with France, and had been almost continuously since 1792. The struggle was worldwide, and England's goal was to prevent Napoleon from dominating Europe and the other places Monsieur Bonaparte eyed, such as Russia, the Caribbean, Egypt, and India. England's military was stretched thin. It had little desire to fight the United States.

At first Britain hoped that diplomacy quickly would end the war, particularly when, on June 23, 1812, the government in London provisionally repealed the Orders-in-Council. Indeed, the British commander in Canada was instructed not to undertake offensive actions lest hopes for a diplomatic resolution be jeopardized. But the Americans insisted that impressment of their sailors be stopped. On this point, England could not and would not yield.

Great Britain's security as well as her economic prosperity depended on her navy. In 1812 this was the largest industrial organization in the world, with more than 590 warships in service. Yet England, with a relatively small population, could not adequately man these vessels. So she resorted to impressment. British nationals, wherever they were and whatever nationality they espoused, legally could be seized and forced to serve. In the event, Americans, both native born and naturalized, were often taken. Between 1792 and 1802, according to one American historian, roughly twenty-four hundred American sailors were forcibly taken from their ships. This same historian, William M. Fowler Jr., writes that during the next ten years the number almost tripled. Not only did this practice of impressment harm the sailor involved, it also was an affront to American honor.

At the start of the war Madison's strategy was to strike at Canada from several locations. This would divide British forces and, hopefully, achieve success before the British army and navy could react. Negotiations would then be held, and, from a position of strength, the Americans would be able to favorably realign borders, remove threats posed by Native Americans, and, quite possibly, have the British withdraw altogether from Canada, whose four provinces and two large islands would become part of the United States.

The strategy was not without merit. Upon embracing it, Madison and his generals envisioned a brief and victorious war. As we shall see they got neither.

On July 12, 1812, Brigadier General William Hull, a veteran of the War for Independence, led a force of twenty-two hundred American soldiers across the Detroit River into Canada. This was the first of three expeditions comprising the overall American plan. Much was expected, but Hull achieved little, and early in August he turned back, re-crossing the river. He and his men settled in at Detroit, then a town of some 150 houses, awaiting the British. The enemy soon arrived. Major General Isaac Brock, British commander in Upper Canada, had seven hundred regulars and a contingent of Indians. On August 15 Brock called on Hull to surrender. In his message to the Americans he said that once the battle was joined, he would not be able to control his native allies. Unfortunately, the British general's observation was not an empty threat. Native Americans often displayed a savagery in and after battle not shown by those trained to European standards. Receiving Brock's message, Hull did the unexpected. He surrendered his entire force, without a fight. He and 582 regulars became prisoners of war. Sixteen hundred Ohio volunteers were paroled home. Some twenty-five hundred muskets and thirty-three cannons were turned over to the British. Yet, for the president, even more bad news was to follow.

The Niagara River flows north from Lake Erie into Lake Ontario. Thirty-four miles long, it was—and still is—a boundary between Canada and the United States. During the War of 1812 it was the scene of several battles. The first took place in October 1812.

Major General Stephen Van Rensselaer was a prominent New York politician and general of militia. It was he who would command the second

American invasion force. With an army of nine hundred regulars and twenty-six hundred militia he chose to attack Queenstown Heights across the Niagara River from Lewiston, New York. On the afternoon of October 13, a Tuesday, he assaulted the Heights. His troops fought well, though several militia units refused to participate, arguing that they were to serve only on American soil. For a time the flow of battle favored the Americans. But the British rallied, and the attack was repulsed. Van Rensselaer had more than 300 men killed or wounded. In excess of 950 were taken prisoner. British losses were less: 14 men killed and 77 wounded, with 21 missing. However, among the dead was Isaac Brock, who in Canada is rightly considered a military hero.

As if the defeats at Detroit and Queenstown Heights were not enough, success also eluded the Americans in Lower Canada (Upper Canada comprised the lands west of the Ottawa River and Montreal). In November, Major General Henry Dearborn, like Hull a veteran of the War for Independence, led a force of three thousand soldiers into Canada from Plattsburgh, New York. Here too American militia chose not to cross the border. Dearborn stayed in Canada for three days without engaging the enemy. He then withdrew, retiring back to Plattsburgh for the winter. His expedition had accomplished absolutely nothing.

Far to the west, and several months earlier, the first action of the war had also had disappointing results for the Americans. On July 17, 1812, a small force of British regulars supplemented by Canadian fur traders and Native Americans took possession of an American outpost on Mackinac Island at the northern tip of Lake Huron. This was done without loss of life and had two important consequences: (1) the British retained the lucrative Canadian fur trade, and (2) the Native Americans of the Michigan Territory saw the Crown as likely victors and, therefore, aided the king's cause.

As the year 1812 came to an end, the American strategy of a quick victory clearly had failed. Hull's surrender, Van Rensselaer's defeat, and Dearborn's inaction had shattered Madison's plan. Moreover, these expeditions had revealed an army that was lacking in leadership. Six months after it began, the United States was involved in a war that quite possibly it would lose.

Yet if America's army had fallen short of success, its navy had not.

In 1812 the United States Navy had but fourteen vessels ready for sea. None of these were ships of the line, the battleships of their day. Only seven were frigates—fast, well-armed ships ideal for scouting and operations against merchant ships. Of these seven three deserve special mention. They were the *Constitution*, the *United States*, and the *President*. Rated as forty-four-gun frigates, these ships were larger and more heavily armed than the standard English frigate. Conceived by the Philadelphia shipwright Joshua Humphreys, they would make their presence known. One of them, the USS *Constitution*, would become an American icon.

In addition to the fourteen oceangoing ships, the American navy had numerous gunboats. Built in response to President Thomas Jefferson's anti-naval policies, these were small vessels, lightly armed, unsuitable for the open sea but potentially useful for harbor and coastal defense. Jefferson believed a blue-water navy would encourage foreign adventures the United States should avoid. So he had produced a large number of these gunboats. They turned out to be of little value.

Yet despite its small size, the American navy was well prepared for battle. Its officer corps was excellent; its crews were fine sailors. Moreover, the navy had combat experience. Prior to 1812 the U.S. Navy had seen action against the Barbary pirates in the Mediterranean and during an undeclared war against France in the Caribbean (in which the thirty-eight-gun frigate USS *Constellation* had captured a French frigate of forty guns). When war broke out in 1812, the navy was ready and confident of success.

This confidence was rewarded when on August 19, 1812, the *Constitution* encountered the frigate HMS *Guerriere* of thirty-eight guns in the mid-Atlantic. The result was a nautical slugfest in which the American ship triumphed. Two months later Stephen Decatur, in command of the *United States*, defeated and took in tow HMS *Macedonian*, also of thirty-eight guns. Earlier the USS *Wasp*, a sloop, had pounded HMS *Frolic* into submission while the USS *Essex,* a thirty-two-gun frigate, captured HMS *Alert*. Late in November the *Constitution* returned to action and, off the coast of Brazil, destroyed the heavy frigate HMS *Java*. Finally, in 1813 the American sloop *Hornet* beat HMS *Peacock*, a sister ship to *Frolic*.

These single-ship actions stunned the Royal Navy (against French and

Spanish ships the British almost never lost). They also shocked a British public unaccustomed to defeat at sea. For the Americans they were cause for celebration, offsetting the setbacks along the Canadian border.

One American ship, the USS *Essex*, made history when in late January 1813 she entered the waters off Cape Horn and became the first American naval vessel to enter the Pacific Ocean. Built at Salem, Massachusetts, and funded by public subscription (101 Americans contributed, including a shopkeeper from Salem named Edmund Gale who gave $10), the ship cost $74,000 to build. Salem citizens raised the full amount. Commanded by David Porter, the ship wrecked Britain's lucrative whaling trade. So many vessels did Porter seize that at one time he gave command of a prize to a twelve-year-old midshipman by the name of David Farragut. Responding to the *Essex*, the Royal Navy dispatched two frigates to the Pacific. In March 1814, they cornered Porter's ship off Valparaiso. *Essex* was well armed, but her guns were short-range carronades. With their longer-range cannons the two British warships stood off and pounded the Americans into submission.

With so few ships, the U.S. Navy had no hope of either neutralizing its British counterpart or halting British maritime traffic, though it proved to be far more than an annoyance, and Decatur and his fellow captains had partners who inflicted great damage on the enemy's merchant fleet. These were the privateers. One British naval historian titles his essay on American privateers during the War of 1812 "War as Business." Privateers were privately owned vessels authorized by governmental bodies to act as warships and—this is the key part—were permitted to retain profits derived from what was essentially legalized pirating. With their strong maritime heritage, the coastal states of America embraced privateering with a vengeance. More than 526 vessels were commissioned during the war. Among the most famous private warships were those built in Baltimore, whose well-designed schooners were admired for both their speed and their beauty.

American privateers sailed in quest of profit and did very well, especially early in the war. Captured British merchant ships totaled 1,444 (the British historian cited above says the number is "nearly 1350"), while the U.S. Navy took a further 254, both warships and merchantmen. True, nearly half of these were recaptured. But the impact of the combined privateer and naval operations against British ships was substantial. Why else did Liverpool merchants in September 1814 censure the Admiralty, claiming that eight hundred vessels from their port alone had been lost?

For the first few months of the war the Admiralty, Britain's naval high command, acted cautiously. The admiral in charge of the fleet's North American station, Sir John Borlase Warren, even put out peace feelers, which, owing to America's views regarding impressment, came to nothing. Warren then was instructed to neutralize American warships. This was to be accomplished either by keeping them in port or by destroying them should they escape. He also was ordered to prevent American merchant ships from sailing. Thus Warren was to employ the tactic that had worked well against the French: the blockade.

In doing so he confronted several difficulties. To start with, the American coastline was nineteen hundred miles long. Then there were the winds—prevailing westerlies that made station keeping difficult. And Halifax, home port for his ships, was isolated and not particularly well equipped. Moreover, Sir John did not have command of a sufficient number of ships. The bulk of Britain's fleet was deployed to the Mediterranean or in home waters.

Nevertheless, Warren did as instructed and instituted the blockade. Initially, New England was exempt (as previously mentioned, Wellington's army needed American grain). So too was the American South. But gradually, as the war progressed, coverage was extended. By late 1814, when Napoleon no longer was a threat, Royal Navy ships were to be found in waters from Maine to Louisiana. Essentially, they crippled America's merchant fleet. By September 1813, 245 vessels were laid up in Boston. In 1805, 250 ships had been registered in Salem. A decade later, the number had fallen to 57. In 1812, there were 45 privateers built in Baltimore. In 1814 only 8 were constructed. The Royal Navy's blockade did not prevent all American ships from sailing, but vessels flying the Stars and Stripes at sea no longer were found in large number. In addition, the blockade caused a loss of revenues, which was serious, as Madison's government depended on customs fees.

The blockade was directed not just at commercial vessels. Warren targeted warships as well. Here too the blockade was effective. The *Constellation* never put to sea. The *Macedonian*, now an American ship, and the *Hornet* were quickly chased back to port. The *President* escaped, but soon was caught by British warships and forced to surrender. However, the USS *Argus* of sixteen guns made a successful cruise in the summer of 1813, capturing twenty British merchant ships. The USS *Enterprise*, also of sixteen guns, later took HMS *Boxer*, while on June 28, 1814, the new American sloop *Wasp* prevailed over HMS *Reindeer*.

Such victories notwithstanding, the Royal Navy's blockade kept most American ships tied up in port. The blockade was a signal feature of the War of 1812. Apparently, Britannia still ruled the waves.

Though not on the Great Lakes.

On March 27, 1813, a young American naval officer reached Lake Erie. Assigned the task of assembling a squadron of ships, he did so most effectively, aided by three master shipwrights: Daniel Dobbins and the Brown brothers, Noah and Adam. Together they built three brigs and several schooners. The strategic objective was to control the waters of the lake, for he who controlled Lake Erie controlled the Northwestern territories of both the United States and Canada.

In late summer, the young officer took his ships to sea in search of the enemy. Like the Americans, the British had been busy constructing ships. The two sides clashed on September 10, 1813. The Americans triumphed, and the young officer, Oliver Hazard Perry, sent his memorable message to General William Henry Harrison: "We have met the enemy and they are ours."

Perry's victory on Lake Erie was soon matched on land. With nothing to fear from the British, Perry transported Harrison's army of thirty-five hundred men across Lake Erie onto Canadian soil, where, on October 5, the future American president defeated the British at Moraviantown along the River Thames. This too was a significant victory. It demonstrated that an American army could prevail in battle. It demoralized a large number of Native Americans who had chosen the British side of the conflict and also removed the possibility of a Native American buffer state. And, although Harrison's troops eventually withdrew, it cemented American dominance in the Northwest.

The United States did less well on Lake Ontario. As on Lake Erie, control of the lake's water was critical to military success. Why? Because the land was such that transport by water was the only practical way to move supplies and men.

In harbors along the shoreline, both sides built ships. But Isaac Chauncey, the American naval commander, and Sir James Yeo, his Royal Navy counterpart, were cautious men. Neither seemed willing to risk a decisive battle. So they sparred, with success eluding them both. Chauncey did undertake a successful raid on the capital of Upper Canada, York (now the city of Toronto), where army troops, contrary to orders, burned the parliament building (considered bad form by the standards of the day). Sir James conducted a less successful raid against Chauncey's base of operations at Sackets Harbor. Yet neither side, despite considerable activity, was able to secure control of the lake.

On land in 1813, save for Moraviantown and the defense of Fort George in May, British forces fared better than the Americans. They won at Frenchtown, Stoney Creek, Beaver Dam, and Fort Niagara. And while the Americans beat off a British attack on Fort Meigs, an outpost south of Lake Erie, they suffered high losses: four hundred men were killed and six hundred taken prisoner.

Nowhere was the superiority of British forces on land in 1813 more evident than farther east. There, along the St. Lawrence River, two battles occurred. The British won both of them. Late in 1813, the largest force assembled by the Americans during the war, eleven thousand men, invaded Canada at two locations along the river. Their target was Montreal. If the city could be taken, the war might end and the United States, despite reversals on land and sea, might claim victory.

Major General Wade Hampton's force came north from Plattsburgh. Farther west Major General James Wilkinson, the senior American officer on the northern frontier, crossed into Canada. Theirs was to be a coordinated attack. Conceptually, the plan was sound. Its execution was not. Neither general appeared equal to his task and both suffered defeat. Hampton lost at Châteauguay. Wilkinson was beaten at Crysler's Farm. Canadians remember the former because British troops were not present. Only Canadians fought the intruders. Hardly anyone remembers Crysler's Farm, though it put a stop to the most serious threat to Canada the British faced throughout the war.

At sea in 1813, the fortunes of the Royal Navy improved. Its vessels now escorted merchant ships in convoys (as they would much later in two world wars), reducing losses to enemy privateers and warships. It conducted raids within the Chesapeake Bay that were intended to—and did—alarm the population and keep American men and material from being sent to Canada. But to the officers of the fleet, the most satisfying event of 1813 was the victory they long had sought over an American frigate. Stung by the successes of the *Constitution* and the *United States* and by the actions of smaller American warships, the Royal Navy desperately was seeking a victory at sea.

On June 1, 1813, the USS *Chesapeake*, a frigate of thirty-eight guns, departed Boston Harbor. She was a fine ship, with a brave captain, James Lawrence. But her crew was inexperienced, and she went up against one of the most capable frigates in Britain's navy. HMS *Shannon*, also of thirty-eight guns, was captained by Philip Broke, who knew his trade exceptionally well. He had commanded *Shannon* for seven years and had trained his crew hard, especially in gunnery. The battle took place in the early afternoon and lasted but eleven minutes. *Shannon* triumphed, pulverizing *Chesapeake*. Lawrence was killed and the severely wounded Broke became a national hero.

For Great Britain more good news was on the horizon. In May 1814, Napoleon abdicated. This freed up military resources for the war in America. The army received fourteen regiments from Wellington's forces in Europe (the duke himself declined the offer to command the army in Canada). The navy in North America received additional ships. As importantly, it received a new commander. Admiral Sir Alexander Cochrane replaced Warren. Cochrane intended to act aggressively. "I have it much to heart," he wrote, "to give them a complete drubbing before peace is made."

Cochrane was true to his word. He extended the Royal Navy's blockade to New England. He ordered the seizure of coastal towns in Maine. And he directed Sir George Cockburn to attack America via the Chesapeake Bay. All of these actions were in support of the principal British effort of

1814: an invasion of the United States from the north. The strategic goal was to inflict such damage upon the Americans that the results of the inevitable peace agreement would be highly favorable to Great Britain.

The Americans understood that with Napoleon gone the British would be able to marshal considerable military resources. They therefore planned to act before these resources could be deployed. And they decided to do what they had done before: invade Canada.

This time, there would be a difference.

In command of the invading force was Major General Jacob Brown, whose force numbered approximately three thousand, divided into two brigades, one commanded by Winfield Scott, the other by Eleazer Ripley. These three gentlemen knew how to fight and were not reluctant to do so. Gone were the likes of Hull, Dearborn, Wilkinson, and Hampton. Brown's army was well trained, and when on July 15, 1814, it met the British at Chippawa in Upper Canada near the Niagara River, the Americans emerged victorious.

Jacob Brown then halted his troops, awaiting support form Commodore Chauncey. With naval assistance, Brown intended to push the British off the lands separating Lake Ontario from Lake Erie. But Chauncey, ever cautious, stopped at Sackets Harbor. This left Brown with insufficient means to continue. So, prudently, he moved his men back to a place called Lundy's Lane, not far from Chippawa.

On July 25, the two armies clashed again. The battle was hard fought and Brown was wounded, as were 572 of his men. His dead numbered 170. The British lost 84 killed and 559 wounded. Both sides had more than 100 soldiers missing. The Americans fought extremely hard and considered the outcome a victory. So did the British. But, as Jacob Brown withdrew to Fort Erie, the British claim seems more convincing.

On the day of the Battle at Lundy's Lane forty-five hundred British soldiers, led by Major General Robert Ross, arrived in Bermuda. They were to be the sharp end of the sword that Admirals Cochrane and Cockburn planned to wield in the Chesapeake Bay. By mid-August Ross was in the Bay. On August 19, he and his troops landed at the mouth of the Patuxent River. They proceeded northward and five days later met a hastily assembled American force at Bladensburg, in Maryland. The result was a rout. The American soldiers were mostly militia and they were no match for Ross's veterans.

That night the British entered Washington. Madison and his government had fled the city. The invaders burned several buildings, including the presidential mansion (which, when repainted to cover the scars of the fire, became quite white). This was in retaliation for the fires set by Americans in York. The next day the British withdrew, quite pleased with what they had accomplished.

But the Patuxent was not the only river on which the British sailed. A smaller force had also navigated the Potomac. South of the American capital, they exchanged gunfire with the Americans at Fort Washington and took twenty-one vessels from the docks of Alexandria. By September, this expedition too had returned to the Chesapeake.

Ross and Cochrane then planned a joint operation against Baltimore. As the city was home to American privateers, the two commanders deemed it a most worthy target. The navy would bombard the town while the army would test its defenses. If all went well, they would attack in force. On September 12, Ross landed troops at North Point. They soon engaged the Americans, and won, but the major general was among the 46 of his soldiers killed. The Americans suffered 163 casualties. The navy did its part. With guns and rockets Cochrane's ships shelled Fort McHenry at the entrance to the harbor. The bombardment was extensive. But at dawn the American flag still flew. Further assaults seemed unwise, so the British withdrew. They left on September 15, 1814. The soldiers went south to the Caribbean. The sailors went north to Halifax.

Were the British expeditions within the Chesapeake a success? In one sense, they were. Twice the British army defeated its American counterparts, at Bladensburg and North Point. It also humiliated the Americans by marching through the streets of Washington. The Royal Navy did its part as well. It sailed the waters of Chesapeake Bay at will and made its presence known at Baltimore. Moreover, together the British army and navy severely frightened the local populations of Virginia and Maryland.

But after doing all this, the British left. There was no follow-up and little lasting impact, save an American national anthem and a coat of paint for the presidential mansion. Shortly after General Ross and his troops left

Washington, Madison and his government returned to the city and continued on as before.

The British attacks along the Maine coast had more staying power. Early in September Lieutenant General Sir John Sherbrooke took two thousand British regulars to the mouth of the Penobscot River. There, without much resistance, they occupied several towns. They also caused the Americans to burn the small frigate *Adams*, then, thirty miles upriver, to prevent its capture. The territory of Maine jutted up between Nova Scotia and Lower Canada. This made communication and travel between the two provinces difficult. Sherbrooke hoped that if they held a few coastal areas, the land would be ceded to Great Britain once the war ended. That, of course, did not happen, and in April 1815, the British departed. That they ever were there is now mostly forgotten.

But it was in neither Maine nor the Chesapeake where the British made their major move of 1814. That came near Lake Champlain, when an army of 10,351 men invaded the United States. This was the most powerful force Great Britain assembled during the entire conflict. It hoped to accomplish what John Burgoyne had failed to do in 1777: thrash the Americans in upstate New York and separate New England from the rest of the country.

In command of this army was Lieutenant General Sir George Prevost. He was the civilian governor of all of Canada as well as its senior military official. So far he had performed both jobs quite well. His most important task had been to hold Canada for the Crown, and he had done so. True, the Americans had invaded often, but whether they had won or lost in battle, they invariably returned to American soil. Prevost's conduct had earned the approval of the duke of Wellington. So when he led his soldiers across the border on September 1, 1814, expectations were high.

Five days later he and his army entered Plattsburgh, a little town in New York State, on the shores of Lake Champlain. Opposing his veteran troops was a small American force numbering about fifteen hundred. Prevost did not attack immediately. He waited for the navy to finish building and outfitting ships so that a combined land-sea assault could be made on the American defenders. This was not a bad decision. The problem was that he did not wait long enough.

As the British were assembling a small fleet for service on the lake, so too were the Americans. Commanding the American effort was another young naval officer, Thomas Macdonough. Aided by the same Brown brothers who had built vessels for Oliver Hazard Perry, Macdonough put together a small squadron led by the *Saratoga* of twenty-six guns.

Soon, however, Prevost became anxious to start, so he ordered the British naval commander to attack. Despite not being ready for battle, the officer did so, on Sunday, September 11. The result was a brief but bloody effort. The Americans had 52 men killed and 58 wounded. Comparable British losses were 54 and 116. When the guns went silent Macdonough had won.

The Americans now controlled Lake Champlain. This made difficult further moves south by Prevost. Yet his army was intact and still capable of inflicting serious damage on the Americans. But Sir George, a cautious man, decided to return to Canada. He and his army marched north. A Canadian military historian terms Prevost's expedition a fiasco.

At Plattsburgh Sir George Prevost ruined his reputation. Thomas Macdonough earned a spot in American history.

As the fighting took place on Lake Champlain, peace negotiations were under way in Belgium. Late in 1813, the British foreign secretary had proposed that each side appoint commissioners to draft an agreement to end the conflict. Almost immediately, President Madison accepted the offer. He knew the war had not gone particularly well and that most Americans would welcome an end to hostilities. For their part, the British were weary of war and of the taxes required to sustain it. In addition, they were irked by the continued success of American privateers not blockaded by the Royal Navy.

So commissioners were appointed and met in Ghent. Considerable time passed before serious negotiations occurred, but on Christmas Eve 1814 a treaty was signed. The government in London accepted it soon thereafter. The United States Senate ratified the treaty on February 16, 1815.

The treaty called for all conquered lands (there were some, but not many) to be returned. It directed that military action with and against Native Americans be stopped. And it said that the boundary between New Brunswick and Maine would be settled by subsequent agreement. Significantly, the Treaty of Ghent made no mention of impressment.

At a time when communication across the Atlantic Ocean took weeks not seconds, news that the war was over did not reach participants for some time, during which several engagements took place at sea and one major battle occurred on land. On February 10, 1815, the *Constitution* captured two Royal Navy frigates, thereby sealing her reputation as one of the world's greatest fighting ships. A month before, Major General Sir Edward Pakenham, Wellington's brother-in-law, made an ill-advised frontal assault against the defenders of New Orleans led by Andrew Jackson. The attack failed, and the British suffered twenty-four hundred casualties, among them Sir Edward who was killed. Undaunted, the British army then proceeded by sea to the coast of Alabama, where it captured the fort guarding Mobile. An attack on the city was called off when word of the treaty arrived.

The final battle of the war took place on June 30, 1815. In the faraway Sunda Strait (a body of water that connects the islands of Sumatra and Java) the American sloop *Peacock* captured the British East India Company's armed brig *Nautilus*. *Peacock*'s captain was told the war had ended, but he did not believe it. He opened fire and killed seven men. After taking possession of the vessel, he was given proof of the treaty and returned the prize to the British. With that, the fighting came to an end.

Which side won the War of 1812?

The British think they did. They point out that their most important objective, which was to retain control of Canada, was achieved. American armies invading Canada were almost always defeated. The Royal Navy's blockade, by and large, was successful. The American capital was occupied. The British were never forced to concede on the subject of impressment.

Americans also believe they won the war. They point to the great victories on Lake Erie and Lake Champlain. They celebrate the actions of the *Constitution* and the other American naval vessels. They remember the defense of Baltimore and Andrew Jackson's victory at New Orleans. They note that in a war against the world's most powerful nation, no American territory was given up. And they note also that after the war Britain no longer seized American seamen.

Each side's position has merit. But the evidence suggests that the British have a stronger claim. Strategically, their primary aim in the war was met. Despite American efforts Canada remained a British possession. Moreover, that the Treaty of Ghent was silent on the subject of impressment indicates that the British kept the American grievance from being redressed. True, the United States won several battles on land and lake, yet the best way to determine who won the War of 1812 is to see whose war aims were achieved, and doing that, it appears the British won.

That does not mean the Americans received no benefits. Indeed, they received several. Two heroes of the war became president of the United States. An army emerged that knew how to fight. Lyrics for a national anthem were written. National identity was strengthened. Perhaps, more important, the War of 1812 created an American naval tradition that would serve the nation well. From Oliver Hazard Perry and Thomas Macdonough, from the *Constitution* and the *Essex*, there was built a heritage that would help make the United States Navy a force to be reckoned with.

3

MEXICO

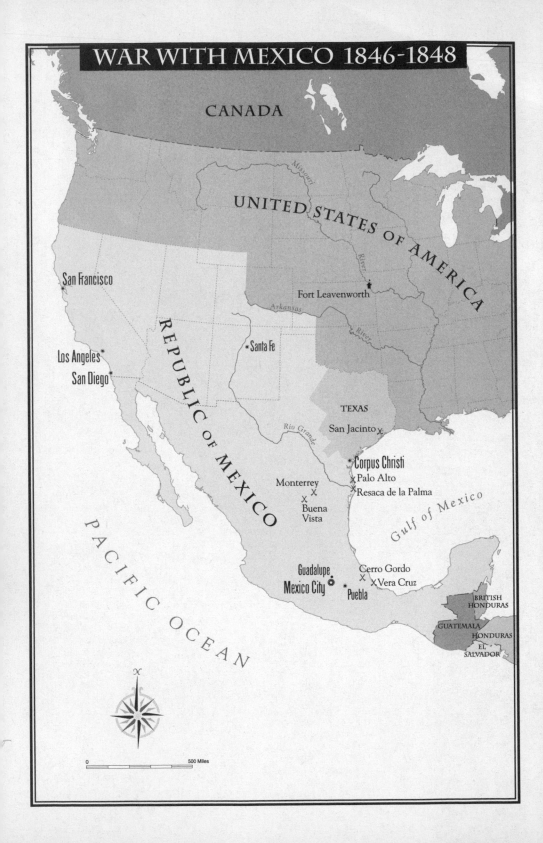

WAR WITH MEXICO 1846-1848

CANADA

UNITED STATES OF AMERICA

Missouri River

Fort Leavenworth

San Francisco

Arkansas

REPUBLIC OF MEXICO

Santa Fe

River

Los Angeles

San Diego

TEXAS

San Jacinto ✗

Rio Grande

Corpus Christi
✗ Palo Alto
✗ Resaca de la Palma

Monterrey
✗
Buena
Vista

Gulf of Mexico

PACIFIC OCEAN

Cerro Gordo
✗ ✗ Vera Cruz
Guadalupe
Mexico City ⊙ • Puebla

BRITISH
HONDURAS

GUATEMALA
HONDURAS
EL
SALVADOR

0   500 Miles

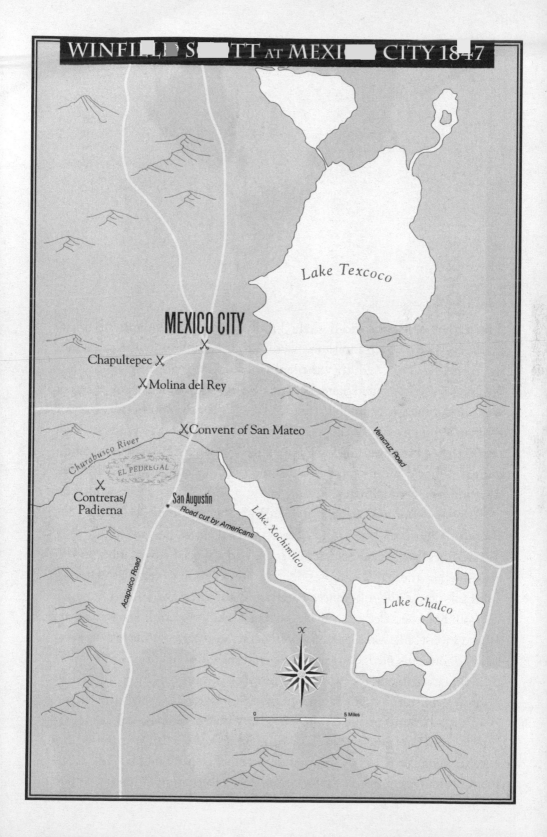

WINFIELD SCOTT AT MEXICO CITY 1847

Lake Texcoco

MEXICO CITY ✗

Chapultepec ✗

✗ Molina del Rey

✗ Convent of San Mateo

Churubusco River

EL PEDREGAL

Veracruz Road

✗
Contreras/
Padierna

San Augustin

Road cut by Americans

Lake Xochimilco

Acapulco Road

Lake Chalco

0   5 Miles

1846–1848

The leaders of Mexico did not take kindly to the independence of Texas, made possible by Sam Houston's victory over Santa Anna at San Jacinto in April 1836. Nor were they thrilled when, a few years later, talk of annexation with the United States began in earnest. Texas, Mexicans believed, was part of the great republic that stretched from the southern border of Oregon to present-day Guatemala. That Texas would merge with Mexico's northern neighbor was unacceptable. Indeed, when the issue of annexation gained political momentum in Washington, Mexico considered itself at war with the United States.

War, however, was not inevitable. With the precedent set by the purchase of Louisiana, the United States several times had offered to buy Texas. These offers had been rebuffed, as had a special envoy, John Slidell, appointed by the American president, James K. Polk, to negotiate a peaceful resolution of the differences between Mexico and the United States.

Polk had been elected in 1844, the first dark horse candidate to win the White House. He was a partisan Democrat, a protégé of Andrew Jackson who honored his pledge to serve but one term. Most historians rate Polk's presidency a success. He achieved a number of his goals, none more important than fulfilling his campaign pledge to bring Texas into the Union.

This accomplishment resulted in war with Mexico, a conflict his political opponents labeled "Polk's War." That he forcefully exercised his constitutional authority as commander in chief is indisputable. Polk was a focused chief executive, not reluctant to direct the nation's military. When the United States Army and its sister service, the navy, completed their mission, the nation they served was considerably larger. Via Polk and the war with Mexico the United States acquired the territory that now comprises the states of Arizona, California, New Mexico, Nevada, Utah, and parts of Wyoming and Colorado. Thus the war was no mere footnote in American history.

As wars do, this three-year conflict caused much blood to flow. The Americans suffered well over twelve thousand deaths, the Mexicans far more. Of U.S. losses only some fifteen hundred were on the battlefield. The rest were the result of disease. In this regard the record of the 3rd U.S. Artillery Regiment is illustrative. The regiment had 224 men killed in the war. Yet only 41 were killed in battle. The others perished from various illnesses. Influenza, smallpox, dysentery, measles, yellow fever—even sunstroke—afflicted the soldiers in Mexico, often fatally.

The first Americans to die in the war were killed by Mexican soldiers who had crossed the Rio Grande into Texas. There, they ambushed an American patrol. Sixteen U.S. troops were killed or wounded. The Americans were part of a much larger force commanded by Brigadier General Zachary Taylor that had been ordered into Texas upon annexation. Its mission was to guard the new American lands and, should there be hostile action on the part of Mexico, to undertake offensive actions. With an army of nearly four thousand men Taylor had the means to do so.

He also had the inclination to fight. Taylor was a veteran commander, not given to pomp and protocol. His soldiers affectionately referred to him as "Old Rough and Ready." He began his expedition into Mexico in the spring of 1846. When he finished, Taylor would be a national hero who soon would become president of the United States.

In late April, Taylor informed the authorities in Washington that hostilities had commenced. War fever in the United States was high, and President Polk had little difficulty in securing from Congress a declaration of war. He then called for fifty thousand volunteer soldiers who, in time, would expand the ranks of the army. Polk also ordered the navy to blockade Mexican ports. The United States was bent on teaching Mexico a lesson, and at least early on, most Americans were fully supportive of Polk and the war. Only a few Whigs, the country's other political party, were against it.

Zachary Taylor, a Whig, was not one of them. He took his army inland and on May 8, 1846, confronted Mexican forces on flat land a few miles north of the Rio Grande, at a place called Palo Alto. At three o'clock in the afternoon, Mexican artillery opened fire, soon followed by cavalry charges. These were repulsed. Taylor's men were army regulars, disciplined and skilled. Eventually, the gunfire ignited the grasses, and a large fire ensued, killing many of those wounded unable to move.

The next morning, the Mexican commander General Mariano Arista withdrew his troops a few miles south, to Resaca de la Palma. There, he held a strong defensive position. Taylor called a counsel of war, at which most of his officers urged waiting for reinforcements. As John S. D. Eisenhower wrote in his book on the Mexican War, that was not Taylor's style. He ordered an attack that, after much hand-to-hand fighting, resulted in victory for the Americans.

In these two engagements Zachary Taylor reported 34 Americans killed and 113 wounded. Many more Mexicans were dead. Indeed, U.S. troops buried 200 of their foe. Among the surviving U.S. soldiers was a young lieutenant by the name of Ulysses S. Grant.

After his victories at Palo Alto and Resaca de la Palma, Taylor was promoted to the rank of major general, at the time the highest rank in the U.S. Army. Perhaps more significantly, his army received additional soldiers. However, these mostly were untested volunteers whose tour of duty was limited. Moreover, the increase in numbers was not matched by a corresponding increase in supplies. So his force, burdened by sickness and by the need to garrison those towns through which it had passed, was far from robust. Still, when he proceeded west toward Monterrey, Taylor had about six thousand men.

Monterrey (not to be confused with the California town Monterey) was the principal city of northeastern Mexico. With a population of approximately ten thousand inhabitants, it was the capital of the state of Nuevo León. Taylor's army reached the city on September 19, 1846. The Mexicans were there in strength, led by General Pedro de Ampudia, who, like Arista, was an experienced commander. Though outnumbered, Taylor chose to attack. He divided his forces (a tactic not always advisable) and came at Ampudia from opposite ends of the town. The battle lasted three days.

Toward the end, the Americans were advancing not through the streets, but literally through the walls of the houses lining the streets. This was the first time the U.S. Army had to fight house to house. On September 24, with the Americans in possession of the city, Ampudia sought terms of surrender. Taylor appointed several of his officers to conduct the negotiations. One of them, a Colonel Jefferson Davis, had commanded the Mississippi Rifles, a regiment that had fought particularly well. Terms were agreed to, and the guns, both American and Mexican, went silent. Polk thought the terms too lenient and was angry with Taylor, but nonetheless, Zachary Taylor had won another battle.

Since gaining independence from Spain in 1821, Mexico had had its share of charismatic leaders, none more colorful than Antonio López de Santa Anna. To the Americans he was the cruel victor of the Alamo who received his just reward at San Jacinto. To his fellow Mexicans he was, intermittently, el Presidente, army commander, patriot, and rogue. In 1845 Santa Anna had been exiled to Havana, his career supposedly over. But with Mexico in political turmoil, he returned the next year courtesy of the U.S. Navy, which, under specific instructions from Polk, allowed him to slip through the blockade. The American president hoped that with a new leader in Mexico, he might be able to negotiate an end to hostilities.

Polk was to be disappointed. With his customary zeal, Santa Anna raised an army. Then, on January 27, 1847, with much fanfare, he and his troops headed north. Their goal was to defeat Zachary Taylor in battle and rid their beloved country of the Yankee invaders. With twenty thousand men under arms—the largest force Mexico would assemble during the war—this goal was well within reach. The two armies met three miles south of the town of Saltillo, in a narrow mountain valley near the hacienda Buena Vista.

Taylor's force, much reduced in effectiveness after Monterrey and, as always, hampered by large numbers of sick and dying, numbered 4,759 men, many of whom had not yet seen battle. At first wishing to attack, Taylor was swayed by one of his senior subordinates, Brigadier John E. Wool, to position his troops defensively at a spot within the valley known as La Angostura (The Narrows). It was a sound move.

Santa Anna arrived in the valley with fifteen thousand men, having lost a quarter of his army from desertion and disease in the march north. Still, he outnumbered Taylor three to one. And his troops were not lacking courage.

On the morning of February 22, 1847, Santa Anna sent a note to Taylor calling on the American to surrender. Old Rough and Ready declined to do so. The next day the Mexicans attacked in force.

The attack was spearheaded by both infantry and the famed Mexican lancers supported by artillery. Taylor's regiments fought hard, stood fast, then on the left flank gave way. General Wool thought the battle lost. Not so Zachary Taylor, who realigned his troops and told Jefferson Davis to shore up the crumbling American line. Davis did so. The U.S. infantry held and, importantly, American artillery began decimating the advancing Mexicans. But Santa Anna did not give up. Again and again, he had his troops attack. The Illinois and Kentucky regiments were in the thick of it. Once again Taylor's cannons found their target and the Mexicans withdrew. On both sides casualties were high. Taylor had 456 wounded and 267 killed. Among the latter was Henry Clay Jr., whose father had opposed the war in the presidential campaign of 1844.

The next morning Taylor and his men waited for Santa Anna to renew the battle. They waited in vain. The Mexican commander and his men had departed. Beaten, Santa Anna had taken his now much depleted army south. There he would raise more troops and defend his country and its capital from a new threat: General Winfield Scott and the nearly twelve thousand Americans who had landed at Vera Cruz.

Scott was the American army's most senior general. An extremely able field commander, he was in addition a fine military administrator and meticulous planner. He also was politically ambitious, a Whig and therefore no favorite of Polk. In fact, the president cared little for either Taylor or Scott, concluding that both were unfit for high command.

Polk had hoped that Taylor's expedition into northeastern Mexico would be sufficient to bring the Mexicans to the bargaining table. When that proved not to be the case, he realized that only if the Americans occupied the Mexican capital would the Mexican government sue for peace. Indeed, any attempt early in the war to negotiate with the United States was seen as treason by Mexico's military and political elites.

So James Polk asked Winfield Scott for a plan to seize Mexico City, which the general duly produced. Once the plan was agreed to, the only question was who would be in charge. Reluctantly, Polk appointed Scott. In truth, he was the logical choice. No other American officer was his equal in stature or skill.

But Winfield Scott was not the only army officer Polk placed in command of an important expedition. On the day the United States declared war on Mexico the president, through Secretary of War William Marcy, directed Colonel Stephen W. Kearny to march west from Kansas to Santa Fe and take control of the lands comprising New Mexico. Once that was accomplished, he was to continue on to California. There, he was to help secure the Pacific territories for the United States.

With 1600 men Kearny departed Fort Leavenworth in June 1846. He had with him also 460 horses, 3,700 mules, 15,000 cattle and oxen, and 16 pieces of artillery. His force was hailed the "Army of the West," and as it trekked through the desert, threats arose from hostile Indians, Mexican patrols, rattlesnakes, and dehydration. But, in mid-August, the colonel and most of his troops arrived in Santa Fe.

Kearny lost no time in establishing an American presence. He claimed the lands for the United States, promised U.S. citizenship to the inhabitants, drafted a constitution for the territory, proclaimed religious freedom, appointed civilian officials, and, along with his soldiers, tasted new foods that were then and now staples of the Southwest. Kearny's energy seemed inexhaustible. Upon determining that all was in order, he moved on. With a much reduced force Kearny entered what is now the state of California on November 25. He had accomplished much, and Polk, in August, had rewarded him with promotion to brigadier general.

Unfortunately, back in New Mexico, the situation deteriorated. The soldiers left behind were behaving badly. Civilians still loyal to Mexico were plotting revenge. And, with a breakdown of law and order, common criminals felt unrestrained. The result was an outbreak of violence, at times brutal. Eventually, American troops pacified the territory, but not before well over two hundred people were dead.

When Kearny reached California, the towns and countryside were far from peaceful. Acting on orders from Polk transmitted via Secretary of the Navy George Bancroft, the American navy had occupied towns along the coast. But in addition to sailors and marines, U.S. Army soldiers had been deployed to California. Some of these were under the command of Lieutenant John C. Fremont, one of those figures in American history who appear larger than life.

Among the inhabitants of California, loyalties were mixed. Some folks wanted the territory to remain part of Mexico. Others favored a semiautonomous region within the southern republic. A few thought California should be an independent nation. Some just wanted to be left alone. A large number thought the future lay with the United States. After a fair amount of bloodshed, political intrigue, and squabbles between Kearny, Fremont, and the senior naval commander, Robert F. Stockton, that brought credit to none of them, the issue was decided. California would join the Union, which it did in 1850, becoming the thirty-first state.

As Kearny was moving into California, one of his officers who had remained in Santa Fe took his troops far to the south, eventually linking up with Zachary Taylor in Monterrey. The officer was Colonel Alexander Doniphan. He commanded about a thousand mounted Missouri volunteers. Besides the extreme hardship of the journey itself, Doniphan encountered elements of the Mexican Army, defeating them twice. When the Americans returned home to the United States, their epic march was over. Doniphan and his men were greeted as heroes.

Doniphan had reached Taylor's camp early in May 1847. Two months earlier Winfield Scott had landed his army on the coast of Mexico, just south of Vera Cruz.

Well fortified and garrisoned by more than four thousand soldiers, Vera Cruz was the gateway to Mexico City, Scott's ultimate objective. His troops came ashore on March 9, 1847. The landing was the first amphibious operation conducted by the United States military. By selecting beaches to the south of the city, Scott's army of twelve thousand men met no opposition during the vulnerable transition from sea to land. The success of the endeavor spoke well of the planning Scott and his staff had conducted and of the skill of the American navy.

Purposefully, Scott eschewed a formal assault upon Vera Cruz. Instead, he brought heavy guns ashore and laid siege, opening fire on March 23.

His artillery pounded the city continuously for seven days. Blockaded seaward by ships of the United States Navy and on land by soldiers of the U.S. Army, the Mexican troops in Vera Cruz had no hope of success. They soon surrendered, on March 29. Only 19 Americans had been killed. Their opponents lost approximately 180, many of them civilians.

Scott lost no time in departing Vera Cruz, heading west to the Mexican capital. He was anxious to avoid the onset of yellow fever, which on the hot and humid coastal plain was always present and often deadly. A small number of troops were left in the city. Throughout the remainder of the war, Vera Cruz would remain the port of entry for American reinforcements and supplies.

To reach Mexico City, Scott chose to march along the route taken by Cortés in 1519. This would take his army through the town of Cerro Gordo. There, Santa Anna, now president of the republic, as well as commander in chief of the army, had deployed some twelve thousand men in a strong defensive position. To his right were steep cliffs overlooking a river. To his left were high hills. The road to the capital ran through the hills. Conditions favored the Mexicans. Scott had but eighty-five hundred men and would be attacking troops well positioned and well armed.

The American commander organized a multipronged assault, one thrust of which was to strike at Santa Anna's rear. This strike was made possible by daring reconnaissance conducted by an army engineering officer who somehow found a path around the Mexican left flank. The officer's name was Robert E. Lee. The attack took place on April 18, 1847, and well before noon, the battle was over. Scott's forces crushed those of Santa Anna. Sixty-three Americans were killed and 337 wounded. The number of Mexican casualties is uncertain, although it was no doubt large. More than 1,000 Mexican soldiers were captured, among them 5 generals. Santa Anna himself escaped, but the wagon carrying coin for his soldiers did not.

At Cerro Cordo Winfield Scott had won a great victory. But his objective was to occupy Mexico City, so he continued west, reaching the city of Puebla on May 28. With a population of seventy-five thousand, the town was among the most important in Mexico. At Puebla the Americans were two-thirds of the way to the capital. Their army numbered about six thou-

sand, although many of these soldiers were in the hospital, unfit for combat. With volunteer brigades leaving for home, with the requirement to
garrison towns along the way, and with the constant presence of men too
sick to fight, the size of Scott's army fluctuated even as reinforcements arrived from Vera Cruz two hundred miles away. Among the reinforcements
to reach Puebla were twenty-four hundred regulars commanded by a
brigadier general, Franklin Pierce. He and his troops joined up with Scott
on August 6.

The next day the Americans broke camp. To hold Puebla, Scott left
behind four hundred soldiers. With them were medical personnel attending eighteen hundred men. According to U.S. Army records the troops
Winfield Scott took out of the city numbered 10,738. Their goal was to
march about a hundred miles through enemy territory, attack a fortified
city with a population of two hundred thousand people, and defeat in
battle an army three times their size. In Great Britain the duke of Wellington, no stranger to military campaigning, is said to have deemed Scott's
position hopeless.

Accompanying Scott and his army was an American diplomat. With
the capture of Vera Cruz Polk and Secretary of State James Buchanan
thought the Mexican government might be amenable to discussing an
end to the conflict. So they appointed Nicholas P. Trist to find out. Trist
was the chief clerk of the Department of State, a lowly sounding title perhaps, but in reality the second-ranking official in the American Foreign
Ministry. His résumé was impressive: Trist had studied law under Thomas
Jefferson, had served as Andrew Jackson's private secretary, and had been
U.S. consul in Havana.

The capital of the Republic of Mexico was situated just west of three
large lakes. To the north was Lake Texcoco, largest of the three. To
the south lay Lake Chalco. Between them were extensive marshlands. The
third lake was to the northwest of Lake Chalco and called Lake Xochimilco. To the west of this lake was El Pedregal, a stony hard lava field
difficult to transit. The simplest way into the city was over causeways that
crossed the marshes. However, easy to defend, these would be difficult if
not disastrous for any attacking force to utilize.

On the advice of his engineers, among them not just Lee but a George B. McClellan, Scott chose to attack from the south, skirting around Lake Chalco and moving northwest, with Lake Xochimilco on his right. On August 17, his troops occupied the town of San Augustin, just nine miles from Mexico City.

Not unreasonably, Santa Anna had expected Scott to approach from the north. When he learned of the Americans' movements, he redeployed his forces, moving General Gabriel Valencia's army to meet the threat from the south. With four thousand troops Valencia moved into a position between two villages, Padierna and Contreras. He expected El Pedregal to complicate the expected American attack. It did, but it did not prevent it. Elements of Scott's army crossed the lava field and defeated Valencia's force. Santa Anna was not pleased. He ordered that Valencia, who had disobeyed an order to withdraw, be shot. Yet Santa Anna could have done better himself. At one time during the battle the Americans were vulnerable to a strike by the Mexican commander in chief's men, who were positioned just north of Valencia's. But Santa Anna stayed put. He thus missed an opportunity to inflict a decisive blow against Winfield Scott.

The battle was fought on August 20 and was over by noon. It was a stunning victory for the Americans. They killed some seven hundred of the enemy and captured more than eight hundred. Additionally, they took possession of substantial numbers of guns, mules, and other military supplies. As one scholar of the war, Robert Selph Henry, put it, Valencia's army "had ceased to exist as a military unit."

But Padierna, or Contreras as it is sometimes called, was only the first of two battles fought that day. The second would be far bloodier.

North of Pedregal was a small river, the Churubusco. The Mexicans had established a strongpoint at one of its bridges and at the Convent of San Mateo nearby. At both locations, Mexican artillery was in place, manned by Irishmen who had deserted from the American army. Known as the San Patricios, these men would fight hard, aware of the consequences should they be captured.

That afternoon the Americans attacked. In three separate actions, Scott's army frontally assaulted the bridge and the convent. The army also

struck at Mexican forces north of the river, crossing another bridge to the
west that was undefended. Winfield Scott committed everything he had
to this fight. At first the attacks were repulsed. Yet the Americans kept
coming, with the bayonet often the weapon of choice. In time, despite
fighting hard, the Mexicans gave way. Scott's army had triumphed again.

But the cost to the Americans was high. The battles of August 20, 1847,
had resulted in 1,016 casualties, most of them at Churubusco. The dead
numbered 138.

For the Mexicans the day—it was a Friday—was a disaster. Santa
Anna's army had been crushed. Four thousand Mexican soldiers were
killed or wounded. Three thousand were taken prisoner. Santa Anna and
the remnants of his force withdrew to the outskirts of the capital city itself.
There they waited, expecting the American commander to regroup and
attack again.

Instead, Scott proposed a truce.

He reasoned that it might encourage the Mexican government to discuss how to end the war, a view concurred with by Nicholas Trist. Moreover, further bloodshed would be avoided and the needs of the army better
served. Scott's healthy soldiers needed to rest. His wounded needed attention. Both were in need of supplies, particularly food. So the general offered
a cease fire, knowing that, if need be, his army could easily engage the
enemy once again.

The Mexicans accepted Scott's offer. On August 20, the two sides signed
an armistice. The agreement called for a cessation of hostilities and an
exchange of prisoners. It forbade military reinforcements and permitted
the Americans to secure supplies from within Mexico City.

Scott hoped that with the guns silent, Trist would be able to negotiate
a peace treaty. But the diplomat was unable to do so. The Mexicans were
not yet ready and the American terms were too stiff. Meanwhile, Santa
Anna, a genius of sorts but not an individual to be trusted, had begun
rebuilding his army (a task for which he showed extraordinary aptitude)
and enhancing Mexican defenses, two activities expressively forbidden by
the agreement. Whether the Mexican general ordered that supplies to the
Americans be limited is unclear, but they were not as easily obtained as

Scott had hoped. On September 6, 1847, the American commander notified his counterpart that the truce was no longer in force.

Two days later American artillery opened fire, in support of infantry that was marching into battle. Their targets were two stone buildings situated outside the capital city. These were known as Molina del Rey and Casa Mata. The former was a foundry Scott believed to be manufacturing cannons. The American force was no small detachment. In total it numbered 3,250 men. One of them, Captain Kirby Smith, wrote his wife the night before that "tomorrow will be a day of slaughter."

It was. The Mexican defenders were well deployed and, as they so often did, fought tenaciously. As the Americans surged forward, General Peña y Barragán organized two counterattacks. These failed, and after hard fighting, Scott's forces, led by Brigadier General William Worth (who, after the war, would give his name to a fort in Texas near the future city of Dallas), carried the day. Worth's men suffered terribly: 653 were wounded, 117 were killed, in total nearly one-fourth of the attacking force. Those who survived, and Kirby Smith was not one of them, were ordered to return to their base. General Scott had envisioned the attack as a raid, not as an assault to win and hold ground. Later, both American commanders learned that no capability to construct cannons existed at the Molina.

The next target for American artillery was the fortified, rocky ridge called Chapultepec. Two hundred feet high, it dominated the landscape. At its top were several buildings that once had served as the summer palace of the Spanish viceroys. In 1847 they constituted the Mexican military college where young cadets learned the art and science of warfare. Chapultepec was significant, not as a military objective, but as the very symbol of the Mexican Republic. To capture it would signal an American victory. To lose it to the invaders would mean Mexican defeat and dishonor.

The battle for Chapultepec was to be the climax of the war.

On September 12 the American bombardment began. It lasted fourteen hours. The Mexican commander on the ridge, Nicolás Bravo, a hero of the effort in 1821 to oust Spain, called for reinforcements. Santa Anna, believing Chapultepec to be vulnerable, denied the request. He preferred to save his rebuilt army for a last-ditch defense of the city itself.

Scott carefully planned his attack. He feinted an assault from one direction and struck from two others. His troops stormed up the muddy slopes. Fighting was fierce, often hand-to-hand. More than once quarter was neither sought nor given. One American lieutenant, James Longstreet, fell wounded. The flag he was carrying was picked up by a fellow officer, George Pickett. The Mexicans fought hard. But the Americans kept coming. They were unstoppable. Two hours after it began, the assault was over. Scott's army controlled Chapultepec, at a cost of 834 casualties.

Mexico had lost the battle, and the war. But it had gained a legend. The cadets of Chapultepec had fought the Americans and died for their country. Their heroism would never be forgotten. Today, as in the past, *los niños héroes de Chapultepec* are celebrated throughout the Republic.

The Americans also gained something memorable. Among the troops assaulting Chapultepec were forty United States marines. Fighting hard, they had reached the top of the ridge, entering what the hymn of their beloved corps would term "the halls of Montezuma."

The bloodshed did not stop with the American capture of Chapultepec. Scott's army pushed on, entering Mexico City. There, as at Monterrey, men fought house by house, street by street. Destructive and bloody it was, but the battle was over by the end of the day. The Americans controlled the capital of Mexico.

Instead of a last-ditch defense of the city, Santa Anna chose to leave. Within the city and at Chapultepec he had lost some eighteen hundred men. Seeing no hope of winning, he and a still substantial number of men evacuated the city. Santa Anna hoped there would be another battle, one that he might win and so turn the tide. No such battle would occur. A few skirmishes perhaps, but no further engagements wherein armies clashed. The Mexican War was over. The United States had won, and decisively so.

Winfield Scott entered Mexico City on September 14, 1847. He had accomplished what he had set out to do. He had taken Vera Cruz, defeated the Mexicans at Cerro Gordo and Contreras, won victories at Churubusco and Chapultepec, and captured the Mexican capital, all in seven months. And he had done so with a relatively small army. Scott had done what a senior commander must do: he had planned, organized, and directed. Others would do the actual fighting. Winfield Scott had performed brilliantly. That few Americans remember him today detracts not at all from his accomplishment.

With Santa Anna gone, the civic leaders of Mexico City met with Scott. Together they arranged the American occupation of the capital. This would last until June of the following year, and was relatively peaceful. Scott himself departed in February.

Once the fighting essentially was over, Nicholas Trist entered center stage. His job was to negotiate a peace treaty. In doing so, he faced several obstacles, two of which were substantial. The first was that the Mexican government was far from organized. Securing legitimacy for discussions with the Americans was difficult, much less agreeing on terms. The second obstacle was more straightforward. Trist was recalled by Polk. The president thought that the emissary's long stay in Mexico conveyed the message that the United States would do practically anything to nail down a treaty. Polk, through Buchanan, ordered Trist home.

Nicholas Trist then did something extraordinary. He ignored Polk's directive. Trist reasoned that the best chance for successful negotiations lay with him already there and at work. So he stayed put. In time, the Mexicans came to the table and they and Trist produced a settlement. It is called the Treaty of Guadalupe Hidalgo after the town in which it was signed.

The treaty established the boundary between Mexico and its northern neighbor. Additionally, the agreement called for the latter to pay the former $15 million for the lands ceded to the United States and to assume payment of certain claims filed against Mexico. Not surprisingly, as Trist had negotiated from a position of strength, terms of the treaty were favorable to the United States. As for the Mexicans, they just wanted the Americans to leave.

Angry with Trist, Polk nonetheless submitted the treaty to the U.S. Senate. Approval was not a foregone conclusion. Some senators wanted even more territory, some less. Some wanted slavery prohibited in the lands gained. To this, senators from the South predictably objected. Some simply wanted to embarrass Polk, as he and "his war" no longer were popular.

Debate in the Senate lasted eleven days, during which there were thirteen roll call votes. Finally, on March 10, 1848, the treaty, in modified form, was brought to a vote. It passed thirty-nine to fourteen. The Mexican Chamber of Deputies and Senate agreed to the same text in May.

On June 19, 1848, amid great fanfare, the Stars and Stripes were hauled down in the center of Mexico City. Replacing the American flag was the green, white, and red banner of the Republic of Mexico. Control of the city, and therefore of the country, reverted to those to whom it belonged.

Why did Mexico not win?

Throughout the conflict Mexico enjoyed several advantages that might have led to victory: On the battlefield the Mexicans usually outnumbered the Americans. They were well armed and not lacking in courage. Indeed, Mexican troops fought hard and with skill. Moreover, they were defending their homeland, a situation that often serves to motivate soldiers. So why did they not defeat the Americans? The answer lies in the skill of their military commanders. The Mexican generals, particularly Antonio López de Santa Anna, were not up to the tasks entrusted to them. They failed the test of leadership.

Why did the Americans win?

The Americans won their war with Mexico because the United States Army performed superbly. At the top were two generals who were expert at their trade. Zachary Taylor both inspired his men and positioned them to win. Winfield Scott organized and led an expedition into the heart of enemy territory and did so brilliantly. In the middle were the lieutenants and captains, many of them graduates of the newly established military academy adjacent to the Hudson River. At West Point these young officers learned skills that served them well at Monterrey and Buena Vista, Cerro Gordo and Chapultepec. Many of these officers—Grant, Longstreet, Lee, and Meade among them—would be heard from again. At the bottom ranks of the U.S. Army were the ordinary soldiers. They were regulars and volunteers, two distinct groups that rarely held the other in high regard. But in battle, each fought tenaciously, matching the courage of their Mexican counterparts.

In support of these officers and men was a branch of the army that deserves special mention. Throughout the war, American artillery was particularly effective, often, as John S. D. Eisenhower has written, "the difference between defeat and victory."

Was the war with Mexico a just war?

The Whigs certainly thought not. Fourteen Whigs had opposed the initial declaration and, as the war continued and casualties mounted, opposition to the war increased. In the 1846 midterm elections Polk's Democrats lost control of the House of Representatives, largely due to the war. Two years later they lost the White House. Whigs saw the war with Mexico as a blatant grab for land or simply as a partisan ploy on the part of Polk. They also saw the war as an effort by Southerners to extend slavery. Subscribing to the last view was a veteran of the conflict and of the one that followed. In his memoirs, Grant wrote that the Mexican War was unjust and, moreover, that the annexation of Texas itself was a conspiracy to bring additional slave states into the Union.

If Grant was correct, then the war clearly was not justified. But there is another interpretation, one that sees the war as not about slavery, but about land. Many Americans, Whigs, and Democrats alike believed that the United States should extend to the Pacific coast. They considered it America's destiny to span the continent. The war to them was simply the means by which destiny was to be realized.

Was the war then simply an effort to acquire land?

If so, and this view has much merit, was the effort an honorable one? Some would say no. They would contend that the United States invaded Mexico and, by force of arms, stripped it of land. Others would see a more complicated picture. They would point out that the land in question was sparsely inhabited, that many of the inhabitants had no love of or allegiance to the Republic of Mexico, and that in the Treaty of Guadalupe Hidalgo the Americans paid Mexico for the land ceded to the United States.

Justified or not, was the war inevitable?

One purpose of diplomacy is to settle differences between nations without either side resorting to force. In the case of Mexico and the United States in the 1840s, diplomacy failed. James Polk tried to negotiate with Mexico but was unable to do so. Once Texas became part of the Union, Mexico considered itself at war. To keep the peace, diplomacy would have had to accommodate Mexican pride and grievances and, at the same time, take into account America's irresistible appetite for new lands. That was not impossible, but only a saint could have brokered a peaceful resolution. None was available in 1846.

Did the Mexican War have a significant impact on the United States?

It most certainly did. The conflict of 1846–1848 shaped the future of the country. Most importantly, and obviously, the war increased the nation's size. The territory that now comprises the states of Arizona, California, Nevada, New Mexico, and Utah as well as parts of Colorado and Wyoming became part of the United States. The dream of many Americans for a nation that stretched from the Atlantic to the Pacific became a reality.

America's military greatly benefitted from the war. Those young West Pointers who served under Zachary Taylor and Winfield Scott gained experience in Mexico. When they rose to command Union and Confederate armies in 1860–1865 they were battle-tested. Historian Douglas V. Meed reports that more than 130 men who saw service in the Mexican War achieved the role of general in the armies of either the North or the South.

The American Civil War began as an effort to preserve the Union. Abolitionists in the North may have wanted to abolish slavery in 1860, but Abraham Lincoln didn't. He wanted to keep the United States together. Had slavery been limited to those states where it had an established foothold, the war might not have been fought. But the expansion of the United

States in 1848 —resulting from the war with Mexico—raised the question of whether the new lands would be free or slave. That caused slavery to be an issue on the national agenda, one that could not be set aside. Extremely contentious, the failure to resolve the issue triggered events that twelve years after the conclusion of the war with Mexico led to Americans again taking up arms, this time against one another.

4

BETWEEN
THE STATES

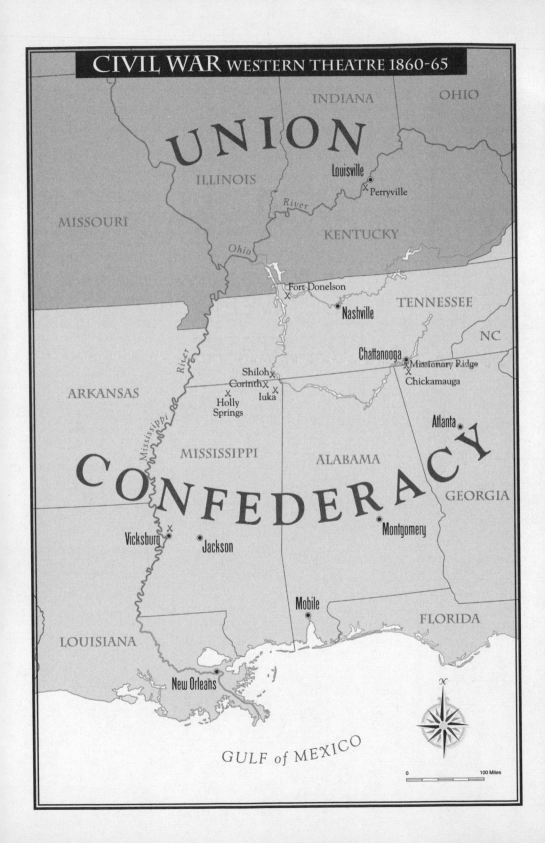

CIVIL WAR WESTERN THEATRE 1860-65

UNION

INDIANA

OHIO

ILLINOIS

Louisville
X Perryville

MISSOURI

KENTUCKY

River

Ohio

Fort Donelson
X

TENNESSEE

Nashville

NC

Chattanooga
X Missionary Ridge
Chickamauga

River

Shiloh X
Corinth X
X
Holly   Iuka
Springs

ARKANSAS

Atlanta

Mississippi

MISSISSIPPI

ALABAMA

CONFEDERACY

GEORGIA

Montgomery

Vicksburg X

Jackson

Mobile

FLORIDA

LOUISIANA

New Orleans

GULF of MEXICO

0   100 Miles

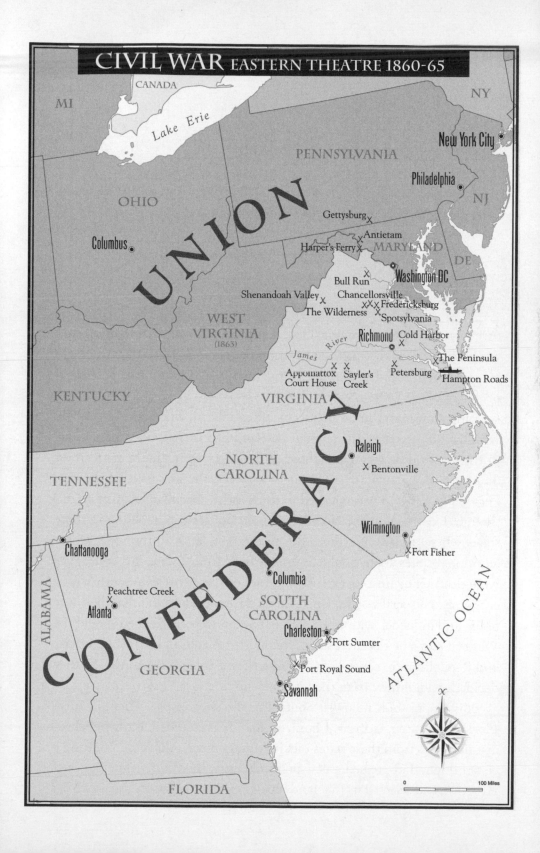

CIVIL WAR EASTERN THEATRE 1860-65

CANADA

MI

NY

Lake Erie

New York City

PENNSYLVANIA

OHIO

Philadelphia

NJ

Columbus

Gettysburg ×

Antietam ×

DE

Harper's Ferry × × MARYLAND

UNION

Washington DC

Bull Run ×

Shenandoah Valley × Chancellorsville

WEST
VIRGINIA
(1863)

The Wilderness × × × Fredericksburg

Spotsylvania

River

Richmond × Cold Harbor

James

KENTUCKY

Appomattox × × Sayler's
Court House Creek

Petersburg ×

× The Peninsula

× Hampton Roads

VIRGINIA

CONFEDERACY

Raleigh

NORTH
CAROLINA

TENNESSEE

× Bentonville

Wilmington

Chattanooga

× Fort Fisher

Columbia

Peachtree Creek

ALABAMA

×
Atlanta

SOUTH
CAROLINA

ATLANTIC OCEAN

Charleston × Fort Sumter

GEORGIA

× Port Royal Sound

Savannah

FLORIDA

0   100 Miles

1861–1865

Five days before Christmas in 1860, South Carolina, in a convention convened to consider the question of secession, chose to leave the American federal union. It did so because Abraham Lincoln had just been elected president of the United States.

Lincoln was an Illinois politician, a Republican, who had been elected with but 40 percent of the popular vote and had carried not a single state in the South. His views and those of his party were anathema to most Southerners, particularly in regard to slavery, the key issue of the day. Personally, Lincoln was opposed to the South's "peculiar institution," although, like many in the North, he would not seek its abolition in those states where it already existed. But in the new lands to the west, where additional states soon would be established, Lincoln and his colleagues were dead set against its extension. States of the American South whose economy and social system depended on slavery understood that their way of life and influence within the national union were threatened should the Western states be declared slave-free. With Lincoln in the White House and Republicans in control of Congress, they feared for the future. So they decided to withdraw from the Union.

Mississippi soon followed South Carolina's example. Then, in turn, Florida, Alabama, Georgia, Louisiana, and Texas seceded. Early in February, delegates from these states met in Montgomery, Alabama. Drafting a constitution, they created a new political entity, the Confederate States of America, and selected its first (and only) president, Jefferson Davis of Mississippi. In addition, they declared their intent to exercise control of federal military assets within the South, including forts along the coast.

Lincoln had no intention of allowing the seven states to secede, nor of transferring military resources to those he considered in rebellion. Cleverly, he maneuvered the South into firing the first shot, which it did on April 12, 1861. That morning Confederate artillery opened fire on Fort Sumter in Charleston Harbor. Thirty-four hours later the fort surrendered. Though no one had been killed, the bloodiest war in America's history had begun.

Two days later Lincoln issued a call for seventy-five thousand men to join the army. Then, on April 19, he proclaimed a naval blockade of the Confederate coast. The blockade would prove effective, though the president would need, and obtain, a far greater number of soldiers.

Meanwhile, Virginia, Arkansas, North Carolina, and Tennessee signed on with the Confederacy. That brought the number of states in rebellion to eleven, all committed to slavery. Four slave-holding states—Delaware, Maryland, Kentucky, and Missouri—remained in the Union.

When Virginia seceded, the Confederate capital was moved to Richmond, one hundred miles south of Washington, D.C. Defending the Southern city was an army that both in its day and in history became legendary, the Army of Northern Virginia. Aiming to seize Richmond was the North's premier fighting force: the Army of the Potomac (Union armies tended to be named after the river in the area where they first assembled). These two armies, each with its eyes on Richmond, would battle each other throughout the conflict, fighting seven of the war's longest battles.

The first one took place on July 21, 1861, at Manassas Junction. This was in northern Virginia, not far from Washington. To reach the enemy, Lincoln's troops had to cross a small stream called Bull Run. In command of the Union force, some thirty thousand men, was General Irwin McDowell, whose army was, up to then, the largest military force ever to be seen in America. But they were an untrained lot lacking in discipline and experience. McDowell pointed this out to Lincoln, who responded that the same was true of the rebels. The Union commander wanted more time to prepare his troops for their first battle, but the political pressure to march "on to Richmond" was such that Lincoln ordered him to engage the enemy, which he did. McDowell's plan was to hold the Confederates' center while moving around to his right, attacking the rebels' left flank. The plan was solid and it almost worked. But Confederate reinforcements arrived at a critical time, and McDowell's army was sent scurrying back to Washington.

The Union defeat at Bull Run (the North tended to name battles by the nearby body of water, while the South called them by the town near where the battle occurred) was followed three weeks later by another defeat, this time in the West. There, in Missouri, a small Union army led by Nathaniel Lyon attacked a larger Confederate force. This proved unwise, as Lyon lost his life and the federals lost the battle. These early setbacks destroyed the hopes of many in the North who, anticipating early success on the battlefield, had expected a quick return to the political fold on the part of the South.

Two additional events associated with the Southern victory at Bull Run are worth mentioning. The first took place during the battle. The second occurred afterward. The first event explains one of the most famous nicknames in all of American history. During the early hours of the fight, when Northern troops appeared to have their Southern counterparts on the run, a senior Confederate commander, Thomas Jackson, effectively rallied his troops. Another Southern general pointed this out to his own wavering men, exclaiming, "There is Jackson standing like a stone wall." Henceforth, General Jackson had a moniker that would stay with him forever.

The second event associated with the July 1861 engagement at Bull Run was the appointment of a new commander of the Army of the Potomac. President Lincoln relieved McDowell, who fades from our story. His successor was a West Point graduate by the name of George B. McClellan.

An extremely capable military executive, McClellan retooled the Army of the Potomac. Under his leadership, the army, dispirited by its performance at Bull Run, became a first-rate fighting force. No longer a collection of amateurs, the Army of the Potomac was transformed into a body of men willing and able to fight. Having selected many of its top officers and attending to the needs of ordinary soldiers, McClellan was revered by the 120,000 he would lead into battle. The Army of the Potomac was his army.

Much was expected of this force and of its commander. Northern newspapers heaped praise on McClellan, who came to see himself, as did others, as the savior of the American republic. Lincoln was more perceptive, but he hoped the young general—McClellan was only thirty-four—would swiftly move his army south and take Richmond.

The general, however, procrastinated. In a pattern that would repeat itself, he delayed his departure, asking for more troops and more equipment, justifying his action by exaggerating the size of the opposing army. Abraham Lincoln said McClellan had "the slows." Frustrated, the president pushed hard to get the general to move, which he finally did, in March 1862.

Instead of taking his army overland to Richmond, McClellan moved south via the navy, landing his troops on the peninsula bounded by the York and James Rivers. Richmond lay not far to the west. He thus kept his supply lanes free from attack and avoided battle while in transit. Methodically and slowly, as was his style, McClellan advanced, eventually coming within five miles of the Confederate capital.

Known to historians as the Peninsula Campaign, McClellan's efforts in late spring and early summer of 1862 did not succeed. A number of battles took place, not all of which the Union army lost. Yet the net result was failure, for Richmond remained under Southern control. Disheartened, the Army of the Potomac withdrew from the peninsula in August.

In one of the early battles on the Peninsula, the general commanding Confederate forces was wounded and had to be replaced. His successor was Robert E. Lee, who, with ninety thousand men, the largest number of soldiers ever to comprise the Army of Northern Virginia, proceeded to outmaneuver the Union forces. However, the cost to the South was high. During the campaign, Lee suffered more than twenty thousand casualties. McClellan, who blamed his defeat on everyone but himself, paid in blood as well: the Union army had more than fifteen thousand killed or wounded.

These losses, as well as subsequent ones, upset McClellan on a personal level. He felt the pain of his men and worked hard to secure medical treatment for them. Given his reaction to the dead and wounded, it's not clear that George B. McClellan had the stomach to do what generals must.

As the Army of the Potomac began its campaign on the peninsula, a clash of a different sort took place at Hampton Roads, a body of water at the confluence of the James and Elizabeth Rivers in southeastern Virginia, immediately north of Norfolk. It was on these waters, on March 9, 1862, that two ships, one belonging to Abraham Lincoln's navy, the other to its Confederate counterpart, fought a battle that forever changed naval warfare.

Upon seizing the Norfolk navy yard in April 1861, Southern engineers rebuilt the partially destroyed Union steam frigate the *Merrimac*. But what they created was an entirely new form of warship. Discarding masts and sails, they constructed an armored warship with sloping sides (the armor and angled structure would cause enemy shells to ricochet off rather than penetrate the vessel) powered by the *Merrimac*'s repaired engine. They armed the ship with ten guns and, in a throwback to Roman times, attached a fifteen-hundred-pound iron ram to the bow. Christened the *Virginia*, this strange-looking vessel first went to sea on Saturday, March 8, 1862. Her commander was Flag Officer Franklin Buchanan, an experienced sailor who had been the first superintendent of the United States Naval Academy.

Buchanan took the *Virginia* into Hampton Roads intent on striking at Union warships that formed part of the blockade Lincoln had ordered the previous year. Buchanan's first sortie was a success. Employing both guns and the ram, his ship sunk the USS *Cumberland*, a twenty-four-gun wooden sloop, and then so damaged the fifty-gun frigate *Congress* that the Union vessel later exploded and was destroyed.

In but an afternoon the *Virginia* apparently had altered the naval equation of the War Between the States. She had demonstrated that the Confederate navy could challenge the much larger Union fleet and, thereby, break the blockade. If the United States Navy's blockade could be rendered ineffective, the chances were good that the South might win its battle for separation from the Northern American states.

However, that same Saturday, about an hour after the *Virginia* had dropped anchor, having returned safely to port, an equally strange vessel, this one belonging to the North, tied up alongside a Union warship in Hampton Roads. Her name was the USS *Monitor*.

She had been built in Brooklyn when Union naval leaders had learned the rebels were constructing an ironclad in Norfolk. Designed for calm, coastal waters, her freeboard (that portion of the side of the hull above the water) was but eighteen inches. She carried neither masts nor sails and had a crew of only 49 (the *Virginia*'s crew numbered 360). Amidships was an armored, rotating turret containing two cannons. No one had ever seen a ship like her.

The *Monitor*'s captain was Lieutenant John Worden. He weighed anchor at 8:10 in the morning and steamed out into Hampton Roads. His goal was to protect a Union ship that had run aground the day before. This was the USS *Minnesota*, a vessel the *Virginia* was determined to sink. Thus began the famous "duel of the ironclads." The fight lasted four hours as the two ships turned and fired, then fired and turned. Neither the *Monitor* nor the *Virginia* was sunk, nor was either seriously damaged. Late that afternoon, they returned to their respective ports. Southerners claimed a victory although the blockade remained in force. Northerners, disputing the claim, simply went to work and built more ships like the *Monitor*.

They also built a large number of shallow-draft, armored steamboats for use on America's rivers. These would play a key role in the war, ferrying troops and supplies and bombarding Confederate fortifications.

Union shipyards were central to the success of Abraham Lincoln's cause. During the war years they built 200 warships. They also helped convert 418 merchant ships into military vessels. At the beginning of the conflict the U. S. Navy had only 90 ships. By 1865, the number was 671.

This huge armada enforced the blockade, no mean task as the Southern coastline extended some thirty-five hundred miles from Virginia to Texas. Confederate blockade runners occasionally slipped through, but the overall effort was to stifle the South's lucrative trade in cotton and to reduce significantly the importation of British firearms. In addition to blockade runners, which used Bermuda, Nassau, and Havana as ports of origin, the South had a small number of oceangoing warships, built mostly in England. They were deployed to intercept Northern vessels far out at sea, much as the tiny U.S. Navy had done in the War of 1812. Perhaps the most famous of the Confederate warships was the CSS *Alabama*. Commanded by Raphael Semmes, she sunk sixty-five ships during her two-year cruise. However, on June 19, 1864, the federal navy caught up with her off Cherbourg in the form of the USS *Kearsarge*, which took but ninety minutes to end her career as a maritime raider.

Whether on the high seas or on fast-flowing rivers, the Union navy had much to do with the defeat of the South, a role that seems overlooked as Americans today recall their Civil War. Yet throughout the conflict sailors and marines were in action. Early in the war, for example, the United States Navy conducted a successful amphibious operation capturing the forts that defended Hatteras Inlet in North Carolina. Two months later, a fleet of seventy-seven vessels, under the command of Samuel F. Dupont, took control of the Confederate forts off Port Royal Sound along the coast of South Carolina. Of greater importance to the Union cause was the seizure in April 1862 of New Orleans by ships directed by David G. Farragut who, three months later, was rewarded with the rank of rear admiral, the first such American to be so invested. Better known is Farragut's later exploit off Alabama. In attacking the Confederate positions guarding Mobile, Farragut shouted, "Damn the torpedoes, full speed ahead," as his ships charged through a narrow channel. The "torpedoes" were, in fact, what today are called mines, a munition which, according to naval historian Jack Sweetman, the South showed great resourcefulness in using to eventually put forty Union warships out of action. Farragut's fleet made it through the channel losing but one vessel, the monitor *Tecumseh*. Subsequently, his ships destroyed several Confederate warships and closed the port to Southern commerce, further tightening the naval screws that so weakened the Confederacy.

One last aspect of the conflict at sea is worth noting. Of the more than 170,000 men who served in the Union navy during the War Between the States, 18,000 were black Americans. Ten times as many served in the Union armies, but, unlike those soldiers, these black sailors were assigned to units in which white Americans served. Thus the Union navy, to a degree, was an integrated force. Congress recognized that black citizens represented a valuable pool of manpower. So in 1862 it authorized military service for African-Americans by passing the Second Confiscation Act in July. This act and other steps led to a large number of blacks donning the blue uniform of the Union army. By war's end there were 166 black regiments in the army's Order of Battle. More than a few were given secondary or menial tasks, yet when called upon to fight they performed well.

When General McClellan withdrew from the Peninsula, contingents of the Army of the Potomac were detached for service with a newly established Union army. Its commander was Major General John Pope, an officer who had had success in the West. He would not have much in Virginia. Abrasive and conceited, he was an unpopular choice. But Lincoln wanted a general who was eager to do battle, and Pope, for all his faults, was that.

Late in August Pope's army met that of Lee. The result was a victory for the South. The battle again took place at Bull Run in Virginia. Union casualties were high: some thirteen thousand soldiers were killed or wounded.

Several of Lincoln's advisors urged him to sack both Pope and McClellan, as neither general had distinguished himself. The president agreed that this was so, but dismissed only Pope. The general's army became part of the Army of the Potomac. Thus this latter army was now a substantial military force. It required a commander who could restore its pride and prepare it for battle. Lincoln knew, better than anyone else, that McClellan would do both.

Meanwhile, in Richmond, Jefferson Davis devised a strategy he believed might win the war. A West Point graduate, the Confederate president planned an invasion of the North, In fact, he set in motion two such endeavors. One in the West would strike into Kentucky. The other would take Lee's Army of Northern Virginia across the Potomac River into Maryland. Kentucky and Maryland were border states with residents sympathetic to the Southern cause. Success likely would bring them into the Confederacy.

Robert E. Lee was fully supportive of this plan. He wanted to relieve his beloved Virginia of the hardship of war. He wanted Northerners to experience firsthand the destruction that accompanies military conflict. He wanted to engage the Army of the Potomac in a decisive battle, one he believed he would win. And, along with Jefferson Davis, Lee wanted a victory up north that might persuade Abraham Lincoln to sue for peace. Moreover, both Lee and Davis were convinced that such a victory would cause Great Britain to recognize the Confederate States of America. Such

recognition would enhance the chances of gaining Southern independence, much as victory at Saratoga in 1777, by bringing about recognition
from France, had aided the American rebels.

The advance into Kentucky began late in August 1862. Commanded
by Braxton Bragg, thirty thousand Confederate soldiers moved from Mississippi to Tennessee, then into Kentucky, a state Lincoln believed had to
remain in Union hands. Defending Kentucky was Major General Don
Carlos Buell, whose Army of the Ohio outnumbered that of Bragg. Buell
was a military professional who rarely moved with speed and lacked an
aggressive approach to war, much like McClellan. The two armies clashed
at Perryville on October 8. Neither appeared to win, but with Confederate
setbacks at Iuka and Corinth, Bragg wisely decided to return home. Buell
did not pursue him and was relieved of command. But, as he no doubt said
to himself more than once, he had kept Kentucky in the Union.

The advance into Maryland began in September 1862, when lead elements of the Army of Northern Virginia began crossing the Potomac River.
Numbering approximately forty-five thousand, the army was structured
as two corps. One was commanded by Jackson, the other by James Longstreet, both extremely capable senior officers. Lee sent Jackson and his men
to capture the federal garrison at Harpers Ferry. Longstreet was to continue
north. Once reunited, the army either would head into Pennsylvania or
turn and fight the Union army that Lee expected would be in pursuit.
Thus Robert E. Lee had split his army in two, a tactic military experts say
is often unwise.

If McClellan and the Army of the Potomac could fall on each of the
Confederate corps separately, they could destroy the South's principal
military force. Such an outcome became a realistic possibility when Union
soldiers found a copy of Lee's orders describing his plan. To succeed, Mc-
Clellan had to move quickly. He did, but not quickly enough.

Troops belonging to Longstreet delayed the Army of the Potomac in
battles at South Mountain in which each side suffered more than twenty-
two hundred casualties. Soon thereafter, Stonewall Jackson took control
of Harpers Ferry, taking twelve thousand prisoners along with much
needed supplies. Learning that McClellan was aware of his intentions, Lee

ordered Jackson to promptly link up with Longstreet, which he did. Lee then placed his entire army just outside Sharpsburg, Maryland, and prepared to fight. Close by flowed Antietam Creek.

When McClellan arrived at Sharpsburg, his army was a powerful force, comprising some eighty thousand soldiers. His plan of attack was to have three assaults in sequence, on the Confederate left, center, and right. This would prevent Lee from moving troops from one spot to reinforce another. The plan was sound, but it required clear communication, constant pressure on the enemy, and precise timing. These three goals the Union army and its commander could not deliver. What the soldiers in blue could deliver was raw courage and murderous firepower, and on that day, September 17, 1862, the Army of the Potomac brought with it plenty of both.

The Union attack began shortly after sunrise. The Union I Corps, commanded by Major General Joseph Hooker, struck hard upon the Confederate left. Across a cornfield they marched, suffering heavily, as did their Southern cousins. A second federal corps entered the fray and it too paid a heavy price. Then to the south, in the middle of the Confederate line, other Union soldiers advanced against the rebels, who were entrenched along a sunken road. There the fighting was furious and long, lasting beyond three hours. The soldiers in blue prevailed, though the cost—on both sides—was high. Further south, on Lee's right flank, a small narrow stone bridge crossed Antietam Creek. McClellan's IX Corps, commanded by Major General Ambrose Burnside, was to cross the creek, push the Confederates back, and envelop Lee's forces to the north. However, Burnside launched his attack late and, instead of fording Antietam Creek in several places, concentrated his men at the bridge. The result was heavy casualties and time lost in crossing the creek. Eventually, his men pushed the defenders back and were able to move north. But not very far north, for his soldiers were exhausted and unable to breach A. P. Hill's division, fresh troops that had arrived from Harpers Ferry truly in the nick of time.

So the Battle of Antietam came to a close. It had been a day unlike any other in American history. From McClellan's army the number of dead totaled 2,108. For Lee, 2,700. Soldiers listed as wounded or missing numbered 10,302 for the North and 11,024 for the South. Thus the butcher's bill at Antietam added up to 26,134. September 17, 1862 was—and still is—the bloodiest day in American history.

Several of McClellan's corps commanders urged him to continue the fight. They pointed out that Lee's army had been hit hard and that their army had fresh troops available to strike again. But McClellan said no. He was satisfied with the results of September 17 and wanted the Army of the Potomac to regroup. Thus the Union army rested as Robert E. Lee took his men back to Virginia.

McClellan claimed a victory. He had confronted the best the South had to offer and had done well, forcing the Army of Northern Virginia to give up its invasion of the North.

Lincoln too saw Antietam as a victory. He had been waiting for such an outcome in order to issue a document of considerable importance. This was the Emancipation Proclamation. One page in length and dated September 22, 1862, it freed the slaves in those states that were in rebellion. Many Republicans wanted a stronger statement. Many Democrats spoke out in opposition. They did not see emancipation as a legitimate goal of the war and they believed that the proclamation would stiffen Southern resistance.

Along with other steps taken by Congress and the president, the Emancipation Proclamation changed the character of the war. No longer just an effort to preserve the federal union, Lincoln's proclamation transformed the American civil war. It was now a crusade. The objective was to rid the United States of an evil that, since 1777, had made a mockery of Jefferson's words that all men are created equal.

If Abraham Lincoln the politician was satisfied with the steps taken to free the slaves, Abraham Lincoln the American commander in chief was not satisfied with the progress of the Army of the Potomac. Lincoln wanted McClellan to pursue Lee aggressively. But that was not the general's modus operandi. Before campaigning again, he wanted more troops and more time. Finally, at the president's direct urging, he marched his army south in search of Lee and the Southern army. But, as usual, he did so at a deliberate pace. Speed was not an attribute of McClellan's leadership.

By late June, Lincoln had had enough. He wanted a commander eager for combat, willing to fight. McClellan, he concluded, was not that man.

So he sacked George B. McClellan. In his place, the president appointed Ambrose E. Burnside, one of the Army of the Potomac's senior commanders.

Burnside had several strengths, but high command was not one of them. He himself thought he was unequal to the task, a view shared by many in the army. Their judgment was vindicated when Burnside bungled the battle with Lee's army at Fredericksburg. In that debacle, for that's what it was, the Army of the Potomac suffered approximately twelve thousand killed or wounded and gained no advantage either tactical or strategic. Confederate casualties on December 13, 1862, were slightly more than fifty-two hundred.

Nothing Burnside did after the battle restored Lincoln's confidence. So, to the surprise of no one, Ambrose Burnside was dismissed. The Union army's new commander was Major General Joseph Hooker. Like Burnside, he had been one of the army's corps commanders, though, unlike Burnside, he had done well at Antietam. Ambitious and aggressive, Joe Hooker intended to give his Confederate counterpart a solid thrashing. But Lee on a bad day was a better general than Hooker on a good day, a point proven at the Battle of Chancellorsville. There, not far from Fredericksburg, Robert E. Lee outmaneuvered a Union army twice the size of his own. For the South, it was a dramatic victory, though costly, for among the dead was Stonewall Jackson, brought down by friendly fire. For the North, it was a humiliating defeat. Once again, the mighty Army of the Potomac had failed, or at least its commander had.

Heartened by his victories, Lee once again turned north. Battle-tested and accustomed to winning, the Army of Northern Virginia swept through Maryland into Pennsylvania. Lee was confident of victory, perhaps too much so.

Once the Army of the Potomac learned of Lee's movements, it followed in pursuit. However, Joe Hooker no longer was its commander. Lincoln had replaced him with George Meade. Major General Meade was a respected officer, a career military man who understood the art of war.

Standard practice with both the Union and the Confederates on the march was to send cavalry forward with an assignment of determining the whereabouts of the enemy. Meade had done so, and, on June 30, 1863, two brigades of federal cavalry led by Brigadier General John Buford rode into a small Pennsylvania town. Buford soon spotted a large formation of Confederate infantry advancing from the west.

The town was called Gettysburg.

Buford realized that he had bumped into the lead elements of the entire Army of Northern Virginia. Calling for reinforcements, he understood the imperative of preventing the rebels from securing the high ground south of the town. Additional Union troops soon arrived. The next day, the battle began in earnest as Lee's men attacked. In furious fighting, the Confederates pushed the Union back through the town. But, in a strategic blunder, they failed to take control of the heights.

By the second day, July 2, Meade and most of his army had arrived on the scene. They were deployed along the ridges and small hills outside of Gettysburg. Their position resembled that of a fishhook, with hills at each end. In between lay a ridge, Cemetery Ridge, south of which a peach orchard and wheat field spread out on relatively flat land. The overall shape of the Union army was that of a shallow convex line. This enabled Meade to move reinforcements back and forth as required. It was a very strong defensive position.

Lee's army was spread out. It also was smaller, comprising approximately 75,000 men against Meade's 112,000. Moreover, Gettysburg was not where Lee had planned to fight. Yet the town was where the two armies had crossed paths. Lee felt he had to attack and so, on three successive days, he did.

On July 2, the second day of the Battle of Gettysburg, the Southern commander launched a full-scale assault on both ends of the fishhook, starting first with the southern tip. Across the peach orchard and wheat field the men in gray advanced. The fighting was fierce. Union soldiers held fast, then gave ground, then held again. At the southernmost point in the Union line, there was a small, tree-lined, stony hill named Little Round Top. If the Confederates could take it, they would be able to swing around and hit Meade's men from the rear. For the Army of the Potomac, holding Little Round Top was vital. The task of doing so was assigned to a brigade of 1,336 men commanded by Colonel Strong Vincent. He ordered one of his regiments, the 20th Maine, to defend that part of the hill that represented the absolute end of the Union line. With fewer than five hundred soldiers, the regiment held fast, rebuffing repeated attacks by men from Alabama and Texas. When the regiment ran low on ammunition, its commander, Joshua Chamberlain—who, three years earlier, had been a professor at Bowdoin College—issued a command of "fix bayonets." He then led his men down the hill into the attacking Confederates and stopped them once and for all. It was a defining moment in the battle, one of the great actions in American military history, and yet, for all the courage it entailed, it was but one event in a day when courage was common and gunfire left oceans of blood on the ground. Two-thirds of the casualties at Gettysburg occurred on July 2.

On the next day, Lee ordered an attack on the Union center. It was to be a massive assault. More than 150 Confederate cannons would bombard the Union line. Then, General George Pickett's division plus men from A. P. Hill's corps, some twelve thousand men in total, would hit the enemy where Lee believed Meade's forces were weakest. General Longstreet thought the attack unlikely to succeed. He preferred an assault on the Union flanks. But Robert E. Lee insisted that the attack on the center be carried out as planned.

At one o'clock in the afternoon the rebel artillery opened fire. The bombardment lasted for two hours. When it ceased, the Confederate infantry moved forward. For sixteen minutes they marched across an open field, twelve thousand men with guns at the ready. An impressive sight, it marked the high tide of the Confederacy as the men in gray advanced into both battle and legend. But the soldiers in blue were ready. The rebel bombardment had failed to dislodge them, and they and their artillery poured such fire into the Southerners as to shred their ranks. Meade's men held their ground. In less than an hour the Confederate assault disintegrated and with it the Confederate hope of victory. Some six thousand Confederate soldiers were killed, wounded, or captured. What became known as Pickett's Charge was more than a failure, it was a disaster, for the Army of Northern Virginia as well as for the Southern cause, a disaster for which Robert E. Lee alone was responsible.

The failure of the July 3 attack meant Lee had lost the Battle of Gettysburg. The outcome gave hope to the North and to the Army of the

Potomac, which now realized that in future engagements it could more than match its vaunted opponent. For Lee, Gettysburg meant a severe and undeniable defeat.

At Gettysburg, the Confederate army suffered 22,874 casualties, of whom 4,637 were killed. The Army of the Potomac listed its dead at 3,149, with 19,664 men wounded or missing. For those three days in July 1863, 45,687 men were either put in the hospital or never left Gettysburg alive. The number bears repeating: 45,687. Never has the United States of America witnessed such bloodshed.

On July 4, Lee began his retreat, marching south, back into Virginia. He moved as quickly as he could, though speed was difficult, as the army's wagon train of wounded soldiers extended seventeen miles. Meade took up the pursuit and battled with the Confederate rear guard, taking some fifteen hundred prisoners. But the bulk of Lee's force escaped. The result was that the war would continue.

Lincoln was displeased that Meade had allowed Lee to get away. The president wanted the Army of Northern Virginia to be destroyed, not just defeated. He realized that once Lee's army ceased to exist, the Confederate cause would collapse, much as the American fight for independence would have fallen apart had the British been able to destroy Washington's Continental army. Nevertheless, Lincoln retained Meade as the commander of the Army of the Potomac.

Because of Gettysburg, George Meade's place in American history is secure. Yet in his day, he did not gain the fame his success in that battle warranted. One reason was Lincoln's dissatisfaction. Another was that he soon became overshadowed by another general. But the principal reason was newspaper reporters. According to historian Brian Holden Reid, General Meade, in 1864, had humiliated a reporter who had written an insulting article about him. The press retaliated by no longer mentioning Meade when writing about the war. As a result he all but disappeared from public view. Perhaps Meade did not care. He had accomplished something significant: he had beaten Robert E. Lee in battle, winning a victory of immense importance. And he had done so while in command of the Army of the Potomac for but three days, having relieved Hooker on June 28,1863. His was an outstanding performance.

By the time of the great battle, the need for more men to serve in the Union army was clear. The thousands who had volunteered at the outbreak of hostilities were an insufficient number. As a result, Congress had enacted a law drafting men into the army. As it was possible to avoid military service by paying a fee of $300, the law fell heavily on the urban poor, whose support of the war was often tenuous. Why? Because they saw freed slaves as cheap labor that would come north and take their jobs. Moreover, racism was not limited to the South. Not everyone north of the Mason-Dixon Line was an abolitionist. The result in New York City was an outbreak of violence. For five days mobs rampaged through the streets. Buildings were set on fire and people killed. Eighteen African-Americans were hanged. Order was restored only with the arrival of federal troops, some of which came from Gettysburg.

Though Lincoln did not fire Meade as he had McClellan and the others, the president was looking for a general who understood the necessity of ruthlessly destroying the enemy's war machine. He wanted an aggressive general. He wanted a man who would seek out and crush the Confederate armies wherever they were.

Out west there was such a general. Lincoln brought him to Washington and placed him in charge of the entire Union army. The general's name was Ulysses S. Grant.

To reinforce Grant's authority, President Lincoln, with the approval of Congress, conferred on him the rank of lieutenant general. Up to then only two men in the United States had held this three-star rank. One was George Washington. The other was Winfield Scott, the hero of the war with Mexico, although his was of an honorary nature. During the American Civil War generals in command of an army or of its principal subdivision, a corps, were major generals, a two-star rank. As a lieutenant general, Grant outranked them all.

In addition to three stars, Lincoln enhanced Grant's authority by appointing him general in command. At the war's beginning the most senior position in the Union army had been held by Winfield Scott. By 1860 Scott was past his prime, though he did propose to Lincoln the sensible strategy of strangling the South by a naval blockade in the East and by taking control of the Mississippi River in the West. For a short period of time

George B. McClellan was general in chief, having replaced the ailing Scott in October 1861. This didn't work out, so the president appointed Major General Henry Halleck to the position. Halleck was Scott's choice for the job, which entailed providing Lincoln with military advice. Halleck, one of the few intellectuals in the army, was considered by many to be an ideal choice. Yet "Old Brains," as he was called, failed miserably in the job. His critics, and they came to be many, considered him a highly paid clerk. When Grant took over, things would be different.

Ulysses Simpson Grant was thirty-nine years of age when he rejoined the army in June 1861. A graduate of West Point and a veteran of the Mexican War, he'd left the service in 1854 to pursue several business ventures. These did not turn out well; nor did the New York investment banking company he established after he left the White House. Historians, of course, judge his two terms as president (1869–1877) a failure. Clearly, Grant was a man neither of business nor of politics. But he was a man of war. In all of American history, no general stands taller.

Grant's first action against Confederate troops, at Belmont in eastern Missouri, was less than fully successful. He and his troops did better early in 1862 when, with the assistance of navy gunboats, he took control of two key Confederate forts in Tennessee. The second, Fort Donelson, was the more important. In seizing it he captured a strategic position. He also took possession of fifteen thousand Confederate prisoners and a huge supply of enemy stores. Given that Union victories early in the war were infrequent, the capture of Fort Donelson pleased Lincoln greatly. For his efforts Grant was promoted to major general.

With the fall of Fort Donelson, the senior Confederate general in the area, Albert Sidney Johnston, retired south to the town of Corinth in Mississippi, just below the state's boundary with Tennessee. He had forty-five thousand men. They were well equipped and ready to fight. Grant, with slightly fewer troops, had pursued him, moving down the Tennessee River to Pittsburgh Landing, just north of the boundary, where he and his men disembarked. Between the two armies lay relatively flat land and a church called Shiloh.

Grant was waiting for additional troops belonging to Don Carlos Buell, who were coming down from Nashville. Upon their arrival, he planned to attack.

No fool, Albert Sidney Johnston struck first. On April 6, 1862, he hit Grant's forces hard and caused them to fall back. While many Union soldiers fought well, a large number simply ran away. As night fell, it seemed that come morning Johnston's men would push Grant and his troops into the river. However, Grant remained calm. He redeployed his men and said he would counterattack the next day and win the battle, which is what he did, albeit with help from Buell, whose soldiers had just arrived.

Shiloh, occurring before Antietam and Gettysburg, was the first true bloodbath of the Civil War. Confederate casualties numbered 10,699, among them Albert Sidney Johnston, who was killed. Grant's army suffered 13,047 killed or wounded. These numbers shocked people in both the North and South. They began to realize that, in human life, the war was to be extremely costly.

Toward the end of 1862 the North had three field armies confronting the Confederacy. To be sure, there were other troops either in training or guarding lines of supply. And elsewhere there were smaller units on the offensive. But the principal threat to Jefferson Davis and friends came from three Union armies. One was the Army of the Potomac then commanded by Burnside. Another was Grant's Army of the Tennessee. The third was the Army of the Cumberland. Its commander was William S. Rosecrans.

Rosecrans was a cautious yet capable general, popular with his men. He had fought Confederate forces at Iuka and Corinth and done well, though Grant thought he ought to have done better. For his efforts, however, Rosecrans received a vote of thanks from Congress and a promotion.

He was then ordered to take the Army of the Cumberland southeast for another crack at Bragg. The purpose was to keep Bragg's army away from Grant in Mississippi. Rosecrans accomplished this, but on September, 19, 1863, his army was defeated at Chickamauga. Only calm steadying of troops by Major General George H. Thomas prevented a Union rout. No small affair, total casualties at Chickamauga numbered thirty thousand. Afterward, the Army of the Cumberland retreated into Chattanooga.

Rosecrans was soon relieved. He was at odds with Lincoln's secretary of war, and by now Grant thought little of him. Command of the Army of the Cumberland went to Thomas. Grant himself became in charge of all Union forces in the West. His army, the Army of the Tennessee, was now led by William Tecumseh Sherman.

While Rosecrans was in Tennessee focusing on Bragg, Grant had been in Mississippi attempting to capture Vicksburg. In July 1863, he finally did so, but it was not an easy campaign.

Vicksburg controlled the central portion of the Mississippi River. Capturing it would cut the Confederacy in half, depriving the Southern states to the east of the food produced in Louisiana and Texas. The river was, as historian Robin H. Neillands has noted, a great commercial highway. Both sides wanted, indeed needed, to control it. By seizing New Orleans, the North had made a strong start. The task for Grant was to finish the job.

He initiated his campaign in November 1862. Trekking through difficult terrain, progress was slow. Then twice disaster struck. In a bold move the Confederates destroyed Grant's supply base at Holly Springs. And General Sherman was defeated in a battle at Chickasaw Bluffs. The result was a withdrawal by Grant to figure out a different approach. Several were devised and attempted. One was to dig a canal in order to divert the river. Another was to send gunboats east of Vicksburg via streams and bayous. Both failed.

Finally, he decided to march the Army of the Tennessee, some forty thousand men, down the western side of the Mississippi River past Vicksburg. The terrain was most difficult, but with great perseverance they arrived at New Carthage, approximately thirty-five miles south of the city. There, they awaited the navy. On the night of April 16, 1863, in a daring midnight sortie, acting rear admiral David Dixon Porter ran his gunboats and transports past the Confederate guns of Vicksburg. He met up with Grant and conveyed the Union army across the river into Mississippi. Grant's plan was bold, some would say foolhardy, because he had no lines of supply to the North. The river current was too strong for Porter's flotilla to sail back. U. S. Grant and the Army of the Tennessee were on their own.

Instead of heading north to Vicksburg, Grant moved east and, after several battles, took control of the city of Jackson, Mississippi's capital. He then marched on Vicksburg, attacking the city twice before putting in place on May 19 a siege the city and its garrison of thirty thousand had little hope of lifting. On July 4, the Southerners surrendered. The day before Meade had defeated Lee in Pennsylvania.

However, all was not rosy for the North. Its Army of the Cumberland was besieged in Chattanooga. Low on supplies, surrounded by Braxton Bragg's army, the Union army in Tennessee was in dire straits. Having become overall commander in the west, Grant had the responsibility of rescuing it.

Grant acted forcefully. He opened a supply line into Chattanooga and then laid out a plan of attack. Sherman and the Army of the Tennessee would attack Bragg's right flank. Joe Hooker, leading two corps on loan from the Army of the Potomac, would hit the left at Lookout Mountain, while General George Thomas and the Army of the Cumberland were to move toward the middle, in front of Missionary Ridge. The two flank attacks were to converge and envelop Bragg's center. As often happens, events in battle deviated from the plan. Sherman's men ran into difficulties, although Hooker's corps succeeded in taking Lookout Mountain. And the Army of the Cumberland, wishing to avenge its defeat at Chickamauga and show its mettle to the other Union units, did more than Grant had anticipated. On their own, without orders, they stormed Missionary Ridge and won the day. Having lost the battle—many in the South believed it to be a catastrophe— Bragg retreated into Georgia. Soon thereafter, he offered his resignation, which Jefferson Davis accepted.

Grant had done well at Chattanooga. Moreover, he had gained a victory at Shiloh and his campaign to capture Vicksburg had been highly successful. Ulysses S. Grant was therefore a soldier accustomed to winning. He was a general who planned well, fought hard, stayed calm, persevered, and, most importantly, won. So hopes were high when Lincoln called him east.

Grant arrived in Washington early in March 1864, checking himself into the Willard Hotel. He did not stay long.

Until Grant, standard practice for the Union army's general in chief was to remain in Washington rather than operate in the field. Scott, McClellan, and Halleck all had done so. Being in Washington facilitated communications with the president and the secretary of war, and made easier the command of the various army staff organizations. But it also imposed heavy social and political obligations, obligations Grant wished to avoid.

So he did something radical. He left Washington and established his headquarters with the Army of the Potomac. George Meade was retained as the army's commander, though it was Grant who gave it direction. He also kept Henry Halleck busy, making him the senior army staff officer in Washington, a position in which Old Brains did some good.

As to fighting, Grant wasted little time in bringing the Confederates to battle. He understood his job was to destroy the two remaining Southern armies, each of which comprised about sixty thousand men. He thus ordered General Sherman to move against Joe Johnston's Army of Tennessee and General Meade to strike at Robert E. Lee's Army of Northern Virginia. As part of this effort Grant directed General Benjamin Butler to march his Army of the James, some thirty thousand Union soldiers, to attack Richmond from the south. He also directed another general, Nathaniel P. Banks, to campaign along the Red River in Texas, hoping that a victory there, in addition to weakening the Confederates, would send a message to Mexico that mischief on its part would not go unanswered.

Both Butler and Banks were among the many nonprofessional generals Lincoln had commissioned in order to secure the political support he considered vital to the prosecution of the war. No president—then or now—can wage war without the support of Congress and the American people. Lincoln was no exception. As a moderate Republican he had to keep the radicals in the party happy, while at the same time holding on to those Northern Democrats willing to continue the war. One way Lincoln did this was to offer military commissions to politicians, most of whom wanted to serve in the army as a means to secure political advantage once the war was over. Banks had been governor of Massachusetts. Butler, like Banks, was a prominent New England Democrat. Neither man, however, was a particularly good general. Banks made a mess of the expedition in Texas. Butler botched his campaign against Richmond.

In 1864 there was to be a presidential election, and without military successes, Lincoln was likely to lose. Many in the North were weary of the war. It had gone on for four years, casualties were extremely high, and despite Union victories at Vicksburg and Gettysburg, the South appeared far from defeated. Democrats in particular were losing their zeal for the war. In fact, many of them favored a negotiated settlement with Jefferson Davis's government. This might not abolish slavery, but it would put a stop to the killing. To carry their flag on the political battlefield, the Democrats nominated none other than George B. McClellan. Many people, Democrats and Republicans alike, expected him to win.

However, Union soldiers and sailors provided Lincoln successes in battle that gave the president a second term in office. In August, Admiral Farragut damned the torpedoes and captured the coastal port of Mobile. In September, two battles on land resulted in victories for the North. General Philip Sheridan defeated Confederate cavalry in the Shenandoah Valley, an area where the South had enjoyed much success. Perhaps most important of all was William Tecumseh Sherman's capture of Atlanta.

Grant had put Sherman in charge of three Union armies, totaling approximately a hundred thousand men. George Thomas, the "Rock of Chickamauga," commanded the Army of the Cumberland. Major General John Schofield led the Army of the Ohio. James McPherson, considered a rising star in the Union army, was in charge of the Army of the Tennessee. Their task was to destroy Joseph Johnston's Confederate army. The way to do this was to move against Georgia's capital, thus forcing Johnston to fight.

Early in May, Sherman marched his troops southeast from Chattanooga into Georgia. Atlanta was about a hundred miles away. Johnston fought a cautious, defensive battle that kept his army intact. Sherman moved aggressively, attempting to outflank his opponent. There were several battles along the way, not all of which Sherman won. But the Union advance was inexorable. By early July, Sherman was at the outskirts of the city.

On July 17, Jefferson Davis, frustrated that Sherman had not been stopped, replaced Johnston. The new Confederate commander was John Bell Hood, a veteran of Chickamauga and Gettysburg. Hood's approach to battle was not terribly subtle: he would attack and then attack again, which is what he did. At Peachtree Creek, Decatur, and Ezra Church, he flung his men at those of Sherman. The battles were hard fought, and on both sides casualties were high (among the dead was General McPherson). Yet each time Sherman prevailed. On September 4, 1864, his troops entered Atlanta, the news of which brought despair throughout the South.

Battered, Hood took his much depleted army north into Tennessee. Sherman detached the Army of the Cumberland to deal with it. George Thomas did just that, defeating Hood twice.

Once in Atlanta, Sherman decided to march to the sea, a distance of 285 miles. His objective was to inflict such damage along the way that Southerners, in uniform and not, would realize the futility of continuing the fight.

The march began on November 16. Averaging about fifteen miles a day, Sherman's men reached the coast early in December. The results were as planned, although there was more destruction than death. After accepting the surrender of Savannah, Sherman took his force, then numbering some sixty thousand soldiers, north into South Carolina. The state was considered by many of his men to warrant special treatment, for it had been South Carolina that had started the conflict. So they wreaked havoc, burning everything in sight. Yet in March, when they moved through North Carolina, they were far less destructive. It was in North Carolina, in Bentonville, where they fought their last battle. A small Confederate force attacked but were driven back. Soon thereafter some of Sherman's soldiers linked up with troops belonging to Meade and Grant.

Sherman's campaign had been a huge success. He had taken Atlanta, destroyed the Confederate Army of Tennessee, marched through Georgia, ransacked South Carolina, and taken control of North Carolina. A large Union force had cut a wide path through the South, destroying whatever stood in its way. Sherman had been its commander and he had performed extremely well. A hero in the North, his name in the South, then and at the present day, brings forth resentment. Yet among military historians William Tecumseh Sherman ranks high.

When in May 1864 Sherman took his troops into Georgia, the Army of the Potomac too was on the march. Generals Grant and Meade broke camp early in the same month and moved south, crossing the Rapidan River on May 4. Their objective was to engage Lee's Army of Northern Virginia and destroy it.

Grant envisioned multiple assaults on the Confederates. In coordination with Meade's advance, Grant ordered Butler to attack from the south and General Franz Sigel to take control of the Shenandoah Valley. In concert with Sherman's invasion of Georgia, the Union forces would be attacking on several fronts simultaneously, offering the rebels no respite. In effect, Grant had crafted a strategy that he hoped would lead to overall victory. It would, but not quickly, and not without great loss of life.

Lee still had some sixty-four thousand soldiers and, most certainly, no intention of giving up. His goal was to keep Grant at bay, hold on to Richmond, and hope Northerners, tired of the war, would agree to let the states in rebellion depart the union. Lee's army was battle-tested. It had bested the Army of the Potomac before and was confident it would do so again.

With approximately 115,000 men Grant first clashed with Lee at a place in Virginia called the Wilderness. This was an inhospitable tract of land, not far from Chancellorsville, some ten miles wide and full of tangled trees and bushes. It was a terrible place to fight a battle, and the ensuing two-day fight was terrible indeed. Many of the wounded, unable to move, died from brush fires started by the gunfire. Their screams were a chorus to the carnage. The Union army suffered sixteen thousand casualties. No one in blue believed they had won.

After the battle most Union soldiers expected the Army of the Potomac to withdraw, in order to rest and rebuild. That is what the army had done in the past. Grant had a different approach. He ordered Meade south to again engage the enemy. The grinding down of Robert E. Lee and his army had begun.

Grant wanted the Union army to occupy Spotsylvania Court House, some eleven miles south of the Wilderness. This was a crossroads, possession of which might cut Lee off from Richmond. But the Army of Northern Virginia got there first. The resulting battle took place on May 12, and once again, American blood flowed freely. According to Robin H. Neillands, "men fought hand to hand with musket and bayonet, sword and pistol." On both sides casualties were high. When it was over, Grant again moved south. He was taking the initiative away from Robert E. Lee.

They next met at Cold Harbor, near the Chickahominy River. There, in several days of fighting, the Union troops attacked their Southern counterparts. In one such assault, on June 3, Grant hurled his men against well-entrenched Confederates, losing seven thousand men—killed or wounded—in a single day. Later in his memoirs he would write that this attack was a mistake.

So far Grant's campaign had been costly. The Army of the Potomac was averaging some two thousand casualties per day. In total, more than fifty-four thousand Union soldiers had been killed, wounded, or gone missing. Critics in Washington, and there were many, were calling Grant a butcher, a perception that has lasted until the present time. In fact, throughout the war Lee's casualty rates were higher than those of Grant. Historian James M. McPherson notes that among seventeen Civil War commanders, both North and South, Lee had the highest percentage of casualties. But the reputation of Grant as a not so subtle killer of men remains. Yet he was doing what he had to do to win. Grant was using the material superiority of the North to hammer the Confederacy's best army. Slowly but surely, he was destroying the Army of Northern Virginia. Grant knew it and so did Lee.

The Union commander was relentless. After Cold Harbor he again ordered Meade to move south, this time to Petersburg. This was a small town directly south of Richmond. It embraced a railroad line on which supplies were transported to both the Southern capital and Lee's army. Take the town and the Army of Northern Virginia would have to move out into the open and fight. Grant wanted such a battle, for he was sure he could win it.

A battle did occur at Petersburg, but not of the type Grant had envisioned. Instead of a few days of assault and counterattack, as had taken place at Cold Harbor and Spotsylvania Court House, the Union army laid siege to Petersburg. For nine months Meade's men kept Lee's penned up. Toward the end of the siege, Union trenches extended some fifty miles. It was warfare that foreshadowed the type of fighting that would later characterize the First World War.

While Grant and the Army of the Potomac were at Petersburg, Sherman was marching through Georgia. And Franz Sigel was attempting to take control of the Shenandoah Valley. Unfortunately for the North, Sigel failed to do so. As did his replacement, General Daniel Hunter. Grant then sent Philip Sheridan to deal with the Confederates. A favorite of Grant, Sheridan was an officer who knew how to fight. He vanquished the rebels, whose commander, General Jubal A. Early, previously had moved troops across the Potomac and threatened Washington. So Grant had dispatched troops from the Army of the Potomac to the Northern capital, and Early wisely withdrew. Washington was safe, and thanks to Sheridan, the Shenandoah Valley was at last no longer in Southern hands.

During the siege of Petersburg an episode occurred worthy of mention. Union soldiers from Pennsylvania, men who had been miners before the war, proposed that a tunnel be dug under the Confederate positions, filled with explosives, and then ignited. The result would be a huge gap in the enemy's defensive structure through which Union troops would pour. The proposal was accepted and the digging began. In overall charge of the project was one of Meade's corps commanders, none other than Ambrose Burnside.

On July 30, 1864, eight tons of explosives were detonated, surprising the Confederates and creating a gigantic crater. But the advance of the Union soldiers was slow. The Confederates recovered, and, worst of all, Burnside's men were unable to move out of the crater once they had entered it. The soldiers in gray poured fire downward and slaughtered the Union troops. The attack failed, with considerable loss of life. General Burnside was relieved of command and the siege continued.

By early 1865 the Confederacy was crumbling. Southern armies in Tennessee and Georgia had been defeated. The Carolinas essentially were out of the war, courtesy of Sherman as well as of General Alfred Terry and Admiral Porter. Early in January, these latter two gentlemen had led a combined army-navy task force that seized Fort Fisher outside of Wilmington. Mobile and New Orleans were under Northern control. The economy of the South was in ruins. The Union navy owned the waters offshore and on the rivers. Confederate forces—particularly the army facing Grant and Meade—were short of manpower and short of supplies. Many of Lee's men lacked shoes. Many more had little to eat.

So the Army of Northern Virginia did what it was good at. It attacked, striking a Union position around Petersburg called Fort Stedman. The assault took place on March 25 and, as in the past, was conducted with skill and courage. But the Union troops, by now a match with their Southern counterparts, recovered and beat back the attack. Grant responded in kind. He sent Sheridan and twelve thousand men to the southeast, where, on April 1, they met up with a force commanded by George Pickett of Gettysburg fame. Sheridan's men demolished their opponents, in the process taking five thousand prisoners. Lee's army was disintegrating. The next day, Grant ordered a full-scale assault along the entire line of siege. Union artillery blasted away and Union infantry swarmed across the Confederate positions. It was an unstoppable tidal wave of military might, and when it was over, Robert E. Lee and his army were in full retreat.

Union forces occupied Petersburg, and on April 3, 1865, the Army of the Potomac marched into Richmond. Lee hoped to reach North Carolina, there to link up with Joseph Johnston's remaining troops. Grant prevented this. He ordered Meade's men to pursue the Southerners. On April 6, Sheridan caught up with the Army of Northern Virginia at Sayler's Creek and inflicted further damage on the Confederate's already depleted force. Lee and his army continued to flee. Three days later Union cavalry overtook them at Appomattox Court House and the Confederate general called it quits.

Grant's terms were generous. He permitted Lee and his men, once they pledged not to take up arms against the United States, to retain their horses and go home, which is what they did. Once soldiers of the South, they were once again simply Americans. With their departure, for all practical purposes, the War Between the States was over.

Could the South have won?

Perhaps, but a Confederate victory was unlikely. The North simply had too great a material advantage. The South was largely an agrarian society, while the North, though full of farms, was replete with companies small and large that could manufacture what a nation at war required. Resources, natural and man-made, favored the North. For example, of the thirty-one thousand miles of railroad track in the United States twenty-two thousand were in the North. Of the firearms produced in the United States only 3 percent were made in the South. The North also possessed the majority of shipyards. Most telling of all were the population figures: there were twenty-two million people in the North, whereas in the South the population was but nine million, of whom four million were slaves.

Hence those states that formed the Confederacy were outmatched. The American War Between the States was far from an equal contest.

How then might the South have won?

The South might have gained independence from the federal union by doing better than it did on the battlefield. Military victory could have led to successful secession. Had Vicksburg not fallen, had Lee routed McClellan at Antietam or beaten Meade at Gettysburg, the North may well have sued for peace. If Sherman and Sheridan had failed in 1864, Lincoln in all likelihood would not have been reelected and the American union of states would probably have split in two. What if sometime in 1863 or 1864 Robert E. Lee had crushed the Army of the Potomac, had beaten it so badly that it simply disintegrated? Were that to have happened, surely the outcome of the war would have been different. But it didn't happen. The great victory parade was held not in Richmond but in Washington.

Might Great Britain have altered the course of the war?

Official recognition of the Confederacy by Great Britain might well have produced a different outcome. In addition to legitimacy and prestige, recognition would have brought much needed supplies to the South. Even without official support, Britain at times aided the Southern cause, in one instance permitting Confederate agents to obtain eight hundred thousand British rifles. At first, before Lincoln's determination to hold the Union together became apparent, Britain's political elites thought the North could never take control of the 750,000 square miles the rebel states comprised. Plus, they had no love for the United States, a country many of them viewed as uncultured and a commercial threat. But they also had no desire to go to war with the United States. The British wanted the South first to win independence on its own, and then they would bestow recognition and its benefits. The South was hoping that the Union naval blockade, in preventing Southern cotton from reaching English mills, would so damage the British economy as to force the government in London to side directly and substantially with the Confederates. The blockade did hurt England's industrial midlands but not to the degree the South had hoped. What decided the matter was the Emancipation Proclamation. Once it became evident that the North was fighting to free the slaves, while the South was rebelling in order to preserve slavery, Britain simply could not side with the Confederacy.

What happened at Gettysburg?

What happened, in essence, is that the Army of the Potomac, under the command of Major General George Meade, decisively defeated the Army of Northern Virginia. In July 1863 Meade stopped Lee's second invasion of the North and, in so doing, inflicted heavy losses on the Confederate army. Responsibility for the defeat rests squarely on Robert E. Lee. In American history Lee is a revered figure. He was a gifted leader and a skilled commander. That he was fighting to uphold the institution of slavery seems not to have lessened the respect in which he was, and is, held. Yet his management of the Battle of Gettysburg requires a reassessment of his talents. Lee failed miserably at Gettysburg. His insistence on directly attacking the Union center on day three was crucially wrong. Pickett's Charge was suicidal, the results catastrophic. A Union general who did what he had done would have been sacked. But Lee was not. He continued on, beloved by his men and respected—then and now—throughout the entire country.

Of course, another view of the Battle of Gettysburg shifts responsibility from Lee to others. Instead of blaming the Confederate leader, credit is given to Meade and the troops he commanded. This view is wonderfully expressed, according to Civil War historian James M. McPherson, by Pickett himself, who, when asked after the war what had led to the Confederate defeat, is said to have replied, "I always thought the Union army had something to do with it."

How best to think about Ulysses S. Grant?

In comparison to that of Lee, Grant's reputation suffers. Much of that stems from his less than successful years as president. Some originates with the widely held view that his approach to battle was excessively costly in blood. And his lack of success in business simply adds to his tarnished reputation.

He deserves better. True, his years in the White House were undistinguished and his talents for business were limited. But as a military commander in the War Between the States, Ulysses S. Grant had no peer. He understood the North's need for a comprehensive strategy. And, unlike his predecessors as general in chief, he was able to implement one. His reputation as a butcher of men is unfair. As noted above, Lee had a higher rate of casualties, and as the Vicksburg campaign revealed, Grant could maneuver an army in the field as well as anyone. What his actions in the East against Lee showed was his determination to do what had to be done to wear down and eventually destroy the Army of Northern Virginia. In thinking about Robert E. Lee and Ulysses S. Grant, it's well to remember who won.

The plain fact of the matter is that Grant was the best of the American civil war generals. That's because he knew how to fight and, more important, how to win. He may not have looked the part— in appearance he was nondescript and in dress ordinary (he usually wore a private plain blue shirt with the stars of his rank sewn on)—but as a military commander he was superb. The American army has had no better general.

What did Philip Kearny, John Reynolds, and John Sedgwick have in common?

They were all major generals in the Union army and they were all killed in battle. During the American War Between the States high rank was no guarantee of safety. Often generals led from the front and often they were killed or wounded. Thousands more of lesser rank lost their lives. Indeed, the years 1861–1865 in the United States saw killing become a common occurrence. The battles between North and South resulted in the death of approximately 618,000 men. Then—and now—that is an enormous number. In 1865 it represented 2 percent of the U.S. population. There was hardly a town in America that did not have someone killed. The war was many things—a sectional conflict, a crusade against slavery, an effort to keep the Union together, a spur of economic growth in the North, and in the South a misguided attempt to preserve the status quo—but, above all, it was a bloodbath. Young men, boys really, marched into battle. Wearing blue or gray, they shouldered arms and advanced in the face of enemy fire. Courage was their companion, as was the angel of death. Again, 618,000 men were killed. The price of union was high, very high.

5

SPAIN

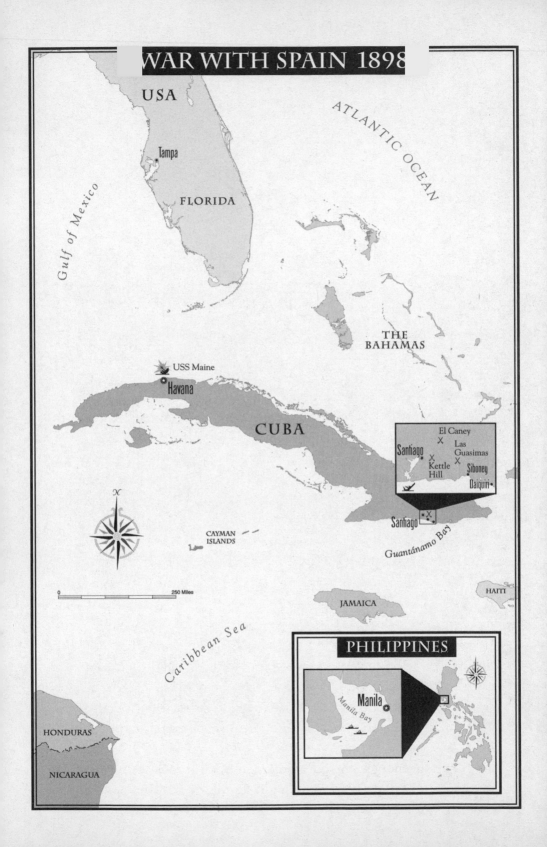

1898

As the year 1898 began, few Americans held kind thoughts toward Spain. They resented a European political presence in the Caribbean, Spain then controlling both Cuba and Puerto Rico. They identified with Cuban insurgents fighting for independence. They were repelled by accounts of Spanish brutality on the islands. Moreover, they blamed Spain for the destruction of the battleship *Maine*, which mysteriously had exploded in Havana Harbor on February 15, 1898, resulting in considerable loss of life. In all these areas American anger was encouraged by widespread newspaper reporting that faulted Spain. That the reports often exaggerated the truth seemed not to matter. Spain was the target of American ire.

So when the president of the United States, then William McKinley, called on Congress to take action, the legislators responded. On April 20, 1898, both the House of Representatives and the Senate adopted a resolution that: (1) stated that the people of Cuba were and should be free and independent, (2) directed the government of Spain to relinquish control of Cuba and to withdraw its military from the island, and (3) required the president to direct the armed forces of the United States to take steps necessary to realize the objectives laid out in (1) and (2). Further, the congressional resolution stated that save for the time necessary to rid the island of Spain, the United States had no intention of exercising sovereignty over Cuba.

Naturally enough, the government in Madrid took exception to the resolution. It withdrew its ambassador to the United States, saying the resolution was equivalent to a declaration of war. Were there any doubt as to what was intended—and there really wasn't—Congress, at McKinley's request, formalized its action on April 25, declaring quite specifically that a state of war existed between the United States of America and the Kingdom of Spain.

It was to be an uneven fight. Spain had neither the economic resources nor the military might to wage a successful war against the United States. The conflict would last less than four months. Casualties would be modest in number, although the consequences for the United States would be great. Senator John Hay called it "a splendid little war." Theodore Roosevelt said it was "a bully fight."

American strategy was straightforward. The U.S. Navy would neutralize its Spanish counterpart in the waters around Cuba and the Philippines, then blockade the Cuban coast. This would enable the army to safely invade Cuba as well as Puerto Rico and, in combat with the Spanish troops, free the islands of control by Spain.

The American navy was up to its tasks. It had several battleships, modern by the standards of the day, and a large number of well-armed cruisers. Among the latter were four ships: the *Olympia*, the *Baltimore*, the *Boston*, and the *Raleigh* (at that time cruisers were given names of American cities, while battleships, larger vessels with bigger guns, were named after the states). These four cruisers comprised the principal assets of the navy's Asiatic Squadron. Based in Hong Kong, this small fleet was commanded by Commodore George Dewey. Days prior to the outbreak of war, Dewey had been instructed to make his ships ready for action. On the other side of the globe, American warships were already at sea, having been ordered by McKinley to institute a blockade of Cuba.

The U.S. Army was less well prepared. No longer the formidable force once commanded by Ulysses S. Grant, the American army at the beginning of 1898 numbered but twenty-eight thousand. This made it one-twentieth the size of Germany's army. Moreover, as historian Edward M. Coffman has noted, the army by then was essentially a frontier constabulary. Given the absence of military threats to the United States, plus America's traditional distrust of standing armies and her reliance on citizen-soldiers, there was no need for a larger, standing army.

Thus, when war broke out, the army had to be, and was, rapidly enlarged. While Congress authorized additional regular troops, the bulk of the increase came from volunteers. Like Lincoln before him, McKinley issued calls for the states to meet the need. The president requested two hundred thousand men be armed and trained. The states responded in full. Practically overnight, the U.S. Army became manpower rich.

But the supply system could not cope. The new troop levels overwhelmed the capacity to provide required equipment. Clothing, tents, transport, medicines, and guns were all in short supply. In both training camps and combat, U.S. troops would face shortages that made their tasks more difficult and more dangerous.

Initially, once the sea-lanes were free of Spanish warships, the army was to attack Havana, the capital city of Cuba. However, this plan was set aside when a Spanish naval squadron led by Rear Admiral Pascual Cervera y Topete evaded the blockade, dropping anchor in the harbor of Santiago de Cuba on the island's southeastern coast. A new plan called for the Americans to land troops nearby and take the city. Once that was done, Cervera's ships would have to sail, into the waiting guns of the U.S. Navy. Entrusted with the assignment of capturing Santiago was Major General William R. Shafter, who, as a younger man, had fought in the War Between the States. He commanded V Corps, which consisted mostly of army regulars, though several regiments of volunteers brought his total force to approximately twenty-five thousand men. Their port of embarkation was Tampa.

It was an unfortunate choice. Tampa lacked the size and equipment required to handle the men and material of V Corps. Additionally, the army no longer possessed the logistical expertise necessary to embark such a large force aboard ships. The result was several days of confusion. Eventually things got sorted out, and most of the men, but not all, and their supplies, but not all of them either, got put into the waiting vessels.

On June 14, the ships sailed. On board were 16,300 soldiers, 2,295 horses and mules, and 34 pieces of artillery. Escorting the thirty-two transports were several naval ships. Among the latter was the new battleship *Indiana*. Her big guns were ready to protect the transports from any Spanish warship that might stumble on the convoy.

George Dewey had no such big ship. As mentioned, cruisers comprised his little fleet. On learning of the declaration of war, he and his ships steamed to the Philippines (a distance of 638 miles), intent on engaging Spanish warships known to be off the waters of Manila. Like Cuba and Puerto Rico, the Philippines was a colony of Spain. Her warships, if they could, hoped to destroy the Americans. If they could not, they aimed to uphold the honor of Spain by not shrinking from a fight.

Dewey arrived at the Philippines on April 30. That night, he led his ships into Manila Bay. In line astern, at intervals of four hundred yards, with the *Olympia* in the van, the American squadron steamed toward the waiting Spanish vessels. These were seven in number and moored in such a way as to be augmented by guns ashore. Unlike the American ships, these vessels were neither modern nor heavily armed.

The next morning at 5:41, when Dewey issued his famous command to the captain of the *Olympia*, "You may fire when ready, Gridley," the battle began. It did not last long. The attacking warships made short work of their Spanish adversaries. Dewey soon ordered his ships to cease firing and the Spaniards surrendered. Their casualties were heavy. Eight hundred and eighty-one sailors were killed or wounded. The American losses were minimal, with but nine men wounded.

News of the battle electrified the American public. Dewey became a national hero and received a promotion to rear admiral (his flagship, the USS *Olympia*, has been preserved and can be seen today in Philadelphia). Later, he helped engineer the peaceful surrender of the Spanish garrison in the city of Manila. The results of his efforts were substantial. Spain no longer held sway in the Philippines. America did.

What the United States would do with its new possession was unclear. Its purpose in sending Dewey to Manila Bay was to neutralize a Spanish naval squadron. It ended up being responsible for a vast new territory, on which a larger number of armed Philippine insurgents had rather strong views as to who should be in charge.

Far from the Philippines and several weeks after Dewey's victory, Shafter's V Corps was approaching Cuba. Because Santiago was well fortified, the American general chose to land his troops sixteen miles to the east, at the little town of Daiquiri. This turned out to be a poor choice. So the next day, disembarkation was moved to Siboney, farther west, toward Santiago. At neither location did the landings—they were unopposed—go particularly smoothly. But, eventually, the soldiers got ashore. The United States military was on Cuban soil.

The story is told that most of the horses in the expedition had to swim ashore, suitable landing craft not being available. Some of the horses, however, began to swim out to sea. An alert bugler, seeing where the animals were headed, sounded recall and the horses turned around and came ashore.

The soldiers at Daiquiri and Siboney were not the first U.S. troops to land in Cuba. That honor belonged to the United States Marine Corps. On June 10, 1898, some six hundred marines had secured the beaches and surrounding hillsides at Guantánamo Bay, forty miles east of Santiago. The bay provided a safe haven for the blockading U.S. Navy ships in the event of a hurricane. It also provided a secluded spot where the ships could refuel. Accompanying the marines was a newspaper correspondent. His name was Stephen Crane, the author of the Civil War classic *The Red Badge of Courage*. With the Corps's encouragement, he made sure the Americans back home knew that the marines had been the first to fight.

The day after V Corps had completed its landing at Siboney, they learned from Cuban insurgents that Spanish troops were nearby. Joseph Wheeler, one of Shafter's senior commanders and a former Confederate general, sent U.S. soldiers to investigate. The result was a nasty little skirmish at a place called Las Guasimas. This was not a town, but simply an intersection of trails. There, the Americans learned that Spanish soldiers were not lacking in courage or marksmanship. For their part, the Spaniards learned that the Americans had no fear of battle. The war, albeit limited in scope and duration, was going to be hard fought.

In charge of defending Santiago was Lieutenant General Arsenio Linares y Pombo. With some ninety-four hundred men he had to keep the insurgents in check as well as stop the Americans. With dwindling supplies this was no easy task. Uncertain as to whether the United States might land additional troops, he spread his soldiers around the perimeter of Santiago.

To the east, in the direction from which the Americans were advancing,

Linares placed soldiers along a ridge known as San Juan Heights. He also dispatched 520 men eight miles to the northeast, to a little town called El Caney. Their mission was to prevent the Americans from outflanking the main line of defense along the Heights. Linares hoped that if he could hold off Shafter and his men for a few weeks, the onslaught of yellow fever in the summer months would destroy the Americans. It was not an unreasonable strategy.

Major General Shafter was aware that tropical diseases soon would cripple his force. Although V Corps contained 150 surgeons and physicians, conditions in Cuba and the state of medical knowledge were such that tropical diseases would cause a large number of fatalities. Shafter was eager to do battle, but he too was short of supplies. Several days passed before the American was able to order an attack. His plan was straightforward. He would send a substantial force to neutralize El Caney, keeping his right flank protected, then have them rejoin the rest of his men for a frontal assault on the Heights. He expected a fierce but short fight. Shafter got the former but not the latter.

The Spanish soldiers at El Caney were commanded by Brigadier General Joachim Vara del Rey. He was a fine soldier and determined to hold on to El Caney. The town's defense was well laid out, with barbed-wire barriers, interconnected trenches, wooden blockhouses, and a stone fort. Though heavily outnumbered—the Americans had sixty-five hundred men—the Spanish soldiers had one key advantage. Their rifles used smokeless powder and, thus, when fired, did not reveal the shooter's position. Not all the Americans had such ammunition, nor did their artillery, which placed them at a disadvantage.

The attack began at 6:35 A.M. Shafter expected the town to fall in two hours. The battle did not end until 3:30 in the afternoon. Moreover, casualties were substantial. The Americans' numbered 441, 81 of whom were killed. The defending Spaniards lost 235 dead, among them Vara del Rey.

The defenses of El Caney brought great credit to the army of Spain. Vara del Rey and his men fought tenaciously but in the end were overwhelmed by numbers. While they did not defeat the Americans, they so occupied their opponents that the attackers did not participate in the assault on San Juan Heights.

To reach the Heights the rest of V Corps had to move down a narrow trail, ford a small stream, advance across an open field, then scale the hills, the top of which was their objective. While doing so, they would be subject to fire from both Spanish sharpshooters and artillery.

The attack began in the early morning of July 1, 1898. The American Signal Corps employed an observation balloon to spot enemy positions. This worked, but, unfortunately, it also revealed the location of the troops advancing to the stream. There, as along the trail, the result was heavy casualties. The soldiers were anxious to move up the hills but had received no orders to do so. Shafter had lost control of the battle, so the necessary orders were delayed. When they arrived, the Americans launched their final assault. This was in two parts. The first involved a hill to the northeast, forward of the ridgeline, called Kettle Hill. Occupied by the Spanish, it had to be taken first. The assignment was given to the 1st U.S. Volunteer Cavalry Regiment and to several regular army cavalry units. (As in the Civil War, the U.S. Army consisted of volunteers who had enlisted for a specific period of time and of regular career soldiers.)

Among the latter were the 9th and 10th Regiments. These were African-American units that, along with the 24th and 25th Infantry Regiments, formed the famous Buffalo Soldiers. They had fought in the West against the Indians, and had done well. In Cuba they would do well again, thereby helping to refute the absurd notion that military skill and courage were functions of race.

The 1st Volunteer Cavalry Regiment was commanded by Colonel Leonard Wood, a regular army officer who, in addition, was a well-regarded physician. When General Joseph Wheeler fell ill, Wood was advanced to brigade commander, leaving the regiment in the charge of its second in command. This was the one and only Theodore Roosevelt.

At the outbreak of war Roosevelt had been assistant secretary of the navy. This was an important position, one that would have involved the future president in significant decision making. But Teddy wanted action. So he resigned and secured a commission in the army. He then helped recruit volunteers to serve in a cavalry regiment, mostly from the American Southwest. Known as the Rough Riders, they would achieve a special place in American military history.

As did all U.S. Army cavalry regiments in Cuba, the Rough Riders and their fellow troopers of the 9th and 10th served dismounted, essentially as infantry. When the orders to attack Kettle Hill arrived, Roosevelt did not hesitate. The Rough Riders and the Buffalo Soldiers charged up the slope, led by Teddy Roosevelt, pistol in hand. Confronting considerable enemy gunfire, they took the hill. Later they moved forward—assisting in the main assault—and charged the northern slope of San Juan Hill. They soon reached its crest, suffering little loss of life. In doing all this, Roosevelt got the action he wanted. He also secured the fame he sought. And the Buffalo Soldiers earned the respect they deserved.

With Kettle Hill secured, the second part of the American assault, the attack on San Juan Hill, which lay to the southeast, began. Here the attack was carried out by the remaining soldiers of V Corps, about sixty-eight hundred men. They were commanded by two brigadier generals, Samuel Sumner and Jacob Kent. Not lacking in courage, the American troops began their climb. More than a few were cut down and the attack appeared to stall. Then four Gatling guns opened fire. Early rapid-fire machine guns, they laid down such murderous fire that the defenders gave way. Those that could retreated into Santiago. The Americans thus controlled the Heights. In doing so, they were in a position to pound the city into submission, or so it seemed.

In fact, Shafter's men were in poor shape. At El Caney and the Heights they had suffered more than thirteen hundred casualties. Moreover, V Corps was seriously short of supplies. The food, medicines, and transportation that were available were insufficient to meet the need. Perhaps more important, disease was beginning to strike the Americans. It would do far more harm that Spanish gunfire ever did.

Still, the American army had won a victory. It had landed on hostile territory, defeated the enemy in battle, and fought quite bravely. Its performance since arriving in Cuba may not have been a textbook example of how to conduct military operations—and it wasn't—but the U.S. Army had accomplished what it set out to do.

Soon it would be the navy's turn.

Inside Santiago, Linares and his men also were suffering. They too were in need of supplies, and desperately so. Although reinforcements had arrived, they proved more of a burden than a blessing. The Spanish commander had enough men to fight. He did not have enough food to feed them. All the while, the civilians, with little to eat, feared for the future.

Among the defenders in Santiago General Linares had been able to deploy were some one thousand sailors, all from the ships of Admiral Cervera. His squadron, four cruisers and two destroyers, was still in the harbor. Now that the enemy controlled the Heights, his ships were vulnerable. He recalled his men and considered his options. There were three. He could haul down his flag and surrender. He could scuttle his vessels, that is deliberately sink them. Or he could weigh anchor and do battle with the enemy.

Spanish honor dictated that Cervera would fight.

On the morning of July 3, 1898, a Sunday, the Spanish ships steamed out of Santiago Harbor. Led by the flagship *Infanta Maria Teresa*, the vessels were in line astern, their crews at battle stations. The adjectives "heroic" and "foolhardy" accurately describe their sortie. Awaiting their arrival were four American battleships: the *Indiana*, the *Iowa*, the *Oregon*, and the *Texas*, along with an armored cruiser, the USS *Brooklyn*, and two smaller vessels.

At approximately 9:30 A.M., the American warships opened fire. Their big guns pounded Cervera's ships. The two destroyers were sunk. Three of the cruisers were set ablaze and deliberately run ashore. So too was the fourth. Of the 2,227 sailors in the Spanish squadron, 323 were killed. More would have died save for the rescue efforts of the Americans. Only one U.S. sailor was killed.

Once again the United States Navy had triumphed, first at Manila Bay and then at Santiago. That later analysis of both battles showed American naval gunfire to be often inaccurate mattered little. The wreckage of Cervera's cruisers along the beaches near Santiago was ample evidence that the Americans owned the waters around Cuba.

In command of the American squadron blockading Santiago had been Rear Admiral William T. Sampson. That Sunday morning, aboard his flagship, the armored cruiser *New York*, he had sailed for a conference with his army counterpart, Major General Shafter. Left in charge of the blockading vessels was Winfield Schley, also a rear admiral. When Sampson learned that Cervera had sailed, he had the *New York* come about and steam to the scene of battle, arriving toward the end of the fighting. Meanwhile, Schley simply had each ship do what was expected of them, which was to pursue and fire at the enemy. Neither admiral controlled the sea battle, though both claimed credit for the victory. Their subsequent public quarrels over who was responsible for Cervera's defeat embarrassed the navy and brought credit to neither man.

The dispute with Schley was not the only disagreement Admiral Sampson experienced. He also differed with Shafter on how best to subdue Santiago, a disagreement less personal than that with Admiral Schley but more fundamental, as it reflected basic differences between the army and the navy. General Shafter wanted the navy to bombard the fortifications of Santiago in order to assist the army's capture of the city. Admiral Sampson wanted the army to subdue the force, making it safe for the navy to enter Santiago Harbor and force the city to surrender.

Such was the disagreement that when General Linares did give up, Shafter chose not to invite Sampson to the surrender ceremony. Their dispute was a failure in command. Neither man rose to the occasion, although the ultimate blame rests with President McKinley. He chose not to appoint an overall commander. Franklin Roosevelt would make the same mistake in 1942.

Santiago surrendered on July 17, but only after much discussion that entailed proposals and counterproposals. When Linares did capitulate, he turned over not only the troops in Santiago, but also the soldiers in all of eastern Cuba, some 22,700 men. In essence, the fighting on the island was over.

Five days before the surrender, eight thousand American soldiers and tons of supplies arrived in Cuba. The troops were under the command of Major General Nelson A. Miles. He was the U.S. Army's senior officer, its commanding general. Miles participated in the negotiations with Linares, but he wished to lead troops in combat. He got his wish when the president approved his plans for the invasion of Puerto Rico. The landings began on July 25 and eventually involved eighteen thousand soldiers. There were several battles, all on the small scale, and all in which Miles and his men acquitted themselves well. The entire island would have been taken by force had the war with Spain not come to a halt.

This came about diplomatically. Spain authorized the French ambassador in Washington to strike a deal with the Americans. The government in Madrid had had enough: Spain's warships had been destroyed and a Spanish army had been beaten. It was time to stop the killing. The ambassador secured an agreement to what is known as a protocol. Dated August 12, 1898, it set forth the basic terms for ending the conflict. Immediately, there would be an armistice. Cuba would become free and independent. Spain would cede Puerto Rico and Guam to the United States. (Guam had been captured on June 21 by sailors and marines of the cruiser *Charleston* as the ship escorted army transports to Manila.) American troops would occupy Manila while the disposition of the Philippines would be resolved in the course of negotiating a formal treaty of peace.

The treaty was to be negotiated in Paris. Discussions began in the French capital in October and concluded on December 10. Tenets of the August 12 protocol were formalized in the treaty. Spain granted independence to Cuba and ceded Guam and Puerto Rico to the United States. Interestingly, Article X of the treaty stated that the inhabitants of the territories relinquished by Spain were to enjoy "the free exercise of their religion."

The treaty also called for the repatriation of Spanish troops and their families in Cuba, at the expense of the U.S. government. America honored the obligation. Aboard sixteen chartered vessels 22,864 men, women, and children were sent home to Spain, at a reported cost of $513,860.

In Cuba, once the Spanish no longer were in control, the Americans worked hard to improve conditions for both Cubans and the U.S. soldiers on the island. Roads were built, hospitals established. A major effort was made to improve sanitation, which, under previous rulers, had been neglected. Hunger was also addressed. Among the first ships to arrive once the blockade was lifted was a vessel belonging to the American Red Cross. Aboard was the organization's founder, Clara Barton, with a great deal of food that was given to Cuban civilians.

Though no longer short of food, Shafter's troops were not in good condition. Disease had struck V Corps and its commander pleaded with the secretary of war to order the soldiers home. In total, disease in Cuba killed 514 servicemen. The troops were transported to a hastily built camp at Montauk Point on Long Island. Once there, 257 additional men died of disease. As in the war with Mexico, enemy gunfire accounted for fewer deaths than disease.

According to a report of the U.S. Army's adjutant general, 345 soldiers were killed in action during the fighting with Spain. Yet 2,565 more died of disease, either in the United States or overseas. The then limitations of medical knowledge plus surprisingly unsanitary conditions in army camps caused the high loss of life. In addition to the war resulting in the deaths of 2,910 Americans, it saw 1,577 men wounded. Total U.S. casualties in the brief conflict numbered 4,487.

Of these 4,487 only a few, 123, occurred in the Philippines. The reasons for such a low number there are twofold. First, except for Dewey's naval battle, little fighting took place in the Philippines, at least initially. Second, the long sea voyage to and from the United States itself was beneficial to the health of the soldiers in transit.

Once Commodore Dewey had defeated the Spanish squadron in Manila Bay, he informed the secretary of the navy in Washington that he had too few sailors to take control of the capital city. The secretary of the navy so informed the secretary of the army who, with the approval of President McKinley, promptly sent 10,850 troops to the Philippines. Commanded by Major General Wesley Merritt, these soldiers soon convinced the Spaniards to haul down the flag.

Thus the future of Manila and the entire Philippine Archipelago were on the agenda in Paris once the negotiations between Spain and the United States began. Ultimately, President McKinley had to decide—or at least approve—the disposition of the city and the islands. He chose annexation. Agreeing to accept $20 million, Spain in turn transferred control of all of the Philippines to the United States.

Most Americans were pleased by their new acquisition (although most of them probably could not identify its precise location). Not so pleased were the thirteen thousand Filipinos who had been in revolt against the Spanish. They had been excluded from participating in the capture of

Manila and, once the Americans had occupied the city, had been told to stay out. To them, the Treaty of Paris simply replaced one set of imperial rulers with another.

However, in administering the Philippines, the Americans were far different than the Spanish. The Americans strengthened native municipal governments. They established schools and reformed both the legal system and the tax code. They improved the Filipino police force and established the Philippine Scouts as an effective partner of the U.S. Army. As important, the Americans brought with them economic prosperity. The result of all this was to make American rule more than acceptable to many Filipinos, though not to all.

Reinforcing this U.S. commitment to the Philippines was an increase in the number of American soldiers stationed there. As tension between the insurgents and U.S. troops grew, Merritt called for additional men. These soon arrived. When, in February 1899, war broke out between the insurgents and the U.S. army of occupation, the Americans were not outnumbered. Indeed, as this new war progressed—and it was a war—even more soldiers were sent. By the fall of 1899, the United States had 17,300 troops on the islands. By December of the next year that number had risen to 69,420.

In battle against the insurgents the U.S. Army did well. They did so well that as a conventional fighting force, the Filipino Army of Liberation dissolved, becoming a guerilla force. Over time, however, it inflicted nearly 4,000 casualties on the Americans, of whom 1,004 were killed. But, once again, disease was a more powerful force. Cholera, typhus, smallpox, malaria, and typhoid fever caused more American deaths than did combat. The War Department later reported that 2,748 men died of disease in the Philippines.

The number of Filipinos killed is uncertain, although casualties far exceeded those of the Americans. Some of those killed or wounded had been subjected to torture, which in the guerilla war made an appearance on both sides.

The last year of the war—President Theodore Roosevelt declared it over in July 1902—saw mostly small-scale actions. Patrols were ambushed, villages overrun, and supply lines attacked. Ten to thirty soldiers might be involved in a firefight. This stage of the conflict was not unlike a later war, in Vietnam, though the outcome was far different. U.S. successes in battle and more peaceful American endeavors in governing the islands caused the insurrection to fade away.

Many of the rebellious Filipinos simply gave up. Many of those then aided the Americans, as did many who were captured. Perhaps the most daring event of the war was the capture of Emilio Aguinaldo, the leader of the insurgents. He was hiding out in the mountains of Luzon. When the Americans learned of his whereabouts, they hatched an audacious plan. Colonel Frederick Funston and several other officers posed as prisoners of Filipino soldiers allied with the Americans, who themselves were disguised as insurgents. They trekked to Aguinaldo's mountain hideout and surprised the Filipino commander. According to David J. Sibley, one of but a few American historians of the war, the plan was "beyond daring. It was suicidal." But it worked. Surprise was complete and Aguinaldo was taken prisoner. The capture took place on March 23, 1901. It was Aguinaldo's birthday. Yet he was to have the last laugh, or more important, realize his dream of Philippine independence. In 1946, when the United States relinquished its claim to the archipelago, Aguinaldo, by then a very old man, was present at the ceremony.

Might Spain, in 1898, have defeated the United States?

The United States quickly and decisively defeated the army and navy of Spain. Could the outcome have been different? Could Spain have won?

It seems unlikely. Her navy was no match for America's. The U.S. ships were modern warships, well armed and well crewed. Spanish vessels were the opposite. Control of the sea was certain to fall to the Americans. This meant that the U.S. invasions of Cuba, Puerto Rico, and the Philippines were not to be contested at sea. Only on land might the Spaniards have successfully confronted the invaders. Their best hope of victory was to have prevented the landings at Daiquiri and Siboney. When they failed to do so, the outcome no longer was in doubt. The American army, despite inadequacies, was not lacking in numbers or courage. Once ashore, it was intent on winning. And so it did. The Spanish might have fought on beyond the August 12 armistice, but the end result would have been the same.

Might the second war, the war in the Philippines, have been avoided?

Once Major General Wesley Merritt and his men took control of Manila, the future of the Philippines became an issue. Who was to govern the archipelago? When the United States decided on annexation, thereby becoming a colonial power, it not only had to put in place a civil administration, it also had to deal with thirteen thousand armed native insurgents who, naturally enough, were suspicious of American intentions. Given that the United States was not going to leave or prematurely grant independence to the island inhabitants, these insurgents were bound to resist, as they had done with the Spanish. War was inevitable. What is remarkable is not that armed conflict broke out, but that the Filipinos did so poorly. The U.S. Army fought well, and triumphed. In this little war—about which most Americans know little—the United States relatively easily subdued those who challenged its control.

Who was responsible for the loss of the *Maine*?

On January 25, 1898, the United States battleship *Maine* dropped anchor in the harbor of Havana. The ship was there to protect American interests and to remind the Spanish of America's military might. Twenty days later, the warship blew up. The ship was a total loss. Of a 358-man crew, 253 men were killed. Americans everywhere were outraged, pointing the finger at Spain. "Remember the *Maine!*" became a battle cry as the United States went to war.

The U.S. Navy immediately convened a court of inquiry to investigate the loss of the ship. Late in March 1898, it concluded that the *Maine* had been destroyed due to an explosion in an ammunition bunker. The cause of the explosion, the court reported, was a submerged mine situated near the bottom of the vessel. Who placed the device close to the ship was not addressed.

Spain denied it had done so. Certainly, blowing up the *Maine* was not in the best interests of the Spanish. The ship's destruction brought war with the United States much closer, a war—as we've seen—that Spain was unlikely to win.

The one group to benefit from the destruction of the American warship was the Cuban insurgents. To rid the island of the Spanish required the intervention of the United States. What better way to achieve this than to do something guaranteed to inflame the American public. No Cuban, then or later, has said they planted the mine. But if the Spanish did not, who did? Assuming the Cuban insurgents were responsible is not a far-fetched proposition.

However, it may be that a submerged mine did not cause the explosion.

As with other warships of the day, the *Maine* was powered by steam generated by the burning of coal. Hence ships carried large quantities of the black fuel. The coal was stored in bunkers, compartments well below the main deck. On occasion, small fires spontaneously broke out in the coal bunkers. These would be detected and extinguished. What if, as many now believe, a fire had started in one of the battleship's coal bunkers and, undetected, had spread to where the ammunition was stored? The result would have been a very destructive explosion. It is therefore quite possible that a small, onboard coal fire and not a mine brought about the loss of the battleship.

In truth, we simply do not know with certainty what caused the explosion that doomed the *Maine*. It may have been a mine set in place by the Spanish, or by the Cubans. Or it may have been a fire in one of the ship's coal bunkers.

Why, for Americans, is the War with Spain worth recalling?

The war itself was brief and won with relatively few casualties. True, men did die and the casualties of the two conflicts are not inconsequential. But the numbers are small and the sacrifice seems long forgotten. Yet the victories of 1898 and of 1902 had important consequences for the United States. Puerto Rico became an American responsibility (and is now a self-governing commonwealth associated with the United States). Guam and Wake, two islands in the Pacific, became American territories. But most important, the United States took control of the Philippines. This meant that America had to govern the archipelago, which, in the event, it did quite well. It also meant that the United States assumed responsibility for the defense of the islands. This required a navy, a rather large navy. With the Philippines as an American outpost, the United States was forced to become a Pacific power. No longer would the president and the military tilt toward Europe and Latin America. Now they would look west as well.

6

WORLD WAR I

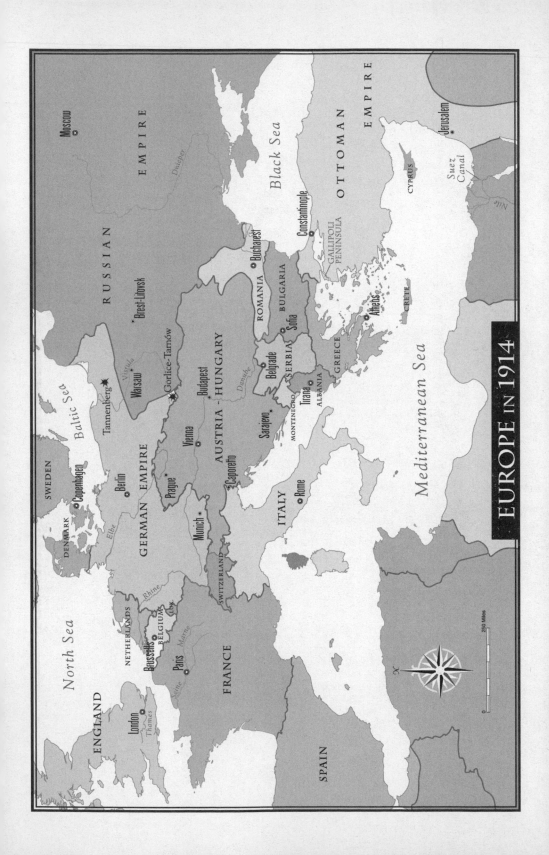

EUROPE IN 1914

North Sea

ENGLAND

London •
Thames

SWEDEN

DENMARK

Baltic Sea

Copenhagen •

Tannenberg ✶

Berlin •

GERMAN EMPIRE

Elbe

Rhine

NETHERLANDS

BELGIUM

Brussels •

Paris •

Seine

Marne

Oise

FRANCE

SWITZERLAND

Munich •

Prague •

Vienna •

Caporetto •

ITALY

Rome •

SPAIN

Moscow •

RUSSIAN

EMPIRE

Dnieper

Vistula

Warsaw •

Gorlice-Tarnów ✶

Budapest •

AUSTRIA - HUNGARY

Danube

Sarajevo •

MONTENEGRO

Brest-Litovsk ✶

Bucharest ✷

ROMANIA

BULGARIA

Sofia •

Belgrade •

SERBIA

Tirana •

ALBANIA

Black Sea

Constantinople •

GALLIPOLI
PENINSULA

OTTOMAN

EMPIRE

GREECE

Athens •

CRETE

Mediterranean Sea

CYPRUS

Jerusalem ✶

Suez
Canal

Nile

N

0   250 Miles

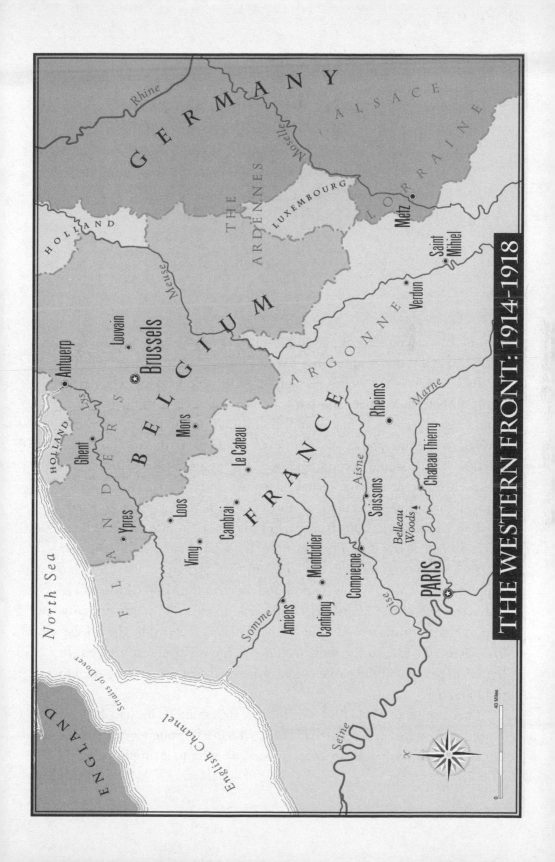

THE WESTERN FRONT: 1914–1918

1914–1918

In June 1914, a single act of political murder in Bosnia set in motion a sequence of events that resulted in a war in Europe, a war that soon reached far distant parts of the globe. The impact of this conflict would be devastating to both individuals and nations. More than eight million soldiers would lose their lives. They would die in mud, in the desert, on snow-covered mountains, and at sea. They even would die in the air. In France, 630,000 women would become widows. In Belgium, Serbia, Turkey, and elsewhere innocent civilians, including women and children, would perish, many of them simply executed. Countries too would die, and maps would need to be redrawn. The Austrian-Hungarian Empire of the Hapsburgs would disappear. The German Imperial State would collapse and its kaiser would move to Holland, emperor no longer. The Ottoman Empire, ruler of what is now Turkey and much of the Middle East, would share the fate of the Hapsburgs and cease to exist. The tsar and Romanov rule in Russia would come to a violent end, replaced by the Bolsheviks. America, late to the war, would emerge relatively unscathed, in better shape than all the nations that earlier had sent their young men to fight and die.

The conflict of 1914–1918 was to be a milestone in human history. Nothing like it had ever occurred. Those who lived through it called it the Great War. Today, less aware of its impact, we refer to it simply as World War I.

Archduke Franz Ferdinand was the heir to the throne of the Austrian-Hungarian Empire. This was an empire that had seen better days. Comprised of many different nationalities—its subjects spoke twelve different languages—the Austrian-Hungarian state in 1914 was a ramshackle affair, conservative to the core, with an army that was large but not terribly effective. On June 28, their wedding anniversary, Franz Ferdinand and his wife Sophie were in Sarajevo, the capital of Bosnia, which, though part of the empire, contained many Serbs. To the south and adjacent to Bosnia was Serbia, an independent nation many of whose people, then, as now, were prone to violence. The Serbs detested the empire of Austria-Hungary, whose rulers reciprocated the feeling.

Thus, no one was surprised when with the complicity of Serbia, a young Bosnian radical shot and killed the archduke and his wife. Correctly blaming Serbia, the empire, with Germany's approval, declared war on its southern neighbor. That upset Russia, which, because of race and religion, considered itself the protector of Serbia. Russia mobilized its armed forces. That in turn alarmed Germany, which saw Russia and its vast number of men eligible for military service as a direct threat to its security. Germany then put its armed forces on notice, which in turn made the French extremely nervous. Forty years earlier, France had been invaded by Germany and, defeated in battle, had ceded to the victor the provinces of Alsace and Lorraine. These the French considered theirs, and they hoped someday to regain them. When the German army mobilized, France naturally enough brought its own military to full alert.

In 1914 most military experts believed that in any war the army that attacked first would win. Armies that found themselves on the defensive, these experts predicted, likely would lose. Once mobilization had been ordered, most generals, and certainly those of the kaiser, believed the war in effect had begun. Once Russia had ordered its army to get ready, German generals considered their country at war.

Though formally at peace with one another, the nations comprising Europe in 1914 were highly distrustful of those countries they viewed as adversaries. Competing desires for empire, rivalry in trade and industry, different political traditions and forms of government, as well as armies and navies that planned for war all made Europe a tinderbox ready to explode. The assassination of Franz Ferdinand provided the spark. True, diplomacy could have doused the flame, but it didn't. The result was that in August 1914, the world went to war, and the killing began.

Geography had not been kind to Germany. To its east lay Russia, to its west France. With good reason, these countries viewed the kaiser's army with alarm. They had an agreement that if one were attacked, the other would come to its aid. Hence, Germany found itself trapped. Each of the two, so the kaiser believed, sought to deny Germany's rightful place in Europe and the world. But France and Russia were not the only nations he considered to be holding Germany back. With its huge navy, Great Britain also stood ready to limit Germany's influence. In response, Imperial Germany, under the guidance of Admiral Alfred von Tirpitz, had built a strong navy. It was not as powerful as Britain's, but it was a force sufficient to command respect.

German war strategy in 1914 took into account both geography and the armed forces of Russia, France, and Britain. First developed by Alfred von Schlieffen, chief of the German General Staff from 1891 to 1906, its essence was retained by Helmuth von Moltke, who in 1914 was the German army's commander in chief. Moltke and Schlieffen reasoned that Russia could not mobilize its troops quickly. Germany's best bet then was to strike first at France and do so with overwhelming strength. The plan was to defeat Germany's enemy in the west, then, by rail, transport the victorious army to the east, there to confront the Russian horde. The kaiser's generals estimated that they had forty days in which to beat the French. After that, the Russian menace in the east had to be addressed. Moreover, given that Russia would grow stronger over time, it would be best to strike sooner rather than later.

France too had prepared for war. It had constructed a series of powerful forts along its border with Germany. Any attack there by the kaiser's troops would run into interlocking fields of fire intended to halt the German advance. But General Joseph Joffre, chief of the French army, wanted to do more than simply hold back the Germans. He wanted his forces to attack. His plan, labeled War Plan XVII, envisioned an offensive into Germany, the goal of which was to retake Alsace and Lorraine.

Aware of the forts and of France's desire to recover Alsace and Lorraine, Schlieffen had developed an extremely bold plan. The German army would strike not across the border with France. Rather, it would attack from the northwest, through Belgium. The army's right wing, its most powerful element, would swing wide, crushing both Belgian and French forces, then sweep south to the west of Paris, coming around the city to hit from the rear those French forces that were facing the rest of the German attack.

Though aware that marching through Belgium might bring Great Britain into the war, Germany's generals were not concerned. The British army was small and not likely to arrive in time. And if it did, it easily could be pushed aside. As to Belgium, its army too was small. The forts on which it relied for defense simply were to be blown to pieces by specially designed heavy guns. Could Moltke and the eight separate field armies he had at his disposal execute von Schlieffen's plan?

On August 4, 1914, German forces crossed into Belgium, heading for France. Two armies were kept home to protect Alsace and Lorraine. Another, the Eighth, was positioned to the east, guarding the nation's border with Russia. Thus Moltke dispatched five separate German armies to hit the French. Two of them, the First and the Second, constituted the strong right wing of the strike force. Commanded respectively by Generals Alexander von Kluck and Karl von Bulow, they together numbered well over half a million men. It was an impressive force. The kaiser and his army commander in chief believed it was unstoppable.

It was true that Belgium's army was small, but when King Albert ordered it to oppose the Germans, it did so, and it did so bravely, delaying the German advance.. The results, however, were as the kaiser's generals had predicted. The forts Belgium had built were destroyed, and those Belgian soldiers not killed or wounded retreated, joining up with the French Fifth Army, which itself was defeated in battle.

Nevertheless, the French commander in chief, true to his desire for offensive action and consistent with War Plan XVII, had sent two armies into Alsace and Lorraine. Attacking along a seventy-five-mile front, the soldiers ran into the two armies Moltke had deployed there. At first the French did well. But by late August they had given way in the face of strong German counterattacks.

By this time, the British too had suffered losses. Once Belgium's neutrality had been violated by the Germans, the government in London had sent most of the British army to France. What was called the British Expeditionary Force (BEF) began arriving on August 14. It went into action almost immediately. At Mons and Le Cateau, the soldiers of King George V fought hard, inflicted casualties on the Germans, but fell back. At Le Cateau, a small village southeast of Cambrai, the BEF had eight thousand men killed or wounded. Not since Waterloo in 1815 had Britain's army seen such combat.

So far the Germans had done quite well. They had pushed aside the Belgians, defeated the French, and caused the British to retreat. Closing in on Paris, they reached the Marne River on September 3. That same day the French government abandoned the capital, setting up shop in Bordeaux, far to the south. Soon, German troops crossed the Marne. Some of their heavy guns began shelling Paris. Victory for the kaiser and his generals seemed close at hand.

However, Joseph Joffre did not panic. Calmly, as the Germans advanced, he redeployed his troops (as each day he calmly enjoyed a lengthy lunch, then a nice nap). He also took note of a gap that had opened between the German First and Second Armies. The former, Kluck's command, had not circled west of Paris. Intent on destroying French forces before him, it had swayed from Schlieffen's original plan. Paris was on its right flank. To its left, but not close by, was Bulow's Second Army.

All along a two-hundred-mile front, the battle raged. Defending the French capital, to Kluck's right, was the French Sixth Army. Among its soldiers were the garrison of Paris. Their commander, General Joseph Gallieni, had requisitioned six hundred Renault taxicabs to transport these troops, five men at a time, to the army. He soon would become known as "the savior of Paris." His vehicles, the taxies, would pass into legend.

Farther to the east, very much in the fight, Joffre had placed the newly created Ninth Army. Its commander, Ferdinand Foch, had performed well in the defense of Nancy, a major city in northeastern France. In 1918, Foch would play a key role in the Allies' final victory. He was a capable commander with an aggressive approach to warfare. In the Battle of the Marne, he drafted a signal that, like the Parisian taxis, would become legendary: "My center is giving way, my right is in retreat, situation excellent. I attack."

The kaiser's troops fought hard. But they had marched a long way since crossing into Belgium. They were tired and no longer at full strength, having suffered numerous casualties. More important, by early September, they were short of supplies. Logistics—that critical component of both ancient and modern warfare—were to be their undoing. The German army simply could not keep its divisions fighting in France adequately supplied. German units were short of practically everything, particularly food. So the kaiser's generals were forced to concede defeat. On September 9, the fortieth day, Bulow ordered his Second Army to withdraw. This meant the other German armies had to do the same. The Battle of the Marne was over.

Joffre had won. "The Miracle of the Marne" had saved France. Church bells rang and the nation celebrated. The cost had been high. In the month of September in the year 1914, the French Army had sustained more than 200,000 casualties. October would see that number increase by 80,000. By the end of the year, after but five months of war, 306,000 French soldiers were dead. Twice that many were wounded.

For Germany, the Marne represented its best chance to win the First World War. Unlike in the successful campaign against France in 1870–1871, the kaiser's armies in 1914 did not crush their opponents or cause a government to topple. Despite successes on individual battlefields, the German efforts in Belgium and France fell short. Yet, though tired and short of supplies, by no means were the German armies a spent force. They retired in good order, retreating to high ground at the Aisne River. There, in addition to emplacing machine guns and siting artillery batteries, they began to dig. So did the French who pursued them. Soon, the trenches that would so characterize the Great War laced the landscape. As winter set in, they would run a distance of 475 miles without a break, extending from the Swiss border to the North Sea.

As a result of the German army's failure at the Marne, Helmuth von Moltke lost his job. His replacement as commander in chief was General Erich von Falkenhayn. By October, given the line of well-defended trenches, the only place where an army might outflank its opponent was to the northwest. The campaign here is often referred to as "the race to the sea." Falkenhayn focused on a small spot in Belgium still held by the French and British. If he could have success there, he would gain control of those ports nearest to England, thus making operations extremely difficult for the BEF, possibly compelling Great Britain to leave the war. Were that to happen, he would be able to concentrate his armies in the west solely on the French. Despite the outcome at the Marne, Falkenhayn saw in this approach an avenue to victory.

The fighting that resulted lasted for more than five weeks. Falkenhayn's soldiers fought Belgian, French, and British troops. Collectively, the engagements are recorded as First Ypres, after the medieval town in Belgium around which much of the fighting took place. This first clash was costly to all involved. Together, more than two hundred thousand men were either killed or wounded. In the end, the Germans failed to advance as Falkenhayn had hoped.

For the British, First Ypres would be a memorable battle. Not because they won, which they did, though with heavy casualties, but because it marked the passing of the small, professional army Great Britain had established to fight its battles on land. By the end of 1914, most of the one hundred thousand men comprising that army were gone. They were either dead or wounded. From 1915 on, the British army would have to rely on volunteers and conscripts, young men with little training whose military skills would take time to develop.

If First Ypres left a mark on the British—and it did—it left a mark as well on the Germans. In pushing forward on the attack, Falkenhayn's forces included a large number of university students who, eagerly, had volunteered for the army. Hastily, they were given uniforms and rifles and, with little preparation, were rushed into battle. The results were catastrophic. Approximately twenty-five thousand were killed. In Germany,

their deaths became known as *Kindermord*, the Massacre of the Inno-
cents. John Keegan, a highly regarded military historian, notes in his fine
book on World War I that the insignia of every German university is
displayed at the cemetery where the twenty-five thousand are buried in a
mass grave.

Holding off the Germans at First Ypres meant that the British and
French retained control of a small slice of Belgium. The rest of that country was occupied by the kaiser's forces. These troops, with the approval of
senior army commanders, acted with extreme cruelty toward Belgian
civilians. They simply took many of them away and shot them. Additionally, they looted and wantonly burned buildings. This barbaric behavior
included the destruction of the ancient university town of Louvain with
its unique library that housed irreplaceable medieval and Renaissance
works of art. What became known as "the Rape of Belgium" appalled
thoughtful people throughout the world. It served to inflame British public opinion, which helped sustain Britain's commitment to battle. It also
contributed to a belief in the United States that Germany did not deserve
to win the war.

Both Moltke and Falkenhayn had concentrated Germany's forces in
the west, hoping to defeat France before Russia was capable of waging war.
But the tsar mobilized his troops more quickly than expected. Two Russian
armies soon attacked, crossing into East Prussia in mid-August. Defending
Germany was a single army, the Eighth. Its commander was a retired
soldier brought back to active duty, Count Paul von Hindenburg. His chief
of staff was General Erich Ludendorff. Together they made a formidable
team. In late August 1914, they crushed the Russians at Tannenberg. One
of the Russian armies was completely destroyed. Mortified by the totality
of his defeat, its commander wandered off into the woods and shot himself.
Casualties were high, but the most notable statistic is the number of Russians captured. At Tannenberg, the German Eighth Army took ninety
thousand prisoners! The battle was one of the great engagements of the
First World War. Germany's victory was complete. Hindenburg became a
national hero. Later on, when Falkenhayn was dismissed, the kaiser appointed Hindenburg as the army's commander in chief. Ludendorff became chief military planner. As the war progressed, Hindenburg became

more of a figurehead, while Ludendorff decided where and when German troops would fight.

For the next three years, 1915–1917, the Germans and the Russians would do battle. Most of the time the Germans won. In 1915 the kaiser's generals scored a huge victory near the towns of Tarnow and Gorlice in what is now Poland (at that time there were Poles, but no independent nation of Poland, the territory being part of the tsar's empire). What is remarkable today is the scale of the battles. Thousands upon thousands of men fought and died. In the campaign of Tarnow-Gorlice, the Russian army suffered nearly one million casualties. In pushing the Russians out of Poland, the Germans took 750,000 prisoners. In 1916, in a rare Russian victory over both German and Austrian troops, General Alexei Brusilov's offensive inflicted 600,000 casualties on the enemy. In the Caucasus, where the Ottoman and Russian Empires collided, the Turks lost more than 60,000 men in an unsuccessful attack on the Russians.

Despite occasional successes, the war did not go well for Russia. Military defeat in the field and political unrest at home led to revolution. On March 15, 1917, the tsar abdicated (and later was executed). The liberal socialist Alexander Kerensky and his government were also toppled (although he was not killed). Vladimir Lenin and the Bolsheviks took control and at once secured an armistice with Germany. The kaiser and his generals were in no mood for leniency. At Brest-Litovsk they laid down harsh terms. The Russians had no choice but to accept. Huge amounts of once-Russian territory were transferred to German control, including what is now Poland, Ukraine, the Baltic states, and Finland. One-third of Russia's agricultural land was lost. Nine percent of its coal reserves were gone. The result of failure in battle, the Treaty of Brest-Litovsk humiliated Russia. Far more than territory had been sacrificed. By the end of 1917, nearly five million Russian soldiers had been wounded; 1,800,000 were dead.

As the Russians were crushed by the Germans, so too were the Romanians. In 1916, emboldened by General Brusilov's initial successes and hoping to gain additional territory once Germany was defeated, Romania went to war. Siding with Great Britain, France, and Russia (the Triple Entente), Romanian forces attacked west, advancing fifty miles into Transylvania, then an area belonging to the Austrian-Hungarian Empire, but in which a large number of Romanians resided. Germany's response was prompt and forceful. One German army, which included troops from Bulgaria and Austria, crossed into Romania from the south along the coast. Another attacked from the north. Together they disposed of Romania's army as well as Russian regiments sent to help. Victorious German infantry entered Bucharest, the capital of Romania, on December 6, 1916. An armistice soon followed, then a treaty of peace. As with Brest-Litovsk, the terms were harsh. Romania possessed four assets: oil, grain, railroads, and part of the Danube. The Germans took control of all four. Romania in effect became a vassal state. However, it would have the last laugh. At Versailles in 1919, in the treaties that formally concluded the First World War, Romania, having chosen the winning side, was rewarded with Transylvania. Even today the region constitutes the northern portion of the country.

Throughout World War I Germany's principal allies were the Austrian-Hungarian Empire and the empire of the Ottomans. The latter was quite large, covering what is today Turkey, Iraq, Syria, Lebanon, Israel, Jordan, and parts of Saudi Arabia (Egypt and Kuwait were British protectorates). Because the empire was in decline, its army needed assistance. This the Germans provided. Indeed, during the last years of the war, the commander of most Turkish forces in Palestine was Erich von Falkenhayn. Among troops at his disposal were eighteen thousand German and Austrian soldiers. In 1916 General Falkenhayn had led one of the German armies in Romania. By 1917 he was in the Middle East. There he had less success. Earlier, British troops had repulsed a Turkish assault on the Suez Canal and retaken Baghdad, the city having surrendered in April 1916. In 1917, Falkenhayn's task was to hold on to Palestine. But in a series of engagements with the British, he was unable to do so. Edmund Allenby, the British commander, defeated the Turks and his German counterpart and on December 11, 1917, entered Jerusalem in triumph.

Of considerable assistance to Allenby were a large number of Arab warriors who had little love for their Turkish rulers. A British intelligence officer, T. E. Lawrence, helped convince them to aid Allenby. They did so in part due to British promises of independence once the war ended. Of course, the British had no intention of honoring these promises, as the Arabs discovered at Versailles.

Like the army of the Ottomans, the army of the Austrian-Hungarian Empire required German assistance. The Hapsburg army was large and certainly not lacking in courage. But in early battles with the Russians along their common border, the army was worn down. By the end of 1914, just months into the war, it had incurred 1,200,000 casualties. Twelve weeks into 1915 saw that number increase by 800,000. Many of these soldiers constituted the core capability of the army and could not be replaced. As the war continued, their absence was felt. The empire's army, while still large, was not effective. It needed help. This came from Germany in the form of men and supplies. In fact, German generals essentially took over command of their ally's army. More than one German commander said that the kaiser's army, to use the phrase highlighted by noted historian Hew Strachan, was "shackled to a corpse."

If there was one nation on which the Austrian-Hungarian Empire wished to wreak havoc, it was Serbia. Since June 1914, revenge for the assassination of Franz Ferdinand was never far from the minds of the Hapsburg leaders. Very early in the war, the Austrian-Hungarians attacked. Remarkably, the Serbs held them off. Despite the setbacks and 227,000 casualties, the Austrians had no intention of quitting. They turned to the Germans and to the Bulgarians, and in the fall of 1915, troops from all three countries invaded Serbia. They were under the command of one of Germany's better generals, August von Mackensen. He had won the great victory at Tarnow-Gorlice and in 1916 would lead one of the German armies into Romania. His efforts in 1915 soon had the Serbs in full retreat. The defenders fought hard, suffering ninety-four thousand casualties. But their opponent was too strong and Serbia's army and government had to flee. Their epic march across Montenegro and Kosovo to the Adriatic Sea, where Allied ships took them off, is today part of Serbian legend.

The soldiers of Austria-Hungary fought not only the Serbs and the Russians, they also fought the Italians. Italy and the Austrian-Hungarian Empire shared a four-hundred-mile border. This was mostly mountains, which favored those waging a defensive battle. Nevertheless, and to their great credit, the Italians attacked, fighting along the Isonzo River (a river near the northeastern corner of the Italian Republic that flows into the Gulf of Trieste). Indeed, in the years 1914 through 1917, they attacked eleven times. For their efforts, however, they gained little ground, while absorbing substantial casualties. Here again, the scale of military operations in the First World War is evident. The total number of men wounded or killed in 1915 in combat between two second-tier states—Italy and Austria-Hungary—on a battlefront considered primary by neither the British, the French, nor the German commanders was slightly more than 424,000.

The number of casualties would increase. In the eleventh battle along the river in August 1917, the Italians suffered an additional 155,000. This time, they made significant gains, so much so that Austria-Hungary, alarmed, requested assistance from Germany.

Germany gathered together several infantry divisions and, with troops from the Austrian-Hungarian Empire, established a new army that attacked the Italians in October 1917. In but a few weeks its troops achieved a great victory, driving the Italians back a distance of some sixty miles. This, the Battle of Caporetto, remains a painful memory for Italy and its army. Ten thousand Italian soldiers were killed and three times that number were wounded. Almost unbelievably—and another indicator of the scale of the 1914–1918 conflict—German troops took 275,000 Italians prisoner. Yet the Italian army recovered. A year later it went on the offensive, supported by British, French, and American units. It fought well and, across a wide front, pushed the Austrians back. This success, achieved right at the end of the war, earned Italy a seat at the head table when at Versailles the Allies redrew the map of Europe. As did Romania, Italy came away with additional territory that remains part of the country today.

Serbia, Romania, the Italian Alps and the Caucasus, Bulgaria, and Palestine are all places far from the trenches of Western Europe. For most Americans, it is these trenches that have come to symbolize the First World War. Yet in each location just mentioned, generals issued orders, soldiers obeyed, and men died. But there are two other places not usually associated with the conflict of 1914–1918 that saw military operations during the Great War. These are Africa and China. Both witnessed the clash of arms.

In 1914 Imperial Germany had an outpost on the northern coast of

China, at Tsingtao. Eager to expand its influence and believing Germany to be otherwise occupied, Japan, with Britain's concurrence, landed sixty thousand troops nearby and, in early November 1914, took control of the city. During the same period, Japan also seized German outposts on the Caroline and Marshall Islands. None of this came as a surprise to the generals and admirals in Berlin, because Japan had declared war on Germany months before, on August 23. In addition to outposts in China and the Pacific islands, Germany also had a presence in Africa. So did other European powers, most notably Britain, France, and Belgium. Germany controlled what is today Togo and parts of Cameroon, Ghana, Tanzania, and Namibia. In all these locations British and German forces went to war, with both sides employing mostly native soldiers (the French brought their African troops north and employed them in the trenches, where no doubt the rain and cold came as quite a shock). Eventually, the British carried the day, although in German East Africa one hundred thousand British troops were unable to decisively defeat fifteen thousand irregulars of the enemy. The latter were led rather brilliantly by the German Paul von Lettow-Vorbeck, who both during and after the war was a national hero.

Lettow-Vorbeck never had to deal with trench warfare, where barbed wire, heavy artillery, aerial observation, and machine gun nests made both attacking and defending a hazardous occupation. Joffre and Falkenhayn did, as did Sir John French, the commander of the BEF. In 1915, all three went on the offensive. The result for each of them was failure. Their armies gained very little ground but suffered substantial casualties. 1915 was a year of slaughter.

The French, in particular, took heavy losses. In the autumn, attacks alone in Joffre's army had 190,000 soldiers killed or wounded. At Loos, in September 1915, the BEF saw 16,000 of its men dead with another 25,000 wounded. Four months before, at the Second Battle of Ypres, a German assault also resulted in numerous casualties. The Germans, who again failed to push the British out of the city, suffered 38,000 casualties. What makes the Second Battle of Ypres particularly noteworthy is that Falkenhayn's forces began their attack by employing chlorine gas. The British responded in kind at Loos. As the war continued, gas remained one of the available weapons, although it did not prove decisive.

The inability of the French and the British to achieve success on the Western Front late in 1914 and early in 1915 led to a decision to seek victory elsewhere. They decided on Gallipoli, a peninsula jutting down from Istanbul adjacent to the Dardanelles, the body of water that links the Black Sea with the Mediterranean Sea and which separates the continents of Europe and Asia. Success at Gallipoli would relieve pressure on the Russians and might well compel the Ottoman Empire to withdraw from the war. It also would boost the morale of the folks back home, who by now had noticed that despite huge loss of life, victory was nowhere in sight.

At first British and French warships attempted to force their way through to Istanbul. That did not work, so the British landed troops ashore in the largest amphibious operation of the war. Among these troops were Australians and New Zealanders. They were known as the ANZACS (the Australian and New Zealand Army Corps) and their exploits at Gallipoli would win them great fame. However, they suffered some 10,000 casualties, for them a substantial number but a small percentage of the 265,000 Allied troops killed or wounded in an expedition that failed. When the British withdrew in December, no one in the British army or government thought the effort had been other than a debacle.

As the British were departing from Gallipoli, Joffre and the new commander of the BEF, Sir Douglas Haig, were planning their campaigns for 1916. The French general believed in offensive maneuvers and in the imperative of removing German soldiers from French soil. Haig believed the only way to win the war was through attrition, engage the German army in battle, defeat it, and do battle again. Their plans for 1916 envisioned a series of strikes, straight at and through well-entrenched German positions.

However, Erich von Falkenhayn struck first, preempting Joffre's attacks. In late February, following a massive artillery barrage, the German general sent his troops forward. Their objective was Verdun, a town on the Meuse River some 150 miles northeast of Paris, a town Falkenhayn knew the French would be unwilling to lose. So began the longest single battle of the First World War. When it was over, 162,440 French soldiers were dead. The number of Germans killed was slightly less. Falkenhayn had hoped to so wear down the French army as to render it ineffective. He came close. But the French commander in charge, Philippe Pétain, one of the few French generals committed to defensive warfare, led his soldiers calmly and courageously and held Verdun. He earned, as Joffre had at the Marne, the reputation of saving France. Given the battle's outcome, Falkenhayn was relieved of command. His failure at Verdun instead had worn down the German army.

If, as it is by many, the First World War is seen as a bloodbath of the first rank, the Battle of Verdun is one reason. Another is the Somme.

One hundred and fifty miles long, the River Somme flows through Amiens into the English Channel. The battle to which the river gave its name began in July 1916 and lasted five months. Haig, a general whom history has not treated well, planned meticulously. His attack was to be preceded by the heaviest artillery barrage the British army could muster: one field gun every twenty yards across a sixteen-mile front. This was intended to destroy the barbed wire and machine gun emplacements the enemy were known to have deployed, as well as kill any Germans unfortunate enough to be in range. As the British infantry advanced, their supporting artillery was to move forward, providing covering fire. It was to be a creeping barrage.

The plan was sound. Its execution was not. The British artillery failed in its task. There were too few guns, they were too small in caliber, there were too many shells that did not explode, and there was too much mud. Moreover, the kaiser's soldiers proved remarkably resilient. For Haig's troops, the results were catastrophic. That first day, July 1, 1916, 19,240 British soldiers were killed. That number needs to be repeated: 19,240 British soldiers died on the first day of the Somme. Total casualties that day numbered 57,470. The battle continued for another forty days. Losses piled up, for the Germans as well and for the French, whose Sixth Army was part of Haig's force.

When the battle came to a close—it's official end is deemed November 18, 1916—the butcher's bill was staggering. Great Britain's official history of the war states that the combined casualties of the British and French forces totaled 623,907. Of this number the British owned 419,654. All for a negligible gain in territory. German losses are more difficult to ascertain, but certainly numbered near to those of their enemy. As John Keegan has written of the British army, the Somme "was, and would remain their greatest military tragedy of the twentieth century, indeed of their national military history."

Yet it must be recorded that the Somme was a victory for the British. Not due to territory gained, a mere three miles that in no way altered the strategic picture, but because having themselves suffered horrendous losses, the German army retreated, withdrawing up to forty miles in some places. They then completed a system of strong defensive positions which the British dubbed the Hindenburg Line. Once there, the kaiser's army, now with Hindenburg and Ludendorff in charge, planned no major offensive. The Somme, wrote an officer on the German General Staff, had been "the muddy grave of the German field army."

While the German commanders were content to remain on the defensive, their counterparts in the French and British armies were not. For them and their troops, 1917 would be a difficult year.

The heavy losses at Verdun had spelled the end of Joffre's tenure as commander in chief of the French army. He was replaced by General Robert Nivelle. An expert in artillery, Nivelle had performed well at Verdun. In 1917, he persuaded the French government that he had battlefield tactics that would bring success against the Germans. He did not. In fact, his tactics were more of the same: massive artillery strikes across a narrow front followed by infantry and continuous, rolling cannon fire. Nivelle's offensive began on April 16, 1917. It lasted just five days. The French army got nowhere, but incurred 130,000 casualties. Nivelle and his offensive were disasters. The result was a broken army. More than a few units refused to do further battle. These were the famous mutinies that inflicted the French army in the middle of 1917. Pétain was ordered to replace Nivelle, and by improving the lot of the ordinary *poilu*, and by not, for a while, engaging in offensive actions, he was able to restore both discipline and morale. He also had 629 soldiers condemned to death, but executed only 43.

The British army too went on the offensive in 1917, several times. Embracing the strategy of attrition Haig wanted his troops to attack, and attack they did. The first assault occurred at Arras and began on April 9. At first, the British troops did well, taking 9,000 prisoners and suffering few losses. But, as happened so often in the First World War, the attack stalled, the Germans struck back, and a slugging match became a stalemate. In the end, the British listed 150,000 men as casualties.

Taking part in the Battle of Arras were four Canadian divisions, some eighty thousand men, operating for the first time as the Canadian Corps. Their attack on Vimy Ridge was successful, earning well-deserved fame for Canada and its soldiers. For the action at Vimy Ridge, the Canadian Corps's commander, Major General Arthur Currie, was knighted on the battlefield by King George V.

The second British offensive of 1917 took place at Ypres, the third time this city and its environs became a battlefield. Its objective was to secure the coast of Belgium, thereby denying submarine bases to the German navy. The attack began with 2,229 pieces of artillery opening fire, ten times the number employed at the Somme. The infantry went "over the top" at 3:50 A.M. on July 31. As with Nivelle's offensive, the outcome was disastrous. After four months, seventy thousand British soldiers were dead. What made the attack fail was the pervasive rain and mud. And, of course, German resistance. Keegan calls the battle "the most notorious land campaign of the war." The battle often goes by the name Passchendaele, a small village outside of Ypres that marked the farthest advance of Haig's army.

The British commander believed the Germans were suffering as much as his army and could less afford the losses. So Sir Douglas attacked again. This, the third British offensive of 1917, took place at Cambrai, a city northeast of Paris, not too far from the border with Belgium. The results followed a familiar pattern: initial success but little gain once the Germans counterattacked. What makes Cambrai significant in military terms is that, for the first time, massed formations of tanks were used. Though slow and prone to mechanical failure, these machines at Cambrai ushered in a new era of land warfare.

During 1917, Hindenburg and Ludendorff, Nivelle and Pétain, and Douglas Haig commanded troops that engaged in battle, in titanic struggles that help define the First World War. Yet 1917 also witnessed two events that marked the beginning of the end of the great conflict. One such event took place in Washington, D.C., in April. The other occurred in Berlin.

On January 9, 1917, at its capital Germany announced its intention to renew unrestricted submarine warfare. "Unrestricted" meant that no longer would a German *unterseeboote*, or U-boat, refrain from sinking neutral vessels or allow time for crew to disembark from a ship about to be torpedoed. Beginning in February, any ship would be sunk on sight. Many people were shocked by this announcement. What the Germans were about to do was considered uncivilized, unnecessarily cruel. But the commanders in Berlin understood that war requires harsh behavior, and besides, submarines had little room for displaced sailors. Moreover, the kaiser's admirals, and his generals as well, understood that after several years of conflict, such U-boat strikes offered the best chance of winning the war. The goal was to force Britain to withdraw from the war, by depriving the island nation of food and essential materials. If Britain were to opt out, France, then alone, could be defeated. This goal had to be achieved before the United States entered the war, which it was likely to do once the U-boats began their campaign. When America joined forces with France and Britain, the battlefield equation would be altered and Germany would lose the war.

Of course, the war at sea had begun well before 1917.

When the German East Asiatic squadron had to abandon Tsingtao late in 1914, most of its ships sailed across the Pacific Ocean to the coast of Chile. There, under the command of Maximilian von Spee, they destroyed two Royal Navy cruisers, killing sixteen hundred British sailors. In London the Admiralty promptly dispatched three battle cruisers, among them the *Invincible* and the *Inflexible*, to deal with the Germans. This they did, totally destroying Spee's squadron in December.

In 1914 Britain may have had a small army, but it possessed a large navy, one which, if it did not rule the waves, came very close to doing so. Upon the declaration of war, the Royal Navy instituted a blockade of Germany. Writing in 1930, Captain B. H. Liddell Hart, a noted military historian, said the blockade "was to do more than any other factor towards winning the war for the Allies." The navy's blockade effectively cut off seaborne traffic to and out of German ports. In time, the blockade imposed severe hardship on the country's industry and civilian population. By 1917, food shortages were causing great distress. By mid-1918, the situation in German cities was such that social unrest was unraveling the political cohesion of the Imperial German state.

With its many warships, Britain hoped to lure the kaiser's quite capable surface fleet into battle. This, it was expected, would result in a great victory, as Trafalgar had been in 1805. In command of the Royal Navy's powerful fleet was Admiral Sir John Jellicoe. On May 31, 1916, he had his chance. The two fleets slugged it out in the North Sea, some fifty miles off the Jutland Peninsula. The statistical results favored the Germans. They lost eleven ships and 3,058 sailors. Jellicoe (about whom Winston Churchill said he was the only man in England able to lose the war in an afternoon) had fourteen ships sunk and twice that number of men killed. But the battle did not alter the strategic picture. Afterward, the Royal Navy still controlled the seas. Germany's fleet returned to port. Never again did it challenge Britain's maritime preeminence.

Only U-boats could, and would, do that.

German submarines registered their first kill early in the war. On October 20, 1914, U-17 sunk the *Glitra*, a small British ship sailing near Norway. Thereafter, the tempo of attacks quickened. The shipping lanes around the British Isles became dangerous places. On May 7, 1915, in waters close to Ireland, a German submarine put a single torpedo into the starboard side of the Cunard liner *Lusitania*, which then took but eighteen minutes to sink. The ship was carrying artillery ammunition for the British army and, thus, was a legitimate target for U-20. Of the 1,195 fatalities, 123 were American. People in the United States, already angry with Germany over "the Rape of Belgium," were outraged. When months later, more U.S. citizens were killed in a submarine attack, President Woodrow Wilson sent an ultimatum to Berlin: halt unrestricted submarine warfare or the United States would sever diplomatic relations with Germany and, in essence, enter the war on the side of France and Britain. Surprisingly, the Germans did so. But by 1917 the situation was such that the German High Command reinstated the policy. That year the kaiser's navy had 111

U-boats in service. Their commanders, armed with skill and courage as well as torpedoes, intended to destroy the maritime lifeline on which Great Britain depended. As the number of ships sunk increased, it looked like they would succeed.

Senior officials in London became alarmed. Among them was Jellicoe, who in June 1917 declared that Britain had lost control of the seas. By then first sea lord, the top position in the Royal Navy, Jellicoe told his colleagues that Britain would not be able to continue to fight in 1918. Needless to say, this message sent shock waves through the British government. Such pessimism could not be tolerated. Jellicoe was sacked. More important, the navy changed its method of combating submarines.

At first, merchant ships sailed singly. Proposals to group them in an assembly of vessels, a convoy, escorted by naval vessels were rejected. The rationale was that a group of ships would be easier for a U-boat to spot and would overload the capacity of British ports upon reaching its destination. However, both analysis and experience eventually showed the rationale to be flawed. Ports could handle the influx of ships. Moreover, the ocean is so large that a submarine is no more likely to find forty ships than it is to find one. And because the convoy would have Royal Navy ships on guard, success by the U-boats would be limited.

Belatedly, Britain's navy therefore required merchant ships to sail in convoy. This produced the intended result. More and more ships arrived safely. April 1918 was the turning point. From then on, Britain received the supplies needed to continue the war effort.

There was a second failure on the part of the kaiser's submarines, one that receives less attention than it deserves. They failed to prevent the transport of American soldiers to France. More than two million "doughboys" crossed the Atlantic to serve in the American Expeditionary Force (AEF). All went by ship. Not one U.S. vessel was sunk. However, what the German submarine campaign did accomplish was America's entry into the war. On April 6, 1917, in Washington, D.C., the United States declared war on Germany.

The United States entered the conflict to save democracy. Added Woodrow Wilson in requesting the declaration:

We desire no conquest, no dominion. We seek no indemnities for
ourselves, no material compensation for the sacrifices we shall
freely make. We are but one of the champions of mankind.

For Wilson, the enemy was German militarism. America was to join Britain and France, themselves democratic states, and rid the world of a government that held in contempt both freedom and justice. Allied propaganda helped sway the Americans and their president. It portrayed the Germans as barbarians, a description seemingly verified by their behavior in Belgium and by their approach to submarine warfare.

Americans were outraged by the sinking of ships without warning, particularly ships carrying U.S. citizens. They also were outraged by Germany's foolish effort to tempt Mexico into the war. Alfred Zimmermann was the kaiser's foreign minister. Early in January 1917 he sent a coded message to the German ambassador in Mexico suggesting that in the event of war between the United States and Germany, Mexico side with the latter. Upon the war's conclusion (with Germany victorious) Mexico would be rewarded with Texas and other lands it had once possessed. The British intelligence service intercepted the message and passed it on to the U.S. Department of State. Neither Wilson nor the American people took kindly to Zimmermann's intrigue. The result simply was another reason to go to war.

Wilson, who in 1916 had campaigned for reelection by proclaiming that he had kept America out of the war, had one additional reason for having the United States enter the conflict. As historian Hew Strachan has pointed out, President Wilson understood that if America were to participate in designing the postwar world, it would have to do some of the fighting. And Woodrow Wilson wanted very much to craft that future world. Indeed, he had at least fourteen ideas as to how to do it.

Both then and now, the army the United States deployed to France in 1917 and 1918 was called the American Expeditionary Force. The AEF's commander was General John J. Pershing.

Known as "Black Jack" because he once had commanded African-

American soldiers, Pershing was a combat veteran of the war with Spain and of the insurrection in the Philippines. In 1916, he led an expedition into Mexico in search of Pancho Villa, who had raided several towns in the United States. Pershing was a tough, demanding officer respected by his men but not beloved. His career, no doubt, had been helped by having a father-in-law who was chairman of the Senate's Military Affairs Committee.

Arriving in France in June 1917 (it was an aide to Pershing not the general who said, "Lafayette, we are here"), Pershing had to assemble, supply, and train a force capable of taking on the kaiser's battle-tested army. This was no simple task, for the Americans getting off the ships were neither well prepared nor properly equipped. The AEF had no artillery, no tanks, no airplanes, and no machine guns. The men themselves were little more than raw recruits. Many had never fired their weapons. To turn them into a combat-ready army required time and instruction. It also required equipment, much of which was purchased from the French. Pershing was able to buy what he needed. The AEF bought 3,532 artillery pieces, 40,884 automatic weapons, 227 tanks, and 4,874 aircraft from French suppliers. When the Americans finally went into battle, they did so because French manufacturers had provided much of their equipment.

Training also was provided by the French, as well as by the British. Veterans of combat, these instructors taught the Americans how to survive and fight in the hellish world of trenches, barbed wire, mud, poison gas, machine guns, and deadly artillery fire.

Pershing himself wanted the Americans to emphasize the rifle and the bayonet. His war-fighting doctrine stressed marksmanship and maneuver. He envisioned the AEF making quick frontal assaults, then breaking through German defenses and advancing rapidly, destroying the enemy as it moved forward. That this approach made little sense in the environment of the Western Front appeared not to register with General Pershing. It certainly made an impact on the average American soldier. Many of them died or were wounded needlessly. The consensus seems to be that the number of casualties suffered by the AEF—255,970—was larger than it should have been.

By war's end the American Expeditionary Force had grown to just over two million men. In total, the United States Army numbered 3,680,458. This was a staggering increase over the 208,034 that constituted the army in early 1917, at which point the American army ranked worldwide sixteenth in size, just behind Portugal.

Transporting the AEF to France was no easy task. It was done by ship, of course, and took time. More than one senior official in London and Paris wondered whether the Americans were ever to arrive. True, at first the buildup was slow, but by the summer of 1918, fourteen months after Congress declared war, U.S. troops were pouring into France.

French and British generals wanted the arriving soldiers to be allocated to their armies. The Yanks were to replenish Allied regiments depleted by three years of warfare. The generals reasoned that the Americans not only lacked combat experience, they also lacked staff organization essential to large military units. Developing these staffs, gaining the necessary experience, would take time, valuable time. Better, they argued, to place the Americans among experienced French and British troops, and do so right away. Waiting for a fully prepared, independent U.S. Army risked defeat on the battlefield. Time was of the essence. The best way to utilize American soldiers was to distribute them among seasoned troops already on the front line.

Pershing said no. Though directed by the secretary of war to cooperate with the French and the British, the commander of the AEF had been ordered to field an independent American army and to lead it into battle. This is exactly what he did.

Senior French and British generals, several of whom thought Pershing was not up to his job, frequently tried to have the American troops amalgamated into their armies. And, just as frequently, Black Jack replied that Americans had come to France to fight as an American army, pointing out, probably correctly, that U.S. soldiers likely were to fight more effectively under American officers in an army whose flag was the Stars and Stripes.

Yet, to Pershing's credit, when in May–June 1918 a battlefield crisis arose and both General Ferdinand Foch and Field Marshal Sir Douglas Haig urgently needed additional troops, Pershing dispatched several U.S. divisions to bolster French and British forces.

The principal fighting unit of the AEF was the division. At twenty-eight thousand men, it was twice the size of British and French counterparts. All forty-three divisions that served in France were infantry divisions. While an AEF division would have its own artillery and support units—plus 6,638 horses and mules—its principal component was the rifleman. The United States entered the war deficient in modern weaponry. As previously noted, the AEF lacked artillery, aircraft, tanks, and machine guns. What it did possess, and what it did contribute, was manpower. By the summer of 1918, the French army was worn out. The British army, still ready for battle, was running out of men. Pershing's army represented a vast influx of men, men whose number and willingness to fight would play a decisive role in the outcome of the First World War.

Two of the forty-three divisions of the AEF were composed of black Americans. These were newly raised units, the 93rd and 92nd Divisions. The former was loaned to the French army and fought extremely well. One of the 93rd's regiments, the 369th "Black Rattlers," served with great distinction. The 92nd had less success. It remained in the AEF and went into battle in September. Due mostly to poor leadership and incomplete training, the division performed poorly. This, unfortunately, left a legacy in the American army. Throughout the postwar years, the army's officer corps were skeptical of the ability of African-Americans to both command and fight.

Racism was alive and well in America during the years of the First World War. This permeated the nation's army, wherein blacks usually were given jobs of secondary importance. In 1916 there were four "colored" regiments in the regular army. None of them served in France. However, some two hundred thousand other African-American soldiers were part of the American Expeditionary Force. Yet most of these men were put to work in what essentially were labor battalions, digging ditches and unloading ships. This, despite the fact that U.S. authorities had established an officer training school for blacks in Des Moines, Iowa, that produced more than eleven hundred officers for the United States Army.

Women too faced discrimination in the army. Given that in 1917–1918 they did not have the right to vote, this is not surprising. About ten thousand women served as nurses in the AEF. Though treated as officers, they were not paid as such. Nor, according to historian Byron Farwell, did the army provide them with uniforms or equipment. Those came from the Red Cross. Despite the inequity, the women's services were indispensable and performed with skill and dedication.

Also performing essential medical services were Americans who, prior to the United States' entry into the war, drove ambulances for the French military. They were volunteers, many of them students or graduates of America's finest colleges. Serving as noncombatants, they transported wounded French soldiers from the battlefield to the hospital. More than two thousand young men so volunteered, eventually carrying some four hundred thousand soldiers to safety.

Nurses were not the only group of women attached to the AEF. To operate the telephone switchboard established at corps and army headquarters, Pershing recruited some two hundred women fluent in French. Trained by the American Telephone and Telegraph Company in Illinois, they were attached to the army's Signal Corps. After purchasing their uniforms in New York, they were shipped to France and went to work. Known as the "Hello Girls," they provided yeoman service and received praise from Pershing himself. What they did not receive was official discharge papers, medals, or veteran benefits. They were bluntly informed that, despite their uniforms and services, they were employees of the army, not members. They were not, therefore, entitled to benefits given to the men of the AEF. Not until 1979 was this injustice rectified, by which time, of course, it was too late for most of these women.

If America's army required months and months to prepare for battle, it's navy did not. On May 4, 1917, just twenty-eight days after the United States declared war, six American destroyers dropped anchor in Queenstown Harbor on the southern coast of Ireland. They and the others that followed would provide needed protection to the merchant ships sailing to and from Britain. Heavier naval firepower arrived in December. Five battleships of the United States Navy, all commanded by Rear Admiral Hugh Rodman, joined the Royal Navy's Grand Fleet. Significantly, they served under British command and were present when Germany's High Seas Fleet surrendered.

The U.S. Navy's role in the First World War is overshadowed by that of Pershing's army. For most Americans the image of the conflict is that of soldiers in trenches surrounded by mud and barbed wire. The navy's contribution receives little notice. Even less is given to Admiral William S. Sims, who throughout the war was in charge of American naval operations in Europe.

In addition to dispatching destroyers and battleships to England, America's navy established a special task force consisting primarily of cruisers that escorted the ships transporting the AEF to France. The navy also provided its air service to the war effort. This comprised some five hundred aircraft distributed among twenty-six naval air stations located in Britain, France, and Italy. And, rather remarkably, the navy sent five very heavy, large naval guns mounted on railroad cars to France, where, in the Allied offensives of September 1918, they pounded German positions near Soissons.

One other achievement of America's navy in World War I deserves mention. As part of the effort to stymie German submarines, the Royal Navy proposed to lay a barrier of mines from northern Scotland across the North Sea to southern Norway. This would seal off the northern perimeter of the North Sea (a similar barrier was to be laid down across the English Channel near Dover). The project would deny the U-boats free access to the Atlantic Ocean. This was to be an enormous undertaking. Two factors initially delayed its start: the Royal Navy had few ships to spare, and, perhaps more important, British mines were defective. Enter the United States Navy. In June 1918, it began laying its own mines. In total, the Americans put 56,571 mines into the water. Britain's navy laid 13,546. Together, they were strung along an underwater belt some two hundred miles long. Jellicoe's successor, Admiral David Beatty, opposed the project. He said it would hinder operations of the fleet and consume resources better spent elsewhere. He had a point. The barrier, the Northern Barrage, to use its customary name, accounted for the destruction of only six U-boats.

Most German submarines operated in the waters around Great Britain and in the Mediterranean. Few made war patrols to North America. One that did was U-156. On July 19, 1918, off the coast of Long Island, the cruiser USS *San Diego* sunk, having struck a mine laid by the German submarine. The cruiser was the only major American warship lost in World War I.

In returning to unrestricted submarine warfare in 1917, Germany had gambled that it could force Great Britain out of the war before America's involvement made much of a difference. The gamble failed. In 1914 Germany had gambled that it could destroy the French Army in forty days before having to move east against the tsar. This gamble also failed. Four years later, in 1918, Germany would take one last gamble.

Hindenburg and Ludendorff, by now running the government as well as the army, decided on one final offensive in the west. It would be a massive affair, employing specially trained storm troopers and army units no longer needed on the Russian Front. The attack began on March 21 with a thunderous barrage. Three separate German armies struck hard, crushing the British Fifth Army, one of four units under Sir Douglas Haig's command. That first day, the kaiser's men killed seven thousand British soldiers and took twenty-one thousand prisoners. The attack was a stunning success. The Germans advanced forty miles, a significant distance, before the British were able to stop them.

A second offensive took place in Flanders, the Germans attacking early in April. Here too they made progress, forcing the British commander in chief to issue his famous "backs to the walls" directive. Sir Douglas instructed his soldiers not to retreat, to hold on whatever the cost. His order was taken to heart. Here are parts of the written orders a young Australian officer issued to his men:

1. This position will be held and the section will remain here until relieved.
2. The enemy cannot be allowed to interfere with this program.
3. If the section cannot remain here alive it will remain here dead, but in any case it will remain here.
4. If any man through shell shock or other cause attempts to surrender he will remain here dead.

The men given this order obeyed. The order was found on the body of one of their dead.

In their spring offensives, the Germans also struck the French. Ludendorff, who planned the attacks, sent his troops to the Chemin des Dames sector, to the northeast of the Reims. There, they crushed a French army and advanced to the Marne River, threatening Paris. In June and July, the Germans, for the fourth and fifth time, again attacked. These attacks were less successful. Nonetheless, French forces had been battered. French troops were in retreat.

All along the front, German troops moved forward, inflicting a large number of casualties. In just the first forty days of combat, Sir Douglas Haig's forces suffered more than 160,000 killed or wounded. French losses in the spring and summer reached 70,000. The British and French armies were bleeding, and bleeding badly.

As the casualties mounted, and the German advances continued, top Allied leaders realized that a change in the military-command structure was needed. Up to now the senior French and British field commanders, at the time Pétain and Haig, and earlier Nivelle and Haig, had acted independently. They consulted with each other, but neither could command the other. The German spring offensives changed that. All came to understand that a single field commander in chief needed to be in charge. Such was the urgency that Field Marshal Haig raised no objection to the appointment of French general Ferdinand Foch to the post (Pétain was considered too defensively oriented). The French general became, as Eisenhower would in the Second World War, supreme Allied commander. At first, he was simply to coordinate the three armies involved, the British, the French, and the American. But, as the German threat increased, Foch was authorized to give orders to their commanders. Only if Haig and Pershing considered these orders detrimental to the national interests of Great Britain or the United States were the two subordinate commanders allowed to appeal. Pétain had no such authority; he was told to follow Foch's instructions. Despite disagreements, some rather testy, this new command arrangement proved satisfactory. Ferdinand Foch, the general who believed the only military course of action worthy of consideration was to attack, became commander of more than five million men. Given his preeminent position in the chain of command and his subsequent record of success, it's not surprising that upon his death in 1920, his body was laid to rest in Paris near that of Napoleon.

As spring gave way to summer, the German offensives appeared to stall. Though inflicting heavy losses on their French and British counterparts, the Germans themselves suffered as well. By the end of April, after just two months, 492,720 of their soldiers no longer were able to fight. They were dead, in the hospital, missing in action, or had been taken prisoner. More German soldiers would be lost in May and June and into July, when, finally, after the fourth and fifth attack, the offensive came to a halt. In total, Ludendorff's spring offensives cost the kaiser 800,000 of his soldiers.

Moreover, the British army, though roughed up, had not been destroyed. Sir Douglas's men, by 1918 the most capable fighting force in Europe, had bent but not broken. So too the French. Pétain's army, one that had experienced both victory and defeat in four years of conflict, still had some fight left in it.

As, of course, did the German army. Yet it was clear, especially to Foch, that the German spring offensives had failed. True, Ludendorff's men had gained considerable territory. But no decisive victory had been attained, nor had the strategic picture changed much. The front, that tangled strip of trenches, barbed wire, and machine gun rests, had been moved to the west. Save for some worried souls in Paris, nothing much seemed to have changed.

In fact, two things had changed, both significant. The first was that the German army was running out of soldiers. A country can produce only a certain number of men capable of bearing arms, and by the summer of 1918, after fighting Russians and Romanians, the British and the French, Germany had just about reached its limit. And the later replacement troops were not as skillful as those who had fought earlier in the war. The second change, one even more ominous to Ludendorff and his field commanders, was that Pershing's American Expeditionary Force was preparing to do battle.

The AEF's first test of combat had come in late May. Assigned to the French First Army, the U.S. Army's 1st Division was given the task of taking Cantigny. This was a small village on a ridge near Montdidier, a town some sixty miles north of Paris. The ridge enabled the Germans to observe what was taking place to the south and west of their positions. Planning the attack was the division's Operations officer, Lieutenant Colonel George C. Marshall. Well conceived and twice rehearsed, the plan had the division's 28th Infantry Regiment directly assaulting the town supported by artillery, tanks, and flamethrowers provided by the French.

The attack began early in the morning of May 28, 1918. By noon, the village was in U.S. hands. The Germans counterattacked several times, and the battle became what author David Bonk has called "a desperate slugging match." Showing notable determination, the men of the 28th held on, despite the premature withdrawal of the French artillery. When the battle was over, the regiment had sustained more than nine hundred casualties. More importantly, Cantigny remained under U.S. control.

The town itself was of no overall strategic value to the Allies. But the fight for Cantigny was important. It demonstrated that the AEF could plan and execute a division-level operation. It also showed that, despite their inexperience, individual American soldiers would do just fine in battle. French and Britain commanders were uncertain how Pershing's soldiers would respond to the ordeal of battle. So too were German commanders, who tried to convince their troops and themselves that Americans were no match for well-disciplined and battle-tested German soldiers. The fight for Cantigny put to rest such nonsense. For Foch and Haig it was reassuring. For Ludendorff it was cause for concern. For General Pershing and his troops, and for the folks back home in the United States, it was a signal that, once fully deployed, the AEF would have soldiers to be reckoned with.

As the 1st Division's fight at Cantigny came to a close, the AEF's 3rd Division was moving into action. Ludendorff's May offensive, code named Blücher, had seen some success with the Germans reaching the Marne. The French, dispirited by their enemy's advances, asked General Pershing for assistance. Recognizing the urgency of the situation, Black Jack put aside his objection to amalgamation and lent the 3rd Division to the French. They ordered it to Château Thierry. This was (and still is) a lovely little town on the Marne River, where today an American military cemetery resides. At Château Thierry the Americans held fast and Ludendorff's troops advanced no farther.

Not far from Château Thierry, to the west, were two villages, Boure-sches and Belleau. In between them stood a small forest. It was called Belleau Wood. In June 1918, it witnessed a fierce battle, one that for the United States of America would become legendary.

That same month, still needing to slow the German advance, Foch requested additional American help. However, he planned not just to halt the German drive. Foch planned to counterattack and wanted some of Pershing's troops to participate. The AEF responded by lending Foch the 2nd Division, which the French deployed to Belleau Wood. This unit was unique in the American Expeditionary Force in that two of its four infantry regiments, comprising the 4th Brigade, were U.S. marines, not soldiers of the U.S. Army.

The 4th Brigade's first task was to stop a German attack, which it did. The story is told that a retreating French officer said to an American that with the Germans advancing, he and his men should fall back. "Retreat, hell," replied the marine, "we just got here."

The second task assigned to the marines was to clear Belleau Wood of Germans and hold on to it. On June 6 they attacked. Their artillery was insufficient, their tactics flawed. But as the marines crossed a wheat field full of red poppies, their determination and courage were in full view. The attack succeeded, although the cost was high. The brigade's casualties that day totaled 1,087. The fight would continue for twenty more days, and at times the marines took no prisoners, and neither did the Germans. It was kill or be killed.

Toward the end of the struggle for Belleau Wood, the 2nd Division's other brigade, the one consisting of two army regiments, went into action. It was ordered to capture the nearby town of Vaux. Quite competently, the brigade took control of the town, for its effort suffering 300 dead and 1,400 wounded. This battle at Vaux received little attention. In 1918—and even today—what captured the spotlight was the marines at Belleau Wood.

By the standards of the First World War, the engagements of Belleau Wood and Vaux were small affairs. In total, the casualty count for the U.S. 2nd Division showed 1,811 men dead and 7,966 wounded. For the armies of France, Great Britain, and Germany, these were numbers unlikely to raise alarm. For the AEF 9,777 in one division was a stiff price. It illustrated that inexperience on the battlefield costs lives. Nonetheless, Vaux and Belleau Wood were victories. As did Cantigny, the two battles bode well for the Allied cause.

The next occasion in which the AEF went into action involved far more men than had fought at Vaux and Belleau Wood. Once the German spring offensive came to a halt, Ferdinand Foch was keen to strike back. He wanted to recover territory lost to the Germans, and he also wanted to damage Ludendorff's army, which he believed by then to be under considerable stress. He directed Pétain to prepare a plan of attack, which the French army's commander in chief did. The plan included substantial participation by the Americans.

Two U.S. divisions, along with a French Moroccan unit, spearheaded the attack. They were part of the French Tenth Army. Pershing had once again agreed to allocate American units to Pétain's forces. Three other AEF divisions were assigned to the French Sixth Army, while a further three were part of the force held in reserve. Ultimately, some three hundred thousand American soldiers were involved. The attack, along a twenty-five-mile front in the vicinity of Soissons, began on July 18. It was over by August 2. Approximately thirty thousand Germans were taken prisoner. Such was the success that afterward the kaiser's son wrote his father that the war was lost.

This battle is usually referred to as the Second Battle of the Marne. One key result of this battle was Ludendorff's decision to call off a major attack against the British in the north. The German commander had hoped once and for all to crush Field Marshal Haig's forces in France. That had been the decisive victory Ludendorff had designed his spring offensives to achieve.

Meanwhile, Sir Douglas had planned an offensive of his own, one to which Foch as Supreme Commander readily agreed. On August 8, the British Army attacked near Amiens. Among the assault troops were Canadians and Australians, whom the *West Point Military Series* account of World War I says were "generally regarded as the finest infantry fighters on the Allied side." The outcome was a stunning success for British arms.

Haig's losses were light, suggesting that the British, at last, had mastered the art of trench warfare. German losses were substantial. Some seventy thousand troops were out of action. Of these, thirty thousand had surrendered without much of a fight. In his memoir, Ludendorff, who offered to resign after the battle, termed August 8 "the black day of the German army."

The British victory at Amiens was one of the more decisive battles of the First World War, but not because of territory gained or men lost. Rather, it was important because of its psychological impact on the Germans. After Amiens the German high command realized that defeat was now likely. For Germany, the war was lost once its generals believed the war was lost. After their drubbing by the British in August 1918, that's exactly what they began to believe.

Two days after the British launched their attack from Amiens, the American Expeditionary Force established a new combat organization. Previously, the AEF had organized divisions as its primary fighting units. As we've seen, these went into battle as components of various French armies. By August, however, the number of American divisions had increased so as to warrant a larger combat unit. On August 10, 1918, the First American Army was brought into being. It was comprised of fourteen divisions organized into three corps. Its commander was John J. Pershing, who remained in charge of the AEF, of which First Army became the principal American combat unit.

By early October, the number of American soldiers justified the establishment of the U.S. Second Army. Its commander was Major General Robert Lee Bullard, who had been in charge of the 1st Division at Cantigny. By then, First Army had a new commander. He was Hunter Liggett, also a major general. Both Liggett and Bullard reported to Pershing, who then was at the same level as Field Marshal Sir Douglas Haig and General Philippe Pétain, each of whose command encompassed several separate armies. Above Haig, Pétain, and Pershing was the supreme commander, Ferdinand Foch.

In early September Foch had been content to have Allied troops conduct limited offensives along the entire Western Front. For the AEF this meant the elimination of the St. Mihiel salient.

In military terminology, a salient is a wedge, a protrusion in the battle line often shaped like an arrowhead. In 1914, the Germans had created such a wedge sixteen miles deep into the French lines, with the tip of the salient at a small town well to the east of Paris. Several times, the French army had attempted to eliminate it. Each time the army had failed.

The St. Mihiel salient was in the American sector of operations. Not surprisingly, General Pershing decided to have his First American Army remove the wedge. Initially, he planned to have the army continue on to Metz, then a heavily fortified German stronghold. Such a move, if success-ful, would have had strategic consequences, threatening the position of all German forces on the Western Front. Foch, however, intervened. He wanted Pershing to abandon the attack on St. Mihiel and strike northwest into the Meuse-Argonne rather than northeast towards Metz. The Supreme Commander also wanted to insert a French army into the attack and place some of the American troops under French command. Pershing reacted strongly to both proposals, and the conversation between the two com-manders became heated. The net result was a compromise. The American army would move against the salient but not proceed beyond it. And it would do so with fewer troops. But, acceding to Foch's desires, the Amer-ican First Army, with a large number of soldiers, then would advance into the Meuse-Argonne, striking northwest as the supreme commander wished.

The attack on the salient began on September 12 with an artillery bar-rage from 3,010 guns. Then, seven U.S. infantry divisions struck from the east. One American division attacked from the west, while French units advanced at the tip. In total, five hundred thousand American soldiers went into battle along with one hundred thousand French troops. Within two days, the salient was reduced. Pershing's men took thirteen thousand pris-oners and captured a large number of enemy guns. American casualties numbered approximately seven thousand.

Among the artillery pieces employed were the fourteen-inch naval guns. Mounted on railroad cars, they shot a projectile up to twenty-three miles and, if on target, were devastating to the enemy. The challenge, of course, was in correctly aiming the gun and properly gauging the ballistics of the projectile. At first the gunners had difficulty in hitting some of their targets. Help came from a young army captain. Edwin P. Hubble, who understood mathematics and the science of trajectories, provided the solutions. He later became an astronomer of note, winning a Nobel Prize. When in 1990 the American space agency, NASA, placed a powerful telescope in low earth orbit, the instrument was named for Dr. Hubble.

St. Mihiel was an American victory and celebrated as such. Once again, as at Cantigny, Château Thierry, and Belleau Wood, the AEF troops had fought hard. Indeed, the German high command took note of the Americans' aggressive spirit. But the sense of victory from St. Mihiel must be tempered. It is generally conceded that a more experienced army would have taken a greater number of prisoners. In addition, the German army, aware of the forthcoming assault and of its vulnerability within the salient, had begun to withdraw. The fight was not as fierce as it might have been. Nonetheless, the American First Army had gone into battle and won.

Next time, at the Meuse-Argonne, the fight would be far more difficult.

Noteworthy in the attack upon the salient at St. Mihiel was the widespread use of aircraft. More than fourteen hundred airplanes took part in the operation. They were flown by American, British, and French pilots (and a few Italians). In command of this aerial armada was Colonel Billy Mitchell, who, postwar, would become a leading advocate of American airpower.

The airplane came of age in the First World War. Armies and navies alike saw opportunities in the use of aircraft. They pushed aeronautical technologies such that planes became faster, more versatile, and somewhat more reliable. They also became weapons of war. Machine guns were carried, though at first their impact was slight. But when interrupter gears were developed so that machine guns could be fired safely through spinning propellers, airplanes became deadly killing machines.

These machines were called pursuit planes, what today are termed fighters. They carried a crew of one, the pilot, and could attain speeds of up to 140 mph. In Germany and Britain, in America and France, and in other countries as well, pursuit pilots became national heroes, especially those who destroyed five enemy aircraft, thus winning the coveted (but unofficial) title of ace. Famous still today is the German ace Manfred von

Richthofen, the Red Baron. His score of eighty kills was the highest tally of any pilot in World War I. The leading American ace was Eddie Rickenbacker who, flying French-built aircraft, knocked down twenty-six German planes.

Despite the fame associated with pursuit pilots, they and their aircraft did not play a decisive role in the war. Nor did the bombers. These were larger machines, multiengine, with a crew of three or four. From 1915 on, they were heavily engaged, bombing enemy troops and installations. But the size and number of bombs they could carry were slight and the accuracy of their aim uneven. So they too played a secondary role.

However, one particular bomber is worth mentioning. This is the German Gotha G IV. Powered by two Mercedes six-cylinder engines, the airplane had a top speed of 88 mph at twelve thousand feet. More noteworthy was its range. The Gotha could fly from Ghent, Belgium, to London and back, which it did on more than one occasion. As did German zeppelins, rigid-framed airships. Together they constituted the first-ever effort at strategic bombing. Even though they killed some fifteen hundred people in England, the damage they caused was insignificant. Their principal impact was to alarm civil and military authorities, forcing both to devise appropriate defenses and, with good cause, to worry about what the future might bring.

The one function performed by aircraft during World War I that did make a difference on the battlefield was reconnaissance. Airplanes were used to locate enemy positions and to track the movement of enemy troops. In 1914–1918 these planes usually were two-seaters. Up front was the pilot. To his rear was the observer who, when the need arose, also functioned as a gunner. Often useful, observation aircraft occasionally proved decisive. In 1914, for example, they alerted Joffre to the gap opening between the German First and Second Armies as the two enemy forces approached the Marne.

Later in the war, observers would employ specially developed cameras with which to photograph the enemy. On both sides, aerial photography was extensive. Such was the extent of this activity that a principal function of pursuit planes was the destruction of enemy aircraft devoted to observation.

Another important task given to observation aircraft was spotting for artillery. The soldiers who fired the cannons needed to know where their shells were striking. Many times in the course of the war they were so informed by aircraft aloft for that very purpose.

The first Americans who fought in the sky did so as part of the French Air Service. Many of these initially served as ambulance drivers, in units supporting the French army. Indeed, as noted previously, the first Americans to see the ugly face of war transported wounded French soldiers to medical facilities in the rear. They had arrived in France well before the United States entered the war in 1917. Such was their service that 225 of them won citations of valor. No recounting of America's involvement in the First World War is complete without reference to their work.

In April 1916, the French Air Service established a squadron of pursuit planes piloted primarily by Americans. Like the ambulance drivers, these pilots were volunteers. Eventually, thirty-eight Americans flew in this squadron that became known as the Lafayette Escadrille. With French officers in charge, the squadron flew more than three thousand sorties and downed more than fifty enemy aircraft. One of the Escadrille pilots, Raoul Lufbery, an American born in France, was an ace with seventeen victories to his credit. Once the United States entered the war, the Lafayette Escadrille ceased to exist, becoming the 103rd Aero Squadron of the American Air Service. Three months later, Lufbery was gone. He jumped (or fell) to his death from a burning aircraft. Pilots back then did not wear parachutes.

In both France and the United States, the Lafayette Escadrille won great fame, not just for its exploits in combat, or because its mascots were two cute lion cubs named Whiskey and Soda. The squadron gained prominence because it represented the desire of many Americans to aid France in that country's hour of need. As time passed and the war continued, more Americans joined the French air corps, many serving with distinction. Today, David Putnam, Frank Baylies, and Thomas Cassady are names no longer remembered. But each flew for France to the regret of more than a few German aviators.

American pilots also flew in British squadrons, even after the AEF arrived in Europe. Forty-one of them scored five kills or more. Among these aces were two brothers from New York, August and Paul Iaccaci. Both flew in No. 48 Squadron of the Royal Air Force, and remarkably, both downed seventeen aircraft. Another of the American pilots in British service was Howard Burdick. He flew the Sopwith Camel, considered by many to be the best of the Allied pursuit planes. Burdick downed six enemy aircraft in September and October of 1918. Years later, during the Second World War, his son Clinton destroyed nine German planes while piloting a P-51 Mustang of the American Eighth Air Force.

In both Great Britain and America, in France and Germany, pursuit pilots were considered to be men of dash and daring, knights of the sky who bravely confronted the enemy in airborne chariots. Less attention was given to their victims, of whom there were many. The top eight French aces of World War I, for example, killed at least 339 German flyers. These men joined 7,873 others of the kaiser's air service who did not survive the war. Britain's Royal Flying Corps and Royal Naval Air Service, combined in 1918 to form the Royal Air Force, counted 9,378 men who died in their aerial operations. Many of these were boys of nineteen or twenty whose flying skills were limited. Due to the demand for pilots they had been rushed into battle. Needless to say, their chances of survival were slim.

The United States had but 237 flyers killed in combat (one of the dead was Quentin Roosevelt, youngest son of Theodore Roosevelt). The number is relatively small, reflecting the limited time the AEF spent at the front. Nonetheless, America's Army Air Service performed extremely well. Its pursuit pilots accounted for the destruction of 781 enemy aircraft, losing 289. As the United States produced no combat planes of its own, American pilots flew machines designed and built in Britain and France. The latter included both the Nieuport 17 and the SPAD XIII, two aircraft the Americans used to good advantage.

Frank Luke was one of these pilots. He flew the SPAD XIII, a fine machine that by war's end equipped most U.S. Air Service units. SPAD was the acronym for the French company that produced the airplane: *Societe Pour L'Aviation et ses Derives*. From Arizona, Luke destroyed eighteen enemy machines. In September 1918 he was shot down by ground fire. His SPAD crashed in enemy territory. Wounded, but still very much alive, Frank Luke drew his pistol and fired at the Germans. They fired back and killed him. Today, Luke Air Force Base in Arizona honors his fighting spirit.

Several of the enemy machines Frank Luke destroyed were observation balloons. Tethered to the ground, these reached heights of up to five thousand feet. With a crew, usually two men, balloons were employed by both sides to monitor the enemy's whereabouts. Filled with gas, often hydrogen, balloons were frequent targets of pursuit planes. But they were not easy to bring down. At their base were numerous antiaircraft guns just waiting for enemy aircraft to appear. This made attacking observation balloons a hazardous venture. Manning them also was dangerous. When struck by incendiary bullets, the balloons burst into flames, creating a spectacular fireball. However, unlike pursuit pilots, balloon crews were issued parachutes. The crew's challenge was to jump neither too soon nor too late.

Observation balloons were in full use when British, French, and American armies began the great offensive that, at last, would bring about the end of the war. Many in leadership positions in both France and Britain thought the war would continue well into 1919. Not Foch. He believed that a massive attack across the entire Western Front in September would crush the German army. After all, he reasoned, the Allies outmatched their enemy in soldiers, supplies, tanks, and aircraft. Accordingly, the Supreme Commander drew up a plan of battle that was complex in detail yet simple in concept: the British (and the Belgians) would strike in the north, and the French would advance in the middle, while the Americans would attack in the south, in the area known as the Meuse-Argonne. With characteristic energy, Ferdinand Foch proclaimed, *"Tout le monde a la bataille."*

The Meuse is a major river, 575 miles long, that flows from northeastern France through Verdun into Belgium and Holland, eventually draining into the North Sea. The Argonne is a region of France, much of it heavily wooded, east of Paris, through which the Meuse flows. In 1918, the area was well fortified by the German army.

The assault by Pershing's army began on September 26 with an artillery barrage purposefully kept brief in order to maintain surprise (one of the artillery batteries was captained by a young officer from Missouri by the

name of Harry S. Truman). Nineteen divisions took part, six of them
French. That meant that Black Jack commanded more than 1.2 million
soldiers. The campaign lasted forty-seven days and was hard fought. One
German officer wrote, "The Americans are here. We can kill them but
not stop them." Throughout the battle the AEF's inexperience showed. At
times supplies ran short and tactics were flawed. Transportation was cha-
otic. Yet Pershing drove his men forward, relieving commanders he considered insufficiently aggressive. Many Americans fought tenaciously. A
few did not. Among the former were the Black Rattlers of the 369th Infantry Regiment, an African-American unit previously mentioned. When
the American attack stalled, Foch proposed to insert additional French
troops into the sector and turn overall command over to a French general.
Pershing refused and simply continued the assault. By early November, his
troops had thrown the Germans back. In the process the AEF had inflicted
some one hundred thousand casualties on the enemy and taken twenty-six
thousand prisoners. American historian Edward G. Lengel says that the
French army could not have done what the Americans accomplished.

Lengel also says that the British army could have and would have done
so with fewer casualties, for the losses of the American army at the Meuse-
Argonne were high. The American dead numbered 26,277. The number
of American wounded totaled 95,923. Writes Lengel in his 2008 book on
the Meuse-Argonne campaign, "Many doughboys died unnecessarily because of foolishly brave officers who led their men head-on against enemy
machine guns." Casualties aside, the Americans clearly had gained a victory. Pershing's men had battled a German army and won.

However, one noted British military historian calls the Meuse-Argonne
campaign unnecessary. In his book on World War I, H. P. Willmott writes
that the battle should not have been fought at all. Why? Because to the
north, British armies had breached the Hindenburg Line.

As did Foch, Sir Douglas believed the war need not continue into 1919.
He thought a strong Allied push in September and October would bring
the war to a successful conclusion. By then Haig commanded five field
armies. Together they represented the most capable military force in the
world.

On September 27 the British attacked. The assault began with a huge artillery barrage, with one gun for every three yards of territory to be attacked. Thirty-three divisions took part, two of them American. The British forces smashed into their German opponents, delivering a blow from which their enemy could not recover.

For Ludendorff and Hindenburg, September brought additional bad news. As American, French, and British troops gained success on the Western Front, an Allied army composed of British, French, and Serbian soldiers, all under the command of French general Franchet d'Esperey, advanced from Salonika in Greece into Serbia and Bulgaria. The latter was an important ally of Germany. It was a land bridge to the Ottomans and gave Germany a position of strength in the Balkans. The Allied army met with such success that Bulgaria withdrew from the war.

The Ottoman Empire too was in trouble. In Palestine, British forces were defeating the Turks, while along the southern Alps, the Italians at long last were gaining ground against the Austrians.

Everywhere Ludendorff and Hindenburg looked they saw defeat. Inside Germany the news was equally grim. In cities across the country shortages of coal, soap, and food caused ordinary Germans to be cold, dirty, and hungry. In Berlin, such shortages and the lack of military success brought about rioting in the streets. In fact, the German Imperial State was disintegrating. Both political moderates and right-wingers feared a Bolshevik-style revolution. In Kiel and Wilhelmshaven, German admirals ordered the High Seas Fleet to sortie for one last glorious battle, but its sailors said they'd rather not and mutinied. The navy thus imploded, while the army high command concluded that the war could not be won. On October 1 Ludendorff told the German foreign minister to seek an immediate armistice. Days later Hindenburg conveyed a note to the new chancellor, Prince Max of Baden, that called the situation acute. Earlier, on September 29, the two generals, the most senior in the army, had told the kaiser the fighting had to stop.

There followed an attempt by the German government to seek an armistice through the good offices of America's president. Prince Max and others assumed that Germany could secure a better deal were the terms first worked out with the Americans. After all, in January 1918, in a speech to Congress, Wilson—a true idealist—had outlined fourteen points that he thought should serve as the basis for constructing the postwar world. However, Wilson's response surprised the Germans. Angered by the harm he believed German militarism had inflicted on the world and by Germany's continuation of unrestricted submarine warfare, Wilson held firm. His terms were tough. Among them was the requirement that the kaiser had to go. Regarding an end to the fighting, President Wilson told the Germans to speak with Foch.

In early November, with the concurrence of the kaiser's army, Prince Max sent emissaries to the Allied Supreme Commander. They were to discuss terms for an armistice.

An armistice is an agreement between opposing military forces to stop shooting at each other. Initiated by field commanders, it is not a treaty, nor does it officially bring an end to hostilities. In the case of the First World War, the conflict would conclude only in 1919 at Versailles, when the governments involved negotiated formal treaties of peace.

After seeing 1.4 million of his countrymen die in battle, a battle for which he believed Germany was responsible, Ferdinand Foch was in no mood to negotiate. Meeting in a railroad car in the woods near Compiègne, the Supreme Commander dictated the terms of the armistice to the German representatives. Not surprisingly, they were severe. In effect, they amounted to a surrender on the part of Germany.

The terms Foch set forth at Compiègne mandated:

- the withdrawal of all German troops from France and Belgium
- the return of Alsace and Lorraine to France
- the transfer to the Allies of large amounts of military equipment
- the internment of the German navy in British ports
- the absence of German forces in German lands west of the Rhine
- the repudiation of the Treaty of Brest-Litovsk
- the payment of reparations to make good on Allied losses

The emissaries had no choice but to accept. Early in the morning of November 11, having first checked with Prince Max and Hindenburg, Germany's representatives signed the document. The armistice was to take effect later that morning. The day before, the kaiser had left for the Netherlands.

And so, at the eleventh hour on the eleventh day, of the eleventh month, the guns fell silent. The killing stopped and the bloody battles of the Great War were consigned to history.

Around the world, but especially in Europe, more than a few people prayed that never again would such a conflict take place.

What caused the First World War?

Clearly, the assassination of the Austrian archduke in June 1914 did not cause the war. It simply set in motion a sequence of events that, given the failure of diplomacy, resulted in European nations declaring war on one another.

The actual causes of the Great War are complex, multiple, and interrelated. They include economic competition and African colonialism, naval ambitions and military alliances, plus extreme national pride and historical animosities. Add to this explosive mix ignorance and fear and the consequences become deadly.

Yet despite this volatility, it is worth noting that Great Britain did not strike the first blow. Nor did France, however anxious the latter was to recover Alsace and Lorraine. Moreover, the Austrian-Hungarian decision to invade Serbia need not have produced a wider conflict, since most European leaders accepted the Hapsburg's need to respond to Franz Ferdinand's murder. There had been localized Balkan wars before, and one more need not have caused Europe to erupt. That leaves Russia and Germany, two nations with little love for each other. Historians see Russia's decision to mobilize its military as a decisive step. Once the tsar called up his army, Germany went to war.

In 1914, Germany was a rising industrial power, eager to gain a larger and more respected role in the world. It also was a nation in which the army wielded considerable political influence. The Germany of Kaiser Wilhelm II was a nation comfortable with the idea of war, which it viewed as an appropriate means by which to conduct foreign policy. To most Germans, Russia constituted a threat to German culture and the country's economic prosperity. So when the tsar called up his troops, Germany took action. Germany did not cause the First World War, but its troops were the first to strike.

How many men died in battle during the First World War?

World War I was an *extremely bloody affair.* Battle deaths, by nation (excluding the United States), are shown below. The list is taken from one of the better books on the conflict, entitled *World War I* and written by H. P. Willmott. Other authors cite similar though not identical numbers.

Russia—*1,800,000*
France—*1,390,000*
British Empire—*900,000*
Italy—*460,000*
Germany—*1,040,000*
Austria-Hungary—*1,020,000*
Turkey—*240,000*
Bulgaria—*80,000*

These numbers total 6,930,000. Add to this total the number of deaths sustained by Belgium, Serbia, and Romania and the number exceeds eight million. Even this figure may be low. Civilian deaths also were high. At least seven million nonmilitary men and women lost their lives as a result of the war.

Casualty figures for the United States reflect its army's late arrival in France and its limited combat role. American battle deaths number 50,280. Fifty thousand dead soldiers is not an insignificant loss. Today, eight U.S. military cemeteries in Europe attest to the sacrifices made by the American Expeditionary Force. Yet, relative to the losses sustained by other nations, the number is quite small.

Pershing's army also had some 205,000 men wounded. This number too is small in comparison to what Britain, Germany, and the others sustained. France, for example, saw 4.3 million of its soldiers in need of medical attention.

Perhaps surprisingly, the First World War was not the most deadly event of the early twentieth century. That dubious distinction belongs to the flu pandemic that struck in 1918 and 1919. Worldwide, the flu took the lives of twenty-one million people and possibly more.

Why did so many men die in the First World War?

The war was a bloodbath because two weapons widely employed were particularly lethal. The machine gun and the cannon were extremely effective at killing soldiers. Machine guns cut down waves of advancing men, while artillery fire, delivered in vast quantities, became highly accurate. It was the latter that caused the greatest loss of life. In his memoirs, written in Sweden shortly after the war, Hindenburg wrote that his army's most dangerous opponent was French artillery.

Another reason why so many men died in the First World War was that the tactics employed by generals such as Haig and Pershing were flawed. Having soldiers attack machine guns head on or having infantry walk line abreast across open fields was a recipe for disaster. Yet both commanders, and other generals as well, did just that.

Was Field Marshal Sir Douglas Haig an incompetent commander?

History has not been kind to Sir Douglas. Although his army was victorious and he won several battles, Haig is seen as the archetypical inept general of World War I, insensitive to the loss of life while remaining comfortable and safe far from the enemy lines. The image is only partially correct. True, he appeared unconcerned about the great losses his army sustained. And he was not exposed to enemy fire (although seventy-eight British generals were and paid with their lives). Nor were his tactics in 1916 and 1917 the best. But commanding generals are not supposed to be on the front line. Their job is to prepare for and manage the battle, and that can be done only in the rear. No one in 1915–1917 knew how to break through tiered layers of defense or, if they knew—and later on some did—the resources available were not up to the task. By 1918, however, Haig's armies employed tactics that enabled British troops to crack German defenses. Massive artillery fire, tanks, and infantry, all coordinated, were the formula for success. When, in September 1918, the British army swept through the Hindenburg Line, Haig and his staff demonstrated that they knew how to wage war.

Still, the carnage of the Somme and of Passchendaele linger, and will be linked forever with the name of Douglas Haig.

Why were parachutes not widely used?

Parachutes were available in 1914 and could have been employed throughout the war. That they were not today seems foolish. Parachutes, however, were issued to balloon crews and, toward the very end of the conflict, to German pilots. But French, American, and British aviators did not have them. At first the reason was one of weight. Early warplanes were light and utilized engines that were underpowered. The additional weight of a packed parachute adversely affected aircraft performance. But as planes grew more robust, a parachute's weight mattered little. Still, the pilots of SPADS, Camels, and Fokker Triplanes were not issued this simple piece of lifesaving equipment. Why? Apparently, because commanders believed that with such a device available, pilots and observers would too readily abandon the plane. Knowing there was no easy exit, pilots, particularly pursuit pilots, would stay in the fight and give it their all.

Were the terms of the armistice too lenient?

By November 1918, the German army was a spent force. Ludendorff and Hindenburg understood that victory was not possible and that Germany needed to sue for peace. At Compiègne, the terms Foch set forth in the armistice amounted to surrender on the part of the German military. But Germany never formally surrendered. No surrender ceremony took place, no such document was signed. German soldiers simply turned around and marched home. In Berlin, a victory parade was held, but its participants were German. British, French, and American troops made no celebratory march through Germany's towns and cities.

This was a mistake. In the years following the war, German citizens and ex-soldiers were able to convince themselves that, as the army had not surrendered, Germany's defeat must have been brought about not by its armed services, but by forces at home. They blamed left-wing radicals, war profiteers, and the Jews. The Fatherland, they agreed, had been stabbed in the back. This contention, false though it was, gained credence in postwar Germany. Among its proponents was a former corporal in the kaiser's army by the name of Adolf Hitler.

Should the Allies have continued to fight past November 11, forcing Germany to surrender? Haig thought not. Why? Because the British army would have had to do most of the fighting and, thereby, would have taken heavy casualties. Foch saw the armistice as entirely sufficient. At Compiègne the French had gotten what they wanted, the return of Alsace and Lorraine, etc., without the need for further bloodshed. Only Pershing disagreed. He thought the armistice premature. Black Jack wanted the troops Foch commanded to destroy the German army, thus making clear to everyone that the Allies had won and that Germany had lost. Otherwise, he believed, another war might have to be fought.

Why did the United States not join the battle earlier?

The United States declared war on Germany in April 1917, thirty-one months after the conflict started. In 1914, most Americans believed that Europe constantly went to war and that nothing was to be gained by participating in conflicts that affected only Europe. Americans would mind their own business and let the French, British, and Germans go about killing themselves. What changed their minds? British propaganda, the type of submarine warfare the Germans resorted to in 1917, and Wilson's desire to influence the postwar world resulted in the U.S. change of heart. That American finances were tied to the success of Britain and France, to whom they had extended significant war credits (loans), was another contributing factor.

How effective was the American Expeditionary Force?

During World War I American soldiers fought hard and with great courage. Yet Pershing's army was inexperienced, and for this inexperience it paid a price. Writing in October 1918, as the Americans were battling in the Meuse-Argonne, Great Britain's most senior field commander, Field Marshal Sir Douglas Haig, described the AEF as "ill-equipped, half-trained, with insufficient supply services."

Rarely does a novice army perform well in its early engagements. Combat is a learning experience, and in 1917, the American Expeditionary Force had much to learn. In his memoirs, Hindenburg wrote of the importance of experience, saying that the losses sustained by the AEF "taught the United States for the future that the business of war cannot be learned in a few months, and that in a crisis lack of experience costs streams of blood."

Pershing and his men struggled to master the art of war. Mistakes were made, yet not once were the Americans defeated in battle. There is little doubt that had the war continued into 1919, lessons would have been learned and the AEF would have become a most formidable fighting force.

Was the United States alone responsible for the Allied victory in World War I?

No, it was not. America played a part in the war's outcome, a significant part, but the United States did not cause the defeat of Germany and its partners.

As Captain B. H. Liddell Hart has written, no single factor can account for the victory of November 1918. However, several factors can be seen as critical. One of these was Britain's naval blockade. This ruined the German economy and weakened the kaiser's army. Another was the grit shown by the French army, which, despite setbacks, continued the fight from the first day of the war to the last. Still another, not mentioned by Liddell Hart, was that Germany took on not only France and Russia, but also Great Britain and the United States. In doing so, Germany was simply outmatched.

Most certainly, Americans contributed to Germany's defeat. In battle, the AEF engaged the German army and helped to grind it down. But America's more important contribution was to lift the spirits of the French and British, both at home and on the field of battle. American involvement made them believe victory was possible. The British and French had been fighting hard since 1914 and, after sustaining horrendous losses, were no longer convinced Germany would be beaten. Enter the United States. In 1917 and 1918, America sent to Europe thousands and thousands of healthy young men eager to fight. Commented Liddell Hart:

> *The United States did not win the war, but without their economic aid to ease the strain, without the arrival of their troops to turn the numerical balance, and, above all, without the moral tonic which their coming gave, victory would have been impossible.*

7

WORLD WAR II

EUROPEAN THEATRE 1941–1945

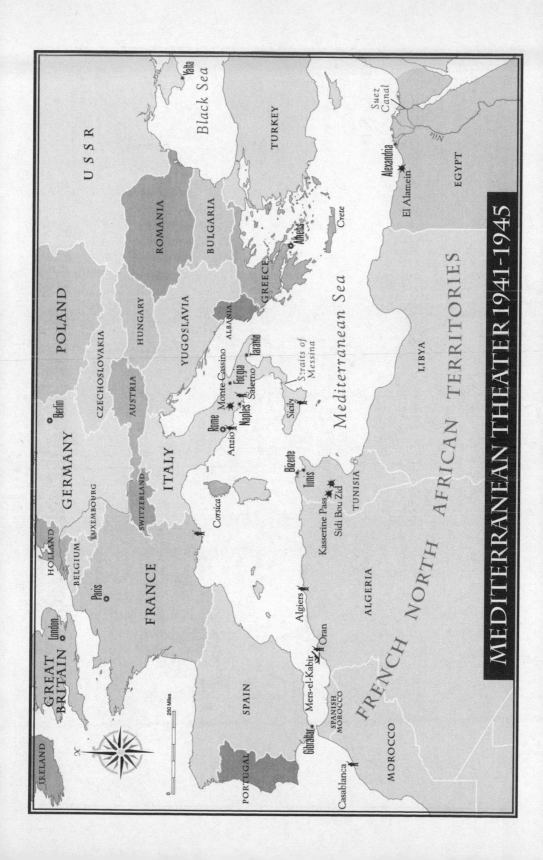

MEDITERRANEAN THEATER 1941-1945

IRELAND

GREAT BRITAIN

London

Paris

FRANCE

PORTUGAL

SPAIN

Gibraltar

Mers-el-Kabir

Oran

Algiers

Casablanca

MOROCCO

SPANISH MOROCCO

FRENCH NORTH AFRICAN TERRITORIES

ALGERIA

HOLLAND

BELGIUM

LUXEMBOURG

GERMANY

Berlin

SWITZERLAND

Corsica

ITALY

Rome

Anzio

Monte Cassino

Naples

Foggia

Salerno

Taranto

Sicily

Straits of Messina

Bizerte

Tunis

Kasserine Pass

Sidi Bou Zid

TUNISIA

LIBYA

POLAND

USSR

CZECHOSLOVAKIA

AUSTRIA

HUNGARY

YUGOSLAVIA

ROMANIA

BULGARIA

ALBANIA

GREECE

Athens

Crete

Black Sea

TURKEY

Mediterranean Sea

Malta

Yalta

Suez Canal

Nile

Alexandria

El Alamein

EGYPT

250 Miles

0

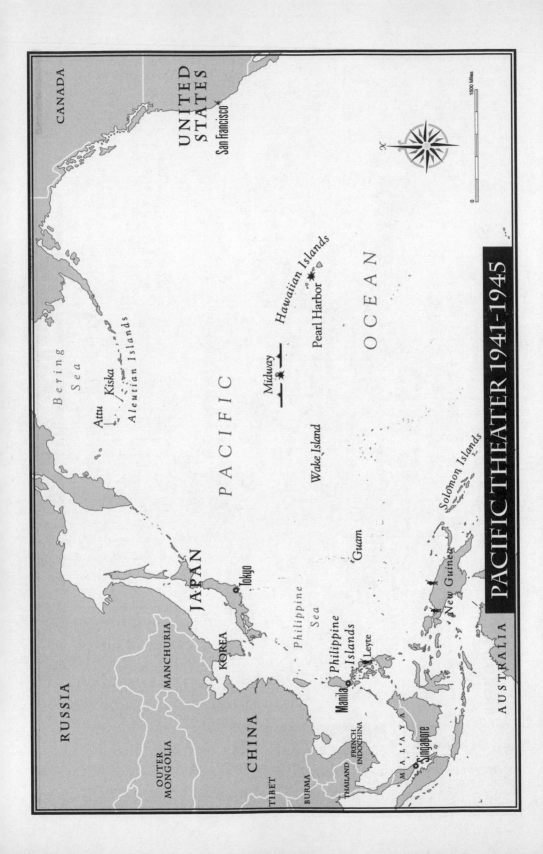

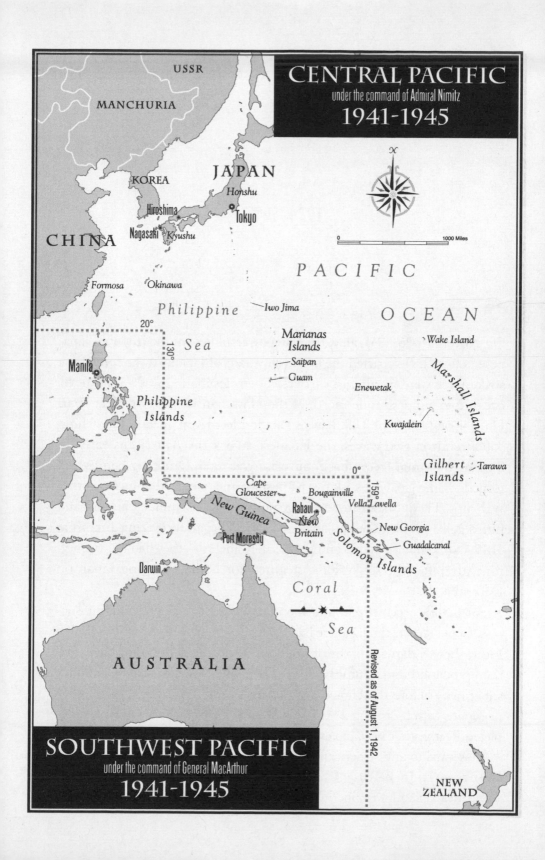

1939–1945

On November 26, 1941, an extremely powerful fleet of the Imperial Japanese Navy (IJN) departed the northern waters of Japan. At the core of the strike force were six aircraft carriers. Their destination was a spot in the ocean two hundred miles north of the Hawaiian Islands, where at Pearl Harbor on Oahu, the U.S. Navy's Pacific Fleet lay at anchor. Launching 350 aircraft in two waves, the Japanese struck the Americans early on Sunday morning, December 7. Surprise was total. Dropping bombs and torpedoes, the Japanese sank five battleships and damaged numerous other warships. They also destroyed a large number of U.S. military aircraft and killed 2,403 people. The six Japanese carriers began recovering aircraft at 11:15 A.M., and with planes and pilots safely aboard—they had lost twenty-nine aircraft—the strike force steamed for home, reaching Japan on December 24.

Brilliantly executed, the attack on Pearl Harbor was a resounding success. In one stroke, the Japanese had dealt a severe blow to America's Pacific Fleet, thereby damaging the one opponent capable of opposing their further expansion into Southeast Asia. Their intent was to achieve military superiority before the United States was able to strike back, then either negotiate with a dispirited America or gain a victory at sea against a depleted fleet. Either way, Japan and its empire would be secure.

Essential to any American military response to the Japanese were aircraft carriers. In 1941 the United States had seven of these vessels. Two were incapable of sustained combat, one being old and the other quite small. Of the remaining five, three were assigned to the Pacific Fleet. At that time, many admirals considered battleships to be the most important warship afloat. But, as events would show, the aircraft carrier was to become the decisive weapon in the war against Japan. Fortunately for the Americans, none of the three Pacific carriers were at Pearl Harbor on December 7. The USS *Lexington* was delivering planes to the American garrison on Midway Island. The USS *Saratoga* was in a naval yard on the West Coast. And the USS *Enterprise* was returning to Hawaii having transported airplanes to the marines on Wake Island. The survival of these three ships meant that the Americans, despite the catastrophe at Pearl Harbor, could mount offensive operations against the Japanese.

If the attack on December 7 was a tactical success—and it was—it was also a strategic blunder. For the attack, undertaken while diplomatic negotiations between the United States and Japan were under way, enraged the Americans. They believed, rather quaintly, that nations first declared war and then attacked, rather than the other way around. "Remember Pearl Harbor" became a rallying cry for a nation intent upon revenge. "December 7," said President Franklin Roosevelt, was "a date that will live in infamy." Few Americans, then, objected when on the next day Congress formally declared war.

Until that date the United States had been a nation divided over whether to engage in foreign wars, especially the one then taking place in Europe. Many Americans believed that the country should remain neutral. They saw the price of involvement as too high in both blood and treasure.

President Franklin Delano Roosevelt, however, was no isolationist. He realized that the United States needed to stop the Nazis. He understood that Adolf Hitler's Germany represented a grave threat to all democratic nations. But the president was mindful of the strong isolationist feelings in the country, especially as he was running for an unprecedented third term. He therefore proceeded cautiously.

But Roosevelt did act. He authorized the United States to sell armaments to Britain and France. He established (to the disadvantage of Germany and the German-controlled French government) a naval exclusionary zone in Latin America. He asked for, and received, from Congress a military draft. He sent fifty overaged destroyers to Britain in exchange for leases of naval bases in Newfoundland, Bermuda, and the Caribbean. And, on January 6, a newly reelected President Roosevelt spoke eloquently of what he called the Four Freedoms: Freedom of speech, Freedom of worship, Freedom from want, and Freedom from fear. As historian C. L. Sulzberger later wrote, "It took no seer to recognize this was a world in which Adolph Hitler had no place."

In January 1933 an elderly Paul von Hindenburg, then president of the German Republic, and earlier the senior commander of the kaiser's army during the First World War, appointed Hitler chancellor of Germany. Hindenburg did so in recognition of Hitler's National Socialist Party having won the largest number of seats in the previous election. In other words, Adolf Hitler came to power legally. Millions of Germans saw him as the country's savior. Two years later, after Hindenburg's death, they voted enthusiastically to combine the vacated presidency with the office of chancellor. By the end of 1934 Hitler's power was absolute. Moreover, he was, as historian Robert E. Herzstein has written, "the heart and soul of the German state." That the man was a thug seemed not to matter.

How had such an individual come to power? Part of the answer lies in his magnetic personality and in remembering that he was a mesmerizing speaker. Part lies in Hitler being able to take full advantage of the chaos then enveloping Germany. Adolf Hitler promised to deliver what the German people desperately wanted—economic recovery, financial stability, social order, and, as important, pride in the Fatherland. The years following World War I had been difficult for Germany. Reparations and the Great Depression had made things worse. To millions of Germans, including those of the middle class, Hitler offered hope.

Once in control, Der Führer moved swiftly. He embarked on a massive program of rearmament and secured from the military's officer corps an oath of personal allegiance. He crushed political dissent, making the Nazi Party the sole legitimate political organization. Internationally, he repudiated the Treaty of Versailles, withdrew Germany from the League of Nations, engineered a union (*Anschluss*) with Austria, and formed a military alliance with Fascist Italy and the Empire of Japan.

As Germany grew in strength and assertiveness, the rest of Europe took notice, but did nothing. In particular, Great Britain and France, two nations that might have restrained Herr Hitler, stood aside. They themselves were in dire economic straits and had no stomach for military confrontation. When German forces reentered the demilitarized lands west of the Rhine, France and Britain remained silent. When Germany dismembered Czechoslovakia, they acquiesced, appeasing the German leader and hoping that a piece of paper Adolf Hitler had signed in Munich would bring an end to German demands.

It did not. Only when the German führer invaded Poland in September 1939 did Britain and France respond. They declared war on Germany, and so began, in Europe at least, the Second World War.

For Great Britain and, later, for the United States, the war was a global conflict, not one confined to the boundaries of Europe and of the Atlantic Ocean. For at the same time Adolf Hitler brought his own brand of misery to the Continent, Imperial Japan was striking hard into China, eyeing the resources-rich islands of the Dutch East Indies and contemplating how best to counter the U.S. Navy's Pacific Fleet.

From 1941 to 1945 President Roosevelt and Prime Minister Winston Churchill never were able to concentrate solely on the war in Europe. They had the Pacific conflict to contend with as well. Because both theaters required men and material, allocating resources to one meant depriving the other. Shipping P-51 fighter aircraft to England meant General George Kenney's Fifth Air Force in New Guinea did not receive the Mustang. Landing craft assigned to marine regiments in the Pacific meant these essential vessels were not available for transporting General Eisenhower's soldiers onto the beaches of Europe. The simultaneous demands of what truly was a global conflict required planning of the highest order and a fair amount of juggling. In retrospect Franklin Roosevelt and Winston Churchill—and their countries' senior military commanders—did both, and did so extremely well.

By the time Mr. Roosevelt had enunciated his Four Freedoms, France had fallen to Germany's impressive war machine and Britain stood alone against the Nazis. Earlier, from August through October of 1940, Britain's Royal Air Force (RAF) had thrown back the Luftwaffe. But this aerial conflict, known as the Battle of Britain, meant only that Britain was not yet defeated. Her army was small, her navy overextended. Her financial reserves were dwindling, and with U-boats prowling the Atlantic, the small island nation, home to the Magna Carta and parliamentary democracy, seemed likely to collapse—unless the United States was to provide massive assistance.

"Give us the tools and we will finish the job," said Britain's bulldog of a prime minister, Winston Churchill. But how to do so, when Great Britain had no money and the United States, at least formally, was neutral?

Roosevelt found a way. He likened the situation to when a neighbor's house is on fire. "You don't," he said, "make the neighbor first pay before permitting him use of your garden hose. You lend it to him, and do so immediately." The president then revived an obscure federal law that allowed the War Department to lease military equipment, and the Lend-Lease Program was established. This program was the means by which the United States provided huge amounts of war material to those nations fighting the Germans and Japanese. The scale of the effort was immense. Britain, for example, received slightly more than $31 billion worth of armaments. Some of this was in the form of aircraft for Britain's Royal Navy. By the end of the war, Fleet Air Arm carriers were well stocked with Hellcats, Avengers, and Corsairs, all of which were manufactured in the United States.

Russia too received Lend-Lease aid. After conquering Poland in 1939, Denmark, Norway, Belgium, and France in 1940, and Yugoslavia and Greece early in 1941, while, for the moment at least, putting Great Britain on the defensive, Hitler turned his attention east. In one of the Second World War's most momentous decisions he ordered his army loose against Russia, which then was constituted as the Union of Soviet Socialist Republics (USSR). Deploying some three million soldiers and 3,330 tanks, the Germans, in Operation Barbarossa, invaded Russia on the morning of June 22, 1941. What made the attack somewhat surprising was that, in August of 1939, Hitler had signed a nonaggression pact with the Soviet Union. Once the invasion began, the Russians resisted, though not very well. At the battle for Minsk, for example, the Germans crushed two Russian field armies and, indicative of the scale of the fighting, took three hundred thousand Russian soldiers as prisoners. By late August the Germans had gained control of much Russian territory. Soon Russia was reeling. Though stretched thin, the German army had victory within its reach. Joseph Stalin, a man who, like Hitler, represented evil in its most pure form, took several steps to save Mother Russia. He poured more and more soldiers into battle. He shot commanders who failed. And he sought American aid.

Eager to strengthen any country combating Nazi Germany, the United States responded, providing assistance via Lend-Lease. Some $11.3 billion in war materials were sent to the Soviet Union. Among the aid were 4,924 Airacobras, planes the Red Air Force used to great advantage against German tanks. Only recently has Russia acknowledged the key role this aid played in the victory the Soviet military achieved in 1945.

Lend-Lease supplies were delivered to Russia by three different routes. Some aircraft simply were flown to Siberia from Alaska. Most aid, however, took a more indirect journey. It first was shipped to Iran and then by road and rail transported north into Russia. U.S. troops operated much of the Iranian National Railway, employing more than forty thousand Iranians to help move supplies.

The third route of Lend-Lease supplies to the Soviet Union was the most treacherous. Material was shipped to Britain (which also provided aid) and then by ship sent in convoy past the Arctic Circle and around Norway to Murmansk and Archangel. Throughout the voyage, the vessels were subject to attack from German submarines (U-boats), surface warships, and aircraft. Yet the most dangerous foe was the weather. High seas and bitter cold made the trip difficult and dangerous.

The legislation authorizing Lend-Lease became law in March of 1941. Late in December of that same year, well after the attack on Pearl Harbor, President Roosevelt gave a radio address to the nation. It was one of his signature "fireside chats." These were seemingly informal conversations in which the American leader spoke directly to the people of the United States. At the time, these addresses were novel, and millions of Americans tuned in to listen. In this particular chat, Franklin Roosevelt coined a phrase that has become synonymous with the United States in regard to the Second World War. Speaking of the need for the United States to supply the tools of war to those willing to do battle with Japan and Germany, Roosevelt said that America should become "the arsenal of democracy." And that is exactly what the United States did.

Shielded from the enemy by two oceans, American industry turned its attention to the manufacturing of military equipment and supplies. Vast quantities of armaments were produced. American workers, many of them women (the symbol of whom was "Rosie the Riveter"), turned out the tools of war in numbers hitherto unimaginable. For example, in 1943 American aircraft manufacturers delivered more planes than Britain, Germany, and Japan combined, and twice the number from the Soviet Union.

Shipyards too were hard at work. During World War II the United States became the world leader in shipbuilding. Yards on three coasts launched more ships than German U-boats could sink and Japanese aircraft could destroy. In addition to warships, the Americans built cargo vessels, lots of them. None were more critical to success than the Liberty ships. These were dry cargo ships of a standard design. In 1943 alone, 140 Liberty ships were launched per month. A California industrialist by the name of Henry J. Kaiser developed the concept of prefabricating the components of the ship and then rapidly assembling them at the shipyard. So efficient was this process that, at the peak of their manufacture, Liberty ships were being built in ten days.

It is no exaggeration to state that America's role as the arsenal of democracy made possible the Allied victory of 1945.

Neither HMS *Prince of Wales* nor the USS *Augusta* were Liberty ships. The former was a British battleship, the latter an American cruiser. The battleship had carried Winston Churchill to the waters of Newfoundland, where, off Argentia in Placentia Bay, he met with Franklin Roosevelt, who had arrived on the *Augusta*. The two leaders had exchanged a great deal of correspondence but were eager to meet face-to-face. Both men understood the importance of stopping Adolf Hitler. On board the two warships, the president and the prime minister, and senior military officers of both countries, held extensive talks from which emerged a joint declaration of democratic values. Known as the Atlantic Charter, the document set forth the political and economic foundations that Great Britain and the United States deemed essential for the future.

Remarkably, the meeting off Argentia took place before the Japanese struck Pearl Harbor. The leader of an ostensibly neutral country was discussing how a postwar world might look with the leader of one already at war. No doubt, Herr Hitler took notice, especially as the charter did not mince words, referring as it did to "the final destruction of Nazi tyranny." ▪

In fact, the British had hoped to secure from Roosevelt a stronger expression of American commitment to the war. Already the president had taken additional steps. He had ordered the U.S. Navy to escort British-bound convoys to a midpoint in the Atlantic, thus easing the burden on the Royal Navy. He also had ordered American armed forces to assume the defense of Iceland. Yet the president resisted the British efforts. He was ever so conscious of the thin ice on which he was stepping. After all, on August 12, 1941, the day he and Churchill signed the Atlantic Charter, the United States House of Representatives approved an extension of the military draft by only one vote.

On Sunday, August 10, Winston Churchill and Franklin Roosevelt, along with their advisors, gathered together aboard the *Prince of Wales* for divine services. Of that morning occasion Churchill later wrote:

> *This service was felt by us all to be a deeply moving expression of the unity of faith of our two peoples, and none who took part in it will forget the spectacle presented that sunlit morning on the crowded quarterdeck—the symbolism of the Union Jack and the Stars and Stripes draped side by side on the pulpit; the American and British chaplains sharing in the reading of the prayers; the highest naval, military and air officers of Britain and the United States grouped in one body behind the President and me; the close-packed ranks of British and American sailors, completely intermingled, sharing the same books and joining fervently together in prayers and hymns familiar to both.*
>
> *I chose the hymns myself—"For Those In Peril on the Sea," and "Onward Christian Soldiers." We ended with "O God, Our*

Help in Ages Past . . ." Every word seemed to stir the heart. It was a great hour to live.

There is a sad postscript to the story of the Atlantic Charter. Along with the battle cruiser HMS *Repulse*, the *Prince of Wales* was dispatched to Southeast Asia in order to defend Singapore, now an independent nation but then a British colony. The Japanese were intent on capturing the city, and the two British vessels were directed to stop them. But the ships lacked air cover, and on December 10, 1941, Japanese aircraft easily sank both of them. The British people took great pride in their navy, so the news of the sinkings hit hard. "In all the war," wrote Churchill, "I never received a more direct shock."

Soon after the attack on the American fleet at Pearl Harbor, Prime Minister Churchill journeyed to Washington, D.C., for the first of several wartime conferences with the American president. At this initial meeting Roosevelt and Churchill made two important decisions. The first was that the fight against Germany would take priority over the one against Japan. The second was that the United States and Great Britain would plan their military operations jointly.

To carry out this second decision, the two men established an unusual, albeit highly successful, military command organization. Known as the Combined Chiefs of Staff (CCOS), it consisted of the leaders of the armed forces of both countries acting as a single unit. For the Americans this meant that General George C. Marshall, chief of staff of the U.S. Army, and Admiral Ernest J. King, commander in chief of the U.S. Fleet, served as members. So did General Henry H. Arnold, who headed America's air force, which at the time was part of the army (unlike in Britain and Germany, where the Royal Air Force and the Luftwaffe were separate services, independent of the army and navy). In addition, Admiral William D. Leahy was a member of CCOS. He served as President Roosevelt's personal representative to the new organization.

These four men and their British counterparts directed the overall war effort. When they were unable to reach agreement, the issue would be referred to the president and the prime minister. What is remarkable is that despite difficulties (the British general on CCOS, Alan Brooke, thought the Americans were amateurs at warfare, while Admiral King intensely disliked the British), the Combined Chiefs of Staff worked well. A common language helped. So did a mutual desire to utterly crush the Third Reich and the Empire of Japan.

By the evening of December 8, the United States was at war with Japan—but not Germany. Yet if America was to combat those that threatened democracy, it needed to fight the Nazis as well as the Japanese. Roosevelt understood that. But how was he to bring the nation into war with a second opponent? After all, Germany had caused little if any harm to the United States. The solution came from Hitler himself. In a hate-filled speech on December 11, he simply declared war on the United States. Benito Mussolini, the Italian fascist leader, followed suit. By the end of the year, the sides were drawn. The Axis powers were Germany, Italy, and Japan. America, Great Britain, and Russia constituted the Allies.

Anxious for American troops to do battle with the Germans, President Roosevelt dispatched General Marshall and Admiral King to England for talks with British military leaders. They were to decide, with British agreement, how best to confront the Third Reich. Roosevelt had mandated that U.S. forces initiate combat against the Nazis in 1942. He knew that American morale required action as soon as possible. He knew also that the Soviet Union was demanding that Great Britain and the United States open up a "Second Front" in order to relieve the pressure on the Red Army. Both the president and Churchill worried that German success in the east might force Russia out of the war, as had occurred in World War I. Were that to happen, the full might of the German war machine would be directed against an outmatched Britain and an unprepared America.

In meetings with the British, the Americans, and particularly General Marshall, favored an early cross-channel invasion of Europe. The British were opposed to the idea, fearing high casualties. The chief of staff, however, soon realized that such an invasion simply could not be accomplished, at least not until the fall of 1943. The necessary landing craft were not available, nor were there a sufficient number of aircraft, tanks, and troops. Consequently the idea was soon discarded.

.In its place, the British and Americans decided to invade North Africa, where German troops had been trying—with some success—to advance toward the Suez Canal. The landings were to be called Operation Torch, for, as the first joint endeavor of British and American ground forces, they were to light the way.

As the U.S. Army's chief of staff during World War II, George C. Marshall had great responsibilities. One was to select officers of senior rank for command of America's field armies. It was Marshall who chose the commander for the Allied invasion of northwestern Africa. The man he chose was a general without combat experience. However, the man was an astute planner, a fine soldier whose personality was well suited to working with the British.

The general's name was Dwight D. Eisenhower.

Although British troops were to participate in the landings, Torch was portrayed as an American operation. This was because northwestern Africa was under French control, and the French were less likely to oppose an American expedition than a British one. Indeed, the hope was that U.S. troops would be welcomed.

When France surrendered to Germany in 1940 (Hitler held the surrender ceremony in the same railroad car at Compiègne in which the Germans in 1918 had signed the armistice that ended the First World War), the victors had taken direct control of the northern half of France, including Paris. The French government, headed by a hero of World War I, the elderly Marshal Philippe Pétain, controlled the southern portion of the country. Headquartered at Vichy, it also administered France's colonial possessions, including those in Africa.

With France no longer opposing Hitler, the British were alarmed lest the French fleet become naval assets of the Nazis. Were this to happen, the British position in the entire Mediterranean area would be vulnerable. Churchill told the Royal Navy to remove the threat. This the navy did, opening fire on the French fleet in July 1940 as it lay at anchor. Most of the French ships were put out of action, with heavy loss of life. Needless to say, the French were not pleased. British troops landing along the African coast thus were likely to receive a hostile reception. Willingly then, the British let Torch be largely an American show. Once U.S. troops were ashore, with the French forces either neutralized or enlisted in the fight against the Germans, British soldiers would join the fray.

The landings took place on November 8, 1942. American troops went ashore at three locations. On Morocco's Atlantic coast some 25,000 men, under the command of Major General George Patton, hit the beaches near Casablanca. In the Mediterranean 39,000 U.S. soldiers landed at Oran. These troops were led by Lloyd Fredendall, also a major general. And, 250 miles farther east, another 43,000 troops landed at Algiers. In total, the United States Army placed 107,000 men onto the northwestern shores of Africa. It was, up to then, the largest military amphibious operation ever attempted.

Once ashore, these soldiers were joined by British troops and by those French forces who decided the enemy was Germany, not Britain or America. Eisenhower, in overall charge of the invading force, hoped to reach Tunis quickly but was unable to do so. One reason was the inexperience of U.S. troops. The other was the German army.

Torch surprised the Nazi high command. But it reacted swiftly. Hitler deposed Pétain and had his army occupy the rest of France. He also sent reinforcements to Tunisia.

The result was a series of nasty little battles in which the Americans initially did poorly. At Sidi bou Zid and the Kasserine Pass, the Germans thrashed Eisenhower's men. In tactical command of U.S. ground forces was Fredendall. Clearly, he was not up to the job. (The senior British general in Africa, Harold Alexander, is reported to have said to Eisenhower, "I'm sure you must have a better man than that." An American commander put it more bluntly, saying, "He's no damn good.") General Eisenhower sacked Fredendall, although, to avoid a public relations disaster, the army promoted him to lieutenant general and gave him a training assignment back in the States.

Patton was put in charge of the American troops, who, gradually but decidedly, learned how to fight. As 1942 turned into 1943, the U.S. soldiers and their allies began to make headway against the Germans. By mid-January, General Bernard Montgomery's British Eighth Army, having defeated Erwin Rommel's Afrika Korps at El Alamein, was closing in from the east. German forces in Africa thus were confronted by Patton to the west and Montgomery to the east. It was not an enviable position.

Montgomery was a very capable military leader. He was battle-tested and, unlike many British generals up to then, had led British troops to victory. He was also rather arrogant. He had an extremely high opinion of his own abilities, and a correspondingly low opinion of those of his American counterparts. Of Eisenhower he wrote—privately—that the U.S. commander in chief "knows nothing about how to make war or to fight battles." Throughout the war, Montgomery never could understand why he was not the Allies' supreme commander. Patton, needless to say, could not stand the man.

By May, the Americans and the British were squeezing the German army hard. Rommel flew to Germany to plead for more troops. Worried more about Russia and judging Tunisia to be a sideshow, Hitler said no. The führer then relieved Rommel of command, ordering him to remain in Germany (losing battles, which the field marshal of late had been doing, was no way to win favor with Herr Hitler). To lead the dwindling German army in Africa the High Command dispatched a veteran of the Russian front, Jürgen von Arnim.

It mattered little who was in charge. Victorious American troops entered the key port city of Bizerte on May 7. British troops took control of Tunis shortly thereafter. Von Arnim is remembered today simply as the commander of 125,000 German troops who surrendered to the Allies.

With the entire northern coast of Africa secure, the question arose of where next the American and British forces would strike. The answer had been given at Casablanca. There, in January 1943, Roosevelt and Churchill had met, joined as always by their respective nations' armed forces chiefs. Several key decisions were reached. The Americans would institute a campaign of daylight strategic bombing of Germany. Preliminary planning for a cross-channel invasion of France would begin. The Allies would stop fighting only when Germany surrendered unconditionally. And, most relevant to our narrative here, Sicily would be the next objective.

Attacking the island of Sicily held several advantages. It would draw German units to its defense, thereby easing the pressure on Stalin's armies. It also would maintain the momentum the Allies had gained by their victory in Africa. Additionally, it would encourage the Italians to get rid of Mussolini. And, much to Churchill's satisfaction, it would reflect the strategy he favored of invading Europe not from England directly, but from the Mediterranean.

American and British troops, about eighty thousand in number, invaded Sicily on July 10, 1943. The campaign to capture the island took thirty-eight days and produced nineteen thousand Allied casualties. Although a large number of German soldiers escaped, the fact was that, once again, American and British soldiers had engaged the enemy and emerged victorious.

Worth mentioning is an incident involving U.S. paratroopers. As part of the invasion of Sicily, some two thousand soldiers of the 82nd Airborne Division made a night jump onto the island. Their planes took the paratroopers over the invasion fleet. Nervous gunners then mistook the American aircraft for German intruders. The results were disastrous. Twenty-three planes were shot down, and 229 paratroopers were killed or wounded. This was not the first incident of "friendly fire," nor would it be the last. It did, however, reflect a risk of warfare, one that remains today. To ensure it did not recur when, in 1944, the Allies invaded Normandy, the commander of the 82nd insisted that the planes carrying the paratroopers make a wide berth of the invasion fleet.

Next up was Italy. The British were eager to proceed, the Americans less so. Generals Marshall and Eisenhower were concerned that a campaign to seize the Italian mainland would divert resources required for the cross-channel invasion. But when they learned that invasion would not occur in late 1943 as originally thought, but in the spring of 1944 at the earliest, they agreed to the venture. The initial goal was to capture the port city of Naples and the airfields surrounding the town of Foggia. Later, this was expanded to include Rome, and later still, the entire peninsula. The result was a major Allied military effort. The campaign would last until April 1945 and cost many, many lives. Author Robert Wallace described the fight for Italy as "one of the most grinding and protracted struggles of the entire war."

It began on September 3, 1943, when British troops crossed over the Straits of Messina and entered the continent of Europe. Six days later, additional British troops landed at Taranto. That same day, American and British soldiers under the command of Mark Clark went ashore on the beaches of Salerno, just south of Naples. German forces contested the landing and came close to pushing the Allied troops into the sea. But, after nine days of intense fighting, the invaders prevailed, though at the cost of thirty-five hundred casualties.

Naples fell on October 1. Days later, the airfields of Foggia were in Allied hands. This enabled the American Fifteenth Air Force, with its B-17s and B-24s, to begin its strategic bombing of Germany, which it did, and which it continued until the day the war ended.

The Italian terrain of mountains and rivers favored the Germans, who proved adept at defensive operations. This, plus the cold weather and lack of roads, made Allied advances extremely difficult.

By early 1944, a stalemate had arisen. So General Clark launched an amphibious operation hoping to outflank the Germans. American troops landed at Anzio, a small coastal town on the western side of Italy, some twenty-five miles south of Rome. The Germans pounded the position, and Anzio became a problem for the Allies. Not until mid-May were the U.S. troops able to break free and then only because the Germans had decided to move farther north.

At Anzio the Americans displayed much courage, none more so than the U.S. Army nurses who served in the field hospitals. These medical stations provided immediate care and, illustrating the scale of the Anzio endeavor, treated more than thirty-three thousand men. Throughout the ordeal German artillery fired on the Americans. Most of the shells hit legitimate targets. Some, however, struck the hospitals, where some two hundred nurses were at work. Six nurses were killed at Anzio. Four won the Silver Star, the first women ever to do so.

The Allied advance from Naples to Rome was never more difficult than at Monte Cassino. The town of Cassino lies midway between the two cities, on the western side of the Apennine Mountains. Its most noteworthy feature was the monastery atop a seventeen-hundred-foot-high hill immediately adjacent to the town. The monastery was a historic treasure. The birthplace of the Benedictine order, it contained medieval manuscripts of great value. It also was a perfect place for the Germans to observe Allied movements.

Respecting the historical significance of Monte Cassino, the German army had not occupied the monastery. The Allies, whose army by then included troops from New Zealand, South Africa, India, and Poland as well as Free French forces, did not know that. They assumed the Germans were watching their every move. Thus the Allies attributed the difficulties they were having in capturing Cassino to the ability of the Germans to pinpoint their positions. After repeated failures to capture the town, they decided to eliminate the monastery and all of the Germans therein.

On February 15, 1944, Allied aircraft dropped bomb after bomb on the monastery, destroying it completely. The unintended result was to create such rubble that once the Germans occupied the hill, which they quickly did, seizing the hilltop became that much more difficult.

At about the same time the Allies finally took control of Cassino, the Americans at Anzio broke out. As Anzio was north of Cassino, the hope was to trap the retreating Germans. This might have happened but for a decision made by the senior American general in charge. Mark Clark decided he'd rather be the first to reach Rome than destroy the retreating German Tenth Army, the unit which so capably had been resisting the Allied advance. Eager for the glory associated with the capture of the Eternal City, Clark directed his divisions north to Rome. They entered the city on June 4. Clark got his reward. But it was short-lived. Two days later, events in Normandy overshadowed the general and the Italian campaign.

The advance up the peninsula would continue. Lasting a total of 607 days, the entire Italian campaign was costly in matériel and expensive in lives. American dead eventually numbered 19,475. Four times that number were wounded. The losses to Britain and the other Allied nations were comparable. It was a high price for an effort than in his memoir General Eisenhower described as a "distinctly subsidiary operation."

Yet the campaign's accomplishments were many. The fighting forced Italy out of the war. It secured the Mediterranean for the British. It provided airfields for the strategic bombing of Germany. It kept the U.S. Army in battle for the year 1943 and gave FDR a response to Stalin when the Russian leader complained that only the Red Army was fighting the Nazis. Most important, at least for George Marshall and Dwight Eisenhower, it tied down twenty German divisions that otherwise would have been available to confront the Allies in Normandy.

Of necessity, this narrative contains few references to individual combat units of the U.S. Army. Numbered field armies and air forces, such as Patton's Third Army, that fought in Normandy and the Fifteenth Air Force are mentioned, but smaller organizations, such as infantry divisions or fighter groups, rarely are identified. One exception is the Army Air Force's 332nd Fighter Group.

This air force unit has become known as "the Tuskegee Airmen." Composed exclusively of African-Americans, all of whom were trained at the Tuskegee Institute in Alabama, the 332nd flew in both North Africa and Sicily. Later, based in Italy and equipped with P-51 Mustangs, the group escorted Fifteenth Air Force bombers on raids into Germany, Czechoslovakia, Hungary, and Romania. Commanded by Colonel Benjamin O. Davis, the group compiled an outstanding combat record. For the loss of fifty-one pilots, the 332nd Fighter Group destroyed 119 enemy aircraft.

This record is even more noteworthy in view of the discrimination these black Americans had to endure. In the early 1940s, the United States was an overtly racist society. African-Americans were denied equal opportunities and equal rights. Few institutions were more racist than the U.S. Army. The 332nd overcame such injustice. The 92nd Infantry Division could not.

The 92nd was composed of African-American enlisted men and white officers. The former were poorly trained. The latter were unhappy in their assignment. The result, not surprisingly, was failure in battle. Only with time would the army rid itself of the absurd notion that black Americans could not fight with skill and courage. During the Second World War, some 961,000 African-Americans served in the armed forces. Most, however, were relegated to support units.

When Churchill and Roosevelt met at Casablanca in January 1943, they reached agreement on an Allied military priority in addition to that of Sicily and the strategic bombing of Germany. The president and the prime minister agreed that the defeat of the enemy's submarine forces was to be Britain's and America's most urgent objective.

Throughout the Second World War, German submarines, the U-boats (*Unterseeboote*), waged a campaign to defeat Great Britain by depriving her of food and war materials. Nazi Admiral Karl Dönitz, commander of the U-boats, reasoned that if his boats were to sink enough of the ships delivering supplies, Britain would have no choice but to surrender. Germany had tried this plan of attack once before, in 1917. She failed then and would fail again. But from September 1939 to May 1945, her submarines would wreak havoc at sea, ultimately sinking 5,140 merchant vessels.

Thus was fought what is called the Battle of the Atlantic. This was not a single engagement, but a host of small battles below, on, and above the ocean. The combatants were the U-boats and those Allied ships and planes attempting to sink them. The battle began the day the war started. It ended on May 4, 1945, when Dönitz signaled the U-boats to cease operations and return to base. In his memoirs Winston Churchill called the Battle of the Atlantic, "the dominating factor all through the war."

Even before the United States entered the war, President Roosevelt had become acquainted with the U-boats. Early in September 1941 the American destroyer USS *Greer* was in the Atlantic south of Iceland. A German submarine fired two torpedoes at her. Both missed. A month later a German torpedo struck the USS *Kearny*, another destroyer. The ship survived, but eleven sailors died. The USS *Reuben James* was not so fortunate. On October 31, 1941, U-568 sank the vessel, killing 115 American sailors. Harold Stark, then one of the navy's most senior admirals, said, "The Navy is already at war in the Atlantic but the country doesn't seem to realize it." Franklin Roosevelt did. After the attack on the *Greer*, he ordered the U.S. Navy to fire on any ship threatening American vessels or those under American escort.

At first, the battle against the U-boats did not go well, for neither Great Britain nor the United States. Once Germany and America were at war, Dönitz sent the U-boats to American waters. There they enjoyed great success, sinking ships from Cape Cod to the Caribbean. Foolishly, the U.S. Navy initially chose not to mandate that merchant ships sail in convoy. This made the job of the U-boats much easier. So did the bright lights of American cities. Only belatedly were they blacked out. The initial result was a maritime massacre. The Germans called the submarine campaign

Operation *Paukenschlag*, best translated as the introductory roll of kettle drums. The U-boat commanders referred to it as "the Happy Times."

Early in the war, the British too had felt the full force of the U-boats. From May through November of 1940, in the waters off England, there had been an earlier Happy Time. In June alone the U-boats sank 173 ships. By then the German submarines had gained an important advantage. With the defeat of France, Dönitz had been able to base his boats at French ports. This shortened their voyages to and from operational areas.

During 1942, despite increasing losses, the U-boats continued to enjoy success. And their numbers grew. At times, Dönitz had one hundred U-boats on patrol in the Atlantic. Sometimes these were replenished at sea. The Type XIV submarine, nicknamed the Milk Cow (*Milchkuh*) carried fuel and food, fresh water and torpedoes. These submarines would rendezvous in mid-ocean with the attack boats, which then would continue the hunt. Often the U-boats would strike in "wolf packs," a number of submarines acting in concert. Pity the convoy they encountered. In 1942, a banner year for Dönitz, his U-boats sank 1,662 Allied ships.

On February 18, 1942, as the Battle of the Atlantic raged, U-578, sank the American destroyer escort the USS *Jacob Jones*. Twenty–five years earlier, as Germany's kaiser sought to control the seas, U-53 had torpedoed an American warship. It too was named *Jacob Jones*.

Yet in May 1943 the Allies gained the upper hand. More escorts, better weapons, plus advances in technology made the Atlantic Ocean safer for convoys and more dangerous for the U-boats. One key factor was the increasing use of aircraft. These would first detect the submarine and then attack. Employing American-built long-range B-24s, Britain's Coastal Command made life difficult for the U-boats. So did escort carriers. These were small warships that operated naval aircraft. Along with destroyers they formed hunter-killer groups. In mid-June 1944, one of them, an American, captured a U-boat. The war prize, U-505, is today on display in Chicago's Museum of Science and Industry.

By the beginning of 1944 the Allies had won the Battle of the Atlantic. U-boat losses were heavy. That year alone, 242 boats did not return. Dönitz attributed the defeat to technological advances in radar and radio detection. He would have been surprised to learn that a principal reason for the Allied victory was that the British Intelligence Services had penetrated U-boat communications and were able to read the encrypted messages that Dönitz and his U-boat captains sent to one another. At first, the British used this knowledge to reroute convoys away from the wolf packs. Later, this highly secret intelligence was employed to direct air and surface forces to where the U-boats were.

Key to this intelligence coup was early work by Polish and French agents. This was built on by the British. At Bletchley Park in Buckinghamshire, some extremely smart men and women analyzed captured German code books as well as Germany's famous Enigma machine (one of which had been plucked from a sinking U-boat). The Enigma machine was a sophisticated electromechanical encoding device, about the size of an old-fashioned typewriter. It was the means by which senior German generals and admirals communicated. That the British were able to intercept and decode these communications was extraordinary. Indeed, it was one of the most remarkable accomplishments of World War II. So critical was this intelligence that only a few individuals were privy to it. The intercepts were labeled ULTRA. Closely guarded—their existence was publicly revealed only in 1977—ULTRA intelligence was of great value to the Allies. In the Battle of the Atlantic, it was decisive.

When Admiral Dönitz recalled the U-boats in May 1945, it marked the end of a titanic struggle. Germany had contested the Atlantic with Britain and America and had lost. During the Second World War, Dönitz sent a total of 859 U-boats on war patrols. A staggering 648 of them failed to return. Toward the end of the conflict, a German submarine leaving port was embarking on a suicide mission. In total, some 30,000 U-boat crewmen lost their lives.

Dönitz survived. Upon Hitler's death, he became head of state. But, not for long, as Germany soon surrendered and the admiral was placed under arrest. At Nuremberg, where the top Nazis were tried postwar, Dönitz received the comparatively light sentence of ten years in prison. He died in 1980. His impact on the war and that of the German submarines were substantial. Winston Churchill expressed it in simple prose: "The only thing that ever really frightened me during the war was the U-boat peril."

As the Royal Navy and its American counterpart fought the U-boats, their comrades in the Allied air forces were engaging the Luftwaffe, the German air force. In 1939 the Luftwaffe was the foremost aerial combat organization in the world. By 1943 it was waging war on three fronts—Italy, Western Europe, and Russia—and the strain was beginning to tell. Yet it remained a formidable foe, as both England's Royal Air Force and the American Eighth Air Force were finding out.

Proponents of airpower in both the United States and Great Britain believed aircraft alone could destroy Nazi Germany, thus making the inevitably costly cross-channel invasion unnecessary. Their plan was to strike Germany from the air with well-armed long-range bombers. They expected to destroy the Nazis' capacity to make war and to break the morale of the German people. In the event, they accomplished neither. But the damage their bombers inflicted was immense and their contribution to victory significant.

The British bombed at night. Their principal targets were German cities. By April 1945, most major cities in Germany were in ruins, thanks to the RAF's Bomber Command. Because thousands and thousands of German civilians were killed, postwar moralists would declare the raids to be inhumane, condemning Bomber Command and its leader, Air Marshal Sir Arthur Harris. Harris, however, simply wanted to win the war. He and his pilots thought what they were doing was eminently reasonable given what the German air force had done to Warsaw, Rotterdam, Coventry, London, and numerous Russian cities.

The Americans bombed in daylight. Their goal in the strategic bombing campaign was to destroy Germany's industrial base. Over a period of 966 days the four-engine B-17s and B-24s of the Eighth Air Force would depart England and fly to the Continent. There, they would bomb shipyards, railroad yards, munitions factories, naval bases, aircraft plants, and the like. By mid-1944, the Luftwaffe no longer could stop them.

The Eighth Air Force was one of fifteen numbered air forces the United States established during the Second World War. Eleven of them were deployed overseas. The Tenth Air Force, for example, operated in Burma and India. The Fifth flew in the southwestern Pacific. The Eighth was based in East Anglia. It operated from sixty-two airfields that crowded this most eastern bulge of the United Kingdom.

The Eighth began its endeavors on February 29, 1942, when seven U.S. Army Air Force officers arrived in Britain. Their job was simple: create an aerial armada that would pulverize the enemy. That is exactly what they did. But the cost was high. Some twenty-six thousand Americans of the Eighth Air Force did not return home alive.

At first, progress in building the Eighth was halting. Airplanes and crew were slow in arriving, and some were transferred to Africa to assist Eisenhower in the battle for Tunisia. Then, General Ira Eaker, the commander of the Eighth, discovered that B-17s and B-24s could not safely fly over Germany without protective escort fighters. Yet the fighter available, the P-47 Thunderbolt, did not have sufficient range. So, consistent with U.S. war fighting doctrine, the bombers went on alone into Germany. The results were disastrous. Luftwaffe fighters destroyed many, many U.S. aircraft. Perhaps the most notorious missions targeted Schweinfurt. On August 17, 1943, and October 14 of that same year, Eaker dispatched first 337 planes and then 420 to Schweinfurt and, on the first mission, to nearby Regensburg as well. The latter was the location of an important aircraft manufacturing plant. Schweinfurt was where most ball bearings in Germany were made. On both days the Luftwaffe hammered the attacking force. Each time their guns destroyed more than sixty B-17s. As one B-17 Flying Fortress carried a crew of ten, the Schweinfurt raids cost the Eighth Air Force no fewer than twelve hundred men.

Another difficulty was the weather. Fog, rain, and high winds either kept the planes on the ground or made precision bombing impossible. The Americans thought their top-secret Norden bombsight would ensure accuracy. It did not. Bombardiers trained in the sunny, peaceful skies of the American Southwest found their jobs much more difficult once in German airspace, especially when antiaircraft guns and Luftwaffe fighter planes were trying to kill them. As Eighth Air Force intelligence officers discovered, the B-17s and B-24s more than occasionally missed their targets.

Yet the Eighth persevered. Its numbers grew, and by late 1944, it could put a thousand bombers into the air. Moreover, when early in that year a new fighter arrived, prospects for success dramatically increased. The new plane was the P-51 Mustang. It was fast, maneuverable, and most important, it could fly to Berlin and back. Hermann Göring, the head of the Luftwaffe, is reported to have said that once he saw Mustangs over the German capital he knew the war was lost.

With the P-51s—and the Thunderbolts—the Eighth Air Force was in a position to destroy the German air force. What the Eighth needed to do was to draw Luftwaffe fighters into battle. This was accomplished primarily in two ways. The first was to mount large-scale raids against factories producing German aircraft. Known as "Big Week," these raids took place in February 1944. The second was to attack Berlin. Early in March, the Eighth struck the German capital. In both cases, the Luftwaffe responded. But the German air force incurred huge losses, and by late spring, the Luftwaffe, short of experienced pilots, was a spent force.

So when Allied soldiers landed on the beaches of Normandy, the German air force was nowhere to be seen.

To command the great invasion, code named Overlord, Churchill had hoped to designate General Sir Alan Brooke, chief of the imperial general staff, the British army's most senior position. By 1944, however, it was clear than an American would have to hold the job, because Americans would constitute a large majority of the troops involved. So the choice was Franklin Roosevelt's. Initially, he planned to appoint George Marshall. At the last minute, the president decided that he needed Marshall right where he was: in Washington directing the United States Army. With General Marshall's full concurrence, Roosevelt gave the most important field command any American would hold in World War II to Eisenhower.

Eisenhower's title was Supreme Commander Allied Expeditionary Force. His deputy was a British airman, Sir Arthur Tedder. Tedder had worked with Ike (the nickname used by everyone save the more formal George Marshall) and shared the American commander's commitment to a staff of British and American officers functioning as a single, integrated unit. The senior naval commander for Overlord also was British, as was the top air force officer.

Eisenhower had wanted Field Marshal Sir Harold Alexander for command of the invading ground forces. An Englishman, he had seen success in Egypt, Tunisia, and Italy. "Alex" was well liked and very good at his job. But Churchill insisted that he remain in the Mediterranean. So the assignment was given to Montgomery. In fact, "Monty" was an obvious choice, though not one Eisenhower relished.

The newly installed Supreme Commander arrived in England on January 15, 1944. By then much planning for the invasion already had taken place. A British officer, Lieutenant General Sir Frederick Morgan, had put in place key parameters of the plan. It was Morgan, for example, who selected Normandy. He also initiated construction of the artificial harbors as well as the oil pipeline that ran under the channel from the coast of Cornwall to the Contentin Peninsula. One of Eisenhower's biographers, Michael Korda, has called Morgan's plan "inventive, audacious . . . and well-prepared." Later, Montgomery would attempt to take credit for Overlord. But Korda reminds us that it was Frederick Morgan who did much of the planning.

When assigned his task, Morgan had been told Overlord would comprise three infantry divisions plus paratroopers. To his credit, Montgomery realized more troops would be needed and that the beachhead needed to be much wider (eventually it would span nearly fifty-five miles), an assessment with which Eisenhower agreed. However, more troops meant more landing craft, more equipment, and importantly, more time. So the date for the invasion was pushed forward. It was to take place on June 5.

By then, indeed even at the beginning of 1944, Germany's generals expected the Allies to invade Western Europe. Their problem was that they didn't know where the landings would occur. Norway was a possibility. So was Holland. The location they themselves would have chosen was in France, at the Pas de Calais. This is where the channel-crossing would be the shortest, and it offered a direct route into Germany. Normandy and Brittany also were possible locations, as was Spain.

To add to the Germans' dilemma, the Nazi commanders did not know exactly when the Allies would strike. It might be in the spring or, possibly, the summer. The fall would be less likely given the weather. But still, September and October could not be ruled out.

To mislead the Germans the Allies engaged in an elaborate program of deception. Through the use primarily of radio signals that the Allies knew the Germans would intercept, the British and the Americans created phony invasion forces, one in Scotland and one in southeastern England. The latter was "commanded" by Patton, who on occasion would appear in public in Kent and Sussex in order to lend credence to the fictitious army. Such a force so close to the Pas de Calais and led by one of America's most dynamic generals helped persuade German officers that the invasion would take place across the Straits of Dover. Hitler, himself, thought Norway was a strong possibility.

This effort in deception by the Allies was highly successful. It threw the Germans off balance and kept troops away from Normandy. Indeed, of the two German armies stationed in France, the strongest purposely was deployed in the area around Calais.

To prepare for the invasion, the Germans constructed an extensive network of coastal fortifications. Known then and now as "the Atlantic Wall," it consisted of guns, beach obstacles, and mines. Of the latter there were many. In order to repel the invaders, the German army planted 6.5 million mines along the French, Belgian, and Dutch coasts.

Further, reasoning that the Allies would require deep water ports to keep their troops supplied, the Germans designated eleven seaports as *festungsbereiche*. These were heavily armed fortress areas. Self-sufficient, they were not dependent on reinforcements and were intended to be impregnable. Deny the Allies ports for their supply ships and the invasion would be contained.

All told, the Atlantic Wall presented a formidable obstacle to Eisenhower and Montgomery. Yet it had one major drawback. It wasn't finished. Moreover, the Germans faced two further problems, both self-imposed. The first was that many of their troops in France were not first-rate. The second pertained to their command arrangements. These were cumbersome, and they hindered rather than aided efforts to defeat the Allies.

The German generals had still another problem. They did not agree on the strategy to be employed once the Allies arrived. Field Marshal Rommel, reinstated by Hitler, and in tactical control of most German troops in France, wanted to meet the Allies head-on at the beaches. He wanted command of all armored forces, which he would fling at the invaders as they were stepping ashore. Other generals wanted to hold the tanks back from the coast, away from naval gunfire. Their approach was first to determine where the principal attack was taking place (there might be a diversionary landing) and then order the tanks into battle. Rommel's reply was that armor thus employed would be subject to Allied aircraft as it moved into position.

Both points of view had merit. The solution was a compromise. Some tanks were placed under Rommel's immediate command. Others were held in reserve, allocated to another general. Still other forces were under Adolf Hitler's personal control. The arrangement was far from satisfactory, especially given that in the absence of the Luftwaffe, German success depended on rapid deployment of armor.

Eisenhower too faced difficulties in the structure of command established for the invasion. One of the difficulties involved control of strategic airpower. The Supreme Commander wanted to employ the heavy bombers of the Eighth Air Force and RAF Bomber Command in a tactical role. He wanted them to pound railroads, bridges, and roads in and around Normandy so that German troops on the coast could not be reinforced. The air commanders objected. Sir Arthur Harris and his American counterpart, Lieutenant General Carl Spaatz, thought their aircraft would be best utilized attacking German industry. In particular, Spaatz wanted to destroy the enemy's petroleum assets. Neither man had much use for Trafford Leigh-Mallory, the RAF officer formally in charge of Overlord's air campaign. They ignored whatever he had to say and went about their business, which, to them, was strategic air warfare. Eisenhower, however, was adamant. He insisted they divert their planes to Normandy and environs. When they continued to resist, Ike threatened to resign. Harris and Spaatz then gave way. The result was that for several months American and British heavy bombers dropped thousands of bombs on targets in Normandy. But in order not to give the Germans a clue as to where the Allies were to land, the bombers struck more often in the area around the Pas de Calais.

With but one exception, the Overlord air campaign was highly success-ful. British and American aircraft kept many of the enemy away from the battle. Those that did arrive were delayed and battered. Of critical impor-tance were the Allied fighter-bombers. These were smallish, single-engine aircraft, exceptionally rugged and armed with both bombs and rocket-propelled explosives. Two such aircraft, the British Typhoon and the Amer-ican Thunderbolt, harassed the enemy every day.

The one exception took place on the day the Allies invaded. American heavy bombers were directed to pulverize the beach areas just before the troops landed. But, fearful of hitting the Americans moving toward the shore, they overcompensated. Their bombs struck well beyond the beaches. Few German soldiers were killed, although the number of cows in Nor-mandy was severely reduced.

Those planes had "bombed long." A more distressing incident involv-ing "bombing short" occurred in Normandy several weeks later. To support the breakout of American troops from the confines of the ground gained in the first weeks of the invasion, the Eighth again was instructed to strike enemy positions immediately in front of the soldiers. Unfortunately, their aim was off. The bombs struck the Americans instead. Many of them were killed and wounded. Among the dead was Lieutenant General Leslie J. McNair. He had been the commander of the huge stateside organization responsible for training and equipping the entire U.S. Army. In Normandy to observe the troops he had trained, McNair was the highest ranking American officer in Europe killed during the Second World War.

Eisenhower faced another difficulty, one over which he as Supreme Commander had no control. This was the weather. Placing thousands of troops on the beaches of Normandy required relatively calm seas to prevent the small landing craft from capsizing. Fair weather also was required for operating aircraft that would fly in support of the invasion. On June 4, the weather was dreadful. Hard rain, high winds, and choppy seas posed too great a risk to Overlord. The forecast was similar for June 5, the date scheduled for launching the attack.

Eisenhower postponed the invasion by one day. Given the prediction for the 5th, this was not a difficult decision. The next one was.

Because of requirements regarding tides and moonlight, few days in

June were suitable for the invasion. June 6 was one of them, but the next date was not until June 17. By June 4 the troops had been moved to their embarkation points and much of southern England was sealed off. Further delay would jeopardize the secrecy that so far had been maintained.

What would the weather be on June 6?

Overlord's chief meteorological officer was J. M. Stagg, a group captain in the Royal Air Force. On June 4, he reported to Eisenhower and the senior commanders that data indicated that on the 6th the weather would moderate. Conditions would not be good, but they would be less severe. The invasion could be carried out. Everyone in the room understood it would be dicey and that there would be no guarantee of success.

At stake was more than the lives of the troops involved. Were the invasion to fail, the consequences would be enormous. There would be no Second Front. Nor would there be a second chance to invade Normandy, at least not for a year or two. Hitler then would be able to concentrate on the east. The outcome of the Second World War, however it played out, would not favor the United States and Britain. A failed Overlord would be seen as a defining moment, a catastrophe that constituted an unparalleled setback to the cause of freedom. And the responsibility would be Eisenhower's.

Should he again postpone the invasion, or despite the weather, should he order the invasion to proceed? The Supreme Commander did not flinch. He gave the order putting Overlord in motion. The Allies, said Eisenhower, were to land in France on June 6, 1944. Writing in 1983, Montgomery's biographer Nigel Hamilton noted, "It was Eisenhower's moment of trial—and he responded with what can only be called greatness."

Transporting 132,700 soldiers across the English Channel to a Normandy occupied by two German armies was not a simple task. Assembled for the trip were some 5,000 vessels, including 138 warships. The latter included battleships, cruisers, destroyers, and the all-important minesweepers that provided safe passage through mine-infested waters. One of the battleships was the USS *Nevada*, which had been damaged but not destroyed at Pearl Harbor.

The plan of attack called for five landing sites. Each had a code name. From west to east, these were Utah, Omaha, Gold, Juno, and Sword. Utah and Omaha belonged to the Americans. Juno was assigned to the Canadians. Gold and Sword were British. Further, three airborne divisions, one British and two American, were to make night jumps on both flanks of the invading force.

American paratroopers numbered approximately thirteen thousand. They were superbly trained, perhaps the best soldiers in the entire United States Army. Carried to Normandy by 822 C-47 aircraft, they were to secure the causeways leading away from Utah Beach and delay, if not prevent, German reinforcements from dislodging the American 4th Division that had come ashore.

The paratroopers, and their comrades who arrived by glider, achieved these goals but at great cost. More than a few C-47s were shot down killing all aboard. The Germans had flooded the environs of Utah, so many paratroopers drowned. Practically none of them landed where they were supposed to. Confusion was great, but somehow the airborne soldiers rallied, and started to kill Germans. When, in August, the Battle for Normandy was over, the two American airborne divisions were in need of rest. One of them, the 82nd—one of America's most famous military units—had endured a 46 percent casualty rate. Their dead numbered 1,142.

The U.S. Navy's big guns opened fire at 5:30 A.M. At Utah the tide carried the troops somewhat south, but the 4th Division was able to secure the beach with relatively light losses. Indeed, the Americans had lost more soldiers in a disastrous training exercise at Slapton Sands on the southeastern coast of England than they did at Utah Beach. Among the soldiers in the first wave was Brigadier General Theodore Roosevelt Jr. The son of the former president, he did well that day, earning the Congressional Medal of Honor. In July, while still on duty, he died of a heart attack. The general was buried in Normandy, in an American military cemetery. Nearby is the grave of his younger brother, Quentin, an aviator killed in the First World War.

At Omaha U.S. infantry and combat engineers landed at six-thirty in the morning. They were met with murderous enemy fire. Those that survived, as well as those that died, passed into legend. Omaha Beach today is one of America's most sacred spots. Loss of life on June 6, 1944, was great, and early on, consideration was given to withdrawing the troops. Part of the difficulty was the terrain. Heights close to the beach provided excellent fields of fire for the defenders. Another was that, unbeknownst to the Americans, a first-rate German division was stationed at Omaha. Still another problem was the absence of U.S. tanks. Most of those allocated to Omaha floundered in the rough water while attempting to reach shore. During the morning, American soldiers, many dazed and wounded, huddled beneath the coastal bluffs. To them and to their commanders, the situation looked grim.

Instead of withdrawing, the soldiers picked up their weapons and attacked. Supported by U.S. warships that moved in close, individual soldiers rallied, motivated in part by Charles Taylor, one of their officers, who shouted, "Two kinds of people are staying on this beach, the dead and those about to die. Now let's get the hell out of here." And they did. By late afternoon, U.S. troops had secured the beach and moved a mile or so inland. The cost, however, was high. Casualties at Omaha numbered slightly over forty-one hundred, of whom at least a thousand were killed.

Hard fighting took place at the other landing sites as well. The British and the Canadians fought tenaciously. By day's end, they had established a presence in Normandy that the Germans were unable to dislodge. After five days, the Allies had landed 326,000 men. Eisenhower's army was on the Continent to stay.

What followed in the fighting that lasted until August 22 is now called the Battle for Normandy. At times, the combat was fierce. Allied commanders proved skillful, and despite occasional setbacks (Montgomery at Caen, for example), they were able to defeat their enemy. When it was over, a great victory had been achieved. Hitler had lost some four hundred thousand men, half of whom were casualties. The rest were prisoners. The Allies too had suffered. Nearly thirty-seven thousand were dead.

On August 25, 1944, Allied soldiers liberated Paris. More and more troops were arriving, so that by September General Eisenhower commanded seven separate field armies. In the north were the Canadian First Army and the British Second Army under the overall command of Montgomery, newly promoted to field marshal. In the center, Omar Bradley, one of Ike's most trusted generals, was in charge of the U.S. First, Third, and Ninth Armies (George Patton, reporting to Bradley, commanded the Third Army). To the south, having come north after landing in Southern France, were the Free French First Army and the U.S. Seventh Army. Both of these were under the direction of Lieutenant General Jacob Devers, who, like Bradley and Montgomery, reported to Eisenhower. In total, the Supreme Commander commanded well over three million men. It was a formidable force, one that many hoped would end the war by Christmas.

That was not to be. In large part because the Allies, despite American expertise in logistics, were running short of supplies. Five hundred tons of food, ammunition, clothing, and gasoline were required each day just to sustain U.S. troops. The needs of British, Canadian, and French soldiers added to the shortage. There was another problem as well. The German army, though defeated in Normandy and battered by the Russians, showed no signs of giving up. In fact, Hitler's men fought increasingly hard as the Allies closed in on the River Rhine.

In June, the Germans had started using a new weapon. Called the V-1, it was a pilotless flying bomb, the first of what are now called cruise missiles. They were aimed at London and at cities in Belgium. The RAF shot down 1,771 of them, but twice that number struck the English capital. Some six thousand civilians were killed. By September, however, the V-1 launch sites were in Allied hands, so the threat they posed subsided.

The Germans then deployed a more deadly device, one for which there was no defense. This was the V-2, the world's first ballistic missile. Developed by Werner von Braun, who later built the Saturn V rocket that launched the Apollo astronauts, the V-2s targeted London. They first struck in September 1944. Eighty-five landed in October. The next month the number rose to 154. Hitler thought it and the V-1 would reverse Germany's declining fortunes of war. They did not. But they illustrated the Third Reich's technical ingenuity and gave the Allies great cause for concern.

In September, two major Allied attacks took place The first was an uncharacteristically bold venture Montgomery had conceived. It consisted of dropping paratroopers behind enemy lines deep into Holland in order to secure key bridges. Unfortunately for the Allies, particularly the British who participated, the attack failed. The second offensive was a drive by the Canadians toward Antwerp. This succeeded, but not quickly and not without considerable casualties.

U.S. troops had better results, at least initially. In October, after hard fighting, the U.S. First Army entered Germany and took control of Aachen, the first city in Germany to be seized by the Allies.

First Army then attacked an area known as the Hürtgen Forest. This became one of the more searing campaigns ever waged by an American army. Virtually unknown today, more than 120,000 U.S. soldiers fought in what authors William K. Goodneck and Ogden Tanner call "a chamber of horrors, combining the most difficult elements of warfare, weather, and terrain." When the battle finally ended on December 13, approximately twenty-four thousand Americans were either dead or wounded, missing or captured.

As the fighting in the Hürtgen indicated, the German army was far from being a spent force. Nevertheless, several Allied generals thought their opponents had little fight left in them. These officers were in for a surprise. On December 16, at five-thirty in the morning, three German field armies, some 250,000 men, struck the Americans in the Ardennes, a region where the borders of Belgium, Luxembourg, and Germany converge. This attack began what is called the Battle of the Bulge (after the indentation it created in the Allied front lines) and, ultimately won by the Americans, was the largest battle fought by the United States in the entire war. Some 81,000 U.S. troops were casualties, of whom 10,276 were killed. The weather was atrocious. There was much snow and extremely cold temperatures. Notable was the American defense of Bastogne and the drive north to Bastogne by Patton's Third Army. Both of these actions are legendary, and rightly so.

Less well known are the events at Stavelot and Malmédy. At both places German troops killed U.S. soldiers who had surrendered. These were SS troops, fanatical Nazis imbued with all the evil Hitler's regime represented. They took unarmed Americans to a snow-covered field and simply shot them. Earlier, in Normandy, SS men had murdered 156 Canadian prisoners of war. These events, particularly the one at Malmédy, backfired on the Germans. Word of the killings spread quickly. The result was that U.S.

troops fought with greater tenacity. Sadly for the Americans, one division did not. This was the 28th. It was an inexperienced unit and, early in the battle, was mauled by the advancing Germans. Some seven thousand of its soldiers surrendered.

These men, along with other Americans taken prisoner during the Battle of the Bulge, were among the ninety thousand U.S. soldiers and airmen held captive in Germany during the Second World War. For the most part, they were treated well. Most received Red Cross packages shipped from the United States to Germany via Lisbon. These contained food and clothing, cigarettes and reading materials.

German soldiers surrendering to Americans were transported to the United States (except for those who called it quits very late in the war). This enabled U.S. troops in Europe to concentrate on winning the war. German prisoners of war (POWs) in America numbered some 370,000 and were held in 666 camps, most of which were located in the South (this kept heating costs low). The prisoners were well fed and provided with decent housing. Many were put to work, in forests and on farms and in selected factories. Receiving pay of 80 cents per day, these prisoners in fact alleviated labor shortages in the U.S.

By January of the new year the Allies were ready to clear the lands west of the Rhine. This meant breaching the Siegfried Line, a series of fortifications on the border erected to halt the Allied advance. In this the Line failed. By March, Eisenhower's armies—British, American, Canadian, and French—were at the great river. The Rhine epitomized the German state. Crossing it, in addition to providing military advantage, would be of immense symbolic value.

One of the armies engaged in battles west of the Rhine, and later beyond, was the U.S. Ninth Army. Overshadowed by Patton's Third Army, the Ninth played a significant role in defeating the Nazis. For example, in crossing the Roer River, necessary in order to reach the Rhine, it displayed both skill and courage, eventually taking thirty-six thousand German soldiers prisoner. Commanding the Ninth was General William Simpson. Eisenhower later wrote of the general, "If Simpson ever made a mistake as an army commander, it never came to my attention."

To cross the Rhine, the Allies assembled a massive force. All four

American armies in Europe participated. More than a thousand assault boats were needed. The force included two airborne divisions, some twenty-one thousand men, who, as at Normandy, would parachute into enemy territory or arrive by glider. The great assault began in March. Troops were ferried across the Rhine, usually under fire, and soon established a secure bridgehead. Eisenhower's armies then advanced into the heartland of Germany. As they did so, they began to see that in towns and villages white flags of surrender hung from windows and balconies.

In the north, Montgomery's soldiers raced into northern Germany, taking control of the Baltic ports. In the south, Devers's two armies (the U.S. Seventh and the Free French First) secured Nuremberg and the surrounding areas. Patton's army, taking a thousand prisoners a day, moved rapidly into south central Germany, eventually reaching Czechoslovakia. First Army occupied the Ruhr Valley. Simpson's Ninth Army reached the Elbe River on April 11, 1945. There, it met up with Soviet troops that had defeated the Germans in the east.

As the Americans and Russians were advancing into Germany, they discovered the concentration camps the Nazis had established primarily to exterminate men, women, and children of the Jewish faith. Auschwitz, Buchenwald, and Dachau, as well as the other camps, epitomized the vile nature of the Third Reich. Over time, the Nazis killed six million Jews. Rarely in human history has such cruelty been perpetuated. With good reason Herr Hitler and his cronies are seen today as the personification of evil.

By mid-April, thousands of Hitler's soldiers were laying down their weapons. Wisely, Germany's führer chose not to surrender. On April 30, 1945, he put a gun to his head and pulled the trigger. By then, Soviet troops were in Berlin and the Third Reich had ceased to exist.

There remained only the formal surrender of the German armed forces. This took place on May 7, at Eisenhower's headquarters in Rheims, France. Three days earlier Montgomery had received the surrender of German armies in Holland, Denmark, and northern Germany. But the Soviets claimed that they were not adequately represented at either event, so a third ceremony was held. This occurred in Berlin on May 8.

The German officer who surrendered to Field Marshal Montgomery soon thereafter committed suicide. The two generals who signed the documents of surrender in Rheims and Berlin later were hanged. Given the death and destruction they and their fellow Nazis had caused, it seemed appropriate.

The Second World War, however, was far from over. In the Pacific, American soldiers, sailors, and marines were engaged in fierce combat with the Japanese. Together with their Australian, British, and Chinese allies, these Americans were taking back the territories Japan had seized early in the war.

The day after the attack on Pearl Harbor, Japanese naval forces took control of Guam. This was a small island in the Marianas, an American outpost that served as a stepping stone to the Philippines.

After Guam, the Japanese struck Wake Island, also an American outpost. On this tiny speck of land the Americans put up a spirited defense, sinking two Japanese warships and damaging several other vessels. But the Japanese soon overwhelmed the defenders, who surrendered on December 24, 1941.

The most important American possession in the Pacific was the Philippines. This the United States had won as a result of victory in the Spanish-American War. By the standards of the day, America's rule in the islands had been enlightened, and the Philippines was due to gain independence in 1946.

Japan, rightly, saw the American presence in the Philippines as an obstacle to its move south to the Dutch East Indies (now the Republic of Indonesia). So it amassed a strong strike force and attacked on December 8.

Defending the Philippines was a sizeable number of American and Filipino soldiers. These were commanded by Douglas MacArthur. He was a former U.S. Army chief of staff, well known to the American public. MacArthur's political supporters in Washington believed he was a military genius, a view MacArthur himself shared. Unfortunately for the United States, his defense of the Philippines left much to be desired.

MacArthur allowed his airpower to be destroyed on the ground and mishandled the land campaign. After abandoning Manila, his troops, some eighty thousand Americans and Filipinos, withdrew to Bataan. This was a peninsula to the west of the capital. Within a short time, with reinforcements unable to be sent, MacArthur's men were in a desperate way. They were short of supplies, undernourished, and in need of medical care. Trapped on the peninsula, they surrendered on April 9, 1942. It was—and still is—the largest capitulation of an American field command in the history of the United States.

About seventy thousand men, American and Filipino, were marched off to prison camps. This was the infamous Bataan Death March. More than seven thousand perished. Some were killed by guards; others were simply too weak to survive.

MacArthur was not one of them. He and several thousand men (plus a few female army nurses) had moved to Corregidor, a small, heavily fortified island at the tip of the Bataan Peninsula. After incessant pounding by the Japanese, it too surrendered. The surviving defenders were sent off to a prison camp outside of Manila.

The Japanese, who considered surrendering a dishonorable act, had little regard for Allied POWs. In addition to beating and starving their captives, they sometimes simply shot them. Only 4 percent of the British and American servicemen taken prisoner by the Germans died while in captivity. The comparable statistic for POWs of the Japanese was 28 percent.

When Corregidor fell, Douglas MacArthur was in Australia. He had been ordered there by President Roosevelt. MacArthur was too well known an American to be captured, so Roosevelt directed him to escape, which he did, departing Corregidor by PT boat. Once in Australia, the general was given command of all American and Australian forces in the Southwest Pacific. He also was given a medal. Anxious to placate MacArthur's supporters in Washington and aware of the need to create American heroes, Roosevelt and George Marshall arranged for MacArthur to receive the Congressional Medal of Honor. Never has the award been less deserved.

By March 1942, the Empire of Japan had achieved great success. In but a short time the Japanese had vanquished their foes, ending the myth of Western superiority. The empire's battle-tested army had triumphed. Its navy, the Imperial Japanese Navy, appeared invincible. In Tokyo the strategy was to consolidate the gains made and await the inevitable American response. One more victory and the Empire of the Rising Sun would be secure. Nothing would then rival its power or its prestige.

America's initial response came in a totally unexpected way. On April 18, 1942, a small U.S. Navy task force appeared off the coast of Japan. On board one of the ships, an aircraft carrier, were sixteen army B-25 medium bombers, twin-engine craft with a crew of five. No one had ever flown a B-25 off a carrier. One by one, the army bombers revved their engines, released their brakes, and roared down the flight deck. All of them made it safely into the air. Led by Lieutenant Colonel Jimmy Doolittle, they bombed Tokyo and several other cities. Damage to the cities was slight and all of the planes save one (it landed in the Soviet Union) crash-landed in China. However, the impact of the raid was huge. Morale in America soared. In Tokyo Japan's generals and admirals were deeply humiliated.

For his efforts, Doolittle was awarded the Congressional Medal of Honor, which (unlike MacArthur) he richly deserved. Prior to the war, he had been a well-respected aviator. During the conflict Doolittle served elsewhere with distinction as well, eventually commanding the American Eighth Air Force in England. But his fame today rests largely on the daring raid he led in 1942. How fitting then that when he passed away in 1993, a lone, restored B-25 flew in salute above his funeral procession.

The military juggernaut that Japan had unleashed in the Pacific was not limited to attacks on the United States. In 1937 Japan had begun its invasion of China. In 1940 Japan took control of what then was called French Indochina and is now Cambodia, Laos, and Vietnam. In late 1941, Japanese forces landed on the coast of Malaya, at the southern tip of which lay Singapore, then a British Crown Colony, and today an independent city-state.

The British considered Singapore an impregnable fortress, able to withstand any assault the Japanese might mount. There was good reason for such optimism. More than eighty thousand troops were on duty in Malaya, far more than Lieutenant General Tomoyuki Yamashita's invading force. Yet the individual Japanese soldier was tougher and better led than his British counterpart. British forces were commanded by Lieutenant General

A. E. Percival, whom no one mistook for a second duke of Wellington. Yamashita estimated the campaign would take one hundred days. It took seventy. Percival surrendered on February 15, 1942. British prestige in the Far East was destroyed.

The ultimate goal of Japan's drive to the south was the Dutch East Indies. These mostly comprised the large islands of Sumatra, Borneo, Java, Celebes, and East Timor. Rich in rubber, metals, and oil—of which Japan had none—the Dutch East Indies were vital to the empire's economic well-being.

Defending the Dutch-controlled islands was a small force that the Japanese easily cast aside. The most noble Allied effort was made by a naval force under the command of Dutch Rear Admiral Karel Doorman. The British, Australian, American, and Dutch navies cobbled together several cruisers and destroyers, which Doorman led into battle. They were defeated decisively on February 27, 1942, in the Battle of the Java Sea. Most of Doorman's ships were sunk and the admiral was killed.

One of the Allied ships sunk belonged to Australia. Perceiving this English-speaking nation as an obstacle to its imperial ambitions, Japan hoped to neutralize Australia either by blockade or invasion. To accomplish either, Japan needed to take control of Port Moresby. This was a harbor town located on the southern coast of New Guinea, not far from Australia itself.

To seize Port Moresby, the Japanese assembled an invasion fleet that set sail early in May. Protecting these ships were powerful warships, including two fleet carriers, both of which were veterans of the attack on Pearl Harbor, and one small aircraft carrier. Aware of the threat to Port Moresby, the United States Navy responded. It dispatched an equally powerful fleet to Australian waters. The results of the ensuing battle favored the Japanese. They sank one of America's most important warships, the carrier USS *Lexington*, plus a fleet oiler and a destroyer. Additionally, they shot down more than sixty American aircraft. United States forces were able only to destroy the light carrier and damage one of the two large fleet units. Strategically, however, Coral Sea was a victory for the Americans because the Japanese invasion fleet turned around and went home. Port Moresby would remain in Allied hands.

The Battle of the Coral Sea was the first naval engagement in history in which the opposing navies never came within sight of each other. All of the fighting, on both sides, was conducted by naval aircraft.

Despite the losses, America's naval aviators had done well in the battle, better perhaps than Uncle Sam's sailors realized. Not only had the aviators depleted the ranks of Japanese naval aircraft by 104 machines, they had heavily damaged one of the large enemy carriers, thus reducing the number of aircraft carriers the IJN had available for the next major engagement at sea.

This would be the Battle of Midway, and it would be one of the most decisive clashes ever waged between two nations at war.

Some eleven hundred miles west of Hawaii lay the tiny islands of Midway, comprising little more than two square miles. In 1942 the islands were an American possession (they still are today). On one of them was an airfield, plus a modestly sized garrison of U.S. soldiers, sailors, and marines. Midway was but a spot in the ocean, but it was of great strategic value.

Admiral Isoroku Yamamoto, the commander of Japan's powerful navy, decided to strike at Midway. The architect of the attack on Pearl Harbor, his prestige within Japan was enormous. Like others in the Imperial Japanese Navy, Yamamoto was embarrassed by the Doolittle raid. He felt that once the Japanese were in control of Midway, it would not be possible for such a raid to take place again. More important, by targeting Midway, Yamamoto understood that he would force the remaining U.S. carriers into battle. The admiral was convinced he would win such a fight. He then easily could occupy Midway, which would serve as a strong defensive outpost for the empire he faithfully served.

Early in June 1942 Yamamoto sent his fleet toward Midway. The fleet's main punch was four aircraft carriers, all veterans of the strike at Pearl Harbor. American intelligence services, however, had broken Japan's naval code and were aware of the Japanese plans. Yamamoto believed the Americans had but two carriers left. In fact, they had three: *Enterprise*, *Hornet*, and *Yorktown* (the latter damaged but not destroyed at Coral Sea). Commanding the U.S. Navy's Pacific Fleet was Admiral Chester Nimitz (for whom the current class of American nuclear supercarriers are named). He ordered the three warships and their escorts to ambush the Japanese. In charge of the American task force was Rear Admiral Frank Jack Fletcher.

The Battle of Midway began when Japanese naval aircraft struck the island's airfield and garrison, causing much destruction. These planes then returned to their carriers to refuel and rearm. Additional aircraft, held in reserve, also were on board. These were being readied for flight operations. Thus, as Yamamoto's carriers were preparing for follow-on attacks, they had on board more than two hundred airplanes, all full of highly flammable aviation gas, that were armed with bombs and torpedoes.

Just then, planes from the American carriers arrived on the scene. They were Douglas TBD Devastators, single-engine torpedo bombers that carried a crew of three, and there were forty-one of them. Attempting to sink the enemy carriers, the Devastators flew low, just above the water, and released their "fish." But the American plane was slow and lightly armed. Above the carriers were numerous Japanese fighters. They were providing essential air cover for Yamamoto's ships. Seeing the American torpedo planes, they swooped down and attacked. All but five of the Devastators were destroyed. None of their torpedoes struck home. The attack of the Devastators was a total failure. Loss of life among their crew was extensive. In one squadron all fifteen planes were shot down and only one man, out of forty-five, survived.

As the American torpedo bombers were crashing into the sea, more U.S. Navy aircraft appeared, well above the Japanese carriers. These were dive-bombers, and with Japanese fighters down low attacking the torpedo planes, they had a clear run at the enemy ships. The results, for the Japanese, were catastrophic. The dive-bombers scored direct hit after direct hit, creating massive explosions aboard the carriers. Three of the big warships were destroyed. Five hours later, the fourth carrier was struck and it too sank. In but a few hours on one day, June 4, 1942, the primary weapon of Yamamoto's fleet, four large aircraft carriers, was sent to the bottom of the sea. For the Japanese, Midway was a staggering blow. No longer would Yamamoto and his navy move with ease across the Pacific. For America, Midway was a stunning triumph.

Despite his defeat, Yamamoto remained in command of the IJN's combined fleet. Indeed, his prestige within Japan seems to have suffered not at all. In April 1943, the admiral was at Rabaul and decided to inspect Japanese air units on Bougainville, an island some 180 miles to the southeast. His staff sent word ahead, providing full details of the trip. U.S. intelligence intercepted the message and informed Admiral Nimitz. Because Yamamoto's destination was within range of American P-38 fighters, a mission to intercept Yamamoto's aircraft was feasible. At first, Nimitz was reluctant to approve such a mission, not wanting to compromise U.S. intelligence capabilities. When assured that steps would be taken to safeguard these capabilities, Nimitz gave the go-ahead. On April 18, 1943, sixteen Army P-38s took off to intercept Yamamoto's aircraft. They flew to where the admiral's plane was scheduled to be, and right on time the airplanes—there were two of them—appeared. Only six Japanese fighters were on station serving as escorts. The Americans attacked and easily shot down the two planes. The admiral was killed, along with everyone else on board. Only after the war, did the Japanese learn that Yamamoto's death was not the result of an unlucky coincidence.

Isoroku Yamamoto's strategy for Midway included an assault on the Aleutian Islands. This was intended to divert Nimitz from concentrating his ships where the principal Japanese effort was to be made. On June 3, the IJN's Northern Force raided the American outpost at Dutch Harbor on one of the Aleutian Islands. Four days later, Japanese troops occupied the islands of Attu and Kiska, farther west.

A chain of desolate islands approximately twelve hundred miles long, the Aleutians form stepping stones between Japan and the United States. In 1942, Japanese and American leaders feared the other side would use the islands as a route of invasion. Hence the need arose in both Tokyo and Washington to control them. Many Americans perceived a Japanese presence in the Aleutians as a direct threat to the continental United States. However, the army's top general in Alaska, Lieutenant General Simon Buckner, took a more realistic view, commenting, "They might make it, but it would be their grandchildren who finally got there, and by then they would all be American citizens."

Buckner's perception notwithstanding, the United States mounted a major effort to seize the two islands. On May 11, 1945, the Army's 7th Division, some eleven thousand soldiers, went ashore on Attu, supported by a fleet of warships that included three battleships. The weather on the Aleutians was atrocious. Fog, high winds, frigid cold, and stormy seas made living difficult and fighting even more so. The Americans persevered, taking control of the island by the end of the month. Japanese resistance was fierce, and fanatical. Of a garrison of twenty-three hundred men, none survived save for twenty-nine taken prisoner. U.S. casualties numbered 1,697, of whom 549 were killed.

Kiska was next. A huge force was assembled. Some thirty-four thousand troops, including fifty-five hundred Canadians, invaded the island on August 15, 1943. To their surprise—and relief—there was no one there. The Japanese had withdrawn. The fighting in and for the Aleutians, truly a dreadful place for combat, was over.

A different but equally dreadful place to fight was Guadalcanal. This is a small island in the Solomons, a tropical rain forest where malaria and the jungle combined to constitute a formidable foe. When U.S. intelligence learned that the enemy was building an airfield on the island, the Marine Corps was given the job of seizing Guadalcanal. On August 7, 1942, the marines went ashore. The resulting six-month battle was a difficult, bloody affair. Some fourteen thousand Japanese were killed, nine thousand more died of disease. American casualties numbered fifty-eight hundred, of whom sixteen hundred died in battle. In 1959, the National Broadcasting Company produced a television documentary on the Second World War. It was called *Victory at Sea*. Of the fight for Guadalcanal, the narrator spoke the following of the American marines:

> *They kept their rendezvous—these men, these grim men, these young old men. And on Guadalcanal there is a lonely grave with an epitaph for each who lost his youth there—*

> *. . . when he goes to heaven*
> *To St. Peter he will tell:*

Another Marine reporting, Sir
I've served my time in hell!

The struggle for Guadalcanal took place not just on land, but also in the air and on the seas surrounding the island. At night, the Japanese would bring reinforcements to the island as well as warships to pound the Americans. The U.S. Navy, less adept at night warfare but having the advantage of radar, would attempt to stop them. More than a few sea battles took place—especially effective were the Japanese long-range torpedoes fired from surface ships—and while the Americans eventually triumphed, they did not always win. Between August 1942 and April 1943, twenty-four U.S. naval vessels were sunk, including two aircraft carriers and six cruisers.

One of the sea battles deserves particular mention. On the night of November 14, a squadron of ten IJN warships led by a battleship steamed south to bombard the marines on Guadalcanal. To prevent them from doing so, the Americans dispatched two new battleships, the USS *South Dakota* and the USS *Washington*, and their escorts. In the fight that ensued the three battleships traded salvos. The *South Dakota* was hit forty-two times but survived. The *Washington*, however, pummeled the Japanese ship, which sunk soon thereafter. That night, no bombardment of U.S. marines took place. The battle was one of the few naval engagements of the Pacific War in which battleships, once the primary weapon afloat, traded gunfire with one another.

For the Americans, Guadalcanal was a significant victory. Unlike their triumph at Midway, which, as had the battle at the Coral Sea, halted Japan's military expansion, the success at Guadalcanal represented the first step in taking back territories the Japanese had conquered. In effect, the road to Tokyo started at Guadalcanal. For the United States the battle had not been easy. But once achieved, victory meant Japan was on the defensive. As to this obscure island in the Solomons, it became enshrined in American military history. When historians write of decisive battles fought by the United States they write not just of Saratoga, Gettysburg, and Normandy, but of Guadalcanal as well.

Concurrent with the struggle for Guadalcanal, General MacArthur, from Australia, was directing U.S. and Australian forces on New Guinea, where, save for Port Moresby and environs, the Japanese were well entrenched. His goal was to drive off the enemy and then seize the island of New Britain. As he did so, to decidedly mixed reviews, U.S. marines and army troops moved up the Solomons from Guadalcanal, taking control of New Georgia, Vella Lavella, and Bougainville. This force, as well as the ships and airplanes that supported it, was commanded by Admiral William Halsey. As with MacArthur, his objective was New Britain. For on the island stood the town of Rabaul, a major base of the Japanese armed forces.

Command of the U.S. forces fighting Japan in the Pacific was divided. General MacArthur was in charge of the Southwest Pacific. Admiral Nimitz (to whom Halsey reported) was in command of the Central Pacific. They competed for resources and proposed different strategies. MacArthur wanted to focus on the Philippines. He saw the army as the nation's primary military force. In the general's view, the navy's role was to support his soldiers. Admiral Nimitz, with Admiral King's full backing in Washington, believed the war against Japan was essentially a maritime conflict, and therefore the navy should lead the endeavor. King, in particular, wanted to advance to Japan via the islands of the Central Pacific. He and Nimitz believed that naval forces would so weaken Japan that an invasion would not be necessary.

Neither the general nor the admiral would budge. In fact the dispute— and it was very real—was between the United States Army and the United States Navy. For each service the stakes were high, and neither intended to give way. The only person capable of resolving the dispute was Franklin Roosevelt.

The president, however, did not resolve the dispute. He simply agreed to let each service proceed as it wished. MacArthur received permission to invade the Philippines (to which, with exaggerated gravitas, he had vowed to return). Nimitz was ordered to seize the islands he had targeted in the Pacific. The arrangement was far from perfect, but it worked.

On December 26, 1943, General MacArthur's troops crossed over onto New Britain. They secured their immediate objective, Cape Gloucester, and prepared to slug it out with the 135,000 Japanese soldiers remaining on the island. Then U.S. commanders reached an important but unusual decision. They decided to bypass Rabaul and leave New Britain to the Japanese. The soldiers there had few airplanes and no means of resupply. They posed little threat. Why then waste time and men in an effort to dislodge them? Besides, Douglas MacArthur's primary goal was to liberate the Philippines.

An archipelago of some seven thousand islands, the Philippines was an essential step in any effort to defeat Japan. The Philippines had been an American colony and its citizens enjoyed a close relationship with the United States. Its liberation was an American imperative, and no one was more anxious to return there than MacArthur.

The first invasion—there were several on different islands—took place on October 10, 1944. Approximately two hundred thousand soldiers ultimately participated, as did much of the U.S. Navy's Pacific Fleet. The fighting was brutal and the death toll high. Capturing Manila alone cost the Americans six thousand casualties while, in defending the capital, the Japanese had sixteen thousand men killed. The city itself was devastated. So too were the island's citizens. In MacArthur's nine-month-long campaign to free the Philippines some one hundred thousand Filipinos lost their lives.

The Imperial Japanese Navy fully perceived the threat posed by the American presence in the Philippines. In response, their admirals mounted a last-ditch effort to destroy U.S. naval forces supporting the invasion. If the American ships could be eliminated, the soldiers ashore would be easy pickings. The IJN assembled most of its remaining warships, including four carriers, and set sail. The carriers were to act as decoys. They had few airplanes on board. Three years of fighting had depleted their supply of both aircraft and pilots. The four ships, steaming north of the islands, were to draw off the Americans' aircraft carriers, leaving the other American ships without protective air cover. These would be sunk by powerful Japanese squadrons sailing from the south and west.

The resulting battle is called the Battle of Leyte Gulf. It was the largest sea battle of the Second World War. Commanding the American carriers was Admiral Halsey (an aggressive commander, the press had nicknamed him "Bull" Halsey, although no one in the navy ever had called him that). Halsey fell for the trap and took his carriers north, leaving the beaches undefended. But the Japanese failed to take advantage of the situation. In two major engagements, their strike forces were defeated by American warships. Among the latter were four battleships, the *California*, the *Maryland*, the *Pennsylvania*, and the *West Virginia*. Each had met the Japanese three years before, at Pearl Harbor on December 7, 1941.

The Battle of Leyte Gulf was decisive. For the Americans it meant the invasion of the Philippines could unfold as planned and that Japan's navy no longer could contest the seas. For the Imperial Japanese Navy, once the most powerful fleet in the world, it meant the war had been lost.

Well before the invasions of the Philippines had begun, Admiral Nimitz launched his campaign to seize islands in the Central Pacific. First on the list was Tarawa. This was a flat coral reef, just half the size of New York City's Central Park. Defending this real estate were 2,600 Japanese. Well entrenched, they were willing to die for their emperor, which all but 17 did. In the seventy-six hours it took to secure the island the United States had 1,056 of its marines killed. The American public was shocked by this number. General MacArthur argued that Tarawa proved that his strategy and approach to combat were preferable to that of Nimitz and the navy's.

But the navy, Admiral Nimitz, and the United States Marine Corps learned from Tarawa. When the marines subsequently attacked Kwajalein and Eniwetok in the Marshall Islands and later Saipan, Guam, and Tinian in the Marianas, their casualties were less.

The pattern for these operations were similar. The islands first would be bombarded from the air. Then a large amphibious force would arrive offshore. After battleships and cruisers pounded the island in question, marines would motor to the beaches in small landing craft. By 1944, America's navy and its maritime soldiers were extremely proficient at this type of operation.

Protecting these invasion forces was the most formidable fleet the world had ever seen. At its core were new American aircraft carriers. Named after the first of its kind, the Essex class carriers were big ships, and fast. They displaced 27,100 tons and carried ninety aircraft. Each of the fourteen that saw action in the Pacific required a crew of more than three thousand sailors. By tradition U.S. Navy carriers were named after American military victories or previous naval vessels. Hence, the carriers included the *Ticonderoga*, the *Bunker Hill*, the *Intrepid*, and the *Wasp*. The navy also named several of the Essex class ships after American patriots: for example the *Hancock* and the *Franklin*. This last vessel, nicknamed Big Ben by her crew, was ripped apart by enemy bombs in March 1945, at the cost of 724 men killed and 256 wounded. But she did not sink. Badly battered, Big Ben sailed home under her own steam.

From late 1943 on, American carrier task forces attacked Japanese bases across the Pacific. These raids severely reduced the number of ships and planes the enemy could muster. Off Saipan, in what became known as "the Marianas Turkey Shoot," U.S. naval aircraft decimated their Japanese counterparts. This helps explain why, four months later in the Battle of Leyte Gulf, the four IJN carriers had few airplanes aboard.

Airfields in the Marianas enabled the United States to mount a strategic air offensive against the Home Islands of Japan. Carrying out the aerial offensive was a brand-new bomber, Boeing's B-29. With a crew of eleven, this four-engine machine could deliver forty 500-pound bombs to Tokyo, a round-trip flight of more than fourteen hours. That the 29's power plant, the Wright Cyclone R-3350, occasionally caught fire made the missions even more eventful.

Initial operations with the B-29 were not successful. High winds, bad weather, inexperienced crews, and Japanese defenses plagued the American bombers. Then General Curtis LeMay, one of the B-29 commanders, made a surprising decision. Instead of high-altitude bombing as the plane's design and air force doctrine mandated, the B-29s, stripped of guns and gunners to save weight, would go in low. Their payload, moreover, would include not just high-explosive bombs, but incendiaries. Japanese cities were full of wooden structures, and LeMay intended to burn them to the ground, which is exactly what the B-29s did.

The most devastating American attack took place on the night of March 9, 1945. LeMay sent 279 B-29s to Tokyo. They were loaded with incendiaries, and coming in low and fast, they leveled sixteen square miles of the city. Approximately eighty-three thousand people were killed. Had the Japanese been rational, they would have surrendered there and then.

But they were not. The slaughter continued. During the ten months of the Marianas air campaign the B-29s flew 190 combat missions, the last one occurring on August 14, when 828 B-29s struck north of Tokyo. By then, LeMay and his airplanes were running low on priority targets.

Initially, the B-29s were based in China. Logistical support there was difficult, so the move to the Marianas was welcomed by all. China itself was a major theater of operations in the Second World War (as was, for the British, Burma). Japan had invaded China in 1937. Chinese forces opposing the Japanese were split. There were the Nationalists led by Chiang Kai-shek and the Communists led by Mao Tse-tung. Chiang and Mao despised each other, and each man intended, once the Japanese were disposed of, to eliminate the other. Franklin Roosevelt thought China to be important and was a strong supporter of Chiang, and so much American energy—and treasure—were expended in aiding the Chinese Nationalists.

When the Japanese cut the Burma Road, the principal route for supplies going to China, American aid to Chiang was delivered by air. Aircraft took off from fields in India, crossed over the Himalayan Mountains, and landed in Kunming. The planes employed were unarmed twin-engine transports. Extremely dangerous, the route was called "the Hump." Beginning in mid-1943, huge amounts of supplies were flown into China, but at a high price. More than fifteen hundred American aviators were killed flying the Hump.

In charge of the U.S. military mission to China was General Joseph W. Stilwell. He also served as chief military advisor to Chiang. Stilwell was in an impossible situation. The area for which he was responsible, China, Burma, and India (known as the CBI) was not an American priority, despite Roosevelt's enthusiasm for China. Making Stilwell's job even more difficult was the Chinese Nationalist leader himself. Chiang Kai-shek was a military leader of little skill who often ignored Stilwell's advice. What Chiang most wanted to do was horde the American equipment he received so it could be used later against Mao. "Vinegar Joe" Stilwell did not succeed in China, but given the circumstances, no American commander could have.

However, there was one American general who enjoyed a modicum of success in China. He was an aviator by the name of Claire Chennault.

Resigning from the U.S. Army Air Corps, he had gone to China to help Chiang fight the Japanese. Recruiting American pilots, Chennault established the Flying Tigers, three fighter squadrons that, in 1942, did well against Japanese aircraft (the pilots, in fact, were mercenaries who received a bonus of $500 for each enemy plane destroyed). When the United States started to aid the Chinese, Chennault was brought back into the U.S. Army. He then commanded the Fourteenth Air Force, which conducted aerial operations against Japan.

Roughly halfway between the Marianas and Japan lies the small island of Iwo Jima. At its southern tip, but dominating the landscape, lies Mount Suribachi, a dormant volcano. Early in 1945, twenty-three thousand Japanese soldiers manned the island's defensives. Understanding that no reinforcements or additional supplies would be delivered, these soldiers expected to die on the island. They were determined to make the Americans pay a high price for Iwo Jima.

American commanders wanted the island as a base for fighter aircraft that then would escort the B-29s on their raids on Japan. More important, the island's airfields would provide Superfortresses returning home to the Marianas a place to land in case of emergencies. Either battle-damaged or with an engine on fire, numerous B-29s were ditching in the ocean, well short of their airfields in the Marianas. In time, once Iwo Jima was in U.S. hands, B-29s would utilize this safe haven more than two thousand times.

To seize Iwo Jima, the Americans assembled the largest formation of United States marines ever to conduct a single operation: three divisions, totaling 70,647 men. The landings took place on February 19, 1945. They were preceded by seventy-three days of aerial bombardment. As was the routine, U.S. Navy warships then pounded the island.

The defenders fought tenaciously. So did the marines. Men were killed on practically every square yard of the island. When the battle was over, on March 19, the Americans had paid a high price. Marine deaths totaled 6,812. The number wounded was 19,217. Very few Japanese, a few hundred perhaps, survived. These numbers reflect the extraordinary level of violence the battle produced. A number that illustrates the courage of the Americans on that island is 27. That was the number of Congressional Medals of Honor awarded to marines and naval medical personnel of the black sands on Iwo Jima.

One remaining piece of the story about Iwo Jima needs to be told. It concerns a photograph, a very famous photograph, one that in the United States became the best known image of the Second World War. Early in the battle, U.S. marines reached the summit of Mount Suribachi. Several of them then raised a small American flag. Other marines cheered and the ships offshore blew their whistles in celebration. Later, wanting a larger flag and hoping to keep the small flag for posterity, six men—five marines and a naval medical corpsman—planted a larger flag. Standing nearby was an Associated Press photographer, Joe Rosenthal. He saw what was happening and snapped a picture. The resulting photograph won a Pulit zer Prize. Much later, the image was reproduced in sculpture form to serve as the official memorial to the United States Marine Corps.

In addition to incendiaries and high-explosive bombs, the B-29s based in the Marianas dropped aerial mines into the waters off Japan. As intended, these took a toll on Japanese vessels. An island nation with few natural resources, Japan depended on its merchant marine for delivery of supplies. Were the Americans able to stop the flow of shipping to Japan, the empire would be brought to its knees.

To do just that, the Americans employed a weapon that proved decisive in the Pacific War. The weapon was the submarine. Operating from bases in Australia and Hawaii, American submarines roamed the Pacific. After a slow start due in part to faulty torpedoes, the U.S. Navy's submarine force scored success after success. In 1944 alone the boats (U.S. submarines are "boats" not "ships") sank six hundred enemy ships. Men such as Slade Cutter, Richard O'Kane, and Howard Gilmore are today unknown to the American public. But these three submarine skippers and many others—seventy-six submarine captains sank five or more enemy vessels each—brought about the defeat of Japan. After the war, Admiral William Halsey, in ranking the tools of war most responsible for the victory over Japan, listed the submarine first. This victory, however, came at a price. Fifty-two U.S. submarines failed to return.

Howard Gilmore's story warrants a few words. During a night action, his boat, the USS *Growler*, collided with a Japanese warship. Gunners aboard the ship fired down on *Growler*'s bridge, killing two men and wounding Gilmore. Apparently unable to move but fully conscious, Gilmore gave the command that sealed his doom, but saved his boat. It is an order that still resonates with the United States submarine service: "Take her down!" Posthumously, Howard Gilmore was awarded the Congressional Medal of Honor.

American submarines did more than just sink ships. They also saved lives.

B-29s and other U.S. aircraft, either damaged or out of fuel, often ditched in the sea. Prospects for rescue seemed bleak. Imagine then the airmen's relief when an American submarine surfaced and hauled them aboard. On lifeguard duty in the Pacific, U.S. boats rescued 504 airmen. One of them was a young naval aviator by the name of George H. W. Bush.

Having captured Iwo Jima and taken control of the Philippines, American strategists set their sights on Okinawa, an island just three hundred miles from Japan. For the United States, Okinawa would be the last stop on the road to Tokyo. Once Okinawa was secured, the next attack would target Kyushu, the most southern of Japan's five major islands. Aware of what the loss of Okinawa portended, Japanese military leaders intended to make the Americans pay an extremely high price for the island.

On April 1, 1945, U.S. forces landed on Okinawa. Commanded by Lieutenant General Buckner (who no doubt was glad to be far from the bitter cold of Alaska and the Aleutians), the force eventually numbered some 169,000 men. Designated the U.S. Tenth Army, Buckner's command included two U.S. Marine divisions in addition to four divisions of the army. It was a large force (the landings at Normandy involved five divisions), one that faced approximately seventy-six thousand Japanese troops. These troops were aided by an additional twenty-four thousand men in support roles, many of whom were native Okinawans.

The Japanese were well prepared. Most of them were deployed in well-protected caves and tunnels on the southern part of the island. The fight to remove them was both difficult and fierce, but making good use of tanks and flamethrowers, the U.S. troops took control of the island, killing most of the Japanese. The battle for Okinawa, the last campaign of the Pacific

War, lasted eleven weeks. While the outcome never was in doubt, the cost to the Americans was high, just as the Japanese had wanted. On Okinawa, U.S. dead numbered 6,319. Americans who were wounded totaled 32,943. Among those killed was General Buckner, who was struck down by enemy artillery fire. He thus joined Lieutenant General McNair as the highest ranking American officer killed in action during the Second World War.

As American forces got closer and closer to Japan, U.S. commanders noticed that the Japanese defenders fought with increased determination. Indeed, as the battles for Iwo Jima and Okinawa indicated, the Japanese were fanatical in their efforts to halt the American advance. Nowhere was this more evident than with the kamikaze. These were suicide strikes in which Japanese pilots deliberately crashed their bomb-laden aircraft into enemy ships.

The kamikazes brought a new form of terror to the war on the Pacific. Eventually, they killed more than three thousand Americans. Their appearance off Okinawa and the Philippines, moreover, was not the result merely of a few crazed aviators. Kamikaze attacks were the result of deliberate decisions made by Japan's senior commanders. Nor were the kamikazes few in number. Nearly four thousand Japanese pilots met their death in such attacks. Many more were waiting to take off when the war ended.

Helping to reduce the number of aircraft available to the Japanese was the newly arrived British Pacific Fleet. Once the war in Europe was over, the British were anxious to have the Royal Navy take part in operations against the Japanese. They wished to repossess Singapore and Hong Kong and, in general, to restore British influence in the region. Moreover, they wanted to avenge the loss of HMS *Prince of Wales* and the *Repulse*. Admiral King had no desire to see the British share in America's victory, but he was overruled. By April 1945, British warships had sailed from Ceylon, attacked oil refineries in Sumatra and Java, and after refitting in Australia, had arrived off Okinawa. The fleet consisted of four large aircraft carriers, two new battleships, and a number of cruisers and destroyers. It was a formidable force, the most powerful Britain had ever put to sea. Yet it was but a fraction of the immense array of warships assembled by the United States. The task of the British ships was to intercept Japanese aircraft being ferried from Formosa to Okinawa. Employing mostly American-built aircraft, the British Pacific Fleet destroyed in total ninety-six of the enemy's planes. While not a particularly large number, it represented a useful contribution to America's victory at Okinawa.

The most spectacular kamikaze attack of the Pacific War involved not Japanese aircraft but a battleship, a very large battleship. The ship was the *Yamato*. She displaced 69,500 tons and carried 9 eighteen-inch guns (the most powerful American battleships—the Iowa class—weighed in at 45,000 tons and was armed with sixteen-inch guns). *Yamato*'s final sortie took place on April 6, 1945. With fuel sufficient for but a one-way trip to Okinawa, the massive vessel hoped to smash American warships in one last glorious engagement. The mission was suicidal. It also was a complete failure. American carrier-based aircraft put ten torpedoes into her well before she reached her destination. When she slipped beneath the waves, so did three thousand Japanese sailors. In sinking the *Yamato* the U.S. Navy lost twelve airmen. No doubt the Americans thought it a fair exchange.

Well before U.S. forces appeared off Okinawa, American strategists were planning the invasion of Japan. The plan consisted of two parts. The first was to have the U.S. Sixth Army, some six hundred thousand men commanded by General Walter Krueger, land on the southeastern coast of Kyushu. This was to be called Operation Olympic and take place on November 1, 1945. The second part, Operation Coronet, was scheduled for March 1, 1946. In this attack, two additional armies were to land on Honshu, near the port city of Yokohama. In overall command of all the armies would be Douglas MacArthur, a command he relished.

Of course, neither Olympic nor Coronet ever took place.

On August 6, 1945, a B-29 nicknamed *Enola Gay* left the Marianas bound for Japan. In the plane's bomb bay was an atomic bomb. That morning, Hiroshima became the recipient of the first nuclear bomb dropped in anger (the first atomic explosion had taken place earlier on July 16, on American soil, in the desert of New Mexico). When the destruction of Hiroshima failed to secure the surrender of Japan, a second bomb was dropped on Nagasaki. Even then, Japan's military commanders wanted to continue the war. They hoped to so bloody the Americans on the beaches of Japan that the United States would seek a negotiated end to the war, an end more favorable to Japan than the one likely to result from surrendering unconditionally. Fortunately for all concerned—Japanese as well as Americans—Emperor Hirohito took the unprecedented step of personally intervening in his government's decision-making. On August 9 Hirohito said it was time to end the war and spare the people of Japan further harm. Reluctantly, Japan's generals and admirals bowed to his wishes.

And so the Second World War came to an end. On September 2, 1945, representatives of the Japanese government and of the Japanese military signed the document of surrender. General MacArthur signed on behalf of the Allied Powers. Signing for the United States was Admiral Nimitz. The ceremony took place aboard the USS *Missouri*, one of the four Iowa class battleships. That day, she was anchored in Tokyo Bay, along with more than 250 other Allied warships. Today, decommissioned, she sits at rest in Pearl Harbor. Close by lies the wreckage of the *Arizona*, a battleship destroyed on December 7, 1941. For Americans, these two vessels mark the beginning and the end of the great war that took place in the Pacific years and years ago.

Why did Japan declare war on the United States by attacking the American fleet at Pearl Harbor?

In the 1930s, Japan hoped to expand its influence well beyond the Home Islands. Governed by zealots and convinced of its citizens' racial superiority, Japan, by 1941, had subjugated Korea, seized Manchuria, invaded China, and taken control of what is now Vietnam. Japan also wanted its empire to include the petroleum-rich Dutch East Indies. The Americans opposed Japan's imperial ambitions. In response to the Japanese actions, the United States froze Japanese assets in the United States. It also forbade the sale of oil to Japan, a step the Japanese considered tantamount to a declaration of war. Further, as both a precautionary measure and as a signal to Tokyo, President Roosevelt transferred the home base of the U.S. Navy's Pacific Fleet from the west coast of America to Hawaii.

The two nations were on a collision course. To prevent a clash of arms, Japan would have had to reverse its policy and recall the troops, especially those fighting in China. But Japan could not do so without losing face, a step inconceivable to the military commanders running the government. If the United States would not peacefully step aside, so the commanders reasoned, it would have to be made to do so. Hence, with little dissent, Japan's leaders chose to go to war.

Many senior Japanese commanders realized that the United States was economically much stronger than Japan. They believed, however, that Americans possessed little physical and spiritual toughness. If the Imperial Japanese Navy could destroy the Americans' Pacific Fleet either at Pearl Harbor or in a subsequent battle at sea, the demoralized Americans, lacking the fiber of the samurai, would acquiesce to Japan's territorial conquests. Rarely have the leaders of a country so miscalculated.

Was it likely that Japan would defeat the United States?

Not really. Japan might win occasional battles, which it did, but the island nation simply did not have the resources necessary to emerge victorious in a full-scale war with the United States. Neither in manufacturing nor in manpower could the empire match the capability of America. By mid-1944, American ships and aircraft were overwhelming their Japanese counterparts. What Japan did have, from the beginning of the conflict to its end, was determination and courage. But as long as the United States was willing to fight a long and costly war, Japan had little hope of winning. After the debacle at Pearl Harbor, the American people were willing to endure the hardship of war to see victory realized.

Did America's insistence on unconditional surrender prolong the conflict?

Yes, it did. In Europe, America's goal was not simply to defeat the German armed forces. It was the elimination of the Nazi regime. To be sure, such insistence stiffened Germany's resistance. Had there been a willingness to strike a deal with Hitler, the fighting probably would have ended sooner and, consequently, with fewer casualties. But the war in Europe was not just a battle over national boundaries and political influence. It was a crusade, a campaign to rid the world of an evil that had infected continental Europe. In both 1940 and 1945, Germany would have been happy to negotiate a settlement that ended the fighting in the west, thus enabling the Germans to concentrate on their most hated enemy, the Soviets. Churchill and Roosevelt would have none of it. Their goal was to crush the Third Reich. Given what the Nazis had done and what they represented, this was entirely appropriate. If that meant additional lives lost, so be it.

Similarly with the Japanese. After December 7, 1941, America's goal was the unconditional surrender of Japan. Leaders in Tokyo—generals, admirals, and civilians—had embarked on a path of military conquest. In so doing, they had caused thousands and thousands to die. The United States went to war determined to eradicate those responsible. The goal was not a negotiated settlement that allowed those in power to remain. It was victory, total and clear-cut. As with Germany, this had the effect of making Japan fight harder. But in the Pacific as in Europe, the Second World War was a fight to the finish.

Why did the Allies, principally Great Britain, the United States, and the Soviet Union, defeat Germany in the Second World War?

The Allies triumphed for several reasons: (1) America's "arsenal of democracy" produced first-rate weapons of war in quantities Nazi Germany could neither match nor imagine; (2) the British intelligence services were superb; (3) the extraordinary talents of scientists in both the United States and Britain led to technologies that made a difference on the battlefield; (4) Franklin Roosevelt and Winston Churchill, unlike Adolf Hitler, provided political leadership of the highest caliber; (5) Allied military commanders were a talented lot; (6) the Royal Air Force and the U.S. Army Air Forces were superior to the much vaunted Luftwaffe, which, from the vantage point of history, turns out to have been woefully inadequate; and (7) British, Soviet, and American soldiers—the Tommy, Ivan, and the GI—proved equal to the dangerous and difficult assignments they were given.

There is an additional reason why the Allies were victorious, one perhaps more important than those mentioned above. In 1940, the Nazis had the resources to combat Britain and France and, with better leadership, could have challenged the United States. What they could not do was to fight all three nations and, at the same time, take on the USSR. By attacking Stalin's Russia in June 1941, Hitler committed Germany to a struggle it could not win, especially given the willingness of the Soviet Union to endure casualties in numbers unacceptable to the people of Britain and the United States. When the Russians threw back the Germans at Stalingrad during the winter of 1942–1943 and later defeated the Nazis at Kursk in July 1943, in the largest tank battle ever fought, Herr Hitler and his Third Reich were doomed.

How many American soldiers and sailors lost their lives in World War Two?

U.S. military deaths during the Second World War numbered slightly more than 405,000. This is a small number (though no less regrettable) relative to the losses other nations sustained, as revealed in the following list. Losses shown cover military deaths only. Note the death toll for the Soviet Union.

> France—*250,000*
> Britain—*240,000*
> Poland—*600,000*
> Germany—*3,250,000*
> Italy—*380,000*
> Yugoslavia—*300,000*
> China—*3,500,000*
> Japan—*1,700,000*
> Soviet Union—*8,700,000*

One notable feature of the Second World War was the large number of civilians killed. The years of conflict, 1939–1945, saw blood flow like rivers, a deluge from which noncombatants were not spared. Often civilian deaths were the result of bombardment. At other times, civilians were trapped in firefights between opposing ground forces. Sometimes, most often on the Eastern Front, they were simply murdered. In the nations listed above more than 37,000,000 civilians did not survive the ordeal of World War Two. Of this number 16,900,000 were inhabitants of the Soviet Union.

Was it necessary for the United States to employ atomic bombs against Japan?

By August 1945, Japan had been defeated. There was no way in which the island nation could have won the war. But Japan had not surrendered, nor did it seem inclined to do so. Her military leaders looked forward to an American invasion, for they intended to make the invaders pay such a price in blood that the American people would demand a negotiated end to the conflict.

Admiral Nimitz thought an invasion was unnecessary. So did Curtis LeMay. The former believed U.S. submarines would deprive Japan of food and other essentials, thus causing the country to collapse. LeMay thought his B-29s would so pound the Japanese that the nation would cease to function. Both men probably were correct. If American submarines were to have continued to sink Japanese vessels, if the B-29s were to have mounted raid after raid, Japan would have been beaten into submission. But both endeavors would have required time. Most likely, the fighting would have continued into November or December, and even then the Japanese might not have given up. They were fanatical in the extreme, and with at least six hundred thousand soldiers in the Home Islands and five thousand kamikaze aircraft at the ready, they still might have dared the Americans to attempt an invasion.

General MacArthur thought the landings were necessary. Air and sea power had not negated the need for army-led invasions of Europe, so he reasoned the same would be true for Japan. Only the seizure of the Home Islands by troops on the ground, declared the general, would secure the victory required.

What the atomic explosions at Hiroshima and Nagasaki achieved were an early end to the war. The two bombs shocked the Japanese as no other action might have, including the entry of the Soviet Union into the war against Japan. The bombs brought about the immediate surrender of Japan, and they did so before the Japanese people either were starved to death by American submarines or burned to death by LeMay's B-29s. Moreover, they made certain that no invasion of Japan took place.

Lives were saved by the two bombs. Fewer people died at Hiroshima and Nagasaki than would have been killed in the four to six months the war would have continued were atomic weapons not utilized. Not only would people have died in the Home Islands. They would have died in Manchuria, where the Russians and Japanese had begun combat operations. In Burma too they would have died, where British troops were fighting the Japanese. In Malaya as well, where British and Indian soldiers were preparing an invasion, many, many people would have died. In China, were the struggle to have continued, the loss of life would have been enormous. The lives lost at Hiroshima and Nagasaki totaled approximately 140,000. It is more than likely that a greater number would have perished were the war not to have ended when it did.

In addition to bringing the Second World War to a close, the dropping of two atomic bombs on cities in Japan conveyed a powerful message to future generations. After Hiroshima and Nagasaki, no one could have any doubt about what atomic warfare would bring. Ever since, that awareness has tempered the actions of national leaders as they contemplate dealing with their countries' enemies. It has funneled strife away from a kind of warfare that, because of Hiroshima and Nagasaki, no longer is unimaginable.

8

KOREA

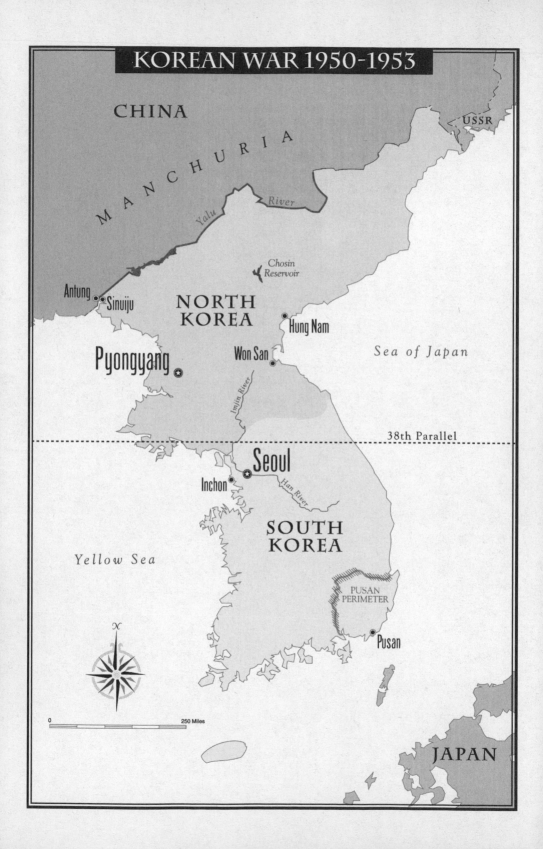

1950–1953

The Korean War was fought for three years, one month, and two days, from June 25, 1950, to July 27, 1953. Losses in the conflict were high. American dead numbered 36,616. Nearly twice that number were wounded. More than 5,000 Americans were declared missing. Korean losses were much higher. At least 1 million people died. Loss of life among the Chinese also was substantial, though difficult to estimate precisely.

How the war began can be traced to the defeat of Japan in 1945. Throughout its history the island nation had coveted its neighbor, finally annexing Korea as a colony in 1910. With the end of World War II the peninsula was divided arbitrarily along the 38th Parallel. To the north lay the Communist regime of Kim Il Sung, a totalitarian state established and supported by the Soviet Union. This Democratic People's Republic of Korea was a disciplined, efficient society in which devotion to the nation and its leader outranked individual choice. To the south lay the Republic of Korea (RoK), a country recognized by the United Nations and led by Syngman Rhee, a fiery Korean nationalist educated in the United States. America backed Rhee's regime as a bulwark against Communism, hoping that he might eventually improve the economic conditions of a people still suffering from years of harsh Japanese occupation.

Kim Il Sung was ruthless, cruel, and ambitious. Syngman Rhee was corrupt, devious, and intolerant. Both men saw themselves as the legitimate ruler of the entire Korean peninsula. Each was intent on destroying the other.

Kim Il Sung struck first. Early on Sunday morning, June 25, 1950, after a thunderous barrage of artillery, the North Korean army—some ninety thousand troops—crossed the border. Kim's goal was a quick victory before assistance to Rhee could be rendered. A worker's paradise would be imposed on a largely agrarian south. Well trained and well equipped, especially with Russian T-34 tanks, the North Koreans overwhelmed their outnumbered RoK counterparts, who, in most instances, fought poorly. What began as an assault soon became a rout. Seoul, South Korea's capital, was captured in three days. Rhee's army lacked competent generals. It also lacked heavy artillery and tanks, purposely so, for the United States feared that a well-armed Syngman Rhee would start World War III by attacking Stalin's puppet regime in the north. To the contrary, as the North Koreans pushed farther south, Kim's goal seemed within reach.

By June 27, the Americans in Seoul had been evacuated. Most left by ship via Inchon, a port city just south of the capital, on the western coast of Korea. They sailed to Japan, from where U.S. Air Force planes soon flew missions in support of the disintegrating South Korean army. Leaders in Washington saw the North Korean attack as an assault on Western democracy orchestrated by the Soviet Union. The object, they believed, was either to test American resolve or to stretch American military resources, thereby making conquest in Europe much easier. So, as President Harry S. Truman was reviewing options, consideration was given to nuclear strikes on Soviet air bases in the northeast, where the border of Korea met that of Russia. The president chose a less drastic approach. He ordered U.S. ground troops into Korea.

Truman's decision was made easier by a United Nations resolution authorizing member states to provide military assistance to the Republic of Korea. This passed the same day the Americans left Seoul and was made possible by the absence of the Soviet Union in the Security Council. Stalin's regime was protesting the exclusion of the Chinese Communists from the U.N. Most Americans supported the presidential decision. Those that did saw the need to confront Communism when challenged. Those that did not thought that Korea simply did not matter. After all, had not Secretary of State Dean Acheson in a speech on January 12, 1950, excluded Korea from areas vital to American interests?

The first American ground troops in Korea were a small combat team of 450 men. Named Task Force Smith, after its commander, the team arrived on the peninsula on July 1, 1950, and soon engaged the enemy. Task Force Smith has since become legendary, but for unhappy reasons. To the shock of many, the North Koreans quickly disposed of the Americans. Smith's bazookas could not stop T-34 tanks. More important, his soldiers were not the equal of Kim Il Sung's. With many casualties, the team withdrew, joining the RoK forces in full retreat. For the Americans the news would get worse before it got better. Additional U.S. troops were thrown into battle. These too failed to do well. One unit in particular, the army's 24th Division, performed miserably, with its commander, a major general, allowing himself to be captured. The reality was that in 1950 the U.S. Army was hardly the armed force that had defeated Hitler's army. American soldiers in the Far East were occupational troops, ill-suited for combat.

As the situation in Korea deteriorated, the United States sent in more troops. Among the arrivals were U.S. marines and soldiers willing to fight. These were joined by a brigade of British troops. As other nations provided small, symbolic contingents, the U.S. effort became, and called itself, a United Nations command. Still, the bulk of the forces opposing the North Koreans were American, specifically the United States Eighth Army, led by Lieutenant General Walton Walker. He was an experienced combat commander, having been one of George Patton's senior officers during World War II. By early August, Walker's men had been pushed back to a small perimeter surrounding Pusan, a port at the southeastern top of the peninsula. Expulsion from Korea was a distinct possibility. For six weeks fierce fighting took place. Mindful of Walker's call to "stand or die," the Americans repulsed determined North Korean attacks. The perimeter held. Pounded by U.S. aircraft and U.S. artillery, the Communists were unable to reach the sea. There would be no Dunkirk in Korea.

Despite the successful defense of the Pusan perimeter, the reputation of the American military had suffered. North Korea had defeated the U.S. Eighth Army though not destroyed it. Yet at the moment of greatest danger to Walton and his troops, the United States would conduct an audacious

maneuver that would shatter the overextended North Korean forces, re-
minding the world of how capable America's military was.

The maneuver was an amphibious landing at Inchon, well up the western coast of Korea, deep behind enemy lines. Conceived by General Douglas MacArthur, the Supreme Commander of U.N. and U.S. troops, the
operation was considered risky by the American Chiefs of Staff in
Washington, D.C. Indeed, as British historian Max Hastings has pointed
out, among U.S. amphibious specialists opposition to the venture was
widespread. Yet the general prevailed. His reputation was such that the
operation took place as planned. On September 15, 1950, U.S. marines and
the army's 7th Division landed at Inchon, carried there by an armada of
260 ships. Together, they constituted X Corps, a force MacArthur kept
independent of Walker's Eighth Army. The Inchon operation was a complete success. Hastings called the landings "MacArthur's master stroke."
By September 27, Seoul had been retaken. In the south, the day after the
landing, Walker's army attacked. Now outnumbered, the North Koreans
gave way. The Eighth Army advanced, linking up with the Inchon forces
on September 26. Badly beaten, though still intact, Kim Il Sung's army
retreated, crossing back over the 38th Parallel, from where, four months
before, it had started the war.

Now came a decisive moment. Would the U.N. forces cross the parallel seeking to destroy Kim's army and with it his regime? The original
purpose of the largely American effort had been met. The Republic of
South Korea had been saved. Crossing the 38th meant expanding the war.

MacArthur wanted to proceed north. He argued that if the North
Korean forces were not destroyed they would be in a position to attack
once again. Moreover, he believed the war to be a part of a Soviet-led Communist conspiracy to destroy the West, an assault on democracy that must
be stopped.

Syngman Rhee also wanted U.N. forces to cross the parallel. He viewed
the conquest of North Korea as a means to unify the country under his
control. Many people believed that Korea should be a single entity, though
not everyone thought Rhee should be its ruler.

America's allies were torn. They worried about further casualties, but
they worried more about the reaction of the Chinese government in Peking

(now called Beijing), which had warned against an American "invasion" of North Korea. But the allies wanted to show support of the United States. In Europe and in the Pacific, they were dependent on America in countering the political and military threats posed by the Soviet Union. Abandoning the Americans in Korea was hardly the way to secure American backing elsewhere.

At the time, MacArthur, his troops, the allies, Syngman Rhee, and the leaders in Washington were caught up in the euphoria occasioned by the success at Inchon. A great victory had been achieved. The North Koreans were in disarray. The war would soon be brought to a successful and definitive conclusion. The troops would be home by Christmas.

Late in September, MacArthur received permission from Washington to cross the 38th Parallel and to continue with the destruction of the North Korean army. Pointedly, he was told to watch for evidence of Chinese or Russian intervention. Under no circumstances was he to advance beyond the Yalu River into Manchuria or the Soviet Union. Having vast influence at the United Nations in 1950, the United States was able to secure passage of a resolution supporting what MacArthur wished to do, in effect approving a military advance into North Korea.

On October 9, 1950, the Eighth Army moved north. That it had been preceded by RoK troops mattered little. The United Nations was now committed to the liberation of North Korea. A momentous chapter in the history of Korea was about to be written. And the U.S. Army would soon receive a most unpleasant surprise.

At first the campaign went well. While meeting resistance, the Eighth Army nonetheless readily advanced along the western side of the peninsula. By October 19 the army captured Pyongyang, the capital of North Korea. Earlier, Kim Il Sung had fled to Sinuiju, a city on the Yalu River, across from the Chinese city of Antung. By November 1, Americans were eighteen miles south of the river. In the east, U.S. X Corps also proceeded north. Additionally, U.S. marines landed at Wonsan and, with army troops, proceeded north to the Chosin Reservoir. The army's 7th Division reached the Yalu itself, from where it could peer into Manchuria.

However, Chinese troops in large numbers had deployed into North Korea. The regime in Peking was alarmed by the approaching "imperialist" forces. Four field armies had been sent across the Yalu and were in position, soon to be joined by two additional armies. Remarkably, approximately two hundred thousand Chinese soldiers went undetected. MacArthur and his officers did not believe the Chinese would enter the war. The evidence that they had was ignored. Moreover, the Americans believed that if the Chinese were to join the battle, the United States easily would defeat them.

On October 25, 1950, the Chinese struck. At first they attacked RoK troops. Six days later they hit the U.S. troops. Both the South Koreans and the Americans were vanquished, and easily so. Loss of territory, though, was limited. Surprisingly, the Chinese soldiers did not follow up these initial victories. Instead they withdrew to the hills and waited.

Why did the Chinese not continue? Were they sending a message to General MacArthur and President Truman? Were they warning the United States not to remain up north, near to the Yalu? If so, the Americans did not listen. They chose an alternate message. MacArthur believed the Chinese had made a face-saving gesture. He expected them to withdraw. He thought they had done their best and no longer were a threat. Rarely has an American commander been so out of touch with reality.

On Thanksgiving Day 1950, Americans throughout Korea enjoyed their traditional turkey dinner. The next day General Walker, in command of troops in the west, launched an offensive he and others believed would soon end the war. The Eighth Army moved out expecting to finish off the North Koreans and any Chinese they encountered. However, the Chinese were the better soldiers. In late November and early December, they inflicted a humiliating defeat on Walker and his men. A few units fought well. Most did not. The U.S. Army's 2nd Division failed totally. Only the marines at the Chosin Reservoir upheld the honor of American arms. They retreated, but the formation brought their dead with them and were evacuated by the navy at Hungnam.

By December 5, the Chinese had recaptured the North Korean capital. A month later, they had retaken Seoul. North Korea no longer was in U.N. hands. Both the Eighth Army and X Corps had been routed. American soldiers, to use the phrase of the day, had bugged out. One American officer called the army's performance against the Chinese "a moment of complete disgrace and shame." But the Chinese advance, extensive as it was, began to run out of steam, hampered by now lengthy supply lines. It came to a halt just south of the Han River, roughly along the 37th parallel.

Two days before Christmas Walton Walker was killed in an automobile accident, his jeep colliding with a truck. His replacement was Lieutenant General Matthew Ridgway, a soldier with a distinguished combat record in World War II. Ridgway energized the U.N. command. He rebuilt the Eighth Army. He commanded all troops in Korea, which Walker had not. American troops in the east, X Corps, had been commanded by Major General Edward Almond, a favorite of MacArthur. Most important, Ridgway brought to Korea skill and leadership, attributes that in Almond and Walker had been lacking.

When Ridgway's forces attacked late in January 1951, they were well prepared. The troops soon pushed the Chinese back across the Han. In the east, the Chinese themselves launched an attack. But this time, the Americans held, with the reconstituted 2nd Division redeeming itself. Supported by massive airpower, the U.S. soldiers shattered four Chinese divisions.

All across Korea Chinese commanders held a low opinion of the American soldier. In the months of January and February 1951, this began to change. Under Ridgway U.S. troops fought well. And they fought successfully. By mid-March, Seoul, by now a city in ruins, was again in U.S. hands. Thirteen days later, American forces had crossed the 38th Parallel. Reaching the Imjin River, some thirty miles north of the city, they dug in.

So did the British brigade. Composed of Gloucester and Northumberland fusiliers (plus a Belgian unit), the brigade was deployed south of the river, some thirty miles north of Seoul, but in the middle of the route traditionally taken by those intent on capturing the capital. What followed, once the Chinese attacked, was a heroic but futile effort to halt the massive enemy advance. One company of Gloucesters, according to Michael Hickey (who had fought in Korea), was "on the verge of extinction . . . when there was a final radio call from the defenders: 'We've had it. Cheerio,' before the radio went dead."

Ridgway expected a new Chinese offensive. This he received. Before the attack materialized, the general was given a promotion he had not expected. On April 11, Douglas MacArthur was fired and Matthew Ridgway became supreme commander of all U.N. forces in Korea.

MacArthur had issued several statements on the war that were contrary to U.S. policy. President Truman, Secretary of State Dean Acheson, and the Joint Chiefs of Staff all wanted to limit the conflict to the peninsula. General MacArthur sought a wider war. With support from influential Republicans in Washington, he advocated attacks on China and saw no reason not to employ nuclear weapons. Moreover, he felt that as Supreme Commander in the field, he, not Mr. Truman, should determine the course of action. Truman, whose standing in the public was as low as MacArthur's was high, reacted to the general's insubordination and sacked him. MacArthur left Tokyo and returned to America, receiving a hero's welcome. He then sought the Republican nomination for president in 1952, but failed. The GOP delegates chose instead another general, one by the name of Eisenhower.

On April 22, 1951, the Chinese launched yet another major offensive, throwing 250,000 men at the Eighth Army, now commanded by Lieutenant General James Van Fleet (as a colonel Van Fleet had led troops onto Utah Beach in Normandy on June 6, 1944). The goal of the offensive and that of another one in May was, once and for all, to evict the Americans and their allies from Korea. The Communists, in what is called their Spring Offensive, were aiming for a decisive victory. They were willing to expend thousands of lives to achieve it. They achieved the loss of life, but not their goal. U.N. soldiers fought tenaciously, retreated a few miles, and held. Then they themselves attacked and pushed the Chinese back several miles.

There, for the next two years, the battle line was drawn. The war in Korea continued, with heavy casualties but little exchange of territory. Peace talks first began in July 1951. They concluded only in July 1953. During that time, the front lines, with trenches and fortified bunkers, resembled those of the First World War. Fighting was extensive. Individual hills were contested. Names such as Pork Chop Hill became legendary. But military gains and losses in any strategic sense were minimal. The Chinese could not drive the Americans into the sea. The United States was unwilling to accept the casualties necessary to push the Chinese back across the Yalu. Nevertheless, American forces suffered. Forty-five percent of U.S. casualties occurred after the peace talks began.

And so the war ended as it had started. Korea was cut in two, roughly along the 38th Parallel. In the north, Kim Il Sung remained in charge of a totalitarian state that still exists today. Then and now its citizens lack material comforts and are deprived of political freedom. In the south, the Republic of Korea continues. However, it is today economically prosperous and a democratic society. Nevertheless, sixty years after the Korean War, armies confront one another halfway down the peninsula. One of them is the United States Eighth Army. This time it is well trained and well equipped. It serves as a deterrent to war and a reminder of a bloody conflict now largely forgotten.

Why did the North Koreans attack across the 38th Parallel?

Kim Il Sung sent his army south in order to place the entire Korean peninsula under his control. Historically, Korea was a single entity, not two separate countries. Kim believed his destiny was to reestablish a unified Korean nation, this time as a Communist state. Moreover, he believed that most South Koreans would welcome the arrival of their northern brethren and that the Americans either would not contest the invasion or, if they did, would be easily defeated. On all three counts Kim was wrong.

Before launching the attack, Kim Il Sung secured Stalin's approval for his action. Indeed, Russian generals helped plan the invasion and provided much of the equipment used by the North Koreans.

The Soviet leader assumed the Americans would not respond militarily to Kim's invasion. The Americans he knew were not prepared for war and were interested in Japan, not Korea. Moreover, like Kim, Stalin had noticed that America's secretary of state had not included Korea when listing territories of importance to the United States.

Why did the Chinese intervene?

The Chinese entered the war in late November 1950, just five months after the conflict began. They did so because an American army was advancing toward their border (the Yalu River being the boundary between North Korea and Manchuria, a part of China). This army was led by a general, Douglas MacArthur, who espoused extreme hostility toward the new rulers of China and their political ideology, and who seemed to have no qualms about employing nuclear weapons. Quite rightly, the Chinese Communists were concerned. They decided to take steps necessary to protect their country.

For several reasons, the Chinese leaders, including but not limited to Mao, saw the Americans as sworn enemies of the state. After all, it was the Americans who had supported their rival Chiang Kai-shek in the bloody contest for control of China. It was the Americans who, with their fleet off Formosa, prevented the Chinese from "liberating" the final piece of Chinese territory over which the Communists did not rule. And it was the Americans who prevented the Chinese in Peking from representing China in the United Nations. With good reason the rulers of China viewed the Americans with distrust and alarm.

Did the Chinese win the Korean War?

They certainly believe they did. From late November 1950 through January 1951 the Chinese army crushed the Americans in battle, causing both the U.S. Eighth Army and X Corps to retreat in humiliating fashion. This victory brought the Chinese great prestige abroad and, at home, remains a source of pride. That the Chinese army suffered enormously high casualties in the effort seems to have been forgotten, or is simply ignored. Nor does it register with the Chinese that, while they defeated the Americans in late 1950 and early 1951, they did not destroy the American forces, which, had their army been more capable, was an outcome within reach. Once Matthew Ridgway took command of the U.S. Army in Korea, the Chinese were unable to push the Americans off the peninsula, which, on several occasions, they attempted to do.

Nonetheless, the Chinese army had beaten the West's most potent military. In doing so, it had kept the Americans away from the Yalu (for the Chinese, a decidedly positive accomplishment) and saved the regime of Kim Il Sung (a more dubious one). So they can claim a victory, although the eventual outcome of the war and the casualties the Chinese incurred suggest the win was far from complete.

The narrative refers to other nations providing symbolic contributions to the U.N. effort in Korea. Which countries were they and what did they provide?

Australia, Canada, Great Britain, the Philippines, Thailand, and Turkey all sent ground troops to Korea, although their numbers were small relative to those of the United States. So did Belgium, Ethiopia, France, Greece, and the Netherlands. As did New Zealand, which, in addition, deployed naval vessels, all frigates.

Canada also contributed to U.N. maritime forces, sending several destroyers to Korean waters. Australia sent an aircraft carrier, HMAS *Sidney*, along with escorts. However, the largest naval contingent, outside that of the United States, came from the United Kingdom. The Royal Navy kept one of three carriers on station throughout the conflict. One of these, HMS *Triumph*, on July 3, 1950, launched twenty-one aircraft that attacked a North Korean air base. This was the very first day of naval strikes against the enemy, strikes that continued throughout the war and constituted a major effort of the American-led coalition.

British and Commonwealth surface warships, primarily cruisers and destroyers, also bombarded North Korean coastal installations. One of the ships that did so, HMS *Belfast*, today remains afloat, moored in the Thames. There, as a museum, it reminds visitors to London of the conflict in Korea, which is now part of Britain's maritime heritage.

Why did America's army at first perform so badly?

In 1950 the United States Army was a shell of what it had been five years earlier. As a result of severe budgetary reductions mandated by President Truman and of the mistaken belief promoted by the newly established U.S. Air Force that airplanes with nuclear weapons were now the primary weapons of war, the army's combat capabilities had become limited. The few troops it had were untrained, and its supplies, particularly ammunition, were inadequate. In Washington, Omar Bradley, then chairman of the Joint Chiefs of Staff, is reported by David Halberstam to have said at the end of the Korean War that the U.S. Army could not fight its way out of a paper bag. That certainly was the case with Walton Walker's Eighth Army. Despite efforts on his part to train the men in his command, Walker was unable to produce an army ready for combat. The results were a foregone conclusion. Both the North Koreans and the Chinese easily pushed aside Eighth Army (as well as Ned Almond's X Corps). Only Walker's pugnacious defense at Pusan saved his reputation. Yet even that was insufficient for him to retain command. MacArthur and the army brass in Washington were about to relieve General Walker. Only his unexpected death kept them from doing so.

What role did the U.S. Navy play in the Korean War?

Simply stated, a significant one. The American navy ferried troops to and from Korea. It bombarded enemy installations. It transported General MacArthur's landing force to Inchon, and evacuated 105,000 men of General Almond's X Corps from Hungnam. It also transported the air force's F-86 fighter planes that were deployed to Korea. Moreover, U.S. Navy helicopters rescued scores of U.S. airmen who had been shot down.

One role the navy played, however, deserves special mention. This was the continuous series of attacks by naval aircraft against targets in both North and South Korea. From aircraft carriers such as the USS *Valley Forge* and the USS *Boxer* operating in the Sea of Japan, F4U Corsairs, AD Skyraiders, and F9F Panthers routinely delivered ordnance to the enemy. But at a not insignificant cost. A total of 564 naval and marine airplanes were lost in combat during the three years of conflict. Of these, sixty-four were Panthers, one of the U.S. Navy's first jet fighters, which, it must be reported, were outclassed in aerial combat by Russian-built MiG-15s, the aircraft favored by North Korean, Chinese, and Russian pilots.

On one such mission, according to historian Richard P. Hallion, a Panther jet attacked enemy trucks near Wonson, and was sent spinning downward after being hit by flak. The pilot, new to naval aviation, nevertheless regained control of the aircraft although the jet's right wing then struck a telephone pole. Somehow, the pilot kept his craft in the air. He flew to more friendly territory and ejected from his damaged jet. Soon picked up, the pilot was returned to his carrier. His name was Neil Armstrong.

How well did America's air force do in the Korean War?

For the United States Air Force, the war in Korea was no small affair. During three years of conflict, it flew 720,000 sorties and lost more than 1,400 aircraft. Moreover, the full array of combat missions were flown. Employing a variety of aircraft, air force pilots flew close air support, interdiction, reconnaissance, strategic bombing, antisubmarine, and air combat missions. Hardly a day went by when the air force was not engaged in the skies above Korea.

The war also brought new developments in air warfare. Helicopters saw their first employment in combat, as did American and Russian jet-powered aircraft. Air-to-air refueling had its wartime introduction. Each of these developments pointed toward the future.

Nearly half the missions flown in Korea were for the purpose of interdiction. This meant the disruption and destruction of enemy supplies and troops well behind the battle line. Having just gained independence from the army, the air force had little interest in focusing on close air support. As strategic bombing targets were limited, the air force concentrated on interdicting the flow of men and matériel. In this, it achieved considerable success. Yet, given the manpower available to the North Koreans and the Chinese, as well as their willingness to accept casualties, interdiction did not achieve its goal of collapsing the enemy's ability to wage war.

Where the air force performed extremely well was in air-to-air combat against Russian-built MiG-15 fighters. The MiGs were first-rate aircraft. Against them, America's best fighter, the F-86 Sabre, nevertheless excelled. Sabre pilots claimed the destruction of 792 MiGs, a number now generally accepted as too high. But only seventy-eight Sabres were shot down by MiGs. Success of the F-86s was due largely to their pilots, who were experienced and well trained. Sound tactics and a superior gunsight made the difference as well. Most of the time, MiG pilots were outmatched. A few did well, particularly a number of Russians, but the majority of those who flew from Antung and the other bases in Manchuria crossed the Yalu at their peril. When, in July 1953, an armistice was signed at Panmunjom, one fact was indisputable: above North Korea Sabres owned the sky.

What, other than the invasion in June 1950 by the North Koreans, were the key turning points of the Korean War?

There were several. The first was Walton Walker's successful defense of the Pusan Perimeter. This meant that Kim Il Sung's army did not achieve its goal of unifying Korea.

The second turning point was MacArthur's successful landing at Inchon. This led to the defeat of the North Koreans and, as important, boosted the morale of the American army and of the American public, neither of whom had much to cheer about as U.S. soldiers retreated down the peninsula.

The next turning point, one of the most significant in the entire conflict, was the move north by the Americans across the 38th parallel. For the United States, this military operation changed the purpose of the war, from repulsing the North Koreans' invasion, to eliminating the regime of Kim Il Sung. Crossing the parallel into North Korea also meant that the Chinese would enter the conflict, thereby changing the nature and outcome of the war.

The Chinese attack of November 1950 constituted the fourth turning point. Chinese involvement led to the defeat in battle of an American army. Their involvement also meant that the U.S. would not unify the peninsula under the rule of Syngman Rhee. Moreover, it ensured that the war would not be limited in duration or in casualties.

The fifth turning point was the dismissal of General MacArthur. The general had overstepped the boundaries of U.S. military field commanders. So Truman's action was entirely appropriate. Nonetheless, MacArthur's removal was a shock to the American political system and a reminder to the American military that in the United States, generals (and admirals) do not outrank presidents.

The final turning point of the Korean War was the arrival in Korea of Lieutenant General Matthew Ridgway as commander of all ground forces.

Ridgway took a dispirited American army and transformed it into an effective combat organization. Under his leadership, the Americans stopped several Chinese offensives, depriving them of control over the entire peninsula, but also advanced north against the Chinese, thus establishing what would become the Demilitarized Zone, close to where the conflict had started, at the 38th Parallel. Rarely has an American commander done a better or more important job. Little wonder then that Matthew Ridgway ranks as one of the country's most capable military leaders.

9

VIETNAM

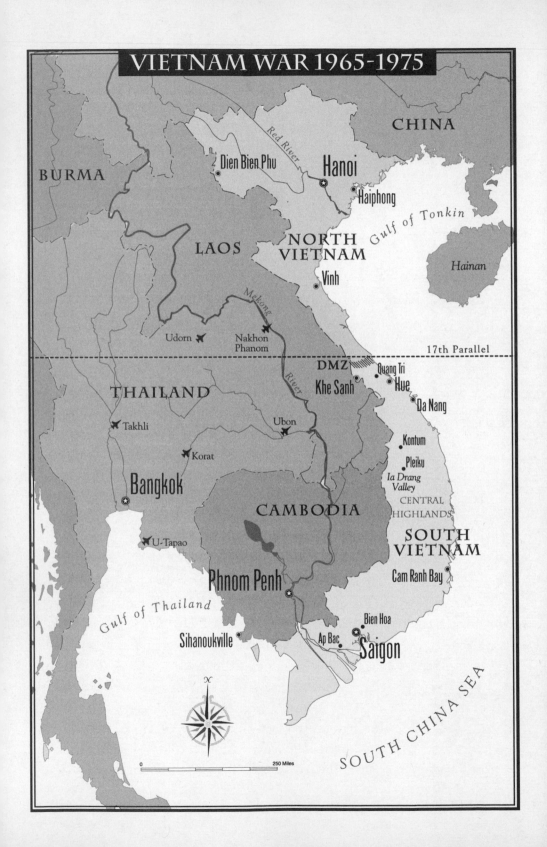

VIETNAM WAR 1965-1975

CHINA

BURMA

Red River

Dien Bien Phu

Hanoi

Haiphong

LAOS

NORTH VIETNAM

Gulf of Tonkin

Hainan

Vinh

Mekong

Udorn

Nakhon Phanom

17th Parallel

DMZ   Quang Tri

THAILAND

River

Khe Sanh   Hue

Da Nang

Takhli

Ubon

Kontum

Korat

Pleiku

Bangkok

Ia Drang Valley

CAMBODIA

CENTRAL HIGHLANDS

SOUTH VIETNAM

U-Tapao

Cam Ranh Bay

Phnom Penh

Gulf of Thailand

Bien Hoa

Sihanoukville

Ap Bac   Saigon

SOUTH CHINA SEA

0   250 Miles

1965–1975

What makes the war in Vietnam unique in American history is its outcome. For no one can doubt that the United States lost the war. Defeat, not victory, was the end result. And the cost was extremely high—thousands of Americans slain and millions of dollars wasted. For the first time, the field of battle belonged to the enemy. The United States had been vanquished, and decisively so.

Much of the responsibility for the debacle of Vietnam rests with Lyndon B. Johnson (LBJ). As president, he directed the American war effort. And when he was in the White House, never far from his mind were the Chinese, whom Johnson was determined to avoid engaging in battle. He remembered that in 1950, when U.S. troops in Korea approached the Yalu River, China had sent wave after wave of its soldiers into battle, crushing an American army. Fifteen years later, in 1965, Johnson did not want to see Chinese troops in Vietnam, a country in which America was fighting a Communist regime based in Hanoi. Nor did he want a war with China itself. The president thus conducted the war in Vietnam with restraint. From 1965 until 1968 the United States did not unleash its military. Indeed, America limited its approach to battle, applying its firepower gradually. This, it was hoped, would keep Chinese troops at home. It also was intended to restrain the Soviet Union. And too it demonstrated to friends of the United States, particularly the Europeans, that America was reasonable when committing its military to combat. *

In Vietnam, Lyndon Johnson most certainly did not want to ignite a world war, a conflict that might well occur were China and the United States to do battle with each other. And significantly the President did not wish to jeopardize his Great Society program. This was an ambitious agenda of legislative initiatives, including a major expansion of health care, that surely would fail were the U.S. at war with China.

Hence LBJ conducted the war cautiously, holding back the admirals and generals who wished to overwhelm the North Vietnamese. These commanders wanted to employ the full might of America's superb army, navy, and air force. They believed that if young Americans were to die in Vietnam, the least their leaders could do was to achieve victory. But Johnson held these commanders at bay. The United States would fight in Vietnam, but not so as to obliterate the enemy in the north.

Why then did the United States fight at all? If the objective was not to destroy the North Vietnamese regime, if at all costs the Chinese (and Russians) were to be kept out of the battle, and if American military leaders were to be held in check, why send troops to Vietnam? After all, according to many experts, America's national security was not at stake in Vietnam. Whatever happened there was unlikely to harm the United States.

The answer is twofold. One reason is that, at the time, the principal focus of U.S. foreign policy was the containment of Communism. As leader of the Free World, the United States was committed to holding back the spread of a ruthless political ideology. Whether Republican or Democrat, America's leaders believed their job was to halt the spread of Communism. So Lyndon Johnson, as well as his predecessor in the White House, John F. Kennedy, dispatched American servicemen to South Vietnam. The two presidents saw in this small country the necessity of standing firm against the beliefs espoused by Karl Marx and Vladimir Lenin.

A second reason for U.S. troops being sent to Vietnam stemmed from American domestic politics. As a Democrat, LBJ remembered how years earlier the Republicans in Washington had savaged the Democrats for "losing" China. That China fell to the Communists in 1949 was interpreted as a catastrophic failure on the part of Harry S. Truman and his fellow

Democrats. In fact, China's American-backed regime gave way to Mao Tse-tung because China's then leader, Chiang Kai-shek, was incompetent. Facts, however, played little part in the partisan warfare then prevalent in the American capital. The Republicans blamed the Democrats for Chiang's defeat. In so doing, they scored political points and were able to defeat the Democrats in the 1952 elections. Lyndon Johnson vowed he never would be tarred with such a brush. So he went to war in 1965. Johnson was determined not to be the president who lost South Vietnam.

America's involvement in Vietnam did not begin with Lyndon Johnson or John Kennedy. It began much earlier, soon after the end of the Second World War. In 1946 the French returned to Indochina, the geographic term employed to describe what is now the countries of Cambodia, Laos, and Vietnam. These had been French colonies, and officials in Paris were eager to reclaim them.

However, many Vietnamese took exception to French rule, particularly Ho Chi Minh, leader of the Vietnamese Communists. Ho and his comrades decided to contest French control of Vietnam. There ensued an eight-year war in which Paris attempted to put down the insurrection. In this the French were aided by the Americans, who, anxious to halt the advance of Communism, financed the effort and supplied large amounts of military equipment. The conflict came to an end in May 1954, when the Vietnamese overwhelmed the French fortress of Dien Bien Phu.

The French army's defeat led to negotiations in Geneva at which the French government agreed to withdraw from Indochina. Laos and Cambodia were declared independent, neutral nations. Vietnam was divided into two parts, separated at the 17th Parallel by a demilitarized zone (DMZ). Each part had its own government. To the north, based in Hanoi, was the government of Ho Chi Minh. South of the DMZ, in what came to be called the Republic of South Vietnam, was a pro-Western government. This soon was run by an ardent anti-Communist, Ngo Dinh Diem. In two years, so the Geneva Accords stated, an election would be held across all of Vietnam. The winner would rule a single, united nation.

The election never took place. Diem knew the outcome would favor

Ho Chi Minh, if only because the population of the north outnumbered that of the south. Ho himself violated several provisions of the agreement, and before long, the two sides were at war. Throughout the conflict, Vietnamese from the north would infiltrate villages and towns in the south. Ho and his comrades hailed these men as liberators. Others did not, especially because their tools of persuasion included terror, extortion, and murder.

In support of Diem, President Dwight D. Eisenhower provided military assistance to counter the growing Communist threat. This assistance included U.S. Army advisors. Their role was to train the South Vietnamese army (known to the Americans by its acronym ARVN, which was pronounced "R-VIN," and stood for Army of the Republic of Vietnam). President Kennedy significantly increased the number of advisors, so that by the end of 1963 some sixteen thousand American soldiers were teaching Diem's troops how to fight. General Earle Wheeler, who in 1963 was the army's chief of staff, called the advisors "the steel reinforcing rods in concrete."

The steel was strong, the concrete less so. In battle, ARVN troops often did poorly. Primarily, they suffered from the absence of capable senior commanders. Diem wanted generals who, above all, were loyal to him. He viewed talented generals as a political threat. Moreover, the good commanders were willing to fight, and this caused casualties, which added to Diem's problems. Shortcomings of the South Vietnamese army were revealed in January 1963 when, near the village of Ap Bac, ARVN troops were routed by the enemy.

Yet the problems for Diem and his American allies were deeper than the South Vietnamese army. The problem was South Vietnam itself. The country lacked political cohesion. It enjoyed no tradition of democracy or of central government. Its population was fragmented: different groups— the Buddhists, the merchants, the army, and the Catholics (who, though a minority, exercised great influence)—were loyal primarily to themselves. They felt little obligation to the state and seemed to thrive on corruption and self-interest. How Diem or anyone else could rule such a land was a question not easily answered.

The battle of Ap Bac revealed another problem that would make dif-

ficult the U.S. Army's campaign in Vietnam. Despite the negative outcome
of the fight at Ap Bac, U.S. commanders in Saigon, the capital of South
Vietnam (renamed Ho Chi Minh City early in 1975), insisted the battle
had been a victory for the ARVN. American media representatives knew
better. They challenged the commanders who, echoing the party line that
the South Vietnamese troops were improving and had carried the day,
refused to acknowledge the truth. And so began the skepticism on the part
of U.S. journalists covering the war toward pronouncements emanating
from the American army. As the war progressed, the skepticism would
grow. At times, the media considered army bulletins less than truthful. In
turn, army officials felt reporters emphasized the bad news and ignored
the good. More than a few army officers in Vietnam believed the media
wished the enemy to win.

Throughout the conflict, the enemy consisted of the Vietnamese native
to the south who were opposed to the government in Saigon, as well as
northerners who had been ordered to move south and challenge the Americans and their Vietnamese allies. Hanoi would claim that the native southerners were an independent entity, without ties to the north. Not so.
Communist leaders in North Vietnam were always in charge. To the
Americans the southern insurgents were the Viet Cong, or sometimes
simply "Charlie." The northerners were regular troops of the North Vietnamese Army known informally as "the NVA." Because President Johnson, in an effort to appear less warlike, had told the government in Hanoi
that the U.S. did not seek its destruction, most of the north's army was
deployed either in the south or next door in Laos and Cambodia. These
troops numbered in the thousands and, as American G.I.s would discover,
were tough, well-disciplined soldiers.

As 1963 drew to a close, the situation in Vietnam, from the perspective
of the United States, was deteriorating. Despite the presence of American
advisors, the performance of the ARVN left much to be desired. As important, if not more so, was the fact that Diem's rule was unraveling. There
was increasingly strong opposition to the man and his government. No
better example of the turmoil exists than the actions of the Buddhist monks
in Saigon. Several of them—to a worldwide audience—committed deliberate acts of self-immolation: they would drench their bodies with gasoline

then set themselves ablaze. So, with American acquiescence, the South Vietnamese army moved against Diem. On November 1, the generals struck. Diem was seized and killed.

There followed a succession of military-led governments, a few of which made efforts to improve not only the army but also the lives of the average Vietnamese, many of whom cared not a whit who governed in Saigon. At times these latter efforts, financed largely by the United States, produced the intended results. But, in the long run, marred by incompetence and by the corruption endemic to Vietnamese society, the programs failed.

President Kennedy had made a second key decision with regard to Vietnam, in addition to that of vastly increasing the American presence. He authorized a covert program of harassment and surveillance along the southern coastline of North Vietnam. South Vietnamese rangers raided the north while U.S. Navy ships conducted electronic espionage offshore. When Lyndon Johnson continued these operations, the stage was set for one of the more important chapters in the story of America's war in Vietnam.

Early in August 1964, the American destroyer *Maddox* was several miles off the coast of North Vietnam, carrying out electronic surveillance. Responding to this intrusion, North Vietnamese torpedo boats attacked the ship. The *Maddox* returned the fire, hitting at least one of the boats. An hour later, U.S. warplanes from a nearby carrier also struck the North Vietnamese craft. President Johnson chose not to reply further, but he did authorize the continuation of the spying missions.

Two days later, on the night of August 4, another destroyer reported (apparently erroneously) that it had come under attack. This time, LBJ hit back hard. He ordered the U.S. Navy to strike the torpedo boat bases. These were located at Vinh, on the coast of North Vietnam some two hundred miles north of the DMZ. Sixty-four planes from two aircraft carriers, the *Ticonderoga* and the *Constellation*, did so, severely damaging the base. Two aircraft were lost; one of the pilots was killed. The other, Lieutenant (j.g.) Everett Alvarez, became a prisoner of war (POW). He would be the first of many, eventually serving eight years in captivity before being released in March 1973 along with 586 other American POWs.

President Johnson's decision to attack the North Vietnamese naval facilities at Vinh served his political agenda. In the midst of the 1964 presidential election, LBJ could use the attack as proof that he was capable of being firm when necessary. This was particularly useful to his reputation as his Republican opponent, Senator Barry Goldwater of Arizona, a hardliner, was projecting Johnson as a timid liberal, unwilling to employ America's military might.

Not satisfied with the attacks on Vinh, Lyndon Johnson sought specific authority to take whatever steps he deemed necessary to repel further aggression against the United States. If he, as president of the United States, were to place America's armed forces in harm's way, he wanted the U.S. Congress alongside, sharing the responsibility. So Johnson went to the legislature and got what he sought. Known as the Tonkin Gulf Resolution, it gave the president a blank check for military action. The House of Representatives passed the resolution 116–0. In the Senate the vote was 80–2. That Lyndon Johnson withheld information regarding the South Vietnamese raids and the American surveillance missions made gaining approval of the resolution easier than it might have been.

Three months after the North Vietnamese fired on the *Maddox*, Americans again were attacked, this time on land and in South Vietnam. On November 1, 1964, the Viet Cong struck a small American air base at Bien Hoa, just north of Saigon. Four Americans were killed, twenty-six wounded. Four airplanes were destroyed. Then, in December, the VC blew up an officer's billet in the South Vietnamese capital, causing additional casualties. In February 1965, the VC struck again, with deadly results. They hit a U.S. Army helicopter base at Pleiku in the Central Highlands. Eight soldiers died. Seventy-six were wounded and several helicopters were disabled. Three days later the Viet Cong blew up a building in Qui Nhon, killing twenty-three Americans. Clearly, the VC were challenging America's presence in Vietnam.

Lyndon Johnson felt he had to respond. And he did. The president ordered U.S. marines to Da Nang in order to secure the airfield there. They arrived, in battle gear, on March 8, 1965. Soon thereafter, they were directed to undertake offensive operations against the Viet Cong. For all practical purposes, the United States had gone to war.

To this war the president fully committed the United States Air Force. Responding to the attacks by the VC, particularly at Pleiku, Johnson ordered American warplanes to strike targets in North Vietnam. Thus began the aerial campaign known as Rolling Thunder. A signature feature of the war in Vietnam, the effort continued, interrupted by several pauses, until the end of October 1968. In the long history of American arms, few operations, whether by land, in the air, or at sea, aroused such controversy as Rolling Thunder.

A typical mission of the Rolling Thunder campaign would involve sixteen or more attack aircraft. These would fly from bases in Thailand and, once airborne, would rendezvous with fighter escorts. Heading north, the aerial armada would refuel from air force tankers (military jets were and are gas guzzlers), receive guidance from nearby electronic warfare planes, and proceed into enemy airspace.

For much of Rolling Thunder the principal strike aircraft was the Republic F-105 Thunderchief. This was a large, single-seat fighter-bomber. The plane was fast (1,372 mph at 36,000 feet) and would carry 14,000 pounds of bombs plus several Sidewinder air-to-air missiles, the latter of which would be useful were enemy aircraft to be engaged (as was the 29 mm cannon carried within the plane's fuselage). Based at Korat and Takhli, the Thunderchiefs flew thousands of sorties. But the cost was high. During the war the U.S. Air Force lost 397 F-105s, nearly half the number built.

Also participating in Rolling Thunder, indeed perhaps the airplane most widely employed by the United States in Vietnam, was the McDonnell Douglas F-4 Phantom. This too was big and fast. But, unlike the F-105, it had a crew of two, a pilot and a weapons-radar officer. In Vietnam, the Phantom was used as both a fighter and as a bomber, as well as a reconnaissance aircraft. Early versions of the F-4 carried no guns. They were armed only with missiles. This turned out to be a mistake and soon was rectified. With its powerful radar and impressive rate of climb, plus the capability to carry tons of bombs, the Phantom was a formidable machine. That its General Electric jet engines emitted lengthy trails of black smoke, making the plane easily visible, was cause for concern. Yet the F-4 did well in combat, especially when crewed by men who knew their trade.

Although the Phantom equipped numerous air force squadrons, the plane was designed and manufactured for the United States Navy, which deployed the F-4 aboard its aircraft carriers (no doubt air force generals winced when ordering a plane its sister service had developed). America's naval air arm played an important part in Rolling Thunder. The navy placed three and sometimes four carriers off the coast of North Vietnam ("Yankee Station") as well as ships farther south ("Dixie Station"). These latter vessels provided air support to friendly troops on the ground in South Vietnam. The aircraft carriers to the north would spend three or four days conducting air strikes, then withdraw to replenish at sea, having depleted onboard supplies of food, ammunition, and the hundred or so odd things necessary to keep a large ship operating.

Both the navy and the air force pilots flying over North Vietnam during Rolling Thunder operated under strict rules of engagement. These specified what could and could not be attacked. Targets in and around Hanoi and Haiphong were off-limits. At first so were enemy airfields. When antiaircraft missile sites were being constructed north of the DMZ, the Thunderchiefs and Phantoms were not allowed to hit them, for fear of killing Russian technicians who were advising the North Vietnamese on how to operate the weapon. Further, the American planes were not to fly inside a twenty-five-mile buffer zone extending from Vietnam's border with China.

Needless to say such restrictions made Rolling Thunder less effective than it might have been. Pilots, in particular, objected to the rules. One F-105 pilot called them "extensive, unbelievable and decidedly illogical." Author Stephen Coonts said they ensured that the United States would not win the war.

Why were the Rules of Engagement put in place? The answer is that Lyndon Baines Johnson, not trusting America's senior military leaders, wanted to make sure that the conflict would not escalate, which it might if the North Vietnamese were to be hit extremely hard. He also wanted to minimize civilian casualties which, were they to occur in large numbers, would pose political problems for the president both at home and abroad.

U.S. generals and admirals chafed at the restrictions. Intent on winning the war, they wanted to bomb Hanoi (a city that, because of the rules air force historian Wayne Thompson described as "one of the safest places in Vietnam"), mine the harbor of Haiphong, cut North Vietnam in half by an amphibious invasion, and generally conduct the war in a manner guaranteed to bring the north, if not to its knees, at least to the bargaining table. If young Americans were to die in Vietnam, these commanders reasoned, did their country not owe them the goal of victory?

But President Johnson was so determined to keep control that he and his secretary of defense, Robert McNamara, instituted a targeting procedure unlike any that had ever been seen. Targets for warplanes striking North Vietnam had to be approved by the White House. Air force and navy leaders would submit proposed targets to the defense secretary, who would massage the list and forward his recommendations to the president. Johnson and a few civilian advisors then would choose what could be struck and what could not. Sometimes, they even decided what size of bomb could be used and what routes the aircraft would take going in and out of Vietnam.

Many targets made military sense. Bridges, rail junctions, and truck convoys were all permitted to be hit. But often, too often to the men who had to do the bombing, the targets seemed hardly worth the effort, or the risk. One F-105 pilot, Ed Rasimus, in a fine book recounting his experiences flying in Vietnam, wrote the following:

> The target itself was described as "approximately fifty barrels of suspected [petroleum]." The pilots had all agreed in the planning room that we must have indeed been winning the war if we were sending sixteen bombers, five SAM-suppression aircraft, eight MiG-CAP, two stand-off jammers, and eight tankers for fifty barrels of something buried at a jungle intersection. The briefing officer seemed a bit embarrassed by the target. . . . It wasn't his

*fault, so we didn't harass him. Credit for targeting rightly belonged
in Washington.*

To say this targeting procedure was unusual would be an understate-
ment. To say it made no sense would be more to the point. Surely, the
president of the United States had more important tasks than selecting
targets for Rolling Thunder. Lyndon Johnson didn't think so. He wanted
to be sure control did not pass to the military. His purpose was to limit the
war in Vietnam, and he thought target selection was one way to do so.

Johnson's strategy for Rolling Thunder was to increase gradually the
aerial violence. He believed that such an approach would induce the North
Vietnamese, who, realizing that even further destruction would be forthcoming, to come to their senses and agree to a negotiated settlement. Johnson believed he was acting rationally and responsibly. He was avoiding
overkill and, by ordering a number of bombing pauses, was giving the
regime in Hanoi an opportunity to act in a similar manner. The Central
Intelligence Agency (CIA) advised the president that this approach would
not work. The agency pointed out that the North Vietnamese Communists
were interested only in victory, which for them meant the removal of the
regime in Saigon, the withdrawal of U.S. troops from Vietnam, and the
unification of the two Vietnams under one rule, theirs. Lyndon Johnson,
a master of political compromise, thought differently. He believed the
North Vietnamese would act as he might act. They would see what he saw
and realize their interests would be served by agreeing to a settlement, thus
avoiding further destruction from American warplanes. But Lyndon Johnson was wrong, his strategy flawed. The North Vietnamese had no intention of agreeing to any settlement that deprived them of victory.

Ed Rasimus survived his tour flying F-105s, completing one hundred
missions over North Vietnam. Other pilots were less fortunate. They were
shot down, and either killed or taken captive. In 1966 and 1967 alone 776
U.S. airmen lost their lives. In total, the United States saw 992 aircraft
destroyed during Rolling Thunder. There were wrecks of Thunderchiefs
and Phantoms all over North Vietnam.

One of those F-4s went down on July 24, 1965, early in Rolling Thunder. What makes the event noteworthy was the cause of the plane's destruction. The Phantom was hit by a Russian-built SA-2 surface-to-air missile (SAM).

Deployed in great numbers throughout North Vietnam, the SA-2 was a modern air defense missile supplied in large numbers by the Soviet Union. With a warhead containing 420 pounds of explosives, the missile could bring down an aircraft at altitudes up to eighty thousand feet. However, the missile was susceptible to electronic jamming, a tool at which the Americans became extremely proficient. Both the U.S. Air Force and Navy produced specialized aircraft and tactics to jam the missile's guidance system. The air force called these planes "Wild Weasles." They were all two-seater warplanes that locked onto SA-2 transmissions and then fired a missile of their own at the launch site. While not always successful, the Wild Weasles put a major dent in the north's missile defense system.

During the war, according to SA-2 historian Steven Zaloga, a total of 5,804 missiles were fired at American aircraft. In the eight years of conflict, SAMs destroyed 205 U.S. planes. However, the impact of the missile was greater than this tally might indicate. That's because the SA-2s caused many of the attacking aircraft to jettison their bombs before reaching their target. Moreover, they forced American planes to dive to lower altitudes, bringing them within range of antiaircraft guns the North Vietnamese had placed all across their country.

The antiaircraft guns and the SA-2s were parts of a triad that together constituted a formidable air defense system. The third element of North Vietnam's air defenses was the MiGs. These were Russian-built jet fighters, and they constituted the core of the small but determined Vietnamese People's Air Force.

While the two air forces met in combat over North Vietnam, aerial battles were not frequent. Nevertheless, the Americans did shoot down 196 MiGs during the war. However, the primary objective of U.S. airpower was not the downing of MiGs. The principal goal was putting bombs on target.

Despite the extensive bombing campaign against North Vietnam, Rolling Thunder was not a success. Why? Because the campaign, though military in character, was essentially an exercise in international politics.

The purpose of Rolling Thunder was to convince the regime in Hanoi that the price it would have to pay to overthrow the government in Saigon was too high and that it should stop the infiltration of men and matériel into South Vietnam (these flowed south through Laos and Cambodia, along a series of trails nicknamed the Ho Chi Minh Trail). Notwithstanding the pounding by American aircraft, neither of these objectives was achieved.

However, Rolling Thunder did accomplish one secondary goal Lyndon Johnson and Robert McNamara had set for the campaign. The goal was to boost morale in the south and buy time for the government there to improve its effectiveness. Rolling Thunder sent a message to leaders in Saigon that, in the fight against the Communists, they were not alone.

More visible evidence of the American commitment was the increasing number of U.S. troops on the ground in Vietnam. After the initial landings at Da Nang in March of 1965, the number of soldiers steadily increased. By the end of that year, the army had 184,000 men "in country." Twelve months later the number stood at 385,000. By April of 1969 there were 543,400 American soldiers stationed in Vietnam. This represented the peak of the army's troop deployment. Afterward, that number declined. By December 1971, only 156,800 soldiers were in Vietnam. By the end of 1972, the number had been reduced to 24,200.

Other nations, allies of the United States, contributed troops as well. Australia, New Zealand, the Philippines, and South Korea all sent soldiers to Vietnam. And their numbers were not inconsequential. Australia dispatched some 7,600 troops, South Korea approximately 50,000. In its battle against the VC and NVA, the United States did not stand alone.

The buildup of troops that began in 1965 was intended to save the regime in Saigon from collapse, which it did. It also had the effect of turning the war into an American effort. Not everyone thought that was a good idea. CIA director John McCone told Lyndon Johnson that such increases meant the United States would get bogged down in a war it could not win. But Johnson, concerned by the political ramifications of defeat, approved the increases.

However, the president did not announce the troop deployments with any fanfare. Indeed, he downplayed them. Worried about the fate of his legislative initiatives, Johnson made every effort to conceal from the American public the expanding scope of the war. This, combined with the optimistic assessments of the conflict regularly issued by the army, would bring trouble in the future for both the president and his generals.

One of those generals was William C. Westmoreland. At one time the services' youngest major general, Westmoreland had attended Harvard Business School and, from 1960 to 1963, was superintendent of the United States Military Academy. More relevant to our narrative, from 1964 to 1968, Westmoreland was the senior American officer in Vietnam. He was the general in charge of the war.

Westmoreland's strategy was to aggressively go after the Viet Cong and the NVA. Despite requesting and receiving more and more troops, Westmoreland did not have the number that would enable him to occupy most of the battlefield (which comprised essentially all of South Vietnam). So he did the next best thing. He pursued the enemy, seeking them out, hoping to crush them via superior American firepower. This strategy came to be known as "search and destroy." Essentially, Westmoreland's plan was to wear down the enemy, to kill so many of the Viet Cong and North Vietnamese regulars that they would either give up or fade away. It was a strategy of attrition. For Westmoreland and his soldiers it was a sensible way to fight. Unfortunately for the general and his troops, it would not have the results he desired. This despite the fact that in combat with the enemy, the U.S. Army in Vietnam never lost a battle.

One of the first battles in which the U.S. Army encountered the NVA gave Westmoreland hope his strategy would prevail. In October 1965, in the Ia Drang Valley, the north had assembled a large number of troops with the intent of splitting South Vietnam in half. U.S. intelligence officers got wind of the plan, whereupon Westmoreland sent the 1st Air Cavalry Division into action. Transported by helicopter, the troops engaged the enemy and, after fierce fighting, emerged victorious. In the battle, the first in which a large unit of the American army participated, at least 600 North Vietnamese were killed. Many, many more were wounded. American dead numbered 305. The outcome helped convince the Americans they would win the war.

One reason for the U.S. Army's success in the Ia Drang Valley was the extensive use of helicopters. Roads in Vietnam were limited in number and size, thus making difficult the rapid movement of men and supplies. Employing helicopters therefore made great sense. These machines gave the Americans an advantage in mobility, which, when combined with the army's firepower, provided Uncle Sam's troops a formula for success.

Helicopters were used in Vietnam to locate the enemy, to carry troops into battle, to resupply them when necessary, to airlift the wounded back to hospital, and to withdraw troops once the battle had concluded. At times equipped with extra machine guns and rockets, helicopters also were employed as attack aircraft spewing forth death and destruction. Helicopters flew every day of the war. Such were their employment that, for Americans both in Vietnam and at home, they became the iconic image of the war. One type of helicopter was ever present. This was the Bell UH-1. Formally christened the Iroquois (as the U.S. Army named its helicopters after Native American tribes), the machine was universally known as "the Huey." Illustrative of the scale of the conflict in Vietnam, approximately 2,500 Hueys were destroyed during the war. Many of their pilots were among the 2,139 helicopter airmen killed in action. Another 1,395 men were lost from non-battle-related helicopter crashes.

During 1966 and 1967 the tempo of the ground war picked up as General Westmoreland moved aggressively to engage the Viet Cong and the NVA. That first year his troops conducted eighteen major operations. In 1967 two of his efforts received much attention. They were called Operation Cedar Falls and Operation Junction City. The first took place in January. Westmoreland sent thirty thousand U.S. and ARVN troops into what was known as the Iron Triangle. Comprising some 125 square miles, this was an area twenty miles northwest of Saigon, heavily infested with the enemy. A month later, the general launched Junction City. This too involved a large number of troops. It occurred in War Zone C, an area of 180 square miles close to the Cambodian border. In each operation, Westmoreland's soldiers did well, inflicting heavy casualties on the enemy. U.S.

casualties were light. In Operation Cedar Falls they numbered 428, in Junction City a little less.

In both endeavors Westmoreland's men won the day. The problem was that, while the general and his troops defeated the enemy, they did not destroy them. During both battles, and in a pattern that was repeated throughout the war, the VC and NVA would fight, disengage, and then escape into Laos or Cambodia (both countries theoretically were neutral, but in fact served as sanctuaries for those Vietnamese fighting the Americans). In other words the Viet Cong and the North Vietnamese regulars would live to fight another day.

Because the war in Vietnam did not involve traditional lines of separation between the two sides—no front lines existed, ahead of which lay the enemy—measuring success was not easy. Westmoreland could not point to a map and say his army had seized from the VC or NVA this amount of territory or that amount of land. How then to measure progress? The general had an answer. As his strategy was one of attrition, success would be measured by the number of enemy killed. Kill large numbers of VC and NVA, and success or failure could be determined. Or so the general argued.

Thus came into being one of the hallmarks of the Vietnam War. This was the body count. After each engagement, commanders reported the number of the enemy who lay dead on the field of battle. This number was reported up the chain of command, eventually reaching the secretary of defense, a man who relished statistics. Because an army officer's performance evaluation was influenced heavily by the number of enemy his unit had killed, the numbers often got inflated. This resulted in a focus on body counts as well as a distortion of the progress being made. That army officers in the field could not always distinguish between civilian dead and enemy killed made the metric even more unreliable.

This emphasis on statistics (some would call it an obsession) extended to the air force as well. Secretary McNamara wanted numbers, so what mattered to the generals in blue were sorties flown and bombs dropped. That the latter more than occasionally missed their target mattered little, and certainly less and less the closer to the secretary the general was. As noted above, Robert McNamara wanted statistics, and because he denigrated those who believed war was as much about morale and tactics, it was statistics he got. Then and now, many would agree that the man went to his grave not understanding the nature of warfare. He thought it was an exercise in accounting.

By the end of 1967, a year in which much fighting had taken place, both sides of the conflict had reason to worry. For the United States, casualties were mounting. Rolling Thunder was not working, and the ARVN still was not the fighting machine U.S. advisors had hoped to create. At home opposition to the war was growing.

In part, this opposition was stoked by the images of violence seen by Americans on their television sets. Vietnam was the first televised war. On nightly newscasts the people of the United States saw for the first time the ugly aspects of war. Often the images were shocking. The result was a conviction on the part of some that war in general was wrong and that this war, in particular, was immoral.

Among those protesting the war were religious leaders who spoke out against U.S. participation in what they deemed a civil war among the Vietnamese. Liberals too opposed the war, often not peacefully. Students, many of them eligible for the draft, took to the streets instead of the classroom. Making matters worse were the racial tensions endemic to an America that overtly discriminated against its citizens whose skin was black (and who, in large numbers, served in the army that was fighting in Vietnam). In 1967 and early in 1968, especially in April of the latter year, when Dr. Martin Luther King Jr. was assassinated, racial tensions exploded. People were angry, and civil discourse often gave way to violence. Yet, despite the dissent, Lyndon Johnson persevered. So did General Westmoreland, who continued to issue optimistic assessments of the progress being made.

In Hanoi no protests were taking place, but Communist leaders had cause for concern. Their casualties too were mounting, American troops were flooding the south, American aircraft were wreaking havoc all across their country, and the government in Saigon—whom they despised— seemed nowhere near collapse, and neither was the ARVN in full retreat. From their perspective the war was in stalemate.

In July 1967, the Communist leaders decided to break the stalemate. They fashioned a plan they expected would topple the South Vietnamese government, shatter the ARVN, cause an uprising throughout the south, and force the United States to withdraw. The plan—they referred to it as the General Offensive—would begin with attacks in the countryside to draw Westmoreland's troops away from densely populated areas. Then, having covertly moved men and supplies into position, they would launch strikes on the cities and towns across South Vietnam. To achieve maximum surprise, the attacks would occur during a traditional Vietnamese holiday when most people would be limiting their daily activities. The holiday, celebrating the beginning of the new lunar year, was called Tet.

The North Vietnamese initiated their General Offensive, which would become known to Americans as the Tet Offensive, as planned. Late in 1967, they and their Viet Cong compatriots began attacking American and ARVN outposts that were far from the populated centers of South Vietnam. One of these, Khe Sanh, became a major battle, longer and bloodier than either side had anticipated.

Khe Sanh was a marine outpost near the Laotian border, just south of the DMZ. When General Westmoreland received intelligence reports that the enemy was amassing troops there—eventually the NVA would deploy twenty thousand soldiers in the hills surrounding the base—he believed they were attempting to repeat their triumph at Dien Bien Phu. Westmoreland welcomed the news, as he was eager to engage the VC and NVA in a pitched battle. The resulting struggle—it began when the Vietnamese attacked the marines on January 23, 1968—lasted seventy-seven days. American casualties in the battle numbered 1,029, of whom 199 were killed. Reflecting the efficacy of American firepower, at least 1,600 of the enemy were dead, with thousands wounded.

In the United States the siege of Khe Sanh received extensive media coverage. Aware that loss of the base would be a political disaster, Lyndon Johnson required his military advisors to state in writing that the base would be held. Were it to fall, the president intended to deflect the inevitable flood of criticism to the military.

One reason the marines at Khe Sanh held the enemy at bay was the massive use of tactical air support. U.S. Air Force and Navy planes pounded the enemy with bombs and rockets, flying some twenty-four thousand air strikes. Joining the battle were the giant B-52s. These huge aircraft conducted numerous missions in support of the marines. Rarely has airpower been so successful.

The Americans believed Khe Sanh was a victory. The marine base was not overrun, while a large number of the enemy were put out of action. Yet the North Vietnamese also considered the siege a success. They argued that General Westmoreland was forced to pour reserves into the fight, thereby weakening the forces available to counter the main thrust of the General Offensive. Their official history of the war states that Khe Sanh represented "a serious military and political failure for the American imperialists. This failure demonstrated the impotence of their strategically defensive posture."

At the task of assembling men and weapons for the General Offensive the North Vietnamese proved masterful (no doubt helped by the fact that their agents had penetrated practically every organization comprising the government of South Vietnam). At having all their teams strike at exactly the same time they were less successful. A few of the teams attacked prematurely, thereby alerting the Americans, who, via intelligence sources, knew that the Communists were planning some sort of attack. When, as a result, General Frederick Weyand, one of Westmoreland's senior commanders, redeployed his troops, the Americans were in a much better position to repel the attacks.

The main strikes took place on January 21, 1968. They were hard-hitting and extensive. Vietnamese teams struck in thirty-six of forty-four provincial capitals, in sixty-four district capitals, and hit many, many military installations. In Saigon, they blasted their way onto the grounds of the U.S. Embassy. The scope of the attacks stunned the Americans. But Westmoreland's men rallied, as did the ARVN. Together, they threw back the attackers. In some places the fighting lasted several weeks. But, when it was over, North Vietnamese casualties were heavy—approximately forty thousand of the attackers were dead. American deaths numbered eleven hundred. Such were the enemy losses that the Viet Cong ceased to be a factor in the war. After Tet the United States was fighting the North Vietnamese Army.

One of the lengthier battles of the Tet Offensive took place at Hue, the old imperial capital of Vietnam. NVA and VC troops initially took control of the city and were thrown out only after fierce fighting, often door to door, by U.S. marines and ARVN troops. Lest anyone think that the Communists were simply freedom-loving Vietnamese seeking to reunite their country, it should be noted that while occupying Hue the Communists rounded up 2,810 individuals they didn't like and summarily executed them.

Atrocities, however, were not just the purview of the Communists. The U.S. Army also stepped over the line of civilized behavior. In March 1968, a small group of American infantry entered the village of My Lai and massacred more than two hundred civilians. At first the army attempted to cover up the incident. Eventually the truth came out and several officers were disciplined (though not harshly). Rarely have soldiers in American uniforms so disgraced themselves and the army in which they served.

General Westmoreland saw Tet as an American victory. He was wrong.

Shocked by the magnitude of the offensive, the American public considered Tet a disaster. Americans had been led to believe that the war was going well, that the end was in sight. Yet here was the enemy with strength assaulting targets all across South Vietnam. Particularly damaging were the reports and photographs of the VC attack on the embassy grounds. Nineteen VC sappers blew their way into the ambassador's compound (but never reached the embassy itself). All nineteen were killed, as were several Americans. The repercussions of this attack and of the Tet Offensive in general were enormous. American support for the war plummeted.

Without this support, Lyndon Johnson could not maintain the course he had charted. He thus took a series of steps that drastically altered the military landscape in Vietnam as well as the political landscape in Washington. He turned down General Westmoreland's request for 206,000 additional troops. He reduced the pace of Rolling Thunder. He convened a group of "wise men" to advise on how to proceed (they recommended he de-escalate the war effort—which he did). He initiated peace talks with the North Vietnamese. And, most dramatically, he announced in a televised speech to the nation on March 31, 1968, that he would not seek re-election.

Tet was a turning point. It caused the United States to back away from the war in Vietnam and forced an American president into retirement. In

Hanoi the regime no doubt rejoiced. Total victory, they believed, was within reach.

⸻

One year after the start of the Tet Offensive, the United States had a new president. This was Richard Nixon, who soon appointed Dr. Henry Kissinger as his National Security Advisor. Together, they made a formidable team. Both were smart, tough, and devious, characteristics that would prove useful in dealing with the North Vietnamese. Their overriding goal was to establish a new balance of power, one in which America played a key role in making the world safer and more prosperous. This meant reaching an accommodation with Communist China and, via the Strategic Arms Limitation Treaty, with the Soviet Union. The situation in Vietnam they saw as an obstacle to achieving this goal, so they embarked on an effort, often secretly, to bring American involvement in Vietnam to a close.

The president knew he had to bring about the withdrawal of U.S. troops, but he wanted to do so in such a way that America's honor was intact. This involved ensuring that a viable government of South Vietnam remained independent of the north. It meant also that he secure the release of the American prisoners held captive in Hanoi.

Most of these POWs were aviators, shot down during Rolling Thunder or later air raids. They numbered a little less than six hundred and constituted an important negotiating chip held by the Communists, who skillfully exploited the desire of the Americans to have these men returned. Their release was a political necessity for any diplomacy Nixon and Kissinger were to undertake.

Ensconced in the White House, the president embarked on four initiatives regarding Vietnam. The first was to begin, and then continue, the withdrawal of troops. By the end of 1969 some one hundred thousand soldiers had left. The second step was to build up the armed forces of South Vietnam to such an extent that they could survive once U.S. forces had departed. Consequently, tons and tons of military equipment were dispatched to the ARVN and to the South's fledgling air force. Next, Nixon had Kissinger begin secret discussions with the North Vietnamese aimed at bringing an end to the conflict. The National Security Advisor went to

Paris for these talks, but little was accomplished, for neither side was willing to make concessions the other considered essential. The fourth initiative was military in nature. Despite his Quaker upbringing, Nixon was no dove. He ordered the air force to strike the NVA hard and to strike it often.

One weapon the president wished the air force to employ more forcefully was the B-52. This impressive airplane could carry a large number of bombs, far more than either a Phantom or an F-105. Moreover, the plane had electronic devices on board that helped shield it from enemy missiles. Used extensively in Vietnam, the first B-52 mission took place on April 11, 1966. B-52s were employed tactically hitting targets in the south. They had not been sent north to Hanoi and Haiphong.

On March 18, 1969, Nixon ordered the big bombers to strike NVA troops and supply depots in Cambodia. Hanoi's forces had long used as a sanctuary Cambodian territory adjacent to South Vietnam. This, of course, violated the country's neutrality. They also had used the Cambodian Port of Sihanoukville on the Gulf of Siam as a major link for transporting supplies. Lyndon Johnson had denied his generals permission to attack these NVA enclaves. Richard Nixon had no such reservations. He sent the B-52s into action. Nixon kept these attacks secret. Not kept hidden was his next move: he ordered American ground troops to raid NVA bases in Cambodia. Some ten thousand U.S. soldiers joined five thousand ARVN troops in the attack. They killed a fair number of the enemy and destroyed large quantities of supplies, but they did not, as hoped, eliminate the NVA's presence.

The invasion into Cambodia lasted from April 29, 1970, through June 30 of that year. Militarily, the raid made sense. But at home it created a political firestorm. Why, asked Mr. Nixon's critics, at a time when the United States was reducing its role in Vietnam, did the army launch a new major offensive against a neutral nation? Students in particular objected. Many protested, some violently. As a result, a total of six students at Kent State University and Jackson State College were killed when fired upon by National Guard troops called out to restore order.

By the end of 1970, approximately 280,000 American soldiers remained in Vietnam. While a large number, it was far fewer than had served when U.S. troop levels peaked in 1969. Clearly, President Nixon was bringing the troops home. As their number decreased, so did their activity. In 1971, for example, General Creighton Abrams, who had replaced Westmoreland as commander of U.S. forces in Vietnam, conducted not a single major ground operation. American aircraft still flew combat missions, but on land the G.I.s no longer were on the attack.

Wisely, Richard Nixon believed the North Vietnamese would respect only force. So when the ARVN struck Communist bases in Laos (like Cambodia, an allegedly neutral state) he ordered U.S. air assets to support the South Vietnamese. No American ground troops were permitted to participate. The operation was called Lam Son 719. Involving nine thousand ARVN troops, it began on February 8, 1971. At first they did well. But soon outnumbered, they fell back, many in disarray. On both sides casualties were heavy. As an indication of the ARVN's readiness to fight on its own, Lam Son 719 was not encouraging.

One positive outcome of the ARVN attack into Laos was to delay the invasion of South Vietnam, planning for which was under way by the NVA. Making such an invasion possible, the Soviet Union had re-equipped Hanoi's army. No longer a lightly armed guerilla force, by early 1972 the NVA was a powerful and well-trained conventional army. It possessed large numbers of tanks, trucks, artillery pieces, and the like. With such a force North Vietnam reasoned it could at last crush the regime in the south. After all, by the spring of 1972, when the invasion began, U.S. troops mostly were gone from Vietnam and, as importantly, so were American aircraft.

———

The invasion began on March 30, 1972. Employing two hundred thousand troops, the NVA first struck across the DMZ, aiming for Quang Tri. Then, from Laos, they attacked in the Central Highlands, targeting the town of Kontum. Not wishing to exclude southern Vietnam, the NVA also attacked in the provinces northwest of Saigon. Known to Western historians as the Eastertide Offensive, the invasion was planned by Vo Nguyen Giap, Hanoi's army chief who had triumphed at Dien Bien Phu. Massive in scope, it also was ferocious in character.

Despite having half a million men under arms, the South Vietnamese army was thrown back, in all three sectors. While several ARVN units performed well, many did not, repeating a pattern all too familiar to U.S. advisors. As the NVA troops progressed, their commander was confident of victory.

General Giap, however, had not reckoned on Richard Nixon.

Responding to the invasion, the president decided to assist the South Vietnamese. Sending in U.S. ground troops was not politically feasible, so Nixon turned to one of America's most potent assets: airpower. He ordered air force and navy pilots back into combat. In one of his more memorable comments, Richard Nixon said, "The bastards have never been bombed like they're going to be bombed this time."

The U.S. aerial response to the Eastertide Offensive was code named Linebacker. In numbers alone the operation was impressive. From the Philippines and Guam, from Korea and Japan, and from airfields in the United States, aircraft returned to their bases in Thailand and South Vietnam. Indicative of the scale of the response, 168 airborne tankers participated in the campaign. Adding to Linebacker's punch were the B-52s, which flew 6,038 sorties attacking targets in the south. Tactical aircraft too were part of the effort: F-4 Phantoms headed north to targets well above the DMZ, as did naval aircraft from the U.S. Navy's aircraft carriers. To illustrate Nixon's determination to pound the North Vietnamese, targets around Hanoi and Haiphong, previously off-limits, were now subject to attack. As one historian of the Vietnam War, Dave Richard Palmer, has written, "Linebacker was not Rolling Thunder—it was war."

In first blunting and then halting the NVA, America's intervention proved decisive. NVA troops, pounded from the air, gave ground and, eventually, withdrew. Battles, however, took place for a period of six months. Quang Tri, for example, which the Communists had seized, was liberated only in September. When the fighting finally ceased, the NVA had suffered one hundred thousand casualties (a number that seemed to disturb Hanoi not at all) and gained little ground. Clearly, the invasion had failed. It's architect, Vo Nguyen Giap, was quietly replaced.

As American airpower was demonstrating its effectiveness, the president's National Security Advisor was in Paris attempting to cut a deal with the North Vietnamese. By November, Dr. Kissinger had announced that the two sides were close to an agreement. But at the last minute the talks broke down. The Americans concluded that the Vietnamese simply were stalling for time, while the north saw revisions to the agreement Kissinger was seeking on behalf of the South Vietnamese government as duplicitous. Regardless of which side was to blame, the talks were deadlocked. No agreement had been reached. Frustrated, Henry Kissinger returned to Washington to consult with Mr. Nixon.

Angry with the North Vietnamese, Richard Nixon once again turned to airpower. In an effort to get the north to sign an agreement, the president ordered his air commander to pulverize Hanoi and Haiphong. And this time the B-52s, symbol of American aerial might, would not be limited to tactical strikes in South Vietnam. For the first time, they were to be sent north. The president wanted the U.S. Air Force to dispatch the big bombers to the two cities and hit them hard. The goal was not to kill civilians (thus, some targets were still off-limits), but to level practically every conceivable military installation.

What followed is referred to as the Christmas Bombings. President Nixon and the air force called it Linebacker II. For eleven days, beginning on December 18, 1972, the B-52s struck the heart of North Vietnam. At first, the Vietnamese put up a stout defense, firing SA-2 missiles at the planes. These brought down fourteen of the bombers. Another B-52 was lost to MiGs, bringing the total number of B-52s destroyed to fifteen. Despite these losses, the air campaign succeeded. Having fifteen thousand tons of bombs dropped on them convinced leaders in Hanoi to resume the peace talks.

Negotiations began again on January 8, 1973, and agreement quickly was reached. That the north had no intention of honoring the terms of the agreement it had signed made little difference. Thanks to Richard Nixon and Henry Kissinger, the United States had found a way to extricate itself from what had been a long and bloody conflict.

Late in February of 1973 a U.S. Air Force C-141 transport plane lifted off the runway at Hanoi's airport. Aboard were former American POWs, now free. At least one of the conditions insisted on by President Nixon, that

Americans held captive be released, had been achieved. The other condition, that South Vietnam be allowed to remain independent of the north, was not to be realized.

Almost immediately after the agreement in Paris had been signed, the regime in Hanoi began planning another invasion. Aided greatly by having thousands of troops already in the south, troops that, by the terms of the Paris Accord, they did not have to withdraw, the Communists assembled men and military equipment for the attack. This took well over a year. By the spring of 1975, they were ready.

The attack began in March. Richard Nixon had pledged to the South Vietnamese that should the north again attack, the United States would come to its defense, as it had during the Eastertide Offensive. But in 1975 Nixon no longer was president. His successor, Gerald Ford, wished to render assistance. However, restrained by an American public tired of the conflict and by the newly enacted War Powers Act that limited presidential discretion in terms of military action, he was unable to do so. Thus Ford allowed North Vietnam's blatant violation of the Paris Accord to go unanswered. This time no American aerial armada would return to Vietnam.

In 1975, the army of South Vietnam still had many men under arms. While underequipped due to cutbacks in U.S. military assistance, the ARVN was battle-tested and seemingly capable of stopping the invaders. Most American commanders thought the army would put up a good fight.

They were wrong.

In perhaps one of the more dismal performances by any army in the twentieth century, the ARVN, when confronting the NVA, quickly collapsed. True, some units fought well, but overall, southern forces easily gave way to the troops of the north. When NVA tanks broke into Saigon's presidential palace on April 30, 1975, the war was over. South Vietnam, a country the United States, with its blood and treasure, had tried to keep afloat, ceased to exist.

The cost of America's failure was high. The war's memorial in Washington, D.C., a stark but compelling black wall, lists the names of 58,261 men and women who died in Vietnam. Their sacrifice appears to have been in vain.

Why did the United States lose the war in Vietnam?

Losing a war requires a definition of winning. In the case of Vietnam winning meant convincing the North Vietnamese to stop its efforts to overthrow the government in Saigon. Said another way, winning for the United States meant securing the independence of the South Vietnamese, enabling their government to be both sustainable and free. Unfortunately for America, Rolling Thunder and the two Linebacker campaigns did not persuade the regime in Hanoi to back off. Neither did the presence of more than half a million American troops.

But the underlying cause of America's defeat, its first in a military history generally characterized by victory, was a matter of political will. The regime in Hanoi was more determined to succeed, more willing to persevere, more accepting of casualties than its counterpart in Washington. Lyndon Johnson and Richard Nixon led a country that soon tired of the war in Vietnam. The United States lacked the stomach to make the sacrifices required. The Democratic Republic of Vietnam, based in Hanoi, did not.

Could the United States have won the war in Vietnam?

Whether the United States could have won is, of course, a matter of conjecture. Academics such as George Herring, author of *America's Longest War*, believe the war was unwinnable. They point to the lack of political cohesion among the South Vietnamese, to the inept leadership of the ARVN, and to the American public's unwillingness to accept casualties. These academics make a strong case.

But so do those who believe victory was possible. These tend to be military men, who argue that the war was fought incompetently, especially from 1965 to 1967, when the North Vietnamese were not as strong as they became in later years. These men note that had U.S. political leaders done what the country's military commanders advocated, the outcome would have been different. The American commanders in Vietnam wanted to hit Hanoi and Haiphong early in the war. They wanted to strike the Communist sanctuaries in Laos and Cambodia. They wanted to land marines halfway up the coast of North Vietnam, thereby splitting the country in half. Had the United States taken these actions, military leaders contend, the Communists would have been forced to halt their aggression in order to focus on the more immediate threat to Hanoi.

Whom to believe? The military men are correct in stating that America fought the war in a limited way. Why? Because as this narrative has stated, Lyndon Johnson did not want a repetition of the Korean experience, where hordes of Chinese soldiers crossed the border and crushed an American army. Whether the Chinese would have done so in Vietnam cannot be known for certain. Had the Chinese intervened, however, it is not unreasonable to believe that America's armed forces would have been able to contain them.

Yet the academics too have a valid point. The government in South Vietnam was not effective and the people there lacked political cohesion, democratic traditions, and allegiance to the state. But with more—and smarter—persistence on the part of the United States, could not a sustainable government in the south have been established? Probably so.

How then to answer the question? Could the United States have won?

America's war in Vietnam, this author believes, could have been won early on, by the more forcible application of military might. But victory was achievable only early on in the conflict, before the NVA gained in strength and before the American people grew weary of body bags. As it is now, the United States was then a military superpower, but its citizens' willingness to accept battle deaths was and is such that victory must be quick, before casualties mount. Otherwise, the country cedes the outcome to its opponent.

10

THE GULF

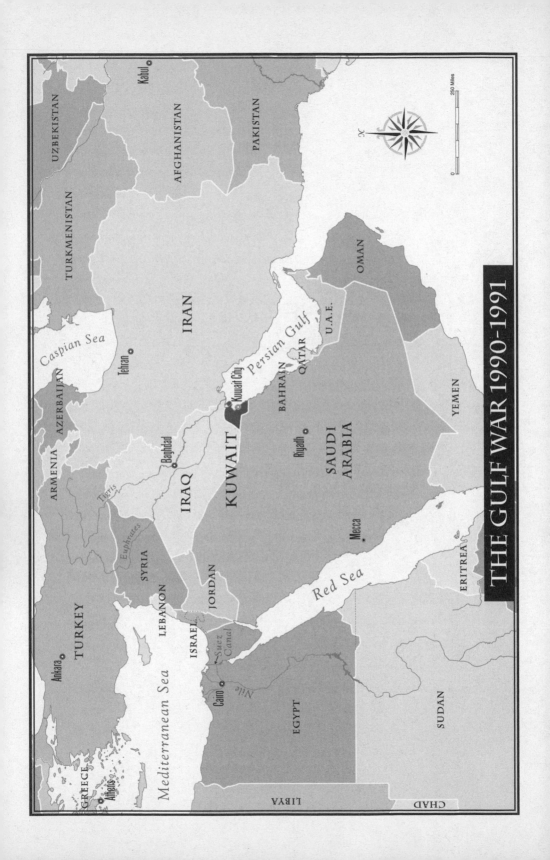

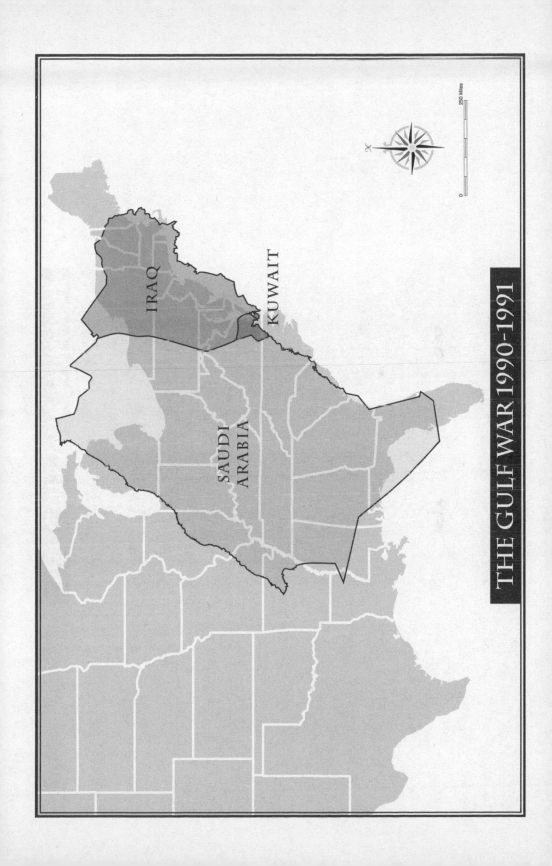

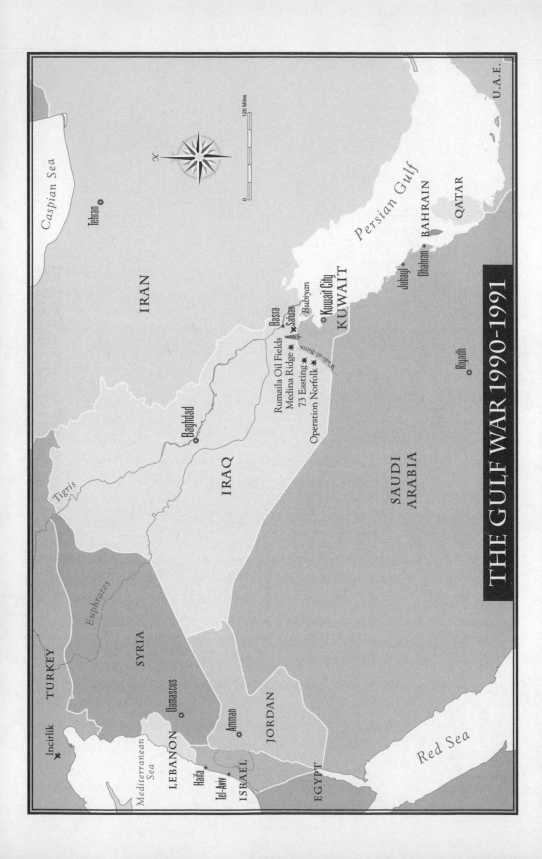

THE GULF WAR 1990-1991

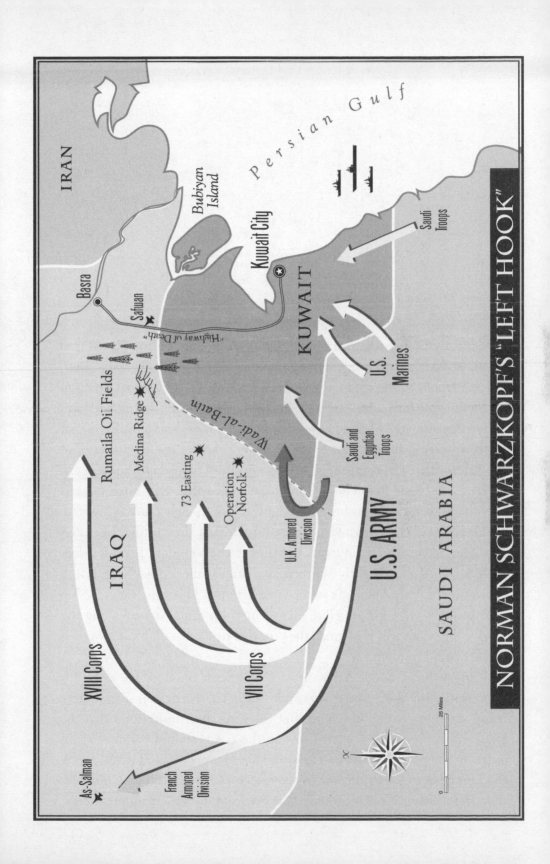

NORMAN SCHWARZKOPF'S "LEFT HOOK"

1990–1991

Late in July 1990, Saddam Hussein, the ruler of Iraq, personally assured Hosni Mubarak, the president of Egypt, that despite the deployment south of Iraqi troops to the country's border with Kuwait, he was not going to invade his much smaller neighbor. Foolishly, Mubarak believed Saddam. Why? Because, in addition to the Iraqi's pledge, there was a tradition that Arab countries did not make war on fellow Arab nations. Saddam, of course, had lied. On August 2, 1990, one hundred thousand Iraqi soldiers, led by tanks of the Republican Guard, the Iraqi army's elite force, crossed over the border, easily pushing aside Kuwait's outmatched armed forces.

Once in control of Kuwait, Saddam increased the number of troops and again redeployed them south, this time to the boundary Kuwait shares with Saudi Arabia. Rightly alarmed, the latter's rulers quickly agreed to consultations with America's secretary of defense. This was Dick Cheney, who brought with him satellite images of Iraqi units massed along the border. These images confirmed the very real threat Saddam's army posed to the Saudi kingdom.

King Fahd of Saudi Arabia was in a difficult position. He knew his conservative Islamic countrymen would object to American military forces being stationed in the kingdom. But the king also understood that the Saudi military was ill-prepared to stop the Iraqis should Saddam again order his troops into battle. The king and his advisors believed that if asked, the United States would come to the rescue of Saudi Arabia. No doubt, they were aware of a letter received earlier from an American president:

I wish to renew to Your Majesty the assurances . . . that the United States is interested in the preservation of the independence and territorial integrity of Saudi Arabia. No threat to your Kingdom could occur which would not be of immediate concern to the United States.

The president was Harry S. Truman. The letter was dated October 30, 1950, and delivered to Abdul Aziz Ibn Saud, then king of Saudi Arabia. Much later, Jimmy Carter and Ronald Reagan would write similar letters. These, like Truman's, merely echoed a pledge made to the Saudis in 1945 by Franklin D. Roosevelt.

Why did American presidents make such statements? The answer is simple. The pledges reflect a simple, well-understood deal: in return for a Saudi commitment to provide a continuous supply of oil to America and the West at a reasonable price, the United States would guarantee the independence of the Saudi kingdom. It was an arrangement that served the interests of both countries.

Before requesting America's protection, King Fahd laid down three conditions. The first was that U.S. forces would leave the kingdom when requested to do so by the Saudis. The second was that the Americans would not initiate combat operations without first obtaining his permission. The third condition, one on which the king placed great importance, was that American soldiers in Saudi Arabia would respect the Saudi way of life. With President George H. W. Bush's concurrence, Cheney accepted the king's conditions. The secretary of defense then set forth one of his own. He said that the Saudis would have to pay for the costs of maintaining U.S. troops in the desert kingdom. When the king agreed, the stage was set for the deployment of American troops to Saudi Arabia.

The first soldiers to arrive were from the 82nd Airborne Division, one of America's most elite combat units. In 1990, the 82nd was the U.S. Army's on-call division, constantly ready to ship overseas should the need arise. On August 7, one of the division's three brigades flew to Dhahran, a Saudi city on the Persian Gulf that became the port of entry for soldiers ordered to Saudi Arabia. A week later, more than twelve thousand troops had arrived.

These were complemented by U.S. marines, whose number eventually would grow to forty-two thousand.

While American military personnel were transported to Saudi Arabia by air, their equipment came by sea. The United States had prepositioned military equipment aboard ships stationed in several locations around the world. These vessels, and others, were ordered to the Persian Gulf so that fairly soon after the troops arrived, so did their equipment.

At first, as the buildup began, U.S. troops would not have been able to stop a determined Iraqi attack. Jokingly, the troopers of the 82nd called themselves "Iraqi speed bumps." Their presence was symbolic. They represented America's commitment to defend Saudi territory. As their numbers increased, and as military aircraft flew in, naval vessels took up station, and the U.S. presence in the Gulf region became formidable. By November, it had grown to comprise well over two hundred thousand men and women. That month, Colin Powell, the chairman of the Joint Chiefs of Staff, America's top military officer, told President Bush that the U.S. forces in Saudi Arabia were sufficient to defend Fahd's kingdom. The operation to build up the force and make it ready to fight had been given the name Desert Shield.

In command of all U.S. forces in the Gulf was Norman Schwarzkopf. He was a four-star general in the American army, the highest rank possible (in World War II Congress had established five-star generals, of which during the conflict there had been only four: Marshall, Eisenhower, MacArthur, and Arnold). Officially, Schwarzkopf headed up Central Command. This was one of six joint commands the United States had established to cover large geographic areas. Encompassing nineteen countries, Central Command focused on the Arabian Peninsula and adjacent waters. At the time, it was the least prestigious of the six.

Schwarzkopf was a good choice for the job. During World War II his father, an army officer, had been stationed in Persia administering Lend-Lease aid to the Soviet Union. As a youngster, Schwarzkopf had spent time there, so he was knowledgeable of the Middle East geography and comfortable with Arabian culture. As chief of Central Command, Schwarzkopf would prove more than capable of handling the diplomatic chores of his position. And, as we shall see, he also knew how to plan a war.

Previously, Central Command had focused on a possible invasion of Iran by the Soviet Union. Prior to Schwarzkopf's arrival that had been seen as the most likely scenario requiring a U.S. military response. Schwarzkopf, however, realized this scenario was no longer realistic. Once established in Florida, where Central Command was located, the general decided to have his planners take a new tack. "I was determined that the scenario . . . would be one in which the enemy was not the Soviet Union, but Iraq."

Two factors explain why General Schwarzkopf identified Iraq as a threat to U.S. interests within the lands assigned to Central Command. The first was the ruler of Iraq himself. Saddam, a thug, was someone who had little respect for the lives of others. Ruling through fear and intimidation, he considered war a tool of statecraft and was unfazed by the resultant loss of life. Moreover, Saddam was unpredictable. What made no sense to an American general such as Schwarzkopf might well seem appealing to the leader of Iraq.

The second factor causing Central Command to redirect its war plans was the Iraqi army. With 1.1 million men under arms, this was the fourth largest army in the world. Well equipped with tanks and field artillery, the army numbered far more than the defense of Iraq required. Additionally, Saddam's army was battle-tested. It had fought—and fought well—an eight-year war with Iran. Its units, especially the Republican Guards, were comfortable with combat, not just with parades in Baghdad.

One aspect of Saddam's military was of particular concern to Schwarzkopf, indeed to any opponent of the Iraqi army. This was its possession of chemical weapons and the willingness to use them. Saddam had employed such weapons against his own people. No doubt, he would be willing to use them in a battle against an enemy force. When the Gulf War began in 1991, nothing worried Norman Schwarzkopf more than the chemical weapons he expected the Iraqis to use against his troops.

Having had their numbers increased shortly after the invasion of August 2, by the following January the Iraqi forces in Kuwait numbered 545,000. This was no token force. It was equipped with several thousand tanks and more than three thousand pieces of artillery. Many of the tanks were Russian-built T-72s. While not the Soviet Union's top tank, the T-72 was well armored, had a powerful main gun, and in trained hands was a weapon to be reckoned with.

Saddam's army in Kuwait was positioned to repulse any effort to dislodge it. Most of the troops were massed along Kuwait's border with Saudi Arabia. Others fortified the Kuwait coast. There also were Iraqi troops in the west, but Saddam did not expect an attack from that direction because an invading force would have to maneuver through miles and miles of desert, something the Iraqi leader thought would be extremely difficult.

The Iraqi army considered itself expert in defensive warfare and with good reason. In the war with Iran, the Iraqis had constructed an array of integrated defensive positions that effectively repulsed many an Iranian assault. In Kuwait, in preparing for a possible attack from the south, the Iraqis built extensive fortifications. They laid down minefields. They rolled out barbed wire. They established supply depots. They constructed oil-filled trenches (to be set afire when the enemy approached). They dug antitank ditches. And they bulldozed large sand berms behind which partially hidden T-72s were deployed. Further, and importantly, they pre-located artillery "kill zones" onto which would rain massive amounts of explosives from the much vaunted artillery of the Iraqi army. Together, these obstacles created a military barrier that no invading force could take lightly.

In front of and behind these fortifications, Saddam's general established two lines, or belts, of men and machines. The first line, nearest the border with Saudi Arabia, consisted of second-tier infantry units. The second line of defense was made up of better equipped armored divisions and artillery brigades. The infantry's job was to slow down and disrupt the invaders, who then, mired in the obstacles constructed, would be destroyed by the firepower of the second line. In reserve, behind the tanks and artillery pieces, were the Republican Guards. These elite troops would be directed to spots where needed and would finish off any of the enemy who somehow survived the devastation wrought by the network of Iraqi defenses.

As the Iraqis concentrated on strengthening their position in Kuwait and Norman Schwarzkopf assembled a force capable of defending Saudi

Arabia, President Bush and his Secretary of State, James A. Baker, in Washington, focused on diplomacy. Their efforts had two targets: the United Nations and those countries that might join the United States in ousting Saddam from Kuwait. In these efforts, Bush and Baker displayed great skill and met with considerable success.

At the United Nations the Security Council acted promptly. It passed a resolution on the day of the invasion itself condemning the Iraqi action. In time, fourteen additional measures would be agreed to. These resolutions tightened the pressures on Iraq, which found itself increasingly isolated. Iraq's standing in the world was hardly helped when Saddam Hussein announced that Westerners in Iraq would be held hostage and placed next to possible military targets as "human shields."

The most significant Security Council resolution was passed on November 29. Frustrated by Iraq's intransigence, the U.N. council authorized the use of force to eject Saddam's troops from Kuwait if the Iraqis did not leave the country by January 15, 1991. With this resolution Bush and Baker had the international community's permission to go to war.

The president and the secretary, however, realized that should the United States be the only nation besides Saudi Arabia to do battle with Iraq, the Arab world might well view the Americans as Westerners typically taking advantage of Arab nations, all for the sake of oil. To counter this interpretation, Bush and Baker worked hard to build a coalition of nations allied to rid Kuwait of the Iraqis.

They started with Egypt, whose president was more than willing to help, given the blatant lie Saddam had delivered. Other Arab states in the region also signed up. These included Qatar, Bahrain, Oman, and the United Arab Emirates. Also joining the Coalition were two nations whose borders touched those of Iraq. These were Syria and Turkey. The former's participation was a surprise as it traditionally had (and still has) little love for the United States. Syria actually provided troops to Schwarzkopf's command, though at the last minute it declined to have them participate in the Coalition's offensive operations.

Turkey's participation in part was made possible by James Baker's visit to Ankara, where he enlisted the Turks' support. A key aspect of this support was permission for the Americans to use the air base at Incirlik, which meant that Saddam had to watch his northern borders and not fully commit military assets to either southern Iraq or Kuwait.

Of course, Bush and Baker targeted America's traditional allies as well. The result was that Australia, Canada, Denmark, New Zealand, and the United Kingdom joined the Coalition. So did Czechoslovakia and Poland, Morocco and Pakistan. In total, the two men, again demonstrating considerable skill, assembled a coalition of thirty nations intent on responding to the Iraq invasion. One of these nations was France, which deployed an armored division to the Gulf.

Perhaps the most important American ally willing to fight alongside the United States was Great Britain. Then possessing a first-rate military, Britain sent tanks, troops, and aircraft of the Royal Air Force. Eventually, British personnel in the Coalition would number some forty-five thousand men and women.

The British also committed naval vessels to the Coalition. Among these were ships essential to success in confronting the Iraqis, but in an arena of warfare that the U.S. Navy had neglected. This arena was mine warfare. The vessels were the Royal Navy's Hunt class boats, perhaps the most sophisticated coastal mine-hunting ships in the world. As the Iraqis had laid more than twelve hundred mines in the confined waters of the Persian Gulf, the British boats became indispensable.

By the fall of 1990, it had become apparent that diplomatic efforts to have the Iraqis leave Kuwait peacefully were not succeeding and likely would not be successful. The Americans began to plan an offensive strategy to remove Saddam's troops by force of arms.

The plan of attack was to be called Desert Storm. However, the number of U.S. troops then in the Gulf, approximately two hundred thousand, was deemed by Schwarzkopf to be insufficient. He wanted more soldiers and greater firepower. The four Americans making the decisions in Washington—Bush, Baker, Cheney, and Powell—gave him what he sought. Reserves were called up, and combat units stationed in Germany were dispatched to Saudi Arabia.

Among these units were two U.S. Army armored divisions. They were equipped with the finest tank in the world, the M1A1 Abrams Main Battle Tank. Previous American tanks had been outclassed by enemy machines. Not so with the Abrams. It was a high-tech wonder. The tank's armored protection was highly advanced, its gun and ammunition were extremely lethal, and its fire control system unequaled. The M1A1 was a superb weapon of war. Its only drawback was fuel consumption. An Abrams tank got 1.8 miles to the gallon.

Joining the two armored divisions from Germany were additional units, including one, the 2nd Armored Cavalry Regiment, that we shall hear of later in this narrative. Together, these forces, soon to include a British tank division, were called VII Corps (in U.S. Army terminology, a corps is two or more divisions and is commanded by a lieutenant general). Eventually, VII Corps would comprise 146,000 men. Its job was to smash the most powerful units of the Iraqi military, the Republican Guards.

A second U.S. Army corps also was assembled. This was XVIII Corps. It too was a powerful unit. As with VII Corps, it was equipped with artillery, infantry, tanks, and helicopters. Placed to the left of VII Corps, this strike force would have a different task, one calling for a quick flanking operation rather than a head-on direct assault.

Of course, the buildup of forces was not limited to ground troops. Aircraft too were deployed. These included the most advanced machines the United States Air Force possessed. One of these, the F-117, was an extraordinary tool of aerial warfare. True, it was small and not very fast. But by the use of exotic materials and radical design, the aircraft was invisible to radar. This meant that at night the F-117 was able to fly undetected to its target and back. In the plan General Schwarzkopf and his air commander, Lieutenant General Charles Horner, were devising, that target was Baghdad.

Also included in the air campaign being put together were aircraft belonging to the United States Navy. Saudi Arabia and Kuwait conjure up images of desert sand and oil derricks, not of ships at sea. Yet Kuwait has a coastline and the Saudi Kingdom is flanked by two bodies of water, the Persian Gulf and the Red Sea. Both would host American aircraft carriers.

The warships ordered to the region were not limited to carriers and minesweepers. They included cruisers, destroyers, frigates, and the always essential supply ships as well. They also included one type of vessel that all navies, save one, had long retired from service.

On October 14, 1990, the USS *Missouri* departed Long Beach, California, and steamed toward the Persian Gulf. She was a battleship, first commissioned in 1944. Heavily armored and packing nine enormous guns, the *Missouri* was the one of four Iowa class boats that had been modernized and returned to sea during the presidency of Ronald Reagan. Each had served its country well. Sent to the Gulf, the *Missouri* and her sister ship the USS *Wisconsin* would provide fire support to Coalition forces attacking Iraqi positions.

As Schwarzkopf received the troops and firepower he needed to conduct offensive operations, the ever present problems associated with assembling, maintaining, and training a large military force became critical. Logistics, the military art critical to battlefield success, was a constant concern to the Central Command leader. Troops arriving by air had to be reunited with their equipment that had come by sea. Tanks painted in dark green had to be repainted in desert sand. Soldiers had to be fed and housed. Medical facilities had to be established and sustained. Everyone in Saudi Arabia had to be issued gas masks and protective gear. By the time Schwarzkopf went on the attack, Central Command personnel numbered approximately six hundred thousand. Keeping them healthy and training them for desert warfare was a logistical challenge of the highest order. Fortunately for the American general, he had on his staff a little known officer who was a genius in the field of logistics.

The officer's name was William "Gus" Pagonis. A major general in the army, Pagonis planned, bargained, and borrowed in such a manner that the massive American effort in Saudi Arabia never once ran out of gas, literally or figuratively. So well did Gus Pagonis perform his duties that during the Gulf War he received his third star, making him a lieutenant general. His was the only battlefield promotion made during the conflict.

During the time of the American buildup an amusing incident took place at Schwarzkopf's headquarters in Riyadh. As noted earlier, the Saudis had agreed to pay for the stationing in country of American troops. One evening in late October the general was handed a piece of paper by a

Central Command staff officer. It was a check from the Saudis drawn on an account at Morgan Guarantee Trust in New York. Signed by Prince Khalid bin Sultan al-Saud, the top Saudi military commander, the check was in the amount of $720 million.

While the buildup gained momentum, General Schwarzkopf wanted to concentrate solely on preparing the Coalition's plan of battle. Of course, he was not able to do so. Other duties interfered, such as meeting with congressional delegations or heading off cultural problems with the Saudis.

The general was not alone in having to deal with distractions. The United States ambassador to Saudi Arabia, Chas Freeman, cabled the State Department in Washington as follows:

> *We understand the need to build and maintain congressional support. . . . It does not necessarily follow that Washington should treat Saudi Arabia as if it were an exotic game park with a four-star general and an ambassador as park rangers. . . . There must be a pause in trekking to Saudi Arabi. . . . Give us a break.*

By "Washington" both men were referring to political leaders who felt compelled to descend on Freeman and Schwarzkopf "to see for themselves" what the situation was in Saudi Arabia. These included U.S. senators and representatives whose support was essential to sustaining American involvement. Apparently, the visits paid off. On January 12, 1991, by which time Secretary Baker's efforts to resolve the crisis diplomatically clearly had not succeeded, Congress passed a resolution authorizing the use of force against Iraq. The vote in the House of Representatives was 250–183. In the Senate the vote was much closer: 52–47.

Despite these forty-seven votes, and what they represented, most Americans strongly supported President Bush's firm stand against the Iraqis, as did Colin Powell. He was pressuring Norman Schwarzkopf to come up with a detailed plan of attack.

In devising such a plan, the Central Command chief had to consider as well *when* an attack should be launched. Two factors affected the timing of an offensive. The first was Ramadan. This was to begin in March and last a month, during which time Arab troops in the Coalition might not fight. The second was that after Ramadan, the temperature in the desert would adversely affect the performance of both machines and men. So Generals Powell and Schwarzkopf, with the approval of the president and the secretary of defense, decided that unless a last-minute diplomatic solution was realized, Coalition forces would strike on January 16, one day after the deadline given to Iraq to withdraw from Kuwait had expired.

Such a diplomatic fix did not emerge. James Baker did meet in Geneva with the Iraqi foreign minister on January 9. But the Iraqi official made unacceptable demands, which the American secretary of state promptly rejected. That meant that eight days later, U.S. military forces in the Gulf, along with their Coalition allies, went to war.

Essentially, there were three ways to invade Kuwait. The first was to land troops on the country's coast via an amphibious landing. The second was to attack directly north from Saudi Arabia. The third was to swing Coalition troops around to the west and strike eastward from inside Iraq.

General Schwarzkopf rejected the first approach. He believed that, given the extensive fortifications and minefields the Iraqis had put in place, an assault from the sea would result in heavy U.S. casualties. However, the general kept twenty-four thousand marines on ships in the Persian Gulf and had them practice amphibious operations. These exercises, along with the presence of two American battleships, convinced the Iraqis that Coalition forces would be storming ashore in a manner reminiscent of the Marine Corps's World War II campaigns. Schwarzkopf wanted to deceive the Iraqis and he did. They kept seven divisions focused on an operation that never took place.

The second way to assault Kuwait, striking north from Saudi Arabia, was also an option the Central Command chief wanted the Iraqis to believe he was employing. Schwarzkopf placed a large number of Coalition troops, including those from Arab countries, on the Saudi-Kuwait border. These forces as well as an American unit in fact would conduct a direct assault into Kuwait, thereby reinforcing the general's intent to have his enemy perceive that this was the principal avenue of attack.

The approach Schwarzkopf adopted was the third option. He decided to have his most powerful strike force, VII Corps and XVIII Corps, at the last minute redeploy several hundred miles west, move into Iraq, and strike to the east. This was the now famous "Left Hook," which the general revealed to his commanders at a meeting in Riyadh on November 14. The plan was audacious, although the inability of Iraqi forces to conduct reconnaissance meant Saddam's troops were unaware that Schwarzkopf had repositioned his troops.

Given the boldness of the plan and the size and experience of the Iraqi army, Coalition casualties in Desert Storm were expected to be heavy. Estimates on the high side numbered 7,000 dead and 13,000 wounded. To accommodate the latter, Central Command had established several hospitals and had made available, according to an official U.S. Army history, 13,350 beds for medical use. The U.S. Navy also prepared for casualties. At the time, the American naval service possessed two hospital ships, the *Mercy* and the *Comfort*. Both were sent to the Gulf.

Prior to the ground attack, Schwarzkopf's plan called for an extensive aerial assault. This was to strike strategic targets throughout Iraq, gain control of the skies above the battlefield, and pound the enemy troops in Kuwait. Saddam and his generals had no idea how destructive this assault was to be.

The first aircraft, six U.S. Army Apache helicopters, lifted off in the early morning hours of January 17 (in Washington, D.C., it was mid-afternoon of the 16th). They struck Iraqi air defense radars just inside the border, thereby creating a corridor through which Coalition planes could safely enter Iraqi airspace. More than six hundred planes took part in this first day of the attacks. They struck targets throughout Iraq, hitting the enemy's command posts, its communications network, and suspected nuclear, biological, and chemical facilities. Among the American aircraft employed were the F-117 Nighthawks. These aeronautical marvels flew to downtown Baghdad and dropped their bombs on target, neither detected by Iraqi radar nor hit by the erratic gunfire the defenders threw up into the night sky.

Only four Coalition aircraft were lost that first night. Throughout the air campaign—which lasted forty-four days—losses were slight. In total, fewer than forty planes were downed by enemy action. Given that Coalition air forces flew 44,145 combat sorties during the war, the number of aircraft lost was minimal.

One reason for the air campaign's success was the dismal performance of Saddam's air force. Though well equipped and by no means small, the Iraqi air arm was outmatched by its counterparts from Great Britain, the United States, and Saudi Arabia. Air forces of the latter two countries flew the F-15 Eagle, then the world's premier fighter aircraft. The Eagles accounted for nearly all of the thirty-four Iraqi machines downed in combat. However, most of Saddam's pilots declined to fight, and more than 120 flew their planes to Iran, where they and their aircraft were interned.

Coalition aircraft controlled the skies above both Iraq and Kuwait. One attack on the former received much publicity as a large number of civilians inadvertently were killed. The target was a reinforced concrete bunker in Baghdad the Iraqis used as a military command center. An F-117 destroyed it with two 2,000-pound "smart bombs." Regrettably, the night of the attack, and unbeknownst to the Americans, Iraqi civilians were inside using the facility as an air raid shelter. Some four hundred individuals, including children, lost their lives. Saddam's propaganda ministry made certain the world knew of the incident.

The use of these smart bombs was a hallmark of the Gulf War. These were bombs that were able to strike their targets with great accuracy. In previous wars bombing strikes were hit-and-miss affairs. Collateral damage often was heavy, because many of the bombs would miss their intended targets. Technology changed that. Targeting systems and the bombs themselves became precision weapons. They now could hit what they were aimed at. This meant not only that nearby buildings and people were left untouched, but also that fewer planes needed to be involved in the attack, thereby reducing the risk to the attacking force.

In the 1990–1991 war against Iraq, smart bombs received their baptism of fire. They also gained considerable public attention as television audiences in the United States and elsewhere became accustomed to viewing Iraqi targets being blown apart by a single bomb. In fact, while smart bombs were employed in the battle against Saddam, their number was limited. Most of the destruction from the air came from old-fashioned, unguided "iron bombs."

One of the new precision weapons first employed in the Gulf War was the Tomahawk cruise missile. Essentially, this was a flying bomb. Launched from a ship it flew at subsonic speed over a long distance and, with a sophisticated guidance system, exploded directly on its target.

During the first night of the air campaign, January 17, six Tomahawks were fired by the battleship *Missouri*, which was positioned in the Gulf several miles southeast of Kuwait. Across the Arabian Peninsula, in the Red Sea, the USS *San Jacinto*, an American cruiser, launched Tomahawks as well. Surface ships were not alone in using the missile. On January 19, 1991, an American attack submarine fired a Tomahawk at a target in Iraq. This was the first time in history that a submerged warship had sent off a cruise missile in wartime.

On that first day of air strikes, 122 Tomahawks descended on enemy targets. In total, 282 of the sea based cruise missiles were dispatched during Desert Storm. Each Tomahawk cost approximately $1.2 million. Several were shot down by the Iraqis. To save money and to not deplete the navy's supply of the weapon, General Powell ordered Schwarzkopf to halt their use, which he did. More than one admiral believed Colin Powell, an army officer, did so because of the favorable media coverage the U.S. Navy received from the success of the Tomahawk.

Cruise missiles were not part of Saddam's navy. Less favored by the Iraqi leader than his army and air force, the Iraqi sea service consisted mainly of small missile boats. The boats were well armed and posed a threat to Coalition warships operating in the Gulf, so they drew the attention of British and American naval commanders. On January 29, near the Kuwaiti island of Bubiyan, aircraft from American and British ships destroyed a large number of the Iraqi boats. The action has been given the name "the Bubiyan Turkey Shoot" for it was a lopsided affair. All the Iraqi missile boats were put out of action, as were thirteen other Iraqi vessels. With Saddam's surface ships no longer a concern, Coalition maritime commanders could breathe easy. But the Iraqi minefields remained a problem. On February 18, they scored a success. Two American warships struck Iraqi mines. Damage was such that both vessels had to withdraw from the battle zone.

One additional naval action deserves mention. To protect Coalition warships, Dutch, Australian, and British ships were assigned air defense duties. This they did well, especially the Royal Navy destroyer HMS *Gloucester*. On February 25, the Iraqis fired two Iranian-built Silkworm missiles at American warships that were shelling Iraqi positions ashore. One of the American vessels was the *Missouri*. As the missiles closed on the battleship and its escorts, one of them fell into the sea, causing no damage. The other proceeded on course. *Gloucester* then fired two Sea Dart missiles, one of which destroyed the remaining Silkworm. The postscript to this episode is that the *Missouri* then located the Silkworm's launch battery and, with its big guns, blew it apart.

As the air strikes continued, Iraqi military assets inside Kuwait increasingly were targeted. The goal was to reduce their combat effectiveness by half, especially the T-72 tanks, which the Iraqis possessed in great number. Whether the air strikes accomplished that goal remains in dispute, although no doubt exists that the Iraqi army's inventory of fighting vehicles was greatly reduced.

Pounded from the air, Saddam responded in kind, but with a weapon far different than what Coalition forces were using. This was the Scud, a crude ballistic missile that carried a very small warhead and was not terribly accurate. As a military device the Scud was little more than a nuisance. But when launched at cities, it became a weapon of political terror, with great psychological impact.

The first Scuds were fired on January 18. They struck the Israeli cities of Haifa and Tel Aviv. By targeting the Jewish state, Saddam hoped to have the Israelis retaliate. Were they to do so, Arab nations in the Coalition would be seen as allied with Israel in a war against another Arab state. This would be unacceptable in the Arab world and would necessitate a withdrawal from the Coalition. Egypt and Saudi Arabia especially could not be seen as partnering with Israel.

Saddam's strategy was clever, but it did not work. At the urging of President Bush and Secretary Baker, Israeli leaders refrained from responding. This represented a significant change in policy, as the Israeli position was to always strike back when attacked. Helping the Israelis exercise restraint was the immediate deployment of U.S. Army Patriot missiles to Israel. These were intended to shoot down any incoming Scuds. An additional incentive to the Israelis was the promise of additional military aid from the United States.

In total, Saddam launched eighty-six Scuds during the war. They caused very little physical damage, save for one strike. This took place on February 25, when a Scud hit a U.S. army barracks in Dhahran. Twenty-eight Americans were killed, and almost a hundred were wounded.

Numerous Patriots were fired in attempts to destroy the incoming Scuds. At the time, the American missiles were seen to be successful. In fact, they were not. Often the Scud broke apart as it nosed down on the target, and the Patriot might hit one of the pieces, with the rest, including the warhead, landing on the city below. The Patriot's value lay less in its actual ability to intercept the Scud than in the belief, at the time, that it was able to do so.

The best way to stop the Scuds was to prevent their launch. British and American Special Forces, therefore, operated inside Iraq trying to destroy their launch sites. Stationary Scud batteries were put out of commission. But mobile facilities (essentially trucks with Scuds) proved difficult to locate, so many remained untouched.

Political pressure to halt the Scud attacks was immense. Coalition aircraft devoted considerable resources to hunting the missiles, with results far from satisfactory. Despite the large number of warplanes allocated to finding them, the Scuds never were put out of action.

As Coalition planes each day struck targets in Kuwait and Iraq, diplomatic efforts to resolve the crisis continued. One last such effort was made by Mikhail Gorbachev, the Soviet leader, who dispatched a special envoy to Baghdad. This, like other diplomatic initiatives, failed. Days later, when Saddam rejected President Bush's final ultimatum to withdraw from Kuwait, the time had arrived for Coalition ground forces to enter the fray. They attacked on February 24, 1991.

Schwarzkopf had deployed forces along the Saudi border with Kuwait. Adjacent to the Persian Gulf were troops belonging to Egypt and Saudi Arabia. Farther west was a second group of Arab soldiers. In between were two divisions of United States marines, supplemented by a U.S. Army armored brigade. Still farther west was Schwarzkopf's "iron fist," VII Corps and XVIII Corps, which included the British and French armored units. In its totality, the Coalition's army—some 620,000 soldiers—was one of the most powerful military forces ever assembled.

Early on the 24th, across a 270-mile front, Coalition troops went on the offensive. Tanks plowed through sand berms, troops carved pathways through the minefields, helicopters flew low firing rockets, artillery lit up the sky (the U.S. 1st Infantry's artillery delivered more than six hundred thousand bomblets within a period of thirty minutes). At the receiving end of this massive firepower were the Iraqi defenders. Poor souls, they were overwhelmed. Some chose to fight and they were killed. Many more simply gave up, and lived. On that first day of combat, some thirteen thousand surrendered.

Along the coast, Egyptian and Saudi troops (and a few Kuwaiti soldiers who had escaped from the Iraqis) made good progress. Supported by naval gunfire, these troops engaged their foe and beat them back. They would be the first Coalition units to enter Kuwait City.

To their left, the U.S. marines also made good progress. By the second day, after beating off Iraqi counterattacks, they were but ten miles from the Kuwaiti capital. Unusual for the marines, they had fought several tank battles, taking on the Iraqi T-72s. By the time the marines had secured Kuwait's international airport, more than three hundred enemy tanks no longer were in service.

To help convince Saddam's generals that the main thrust of the Coalition forces would be a northward strike into southern Kuwait from Saudi Arabia, Schwarzkopf had directed that those U.S. troops in the west not part of the Left Hook also attack the Iraqis directly opposite them. This took place and was carried out by the American 1st Infantry Division. Its commander, Major General Thomas Rhame, wanted to win quickly and with, he joked, "enough of us left to have a reunion." The division accomplished the former and no doubt later enjoyed the latter.

The most striking element of Norman Schwarzkopf's plan of battle—and the most risky—was the flanking maneuver required of his two most powerful units. They were to charge into the southern Iraqi desert then turn ninety degrees and hit the Republican Guards from the west. The two units, VII Corps and XVIII Corps, were well equipped for the job. As has been noted, they were armed with tanks, helicopters, and artillery, all of which were high-tech and deadly.

The role of XVIII Corps, and its 118,000 soldiers, was to race north from a point 350 miles inland to the Euphrates River and, once there, to (1) block the retreat of Republican Guard forces from Kuwait, and (2) then alter course and join the assault toward Kuwait City. With considerable skill and speed, the corps did both. One of its component units, the 101st Airborne Division, conducted the largest combat air assault in history when three hundred of its helicopters transported two thousand of its soldiers into battle.

VII Corps's role was to smash the Republican Guard units in Kuwait. In February 1991 it fought a series of small but nasty engagements close to the Wadi al-Batin. This is a lengthy dry riverbed that essentially marks Kuwait's western border with Iraq. Together, these engagements, at 73 Easting, at Medina Ridge, at Norfolk, and at other locations (including one designated Waterloo where British tanks defeated the Iraqis) have been given the name of the Battle of Wadi al-Batin. They were all limited in duration but violent in character.

Seventy-three Easting was simply a place on U.S. Army maps (initially such was the shortage of maps that the Pentagon's Defense Mapping Agency had to produce 13.5 million of them). The desert terrain was so featureless that American units depended on artificially drawn grid lines to identify where they were and where they were going. In the Iraqi and Kuwait deserts there were no towns, rivers, or hills to serve as points of reference. Seventy-three Easting was inside Iraq, several miles north of VII Corps's departure point. Late in the afternoon of February 26, the Corps's forward reconnaissance unit, the 2nd Armored Cavalry Regiment, did what it was supposed to do. It found the Iraqi Republican Guard armored units. These were dug in, with their tanks half-buried on the downward slope of a rise in the desert, waiting to ambush the Americans. It was a classic defense position, one the Iraqis believed would lead to victory.

It did not. The Iraqis were too far back and their aim was off. The Abrams fired on the move, making Iraqi artillery fire ineffective, and the tanks' lethal shells blasted through the sand barricades, destroying the T-72s.

Douglas Macgregor, an American officer who fought in the battle, described the action. His account, while referring to the engagement at 73 Easting, applies as well to the other battles along the Wadi al-Batin. Writes Macgregor:

> *Metal smashed against metal as killing round after killing round slammed into the Iraqi army's Soviet-made tanks. A few hours later, the few surviving Republican Guards, exhausted men in dirty green uniforms, huddled together as prisoners of war in the nighttime cold.*

Macgregor also described the violent character of modern combat between tanks:

> *Armored warfare is hair-trigger fast, frighteningly lethal, and unforgiving. Men are vaporized, eviscerated, blown apart, asphyxiated, or burned to death when an incoming tank projectile or missile strikes, and the margin between victor and vanquished can be a fraction of a second.*

The speed at which the "frighteningly lethal" combat between American and Iraqi tanks occurred at 73 Easting is illustrated by noting that the 2nd Armored Cavalry Regiment destroyed thirty-seven T-72s in less than six minutes. A somewhat similar outcome took place at Medina Ridge. There, the Iraqis lost 186 tanks in a matter of hours. The two battles and several others demonstrated the superiority of the Abrams and their crews. In total, during its eighty-nine hours of combat, VII Corps destroyed 1,350 enemy tanks and more than 1,200 armored personnel carriers, against the loss of four tanks and a small number of armored vehicles. Victory belonged to the Americans.

Schwarzkopf's plan had worked, and brilliantly. The Republican Guards had been defeated. But they had not been destroyed. The Central Command chief thought he knew why. VII Corps had moved too slowly.

During the battle, he had let his impatience be known to the VII Corps commander, Lieutenant General Fred Franks. Franks, a cautious field commander, had wanted to concentrate his assault forces and have them ready logistically. This took time. Moreover, he wanted to be sure that, once his soldiers pulled the trigger, they were not inadvertently aiming at fellow Americans.

Who was correct? Swiftness in battle is often a virtue. But so is preparation. Significantly, in his memoirs, Schwarzkopf backed off his criticism of Franks, writing:

> *I . . . also decided that I had been too harsh in my criticism of VII Corps' slow progress during the ground battle. . . . Franks was a fine commander who had carried out his assigned mission as he had seen it. . . . What I did know was that we had inflicted a crushing defeat on Saddam's forces and accomplished every one of our military objectives. That was good enough for me.*

With the Iraqis' defeat in battle and with their subsequent withdrawal from Kuwait, President Bush directed that a cease-fire be put in place. It took effect in Iraq on February 28. One highly visible event encouraged the American leader to believe the time had come to end the loss of life.

Highway 6 links Kuwait City and the Iraqi town of Basra. As the Iraqis were fleeing toward Basra on the highway, they were attacked by Coalition aircraft. The planes wreaked havoc on the Iraqis. More than fifteen hundred vehicles were destroyed, and initially the number of people killed, civilians among them, was estimated to be extremely high. Images of this "Highway of Death" were flashed around the world. The gruesome pictures suggested that the Coalition clearly had triumphed and that further killing would be inhumane.

Despite the cease-fire, one last firefight took place. On the morning of March 2, a Republican Guard unit, seeking to return home, fired on the 24th Mechanized Infantry Division near the Rumaila oil fields. The Americans did more than just return fire. They launched a full-scale counterattack. The result was the same as at 73 Easting and Medina Ridge. The Iraqis suffered heavy losses while the Americans lost only a single tank.

Formal cease-fire talks took place on March 3, at an Iraqi airfield near the village of Safwan. Conducting the talks inside Iraq, Schwarzkopf believed, would emphasize to the Iraqis that indeed they had lost the war. Representing Saddam's side was the deputy chief of staff at the Iraqi Ministry of Defense, a three-star general. For the Coalition the two senior officials were the Central Command chief and Khalid Bin Sultan al-Saud, Saudi Arabia's counterpart to Schwarzkopf. To further emphasize to the Iraqis their defeat in battle, their delegation had to arrive at the airfield through a cordon of Abrams tanks while Apache helicopters circled in the skies above.

Discussion at the airfield centered on the return of prisoners, accounting of the dead, the identification of minefields, and the release of Kuwaiti citizens held by the Iraqis. In addition, there were to be restrictions upon the Iraqi air force, although, at the special request of the Iraqi three-star, Iraqi helicopters were given permission to fly. They were allowed to do so in order to be able to move people and supplies throughout the country. That Saddam later would employ these airships to repress groups in Iraq he did not care for was, for the Americans, an unintended result they came to regret.

U.S. casualties in the Gulf War were light, although sources differ as to the exact number. One reputable publication, produced by the Naval Institute Press of Annapolis, lists the total number of American dead at 304, of which 122 came about from combat. The rest were the result of either accidents or natural causes. Regrettably, of the combat deaths, 35 came from friendly fire.

The number of Iraqis killed is but an estimate. At least 10,000 soldiers and civilians appear to have lost their lives, although the number might well be greater. What is not uncertain is that in defeat the nation of Iraq saw many, many of its citizens pay dearly for Saddam Hussein's folly in invading Kuwait.

Why did Saddam invade Kuwait?

Saddam believed that the lands comprising Kuwait historically belonged to the empires from which modern-day Iraq emerged. Moreover, he considered Kuwait to be an artificial construct of the British (which it was, although its legitimacy as an independent nation was recognized by most nations in the world). Additionally, Saddam claimed that the Kuwaitis, by drilling at an angle, were stealing petroleum from Iraq's portion of the Rumaila oil field. This huge oil deposit lay beneath the borders that delineate Kuwait and Iraq. Perhaps equally important, Saddam wanted the access to the Persian Gulf which Kuwait possessed and Iraq did not. Then, of course, there's the enormous debt Saddam had incurred as a result of his war with Iran. Arab nations, including Kuwait, had loaned Iraq large sums of money. The Iraqi leader argued that he had fought the war on behalf of his Arab brothers and that they, therefore, should reduce the debt, if not forgive it altogether. He particularly wanted Kuwait to forgive its share of the debt. Kuwait offered to reduce the amount owed, but not to eliminate the entire debt. This left Saddam angry with the Kuwaiti leaders, and his country in financial difficulty. What better way to solve the problem and other concerns than to remove Kuwait itself from the scene?

Why did Saddam believe the United States would not go to war over Kuwait?

He had good reason to so believe. America had been supportive of Saddam's war with Iran, and when the United States ambassador to Iraq, April Glaspie, met with him prior to the Kuwait invasion, she, following State Department instructions, did not state with specificity what the U.S. response to an invasion would be. She said merely that the United States wished to see a peaceful solution to the dispute.

Yet Saddam, in his own mind, had a more compelling reason to conclude that the United States would stand idly by as Iraqi forces took control of Kuwait. He believed America and its citizens lacked the stomach for any military action likely to result in heavy loss of life. After all, had not U.S. marines ignominiously left Beirut after losing only two hundred of their men, when Ronald Reagan had deployed troops to the Lebanese capital? If the United States did send troops to aid Kuwait, Saddam foresaw "the mother of all battles" in which America would have thousands of men killed. Iraq, he knew, would accept such losses. He was convinced the United States would not.

Did the Iraqis have any realistic chance of winning the war?

No. Coalition forces, particularly those of the United States and Great Britain, simply outclassed Saddam's military. In both equipment and personnel what the Coalition put onto the battlefield was superior to what the Iraqis possessed. American (and British) forces were well trained and well led. And, with their technological edge on the field of battle they crushed their Iraqi opponents.

Did the Iraqis fight poorly?

Certainly the Iraqi air force did. That some eighty-six thousand Iraqis were taken prisoner by Coalition forces suggests that Saddam's army underperformed as well.

Why did Saddam not employ his chemical weapons?

Because the Iraqi leader was uncertain how the United States might respond. No doubt, the U.S. government conveyed to the Iraqi leadership that in the event of chemical attacks, America would respond in a manner that would bring enormous harm to Iraq.

Why did the Coalition forces under General Schwarzkopf, once the Iraqis had left Kuwait, not proceed to Baghdad and finish off Saddam and his regime?

It's true that Schwarzkopf's army could have continued on to Baghdad, destroying both the Republican Guards and Saddam's regime. But that's not what President George H. W. Bush had defined as his objective or what the United Nations had authorized. Moreover, most Arab nations, however much they despised Saddam Hussein, were uneasy with the prospect of an American army unseating an Arab government whose legitimacy they accepted. Had the Americans and British made known their intention to march on the Iraqi capital, the Coalition that President Bush and his secretary of state had so skillfully put together, would have splintered, thus jeopardizing the effort to remove the Iraqis from Kuwait.

**Was there a lesson from the Gulf War
that has ill-served the United States?**

Yes. The Gulf War was won quickly and with little loss of American lives. Many Americans came to believe future conflicts would produce similar results. Yet all wars are different, and there can be no guarantee of either an easy victory or light casualties when the United States embarks on future combat operations.

11

IRAQ

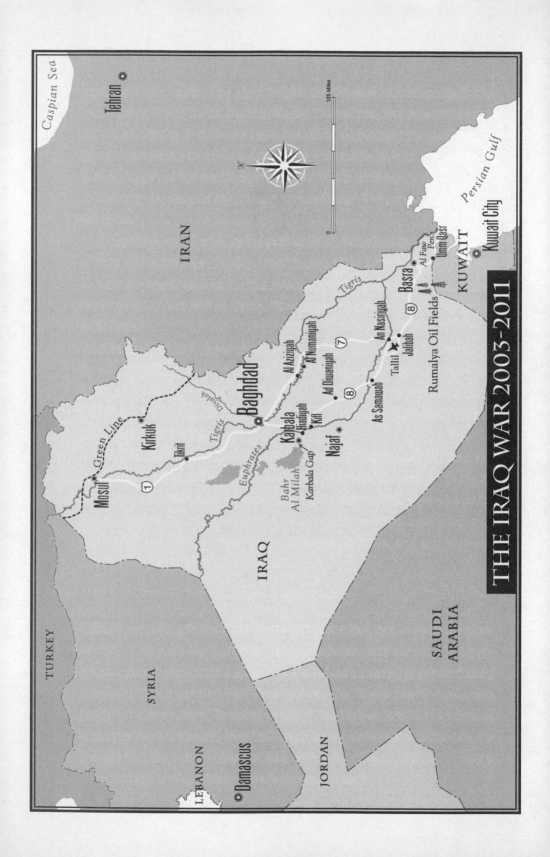

THE IRAQ WAR 2003-2011

2003-2010

On March 20, 2003, American and British troops, staging from Kuwait, invaded Iraq. Superbly equipped, these troops constituted a small but lethal military force. As they pushed through the sand berms at the Iraqi-Kuwaiti border, the invaders had two simple objectives: they were to remove Saddam Hussein from power and bring an end to his Baathist regime.

For years, as the rulers of the country, Saddam and his thugs had terrorized the people of Iraq, and twice they had brought war to the Middle East. By 2003, armed with chemical weapons and having both the capability and desire to develop nuclear devices, Saddam's Iraq posed a threat to the stability of a region critical to countries dependent on oil. Most leaders of the worlds' nations seemed content to tolerate Saddam. One leader did not. This was George W. Bush, the president of the United States.

At the urging of the British prime minister, Tony Blair, and of his own secretary of state, Colin Powell, Mr. Bush had gone to the United Nations to seek authorization to move against Saddam. The Iraqi leader had ignored numerous U.N. resolutions aimed at correcting his country's unacceptable behavior, particularly in regard to nuclear weapons. Increasingly, the international body was receptive to the employment of force. In September 2002, the president had told the U.N. that Saddam was a threat not only to peace, but also to the credibility of the United Nations itself. The next month, the U.N. Security Council unanimously adopted Resolution 1441, which threatened serious consequences if Iraq did not meet the U.N.-imposed obligations. When Saddam continued to defy the U.N., the

American leader, who previously had labeled Iraq as part of an "axis of evil" (along with Iran and North Korea), decided to take action. France, with substantial economic ties to Iraq, objected. Dominique de Villepin, the French foreign minister, argued that before military force was used another resolution was required. The United States disagreed. To George Bush and his vice president, Dick Cheney, 1441 was more than sufficient. Having been told by American, British, and other intelligence agencies that Saddam was building nuclear weapons, they believed the time for debate and diplomacy had ended.

In addition to the United Nations, the American president also sought approval for the use of force from the American people. And he got it. In October 2002 both houses of Congress passed resolutions supporting military intervention. In the Senate the vote was 77–23. In the House of Representatives it was 296–133. In effect, the United States had voted to go to war.

On March 17, 2003, the president issued an ultimatum to Saddam to leave Iraq within forty-eight hours. A refusal to do so, he said, would result in armed conflict "at a time of our choosing." Saddam stayed put. Three days later, American and British tanks crossed the border.

In overall command of the forces deployed to oust Saddam was Tommy Franks, a four-star general in the U.S. Army. Officially, Franks was in charge of Central Command. This was one of six joint commands the United States had established to cover large geographic areas. Encompassing nineteen countries, Central Command at the time had two principal concerns. One was Afghanistan, where U.S. troops were at war with Islamic fundamentalists allied with those responsible for the 2001 terrorist attacks of September 11. The other was Iraq. After the Gulf War, despite two no-fly zones and U.N. sanctions, Saddam Hussein was in Baghdad, still in charge. He continued to repress Iraqi citizens and to threaten the stability of the lands under Central Command's purview.

As chief of the Command, General Franks had senior officers reporting to him. One of these was Lieutenant General David McKiernan, who was in charge of all ground operations. McKiernan would lead the effort to unseat Saddam. With input and approval provided by Tommy Franks, McKiernan devised a detailed plan of battle. The American came up with an audacious scheme, which was given the name Operation Iraqi Freedom (OIF).

His plan called for two powerful armored strike forces to move quickly north to Baghdad. One of the forces, comprising several U.S. Army divisions, would approach the Iraqi capital via the Euphrates River. The other, made up of U.S. marines and located to the east, would advance along the Tigris. The two armored units would surround Baghdad, sealing off the city, and then prevent enemy movements into and from the city. The plan emphasized speed and the need to avoid costly battles in the towns along the way. These towns would be sealed off but not fought over and occupied. American casualties thus would be kept low and the war not turned into a lengthy conflict. The hope was that if Baghdad were rapidly cordoned off, Saddam and his regime would collapse.

Other elements of the plan envisioned British troops seizing Basra and the Al Faw Peninsula, including the port of Umm Qasr. Additionally, U.S., British, and Australian Special Forces would operate in the Iraqi western desert, shutting down missile sites and keeping enemy troops away from Baghdad. Other Special Forces would work in the northern part of Iraq both aiding and keeping in check Iraqi Kurds who had their sights set on the oil fields near the cities of Mosul and Kirkuk.

Of course, America's war plan called for air strikes. These would be extensive and involve U.S. naval aircraft as well as those of Britain's Royal Air Force. In the Gulf War airpower had played a significant role, and it would do so again in this conflict. This time around, there was to be a major difference. Franks and McKiernan wanted no preliminary air campaign as had occurred in the 1990–1991 conflict. They believed lengthy air strikes prior to ground-level attacks would give advance warning to Saddam and his generals, enabling them to better prepare their defenses. The two American commanders thought that by attacking first with soldiers and marines they would surprise the Iraqis, throw them off balance, and deliver a shock to Saddam's political and military infrastructure.

One element of the plan put together by Tommy Franks and David McKiernan was never to be realized. This called for a strong ground force to strike into northern Iraq from Turkey. Such an attack would have required Saddam to fend off American forces from several directions. This made sound military sense, but unfortunately for the Americans, the Turks objected and refused access to their territory. The result was that no attack occurred from the north.

During Operation Iraqi Freedom David McKiernan directed several U.S. Army units that, taken together, were designated as Third Army. The unit's name was rich in American history. In June of 1944, the Third Army had been established in Normandy, soon after the D-Day landings. Its commander was George Patton, who, utilizing the speed and firepower afforded by its many tanks, defeated German forces as the army drove through France. Patton's campaign began as part of Omar Bradley's Operation Cobra, which saw the Americans break out of the French bocage and begin the drive to the German frontier. With a sense of history and the desire to replicate Third Army's success, General McKiernan named his ground attacks Operation Cobra II.

Throughout the planning process and the campaign itself, there was one scenario that deeply concerned the Americans. This was the possibility that as they drew near to Baghdad, Saddam would employ weapons of mass destruction (WMDs), principally chemical weapons and possibly biologicals, in order to halt the invaders. Saddam had employed the former against his own people, so why would he not use them against the Americans? In response, all Coalition troops in the region were issued protective gear. Moreover, special units, including several from Germany and the Czech Republic, were deployed to detect the presence of various toxins. While no doubt Saddam had been warned not to use the WMDs, U.S. leaders were fearful that the Iraqi leader, concluding that he personally had little to lose, would target the approaching Americans with the deadly devices.

Among the American leaders concerned by an Iraqi deployment of such weapons was Donald Rumsfeld, President Bush's secretary of defense. Rumsfeld was a strong advocate of removing Saddam Hussein by force. He also, during his tenure at the Pentagon, was attempting to remake the American military, especially the army. The secretary believed the U.S. Army needed to field units that emphasized speed, lethality, and new sophisticated tools of warfare that only America could bring to the battlefield. Rumsfeld wanted his generals to gain victory through technology, mobility, and firepower. Thus, when Tommy Franks first presented him with a plan for invading Iraq that called for 450,000 troops, Rumsfeld said no. The secretary wanted—and obtained—a much smaller strike force. When General McKiernan's soldiers and marines attacked on March 20, they numbered only 145,000.

When Operation Cobra II began, Apache attack helicopters and the ever-accurate American artillery struck the Iraqi early-warning sites along the Iraqi-Kuwaiti border. Putting these out of commission enabled McKiernan's troops to surprise the Iraqis, especially since no air campaign had signaled the war's start.

In fact, the war with Iraq did not begin with the ground attacks of March 20. The day before, America's Central Intelligence Agency received what it considered reliable information that Saddam Hussein would spend the night at a compound called Dora Farms, located in an eastern suburb of Baghdad. President Bush made the decision to strike the compound in the hope of killing the Iraqi leader. Although cruise missiles were launched as part of the strike, the principal attack was delivered by two F-117 Nighthawks. These were slow but stealthy aircraft, each armed with two large, precision bunker-busting bombs. Arriving over Baghdad just before sunlight (they flew combat missions only at night), the planes released their deadly payloads and destroyed Dora Farms. But Saddam was not there, so the mission, executed with considerable skill, went for naught. Saddam, however, took notice. He ordered a retaliatory strike sending a Chinese-built sea-skimming missile into Kuwait. It landed near the U.S. Marine Corps headquarters in that country, but caused no damage.

Between March 21 and April 3, 2003, the Iraqis launched seventeen missiles at the invading Americans. Of these, eight either crashed prematurely or targeted nothing of value. The remaining nine were intercepted by U.S. Army Patriot missiles. The Patriot was an air defense system in which the Pentagon had invested heavily. Earlier models of the missile had performed poorly in the previous war against Iraq. This time, apparently, the Patriots earned their keep.

As the troops under David McKiernan's command advanced toward

Baghdad, they were aided greatly by the firepower of British and American warplanes. Because Iraq's air force made no effort to interfere, these aircraft enjoyed air supremacy. And, given that Saddam's ground-based air defenses had been weakened by two no-fly zones put in place at the conclusion of the Gulf War, the American and British pilots operated in an environment that kept losses extremely low.

Tommy Franks and his air commanders planned an opening round of air strikes—referred to at the time as "shock and awe"—that would signal to the Iraqis that this time, the gloves were off. Significantly, however, a number of normally legitimate targets were off-limits. Bridges were kept intact because the Central Command chief wanted them available for use by McKiernan's forces once they reached the city. Power plants also were left alone. Their output would be needed once the war was over. The goal of the war, after all, was the removal of Saddam and his regime, not the obliteration of Iraqi cities and towns. This restraint by General Franks served another goal as well. It helped reduce civilian casualties. Critics of the American military seek to portray it as insensitive to the loss of life. In fact, the opposite is true. Such was the concern over the death of Iraqi civilians that any target the U.S. Air Force wished to hit had to have the personal approval of the secretary of defense should estimated civilian deaths number thirty or more.

The scale of the initial air strikes can be seen in the fifteen hundred sorties flown during the first four days (a sortie is one plane flying one mission). Aircraft taking part in the aerial offensive flew from bases nearby in Kuwait and Qatar and as far away as Diego Garcia and the United Kingdom. There even were missions by American aircraft based in Missouri. During the entire twenty-three days of air attacks 36,275 sorties were flown, an astonishing number and one that reveals the extent of the aerial assault. Keeping the airplanes' fuel tanks full required an enormous effort as modern military aircraft are notorious gas guzzlers. Through April 11, tanker planes, via in-flight refueling, delivered more than forty-six million gallons of jet fuel.

Many of the strike aircraft operating over Iraq were deployed not in a strategic sense, but tactically, in missions designed to assist ground forces. These planes alerted McKiernan's troops to the nearby presence of enemy troops and, more important, pounded Iraqi tanks and bunkers that stood in the way of advancing Americans.

———————

Early in the advance north the U.S. 3rd Infantry Division, one of General McKiernan's principal fighting units, took control of an Iraqi airfield southwest of An Nasiriyah. The airfield, Tallil, would become an important logistics base as the Americans continued their drive toward Baghdad. An Nasiriyah, a town of approximately three hundred thousand, stood astride the Euphrates River. For the Iraqis, it could be a place to intercept enemy troops and their supplies. For the Americans, securing An Nasiriyah was essential if the invasion was to proceed as planned. McKiernan wanted his soldiers to seal off the town and avoid a slugfest that would slow the advance. Having done so, his troops were to turn responsibility for An Nasiriyah over to the marines, who, while leaving a sufficient number of troops to control the town, would cross the Euphrates at that point and head north to the Tigris, thus approaching Baghdad from the east.

McKiernan's plan was executed. The marines took charge of An Nasiriyah and the 3rd Infantry moved north to As Samawah. In both towns, however, U.S. forces received a nasty surprise. They had been told Iraqis in the southern part of the country, being Shiite, would welcome American troops. That turned out not to be the case. Moreover, the soldiers and marines confronted an enemy they had not anticipated. This was the fedayeen. They were fanatical Muslims, full of hatred for America. Many were Syrians, paid by Saddam. Poorly trained and equipped with only light weapons, they made suicide attacks against the American armored vehicles. That they did so demonstrated a certain kind of courage. That they murdered Iraqis they disapproved of, and fired from within mosques and schools, suggested their rules of combat differed from those of their opponents.

The 3rd Infantry soldiers arrived at As Samawah on March 23. They were warmly greeted—by enemy rocket-propelled grenades, mortar rounds, and machine gun fire. The result was a two-day-long firefight that left a considerable number of the defenders no longer alive. Among the highlights of the battle was the use by the fedayeen of innocent women and children as human shields.

Next stop for the Americans was the city of Najaf. It sat on Highway 8 and, like An Nasiriyah and As Samawah, had to be contained in order for supplies to reach the advancing combat troops. The fighting at Najaf was brutal. It began on March 24 and lasted for four days. U.S. troops employed the full array of their capabilities—tanks, artillery, and air strikes. The enemy, Iraqis as well as the fedayeen, were outmatched but fought hard. They would fire their weapons and then, more often than not, be killed. When the battle was over, approximately one thousand of them were dead.

About this time Mother Nature intervened. A massive sandstorm struck the entire area. Called a *shamal*, the storm combined high winds, sand, and rain. It blinded soldiers, kept helicopters on the ground, and made difficult simple tasks such as walking, eating, and trying to clean one's rifle. However, American artillery and the air force's precision-guided weapons were less affected. Iraqi commanders, believing the invaders were as blinded as they were, decided to reposition their troops, expecting the *shamal* to hide their movements. It did not. American high-tech bombs and artillery shells found the Iraqis and inflicted serious damage.

The sandstorm coincided with a pause in the American advance. After several days of hard fighting, little sleep, and a trek of many miles, McKiernan's soldiers, principally the 3rd Infantry Division, were in need of rest. Moreover, they were running short of supplies. So the general ordered a pause in the action.

The time was well spent. Recognizing the requirement for his now lengthy supply lines to be secure, McKiernan directed two of the U.S. Army's most elite units, the 82nd Airborne Division and the 101st Air Assault Division, to relieve the 3rd Infantry at As Samawah and Najaf. Their task was to ensure the flow of supplies north and to seize control of both towns. This they did, though not without a fight.

No longer tied down at As Samawah and Najaf, the 3rd Infantry Division was now at full strength. It would spearhead the army's drive into Baghdad. The question was how best to have it move on the Iraqi capital. Once again, the pause was useful. McKiernan and his senior commanders used the time to fix on a plan for the attack. For America's army, this meant a series of feints to confuse the Iraqis and then a Patton-like push through a slice of Iraq's territory known as the Karbala Gap.

America was not the only country to invade Iraq. The United Kingdom also participated in the campaign to remove Saddam Hussein. The British contribution was substantial. It numbered forty-six thousand service personnel. Among these were sailors who manned thirty-three warships the Royal Navy deployed to the Persian Gulf. The ships included HMS *Ark Royal*, Britain's largest warship, and six small mine-clearing vessels. The latter performed the essential task of clearing the narrow waterways to Basra and Umm Qasr, Iraq's two ports.

Another British warship deserves mention by name. This is HMS *Turbulent*, a nuclear attack submarine. When sent to the Gulf, she had not seen England for more than ten months, having traveled fifty thousand miles, forty thousand of them underwater. *Turbulent*'s contribution to the campaign was a salvo of Tomahawk cruise missiles, launched from beneath the sea, that hit their targets in Iraq miles and miles away.

On March 20, 2003, British land forces took part in the opening assault of Operation Iraqi Freedom. Their objectives were the Rumaila oil fields and the oil terminals of the Al-Faw Peninsula. American and British commanders feared the Iraqis would torch the former and open the spigots of the latter, thereby causing environmental harm and economic loss. With assistance from U.S. marines both objectives were met. But the effort was not easy. The British troops encountered considerable opposition, especially from Iraqi tanks and artillery.

> *We go to liberate not to conquer. We will not fly our flags in their country. We are entering Iraq to free a people, and the only flag which will be flown is their own.*

So spoke a British army officer to his troops prior to the start of the war. Having secured the oil fields and occupied the Al-Faw Peninsula, the twenty thousand soldiers comprising Britain's assault force advanced on

Basra. With a population of 1.5 million people, this was Iraq's second larg-est city and key to the southern region of the country. British troops reached the outskirts of Basra on Day Two of the war. But they made no attempt to enter. Instead, they cordoned off Basra, and conducted raids into the city. In turn, Iraqi forces more than once attempted to break out, often employ-ing T-55 tanks. The British were equipped with their own tanks, the first-rate Challenger 2, and beat back the Iraqi forces.

On March 30 the British staged an attack of their own, at a suburb of Basra called Abu al-Khasib. In a nineteen-hour firefight against numerous Iraqis, they carried the day, killing seventy of the enemy and taking three hundred Iraqis prisoner. The next day, in another fight, twenty-five Iraqi tanks were put out of commission, as were two hundred Iraqi soldiers. Soon thereafter resistance in the city melted away, and the British occupied Basra.

What they found was a city whose population was in dire straits. Food was scarce, medicines were in short supply, and city services were in need of fixing. Moreover, Saddam's men, many of them fedayeen, had exercised a firm control, killing those Iraqis they deemed insufficiently loyal.

Responding to the challenges, the British shipped humanitarian aid to the Iraqis. This had to be delivered by sea, which is why Umm Qasr had been seized. British troops had captured the port at the end of March, though not without a fight. During the battle the British defense minister described the Iraqi port as similar to Southampton. To which a British commando replied, "It's not at all like Southampton: there's no beer . . . and they're shooting at us."

The United States Marine Corps is rightly proud of its capability to conduct amphibious operations. In the war to remove Saddam Hussein, the Corps would play an important role, but its role was similar to that of the army's 3rd Infantry Division. The marines would conduct a land campaign. There would be no assault from the sea.

For the campaign, the American marines deployed a substantial portion of their overall strength. Slightly more than sixty thousand marines took part in Operation Iraqi Freedom. At 8:30 P.M. local time on March 20,

2003, pursuant to David McKiernan's plan, the marines drove through the sand berms and entered Iraq.

Initial resistance was light, although the first American to be killed in combat was a marine. Along with the British, the marines' initial task was to secure the Rumaila oil fields, and then they were to proceed northwest to An Nasiriyah. Once there, they were to relieve the army's 3rd Infantry Division and take control of the town. The latter task was necessary because at An Nasiriyah, as noted above, the marines were to cross the Euphrates River and then advance along Highways 1 and 7 to the Tigris. All this they accomplished. But it was at An Nasiriyah that the fedayeen made their debut. Looking like civilians (because they were civilians), these irregulars were Islamic fundamentalists eager to kill Americans. In combat with the marines and McKiernan's soldiers, the fedayeen posed a serious threat. Moreover, they seemed willing, even anxious, to die.

There were three bridges at An Nasiriyah that the American marines needed to control. Because the city was largely Shiite, the U.S. forces expected only minor resistance. But the presence of the fedayeen along with Iraqi army troops turned An Nasiriyah from the anticipated cakewalk into a bloody brawl that lasted for more than a week. When the battle concluded, the bridges, and the city, belonged to the Americans. But the cost was high: nineteen U.S. marines were dead and fifty-seven were wounded. Their opponents, however, suffered far greater losses. The marines believe they killed two thousand of their enemy.

The marines fighting at An Nasiriyah were a unit independent of the main marine strike force that eventually would reach Baghdad. With some five thousand men, the unit was called Task Force Tarawa. The name came from one of the Corps's more brutal (though successful) battles of the Second World War, Tarawa being a once-obscure island in the Pacific. The fight for the bridges at An Nasiriyah was not equal in scale to that of Tarawa, but like the 1943 fight, it has earned a place of honor in the history of the Corps.

Unfortunately for the Americans, the first U.S. troops to enter An Nasiriyah were neither the marines of Task Force Tarawa nor the 3rd Infantry soldiers they had relieved. The first troops in the city belonged to the U.S. Army's 507th Maintenance Company. These were support soldiers, driving supply trucks to combat forces farther north. Their convoy had split into sections, one of which, with sixteen vehicles and thirty-three soldiers, arrived at An Nasiriyah on the morning of March 23, 2003. There, they were to turn left and proceed northwest. Instead, they continued straight and drove into the Iraqi city. After crossing several bridges they realized their mistake, turned around, and retraced their steps. This took them down a two-mile road later dubbed "Ambush Alley." The first time through, the Iraqis had just stared, surprised by the absence of American weaponry. The second time, when the Americans returned, the Iraqis and their fedayeen allies opened fire. The result was a mini-massacre. Eleven soldiers of the 507th were killed. Six became prisoners of war (one of them a woman, Private First Class Jessica Lynch, who later was rescued).

March 23 was a day the Americans would like to forget. That day the 507th Maintenance Company was hammered along Ambush Alley. Then several marines were killed in an effort to secure An Nasiriyah. That same morning, the army's vaunted Apache helicopters failed to perform as advertised in a strike against an Iraqi army division. On March 23, in executing the attack, an Apache crashed on takeoff, one was shot down, and the remaining thirty-two machines were heavily damaged. Compounding the failure, very little harm was done to the Iraqi unit.

The Americans experienced one further setback on March 23. Using the Patriot air defense missile system, they inadvertently shot down a British warplane, killing both crew members. So, most appropriately, the U.S. Army's account of Operation Iraqi Freedom calls March 23, 2003, "the darkest day."

Once An Nasiriyah was under control, the marines were in position to start their drive to the Iraqi capital. One force of marines drove north along Highway 7. Another advanced to Ad Diwaniyah along Highway 1. They met at An Numaniyah, crossing the Tigris at that point. Task Force Tarawa was given the job of securing the ever-lengthening supply lines. This was no easy task as its area of responsibility equaled the size of America's South Carolina. Supplies, of course, were vital to the advancing attack force. Marine requirements for food, ammunition, and fuel were high. Each day, supply trucks needed to deliver 250,000 gallons of gas to keep the combat vehicles moving. As the marines advanced, these trucks, starting their journey in Kuwait, had to travel some three hundred miles.

The terrain that the marines traversed was one of agricultural lands, laced with small rivers and canals. Unlike the army troops, the marines had little desert to deal with, for they fought largely on lands between Iraq's two great rivers, the Euphrates and the Tigris.

They reached the latter, at An Numaniyah, on April 2. But it had not been an easy journey. Iraqi troops fought hard and the fedayeen were out in force. The marines moved forward in tanks, armored personnel carriers, and the ubiquitous Humvees. Artillery and Apaches provided protection. Nonetheless, ambushes were many and the marines took casualties.

As the marines got close to Baghdad, Iraqi resistance stiffened. Tanks and artillery were employed to stop the Americans. Near Al Aziziyah, forty miles south of the capital, an eight-hour battle took place, which Williamson Murray and Robert H. Scales Jr., in their book *The Iraq War: A Military History*, described as "the most significant battle against enemy conventional forces during the war." Once again the Americans won the day. It seemed like nothing could stop the marines; at least the Iraqis couldn't. But as the army's history of the campaign states, "getting to Baghdad looked easier on the map than it was in practice."

The marines arrived in the environs of Baghdad on April 6. The next day, under fire, they crossed the Diyala River, a small waterway that flows into the Tigris River just east of the city. Using tanks, amphibious vehicles, helicopters, and artillery, the American force moved into the Iraqi capital, staying east of the Tigris. By then, many in the Iraqi military had taken off their uniforms and, to employ a phrase a number of observers later used, "melted away."

The marines' campaign had been a success. Starting at the Iraqi-Kuwaiti border, America's maritime soldiers had fought their way to Baghdad. Skeptics would say they had faced a third-rate adversary. Perhaps, but this adversary was well armed and, more than once, fought tenaciously.

The campaign was not over when the marines crossed the Diyala. There would be several days of combat in the city itself before the marines were able to lay down their weapons. What they had accomplished no longer may be of interest to an American public tired of the quagmire Iraq became. But historians, at least some of them, may take note of the U.S. Marine Corps' Iraqi campaign. One British observer, as reported by Murray and Scales, called it "one that should be taught in staff colleges for years to come."

The American assault on Iraq in 2003 encompassed six separate military endeavors. These were mutually reinforcing and, in fact, constituted a single, integrated campaign. In no particular order the six were: (1) the U.S. marine advance to Baghdad via An Nasiriyah and the Tigris, (2) the British operations in the south, (3) the naval efforts from warships in the Persian Gulf, (4) the aerial strikes that so greatly aided U.S. and British ground troops, (5) the U.S. Army's drive to Baghdad along the Euphrates River, and (6) Special Forces operations north and west of the Iraqi capital.

As noted earlier, Special Forces in Iraq had several tasks. They were to shut down Iraqi Scud missile operations, keep enemy army units in the north from reinforcing the defenses of Baghdad, and both assist and restrain the Iraqi Kurds who inhabited much of Iraq's northern lands. When the war ended, the Special Forces had successfully carried out all three tasks.

The Kurds were an Islamic people who, while Iraqis, enjoyed semi-independence from Saddam's regime. They lived north of what was called the Green Line. This was a one-hundred-mile-long line of demarcation, the south of which was controlled by Saddam. The Kurds had little love for the Iraqi ruler and, thus, welcomed the presence of U.S. Special Forces. Complicating an already complex political situation were the Kurds living in eastern Turkey. They wished, as did many of the Iraqi Kurds, to establish an independent Kurdish nation. This desire greatly upset the Turks. They saw in American support of the Iraqi Kurds the possibility of consequences that would lead to a new country, Kurdistan, part of which would be carved out of their own territory.

During late March and early April, the American Special Forces, augmented by regular U.S. Army troops and marines, and enjoying firepower delivered by American aircraft, defeated their Iraqi opponents on more than one occasion. At the same time they supported the Iraqi Kurds, providing weapons, medicines, and tactical advice.

Three specific military operations in the north were particularly noteworthy. The first, which began on March 26 and lasted four days, was a
successful attack on an Iranian-backed group of al-Qaeda terrorists known
as Ansar al-Islam. The Kurds detested this group and, with 6,500 men,
supported by U.S. Special Forces and American airpower, assaulted their
mountain strongholds, killing many of the terrorists.

The second operation was an all-American action. One thousand soldiers of the 173rd Airborne Brigade parachuted onto an airfield in the
Kurdish-controlled portion of Iraq (this was the forty-fourth combat jump
in the history of the U.S. Army). The next day, March 27, additional paratroopers were flown in, as were tanks and supplies, the latter for both the
Americans and their Kurdish allies.

The airborne operation showcased U.S. military strength in northern
Iraq. It also bolstered the morale of the Kurds and reinforced the incorrect
belief held by the Iraqis that the Americans would employ paratroopers to
seize Baghdad. That the brigade's drop zone already had been secured by
Special Forces did not detract from its value.

The third military operation that deserves mention took place early in
April. At that time, U.S. Special Forces and the Kurds were preparing to
attack Kirkuk. This city, two hundred miles north of Baghdad, and its
environs were rich with oil reserves. Those who controlled the city controlled the oil. The Kurds were eager to seize Kirkuk. However, before
the attack occurred, the Iraqi defenders left. The Kurds then occupied
the city. For the Americans, this was unacceptable. It constituted a possible
prelude to Kurdish independence, which, in addition to bringing about
likely action by the Turkish armed forces, jeopardized the territorial integrity of Iraq. The latter possibility concerned the Americans, who, after
all, had invaded Iraq to remove Saddam and his regime, not to dismem-
ber the country. The U.S. Special Forces acted immediately. Exercising both political skill and military muscle, they persuaded the Kurds to
withdraw.

Once the great sandstorm—the *shamal*—had subsided, the U.S. soldiers
that had reached Najaf were ready to move on Baghdad. The march "up

country" was over. The time had come to first surround and then seize the Iraqi capital.

One issue Americans had to consider was where to cross the Euphrates River. Their commanders decided to do so in the narrow gap between the town of Karbala and the large lake to its east, Bahr al Milh. With Karbala just fifty miles south of Baghdad, McKiernan expected the Iraqis to put up a stiff resistance. And if Saddam was ever going to employ weapons of mass destruction, the American general assumed he would do so as they approached the Iraqi capital.

To confuse the Iraqis and to have their focus on somewhere other than the Karbala Gap, the Americans conducted a series of feints. These were five simultaneous attacks each of which McKiernan wanted Saddam to conclude might be the principal attack. One of the feints was at Hindiyah. Another was at Kifl, a town north of Najaf but east of the great river. Kifl was full of fedayeen who used it as a transit point for deployment farther south. The resulting battle in and around Kifl turned out to be more of a fight than the Americans had expected. But the outcome was similar to other battles in Iraq: U.S. troops carried the day.

The drive through the Gap began at midnight on April 1. Abrams tanks and Bradley armored personnel carriers led the way. Their immediate objective was the bridge at Yasir al-Khuder. This spanned the Euphrates and was just twenty miles from Baghdad. The Iraqis, who had repositioned troops away from the Gap in response to the feints, nevertheless fought hard. Using T-72s, Russian-built main battle tanks, and artillery, Saddam's soldiers made a determined effort to halt the Americans. They failed, but punctured the belief now held by many that the Iraqi army was incapable of striking back.

By April 3, McKiernan's troops were closing in on Baghdad's main airport, which lay to the west of the city. The next day, a fierce battle took place as the Iraqis attempted to repel the invaders. When the fight was over, thirty-four T-72 tanks had been destroyed and many Iraqis killed. The Americans controlled the airport and, with the marines approaching the Diyala, the encirclement of Baghdad had begun.

To prevent Iraqi troops from either reinforcing or leaving the capital, McKiernan's soldiers established five operating bases south and west of

Baghdad. These also placed the Americans in position to take control of the city. Each of the five were named after an American professional football team. Thus, Objectives Bears, Lions, Texans, Ravens, and Saints ringed much of Baghdad. Objective Saints was an area where two key highways intersected. The Iraqis fought hard to keep the Americans from securing this pivotal location. Employing tanks and artillery as well as commandos, Saddam's men attacked. But to no avail. The battle took place on April 3 and 4, and when it was over, Objective Saints was in American hands.

Throughout the war the news media covered the Americans' advance. To make possible more accurate and extensive coverage, Secretary of Defense Rumsfeld permitted reporters to be embedded in U.S. combat units. These media personnel shared the hardships endured by the American troops. They also faced the dangers inherent when the shooting started. One of the embedded reporters was Michael Kelly of the *Atlantic Monthly*. He died during the attack on Baghdad's airport, when the Humvee in which he was a passenger plunged into a canal, landing upside down.

While the American public and others were kept informed of the war's progress by these reporters, Iraqi citizens had to rely on information provided by Saddam's government, particularly by the Ministry of Information. Heading up this organization was Mohammed Saeed al-Sahhaf. He gave numerous briefings to the many journalists still stationed in Baghdad. These always were upbeat, positive accounts of the war in which Iraqi forces were triumphant. That they were fanciful in the extreme al-Sahhaf seemed not to realize. In fact, the minister was living in a fantasy world. "Yes," he stated as U.S. forces moved through the Karbala Gap, "the American troops have advanced further. This will only make it easier for us to defeat them."

The U.S. troops in Iraq nicknamed al-Sahhaf "Baghdad Bob." To them, he was a source of amusement as he made pronouncements they knew to be untrue. But the minister and his comments also were an irritant. The words he spoke received attention worldwide. They challenged the American account of the war and gave heart to many in the Arab world who wished to see the United States defeated by one of their own.

By April 5, with the marines at the Diyala and the army's five operating bases secured, the Americans were poised to take control of Baghdad. Generals Franks and McKiernan believed that once the U.S. military controlled the city, Saddam and his regime would be finished. They also believed that the effort to seize Baghdad could lead to protracted urban warfare. This they wanted to avoid. Such combat would be extremely destructive and, more important, would result in numerous casualties, both American and Iraqi.

The two generals knew that the number of troops they had available to assault Baghdad was not large. The capital, after all, was a city of six million people spread out over 440 square miles. How then would the Americans proceed? What was their plan of attack?

They decided to act with caution. There would be no frontal assault, by either the marines or the army troops. Instead, like the British at Basra, the Americans planned a series of raids into the city. These would increase in scale and tempo, gradually wearing down the Iraqis. But before they were to begin, the U.S. Army conducted an operation that became one of the war's most celebrated episodes.

The operation was called "Thunder Run." Carried out by a small armored task force, it was a mission of reconnaissance the purpose of which was to ascertain how the Iraqis would fight within the confines of Baghdad. But Thunder Run had more than one purpose. "The task," said Colonel David Perkins, who commanded the unit to which the task force belonged, "is to enter Baghdad for the purpose of displaying combat power, to destroy enemy forces—and to simply show them that we can."

U.S. Army doctrine said tanks were not to operate in cities. Urban areas limited their maneuverability, restricted their lines of fire, and exposed tanks to attacks from above. Thunder Run proved the doctrine wrong.

At 6:30 A.M. on April 5, twenty-nine Abrams tanks and several other combat vehicles drove into the city. They traveled up Highway 8, a modern roadway much like an American interstate. What followed, according to Mark Bowden, author of *Black Hawk Down*, was "the most bitterly contested moment of the war." It ended two hours and twenty minutes later when the task force, as planned, arrived at the Baghdad airport. One American was dead and one Abrams was destroyed. Estimates of Iraqi losses vary, but at least a thousand men—many of them fedayeen—no longer were alive.

One amusing event occurred during Thunder Run. An Iraqi brigadier general, a staff officer, was driving to work that morning, as he did every workday. Unaware that the Americans were nearby (apparently, he listened to al-Sahhaf's broadcasts), he turned the corner and promptly drove his Volkswagen Passat into the side of an Abrams M1A1 tank. Needless to say, the car fared poorly and the general, one very surprised Iraqi, became a prisoner of war.

Two days later, a second Thunder Run was conducted. But this was a different kind of mission. The tanks were to drive to the center of the city, a distance of eleven miles, and then remain in Baghdad. The tanks and Bradleys would deploy in a circle, in the middle of the city, and challenge the Iraqis to dislodge them.

Whether the Americans, who reached the city center at 8 A.M. on April 7, would be able to stay in the city depended on the army's ability to deliver supplies to the task force. This force consisted of 570 soldiers in sixty tanks and other vehicles, and their requirements were substantial. Food, ammunition, and fuel had to be trucked to them. The supply route was up a highway on which three overpasses gave the Iraqis strong positions from which to fire on the convoys. For the U.S. troops, these overpasses had to be taken and held. Given the names Larry, Moe, and Curly, they all saw ferocious firefights. The Americans prevailed, but at times, it was, as the British would say, "a near thing."

Within the city, firefights took place as well. For two days the Iraqis and the fedayeen tried to kill the Americans, who, having been resupplied, were able to respond in kind. The violence of the combat within Baghdad and at the three intersections, indeed throughout the campaign, can be seen in the following account of one incident as told by David Zucchino in his book about Thunder Run. Captain Stephen Barry was an American officer in Baghdad during the fighting. At one point, his unit sees a white sedan moving directly at it. Barry then gives the order to fire.

Three tanks opened up. . . . The sedan caught fire and crashed. Two men climbed out and both went down, killed instantly. . . .

Thirty seconds later, a white Jeep Cherokee sped down the bridge span. . . . 50 caliber rounds shattered the windshield. The Cherokee exploded. The fireball was huge—so big that Barry was certain the vehicle had been loaded with explosives. He knew the difference between a burning car and the detonation of explosives. This was a suicide car.

And they kept coming—sedans, pickups, a Chevy Caprice, three cars in the first ten minutes, six more right after that. The tanks destroyed them all. It was incomprehensible. Barry kept thinking: What the hell is wrong with these people? They were trying to ram cars into tanks. It was futile—absolutely senseless. It was like they wanted to die. . . . Barry hated slaughtering them. And that's what it was—slaughter.

They were the enemy . . . but it gave Barry no pleasure to kill them.

On April 10, just five days from when U.S. armored units had made their first foray into Baghdad, organized resistance ended. Within the city, the fighting had produced casualties—most of them Iraqi and fedayeen—but McKiernan's troops now controlled the capital. Saddam had fled and his government had collapsed. Four days later, on April 14, the United States declared major combat operations to have ended.

"Mission Accomplished" read a banner on the USS *Abraham Lincoln*, one of the aircraft carriers that had participated in Operation Iraqi Freedom. In just twenty-six days the Americans had taken control of Iraq. Little did they expect that the hard part was just beginning.

The war against Saddam and his army had been a success. The occupation that followed was not. Throughout Iraq, especially in the cities, American troops first hailed as liberators soon came to be seen as foreigners occupying a country in which they did not belong and governing a people they did not understand.

The immediate problem was one of looting. Once Saddam's regime collapsed, law and order disappeared. Iraqis responded by breaking into stores and office buildings, and walking off with whatever they could take. U.S. soldiers and marines just looked on, unwilling to stop the thefts. "We did not come to Iraq," said one American commander, "to shoot some fellow making off with a rug."

The looting foreshadowed the violence that was to permeate postwar Iraq. Once Saddam's hold on power ceased, Iraqis chose to seek vengeance on other Iraqis. Shiites killed Sunnis. Sunnis murdered Shiites. Revenge was sweet. Baghdad became a bloody city whose inhabitants were at war with one another. American troops were the only force potentially capable of freeing Iraq from violence. But they were too few in number. Secretary of Defense Rumsfeld had mandated a small military presence in Iraq, expecting the Iraqi army and police force to maintain order once the combat was over. Yet the army had disappeared. Soldiers simply had taken off their uniforms and gone home, while the police were incompetent, capable of little more than traffic control. So as spring turned to summer and summer gave way to fall, Iraq was home to a rampage of killings that the Americans were unable to prevent.

Only in time and when President Bush ordered a surge in the number of troops stationed in Iraq did the violence recede. But for several years following the ouster of Saddam, Iraqis targeted American soldiers and workers. U.S. casualties were many, and constant. Extremists wanted either to destabilize the governing authorities or force the Americans to leave. Not surprisingly, back in the United States, the country's citizens were angered by what they saw happening in Iraq. Bombs were exploding and people were dying. Opposition to the American presence in Iraq grew as many Americans came to believe that the war had been wrong and the occupation a failure.

As the killing continued—often by suicide bombers—the United States was attempting to rebuild Iraq. Funneling literally billions and billions of dollars into the country, America hoped to create an infrastructure equal to that of any modern country. In this effort the success would be limited.

The difficulties were threefold. The first was the task itself, which was much larger than the U.S. had expected. The second was the corruption that seemed to permeate Iraqi society. The third difficulty, and the most serious, was the lack of security. Workers attempting to rebuild the country's infrastructure were the target of attack by Iraqis attempting to foil America's reconstruction efforts.

The result was that the rebuilding of Iraq was less successful, took longer, and cost more than the Americans expected. Iraqis, at least those without blood on their hands, were frustrated. While during the days of Saddam electric power had been limited, those in Baghdad could not now understand why it remained so. How, they asked, could a nation that had landed men on the moon not be able to provide ample electricity to Iraq's capital?

Despite the violence and the slow pace of rebuilding, the United States did enjoy a few successes in postwar Iraq. Preparations had been made in case food shortages emerged. They did not, but nonetheless, no Iraqi went hungry once American troops controlled the country. Iraqi currency, festooned with images of Saddam, was swiftly and successfully replaced. Much later, in 2005, the United States prodded the Iraqis into drafting a new constitution and holding free and open elections, activities then rarely seen in the Arab world.

At first, the American effort to rebuild Iraq was given to the newly established Office of Reconstruction and Humanitarian Assistance. This was led by Jay Garner, a retired senior American army officer. One of his key staff members, David Nummy, wrote that Garner

> *struck me as one of those people who had successfully made the transition from warrior to statesman. He was a natural leader and understood the differences between waging war and establishing peace. From my perspective, he had the correct vision for post-invasion Iraq—to get life back to normal as quickly as possible and turn the country back to the Iraqis.*

However, with insufficient resources and an environment marred by violence, Garner had no chance of succeeding and did not. He was replaced by Ambassador L. Paul Bremer, who, reporting to Rumsfeld, essentially ruled the country. Bremer inherited an extremely difficult situation, made worse by two of his early decisions. He chose not to immediately reconstitute the Iraqi army, and he forbade most of Saddam's Baathist Party members from participating in the rebuilding efforts. The former meant security forces were insufficient to keep order, while the latter deprived the effort of individuals capable of carrying it out.

The occupation of Iraq can be said to have ended on August 18, 2010, when, at the direction of President Barack Obama, the last U.S. combat troops left the country. For the United States, the experience had been a painful one. After nearly nine years in Iraq, more than 4,480 American soldiers and marines were dead.

During the time when U.S. soldiers and marines were on patrol in a postwar Iraq, when combat with Iraqi army units had ended, many Americans questioned the wisdom of the war itself, especially as body bags kept arriving at Dover Air Force Base in Delaware. These Americans viewed the conflict as a grave mistake. After all, they pointed out, no nuclear weapons were ever discovered. And Saddam's alleged possession of such devices had been a primary justification for the invasion.

Others disagreed. They noted that Iraq became, if slowly, a land with a much reduced level of violence. And they pointed out that the country's leaders had come to power via free and open elections. Regardless of how history judges Operation Iraqi Freedom, there is no doubt that the United States military, spearheaded by American armored forces, performed extremely well. George Patton would have approved.

Did Saddam have any realistic hope of defeating the American and British forces that invaded Iraq?

No, he did not. In equipment, training, tactics, and leadership, the British and Americans outclassed the Iraqis, who, at times, fought courageously, but never in a manner that would result in victory.

Did President Bush rush into war with Iraq?

His critics certainly think so. But Mr. Bush gave Saddam ample opportunity to comply with the United Nations resolutions and thus to avoid armed conflict. Moreover, well before the March 2003 invasion, the American president went to the U.N. and secured a resolution that he and others believed authorized the use of force.

Did Saddam's government possess nuclear weapons?

American and other intelligence services had told President Bush that a very strong case could be made that Iraq had nuclear weapons. However, postwar searches failed to discover any. To be sure, Iraq had the capability to develop such devices. But, in fact, Saddam did not have these weapons in his military arsenal.

In what other way did the American government miscalculate?

Incredibly, the Department of Defense, having made and executed extensive plans for the defeat of the Iraqi military, made few plans for the administration of Iraq once combat had ended. Secretary Rumsfeld and his colleagues incorrectly assumed that American troops would be able to leave Iraq soon after Saddam's regime had been ousted. "There is no plan," said Richard Perle, one of these colleagues, "for an extended occupation in Iraq." But Secretary of State Colin Powell had warned President Bush that once the United States "broke" Iraq, it would "own" the country. Having done the former, America became responsible for Iraq, at least for maintaining order and for helping to rebuild the country. In the event, both tasks proved difficult and expensive. The U.S. Treasury would send bundles of dollars to Iraq. More importantly, coffins containing the bodies of dead American soldiers would be flown home from Iraq for years after the fall of Saddam.

What happened to Saddam Hussein?

As American armored units entered Baghdad, Saddam went into hiding. Not until December of that year, 2003, was he found, in an underground hole near Tikrit, north of the capital. The Americans who located him interrogated the former ruler and then turned him over to the Iraqis. They brought him to trial and, not surprisingly, found him guilty. On December 30, 2006, they hung Saddam Hussein.

12

AFGHANISTAN

2001–2014

On Christmas Eve of 1979, the Soviet Union, intent on establishing a more pliable regime, invaded Afghanistan, its neighbor to the south. Ten years later Soviet forces departed. Their efforts to subjugate this strategically located country had failed. Wrecked Soviet tanks and helicopters littered the countryside, while more than fourteen thousand dead Russian soldiers testified to the fiasco. Native Afghan forces, financed by the Saudis and armed by both the Americans and the Pakistanis, had defeated a much larger, more powerful invader.

What followed was a period of political instability and armed conflict. Afghanistan was (and is) a hyperbolic mixture of tribal loyalties, religious fervor, and incompetent central governments. Yet, by 1996, when the capital city of Kabul fell, a new political-religious movement had gained control. This was the Taliban. They were Islamic fundamentalists full of hatred for anyone who did not share their beliefs. By Western standards, their values were primitive. They forbade women to work or to be educated. They closed movie theaters and banned music. They forced men to grow beards and punished theft by amputating hands. In general, they created a civic society few admired. Among the Taliban's more reprehensible actions was the deliberate destruction of one of the world's great archaeological treasures, two 115-foot-high sandstone statues of Buddha in the city of Bamiyan. At least this action killed no one, unlike the massacre of the ethnic Hazaras who died by the thousands.

Not surprisingly the Taliban enjoyed little support outside their own country. However, one nation aided the fanatics. Pakistan supplied the Taliban with weapons and financial aid. Other entities also supporting the Taliban were wealthy Islamic extremists. One of these was an individual who would play a key role in American military history.

His name was Osama Bin Laden.

Bin Laden was a Saudi who loathed the United States. The founder of the terrorist group al-Qaeda, Bin Laden dedicated his life—and his fortune—to killing Americans. Their coarse behavior and presence in the Middle East, as well as their support of Israel, made them, Bin Laden believed, enemies of Islam.

In 1992 al-Qaeda conducted its first operation against the United States, a bombing of a hotel in Yemen that on occasion housed American troops. Ten months later, in February 1993, one of its disciples attempted to bring down the World Trade Center in New York by exploding a bomb that killed six people and injured more than a thousand. More successful, at least judging by the number of dead, was the subsequent attack upon the U.S. Embassy in Nairobi, Kenya, which killed 224 individuals, not all of them Americans. And in October 2000, Bin Laden's group struck an American naval vessel, the USS *Cole*, in the harbor of Aden, in Yemen. Seventeen sailors were killed.

By then, U.S. intelligence was aware of Bin Laden and his al-Qaeda organization. In response to the earlier attacks, the United States, at the direction of President Bill Clinton, had conducted a missile strike against an al-Qaeda training camp in Afghanistan. But this attack, and what Bin Laden had so far done, were but minor preludes to what would follow.

At 8:42 A.M. on September 11, 2001, a commercial airliner, hijacked by al-Qaeda operatives, deliberately flew into the north tower of New York's World Trade Center. On board the American Airlines Boeing 767 were ninety-two individuals, including the hijackers. Eighteen minutes later, a second plane flew into the south tower. The two crashes soon brought down the Twin Towers and, in total, caused the death of 2,752 people. But al-Qaeda was not finished. At 9:43 A.M. another hijacked airliner, again in kamikaze style, struck the Pentagon, home to America's military, located across the Potomac River from Washington, D.C. A fourth airliner, United Airlines flight 93 heading for San Francisco, also was hijacked. But its passengers, aware of what had occurred in New York and Washington, stormed the hijackers. This caused the plane to crash in a field southeast of Pittsburgh. Most likely, the plane was targeting the White House or the Capitol. All aboard were killed.

September 11, 2001, became, as December 7, 1941, was, a date that for the United States will live in infamy.

Al-Qaeda seemed to have triumphed. It successfully struck the American homeland. And by destroying the World Trade Center and damaging the Pentagon, al-Qaeda had hit two major symbols of American power. While most people around the world were appalled by the events of September 11, many in Islamic countries rejoiced. They believed that the United States and its citizens had gotten what they deserved.

Most certainly, Bin Laden believed that. In 1998 he had published an edict that called on Muslims everywhere to kill Americans wherever and whenever possible. For the al-Qaeda leader, September 11, 2001, was a great victory. He had planned and executed a mighty blow against the infidels.

America's response was swift. Within two weeks U.S. Special Forces and Central Intelligence Agency (CIA) personnel landed in Afghanistan, where al-Qaeda was based and where its leader lived, courtesy of the Taliban. Arming Afghans opposed to the Taliban and simply bribing others, these U.S. forces and their Afghan allies, augmented by high-tech American air assets, overthrew the Taliban, killing many and causing Bin Laden and his people to retreat into the caves of Tora Bora in the mountains that line Afghanistan's border with Pakistan. Despite extensive efforts to find him, efforts that included B-52 air strikes, Bin Laden escaped. He took up residence in Pakistan, from where, often with the complicity of Pakistanis, he would remain for more than ten more years, plotting to kill Americans.

In the aftermath of the September 11 attacks, President George W. Bush vowed that the United States would bring the al-Qaeda leader to justice. Vast American resources, both human and financial, were allocated to this task. For many years, Osama Bin Laden survived, managing his cohorts, hoping to repeat the success of September 11. The latter he was unable to achieve, though not for lack of effort.

Then, on the night of May 2, 2011, U.S. Navy commandos raided a compound in Abbottabad, a town in Pakistan that is home to that nation's military academy. American intelligence officials suspected the compound to be housing Osama Bin Laden. Their suspicions proved correct. He was there. The Americans shot him dead and took his body with them as they departed. Shortly thereafter, his remains, having been placed aboard an American warship, were deposited into the sea.

The raid was daring in the extreme, especially given that the Pakistanis were not told of the incursion. This time it was Americans who rejoiced.

While the Taliban was overthrown in 2001, they had not been eliminated. Many found sanctuary in Pakistan. They would hide—and thrive—in the country's western mountains. Known as the Federally Administered Tribal Areas, these were lands in which Pakistani control was limited. Other Taliban dispersed to the Afghan countryside. There, by coercion or camaraderie, they would rally Afghans to their cause and become a threat to the government that had replaced them.

This government was led by Hamid Karzai. He enjoyed the strong support of the United States and many in Afghanistan as well, including regional warlords whom he constantly would need either to appease or intimidate, or simply bribe.

For Karzai, governing Afghanistan was not possible without massive aid from external sources. This meant primarily the United States, although other nations were called upon to contribute. The United States, in particular its secretary of defense, Donald Rumsfeld, did not believe in "nation building," the phrase that came into use to describe the efforts required to transform Afghanistan into a modern state, one capable of delivering services and security to its citizens. Rumsfeld argued that rebuilding Afghanistan would require huge sums of money (and he was correct) and that it simply was not the task of the United States to construct a nation in Southeast Asia. That responsibility, he believed, belonged to the Afghans themselves.

The result was that, at least initially, America exercised in Afghanistan what scholar Seth G. Jones called "a light footprint." Withdrawals from the U.S. Treasury for the Karzai government were limited, as was assistance from the Pentagon. While eight thousand American soldiers were stationed in Afghanistan in 2002, their role was limited. They were there to kill al-Qaeda operatives and, if necessary, to do the same to the Taliban. They were not there to rebuild the country.

Assisting these troops were soldiers from Britain, Canada, France, the Netherlands, and other countries. They belonged to the North Atlantic Treaty Organization (NATO) and, together with forces from other countries as well as the United States, comprised the International Security Assistance Force (ISAF). Why NATO? Because one of its members, the United States of America, had been attacked. Article V of the treaty states that an attack against one of its member states shall be considered an attack on them all.

The problem was that while the British, Dutch, and Canadians were willing to fight, and did, several other NATO states—Germany and Italy among them—refused to place their soldiers in harm's way. They were unwilling to incur casualties for the sake of Afghanistan. This made ISAF less effective than it might have been.

There was another problem as well. The focus of American leaders, both in the military and at the White House, was shifting. In Washington, Iraq was claiming center stage. Interest in Afghanistan waned as that in Iraq increased. In his fine book *In the Graveyard of Empires*, Professor Seth G. Jones quotes Admiral Mike Mullen, chairman of the Joint Chiefs of Staff: "It is simply a matter of resources, of capacity. In Afghanistan, we do what we can. In Iraq, we do what we must."

By 2005, the situation in Afghanistan had deteriorated. While there had been successes—schools had been built, elections had been held—the failure of the Karzai government to provide security and services to much of the population led to the resurgence of the Taliban. Many people outside Kabul had little use for the central government. They saw it as incompetent and corrupt.

One sign of how bad things had become was the departure from Afghanistan of the French organization Doctors Without Borders. Held in high esteem throughout the world, it had served in Afghanistan for more than twenty years. When four of its workers were shot in the head, the group concluded that Afghanistan was no longer a safe place to provide medical services.

In opposing the Karzai government and the ISAF, the Taliban were ruthless. They kidnapped journalists, threatened schoolteachers, killed civilian aid workers, and assassinated government officials. Confronted by such tactics, American-led forces and their Afghan cohorts were overmatched. Nowhere was this more evident than in the Afghan army and the national police force. Each of these organizations was too small, ill-equipped, and poorly trained. In 2005 and 2006 neither could function effectively.

Recognizing that a fundamental change in America's approach to Afghanistan was necessary, the Bush administration acted. It began to send large numbers of troops to Afghanistan. So did its successor. In March 2008, President Barack Obama ordered twenty-two thousand additional soldiers to be deployed. Late in 2009, he directed that a "surge" in troops take place, which caused thirty thousand more troops to arrive in Afghanistan. By October 2011, after ten years of fighting, the number of U.S. troops in the country had reached ninety-eight thousand.

As commander in chief of the armed forces (a role given to the president by Article II, Section 2 of the U.S. Constitution), President Obama did more than increase troop levels. He fired the troops' commanding officer, General David McKiernan. Advised by the secretary of defense, Robert Gates, Obama believed the general's tactics would not lead to success. McKiernan focused on killing the enemy. Gates wanted a more counter-insurgency effort that aimed at protecting Afghan citizens. The approach was advocated by McKiernan's successor, General Stanley A. McChrystal (who himself was sacked when his indiscreet remarks to a popular newspaper were made public). McKiernan's relief highlighted a fundamental issue confronting the American military in Afghanistan. Should the emphasis be on safeguarding the people of Afghanistan or should the Americans concentrate on taking the fight to the Taliban and al-Qaeda?

Both groups were aided greatly by their ability to use eastern Pakistan as a safe haven. Al-Qaeda operatives would cross over into Afghanistan to strike at their foes, then retreat back into their camps in the Federally Administered Tribal Areas. At times, the Pakistanis assisted the Americans in locating and killing al-Qaeda personnel. Particularly effective in this effort were American unmanned aerial vehicles. The United States employed these lethal devices often, over the public objections of Pakistani leaders. At other times, these leaders, especially those in Pakistan's intelligence service, would provide support to al-Qaeda and to the Taliban. Pakistan's goal was to have a friendly regime along its eastern border. These leaders saw no conflict in helping both sides.

In addition to raising troop levels in Afghanistan, Presidents Bush and Obama increased financial aid. Rejecting the notion that nation building was not an American role, the United States began an effort to rebuild that country. The funding allocated to Afghanistan was substantial. By 2010, it added up to $18.8 billion, with most of that coming in the later years. By 2011, the monthly expenditure was $320 million.

What was this money spent on? The answer is roads, schools, hospitals, generating plants, agricultural assistance, and other worthwhile endeavors. Although large sums evaporated due to waste and fraud, many projects were deemed successful. For example, according to the *Washington Post* of June 9, 2011, 680 schools were constructed or repaired. And these, no doubt, were open to females.

Despite some successes, failures in the reconstruction effort were numerous. For example, an American-led project to upgrade southern Afghanistan's Kajaki hydroelectric plant went awry, with some $260 million expended. A project to upgrade a power plant in Kabul also failed, as the plant remained largely idle after the United States invested approximately $300 million. But the most compelling example of the difficulty the United States faced in building a modern Afghan state centered on road construction, something an infrastructure-poor Afghanistan desperately needed. Over a period of several years, the United States directed vast sums of money into the building of roads. Yet, as the *Wall Street Journal* reported, roads indeed were built, but they cost more than they should have and covered far fewer miles than planned. "You can find programs and projects that have been successful," said Kai Eider, a Norwegian diplomat running U.N. activities in Afghanistan for a time, "but for me it is quite obvious that huge amounts of money have been misspent." The newspaper pointed out one such example: a typical gravel road in Afghanistan was supposed to have cost some $290,000 per mile. Yet for every mile constructed, America's Afghanistan Strategic Roads Project spent $2.8 million.

Another example of the failures the United States experienced in its nonmilitary efforts in Afghanistan dealt with the effort to build a consulate in the northern region of the country. This time, it was the *Washington Post* that reported the story. The consulate was to be constructed in the town of Masar-e Sharif. Yet, after spending some $80 million, the project was abandoned. The reason given was security concerns. With U.S. troops leaving the country and Afghan national forces unequal to their task, it became too dangerous for U.S. officials to work there.

The huge expense incurred to aid Afghanistan troubled many in the United States. Concerned with their own country's fiscal well-being, they were troubled by the mismatch at home between revenues and expenditures. Concerns increased during 2010 and 2011, becoming a factor in Washington's decision making. Of greater significance, however, was the number of casualties the war was causing. As of July 2013, 2,236 U.S. soldiers had been killed in Afghanistan. More than 12,000 had been wounded.

The cost to Americans of their Afghan endeavor, both financial and in lives lost, was such that opposition to the war became substantial. Aware of these concerns, believing al-Qaeda had been neutralized, and anxious to redirect U.S. resources to the home front, President Obama announced a timetable for the withdrawal of U.S. troops from Afghanistan. By the summer of 2012, thirty-three thousand men and women were to be withdrawn. That would leave sixty-eight thousand troops in country. Their departure would continue during 2014, so that, by that year or the following, America's military presence in Afghanistan would be minimal. "America," said the president, "it is time to focus on nation-building at home."

When the U.S. troops are home and the ISAF is disbanded, will the effort, again one that has consumed American dollars and American lives, have been worth it? Many will say no. Others will answer in the positive, pointing to the damage done to al-Qaeda and to the progress made in improving the daily life of ordinary Afghans.

The key issue is whether the progress will be sustainable once the Americans have left. That depends on whether the Karzai government and its successors can survive without having U.S. troops on the ground.

That, in turn, depends on the capability of the new American-trained Afghan National Army. Will it fill the vacuum created when Uncle Sam's soldiers no longer are present? Perhaps it will, but maintaining this army is estimated to require approximately $4 billion each year, money the Afghan government does not have.

Even if it did, the Afghan central governments are not likely to make Afghanistan a place where its citizens are safe and free, and where the progress made so far can continue. A culture of corruption—so prevalent in Afghanistan—will remain as will the pull of tribal loyalties. Assassinations and rebellion, moreover, are part of the country's political traditions, and there is no reason to believe they have been forsaken. Add to these the tenacity of the Taliban and future prospects become rather bleak.

In the days of its empire, the British tried and failed in Afghanistan. Much later, so did the Soviets. Regrettably, America is likely to follow their examples.

Was America's entry into Afghanistan necessary?

Yes, it was. Bin Laden and al-Qaeda had declared war on the United States and its citizens. They intended to bring great harm to Americans, and had done so already. President Bush's response was swift and effective. He ordered CIA personnel and U.S. Special Forces to enter Afghanistan and destroy al-Qaeda and its Taliban hosts. They arrived shortly after September 11, 2001, and, with great skill, toppled the Taliban and sent Bin Laden fleeing into Pakistan.

How did the CIA and Special Forces defeat their enemy?

Instead of employing massive conventional forces, as the Russians had done, the United States mounted a military campaign featuring small detachments of U.S. Special Forces and CIA operatives, armed with AK-47 assault rifles, medical supplies, sophisticated communications gear, and, according to *MHQ* journal, "three large boxes whose contents tipped the scales at 45 pounds: the weight of three million dollars in $100 bills." These units—there were only seven of them—allied with Afghans opposed to the Taliban and went into battle. Employing both modern weapons and some not so modern (horse cavalry), they defeated their foe, though not without the assistance of considerable American airpower. The campaign lasted just twenty-seven days, from October 19, 2001, to November 14. 2001. No Americans were killed. Taliban and al-Qaeda deaths were in the thousands.

Did other nations besides the United States engage in Afghanistan?

Yes, they did. True, the bulk of the military effort to stabilize Afghanistan once the Taliban were removed from power was American. But Britain, France, Germany, and other nations participated. Germany sent 4,701 troops to Afghanistan, though, as mentioned earlier, they were limited to no-combat roles. Not so the French. In addition to ground troops, they deployed units of the *Armee del'Air*, the French air force. It began operations early on and, employing Mirage and Super Entendard jet fighters, flew some seventy-two hundred sorties over a period of six years.

One nation that goes to war when the United States goes to war is Australia. In Korea, in Vietnam, in the Gulf, and in Iraq, troops from "Down Under" joined their American comrades in battle. So too in Afghanistan, where Australian Special Forces displayed their usual skill and courage.

What is likely to happen once the Americans depart in 2014?

If, as planned, the American military leaves Afghanistan in 2014, the security of its citizens and of the central government will rest on the shoulders of the Afghan national police and Afghan army. Neither organization appears equal to the task, despite efforts by ISAF troops to train and equip the personnel involved. Additionally, the central government is in need of financial assistance. Recognizing this need, donor nations, urged on by the United States, in July 2012 pledged $16 billion over four years. These funds, if they materialize, are to be directed toward civil projects. The hope is that they will enable the government in Kabul to continue the construction of a modern state, one that provides security and prosperity to its citizens.

What of the military situation? What will prevent a resurgence of the Taliban when the United States and other ISAF troops no longer are present? The hope is that the Afghans themselves will keep the Taliban from power. However, in May 2012 Leon Panetta, the American secretary of defense, said the United States would have "an enduring presence" in Afghanistan after 2014. What he meant was that U.S. troops would continue to train and support the Afghan forces. Whether they will engage in combat was not addressed.

If they do not, if American soldiers keep to the sidelines when the bullets start to fly, then the Taliban and al-Qaeda will gain in strength. The result will be pressure on the government in Kabul. Whether it will then survive is a problematic question to answer. If the government doesn't survive, America's war in Afghanistan, its longest war, will have been in vain, because al-Qaeda and the Taliban will rise again.

SELECTED READINGS

ONE—INDEPENDENCE

Allison, Robert J., *The American Revolution: A Concise History*, Oxford University Press, Oxford, 2011.

Billias, George Athan, editor, *George Washington's Generals*, William Morrow and Company, New York, 1964.

Ferling, John, *Almost a Miracle: The American Victory in the War of Independence*, Oxford University Press, Oxford, 2007.

Golway, Terry, *Washington's General: Nathanael Greene and the Triumph of the American Revolution*, Henry Holt and Company, New York, 2005.

Hairr, John, *Guilford Courthouse*, DeCapa Press, Cambridge, 2002.

Harvey, Robert, *A Few Bloody Noses: The Realities and Mythologies of the American Revolution*, The Overlook Press, Woodstock and New York, 2001.

Hibbert, Christopher, *Redcoats and Rebels: The American Revolution Through British Eyes*, W.W. Norton and Company, New York, 1990.

Ketchum, Richard M., *Victory at Yorktown: The Campaign That Won the American Revolution*, Henry Holt and Company, New York, 2004.

Marston, Daniel, *The American Revolution 1774–1783*, Osprey, Oxford, 2002.

Matloff, Maurice, general editor, *The Revolutionary War*, David McKay, undated.

Mitchell, Joseph B., *Decisive Battles of the American Revolution*, Westholme Publishing Company, Yardley, 1962.

Stephenson, Michael, *Patriot Battles: How the War of Independence Was Fought*, HarperCollins, New York, 2007.

Wood, Gordon S., *The American Revolution: A History*, Weidenfeld and Nicolson, London, 2003

TWO—1812

Benn, Carl, *The War of 1812*, Osprey, Oxford, 2002.

Bickman, Troy, *The Weight of Vengeance: The United States, the British Empire, and the War of 1812*, Oxford University Press, Oxford, 2012.

Daughan, George C., *1812 The Navy's War*, Basic Books, New York, 2011.

Dudley, Wade G., *Splintering the Wooden Wall: The British Blockade of the United States, 1812–1815*, Naval Institute Press, Annapolis, 2003.

Fowler, William M. Jr., *Jack Tars & Commodores: The American Navy 1783–1815*, Houghton Mifflin Company, Boston, 1984.

Gardiner, Robert, editor, *The Naval War of 1812*, Chatham Publishing, London, 1998.

Hitsman, J. Mackay, updated by Donald E. Graves, *The Incredible War of 1812: A Military History*, Robin Brass Studio, Toronto, 1999.

Latimer, Jon, *1812: War with America*, Belknap Press, Cambridge, 2007.

McCranie, Kevin D., *Utmost Gallantry: The U.S. and Royal Navies at Sea in the War of 1812*, Naval Institute Press, Annapolis, 2011.

Rutland, Robert Allen, *James Madison: The Founding Father*, Macmillan Publishing Company, New York, 1987.

Robotti, Frances Diane, and Jame Vescovi, *The USS Essex and the Birth of the American Navy*, Adams Media Corp., Holbrook, 1999.

Sweetman, Jack, *American Naval History,* Naval Institute Press, Annapolis, 1991.

THREE—MEXICO

Bauer, K. Jack, *The Mexican War 1846–1848*, University of Nebraska Press, Lincoln and London, 1974.

Eisenhower, John S. D., *So Far from God: The U.S. War With Mexico 1846–1848*, University of Oklahoma Press, Norman, 2000. Originally published by Random House in 1989.

Henry, Robert Selph, *The Story of the Mexican War*, DeCapo Press, New York. Copyright 1950 by the Bobbs-Merrill Company.

Meed, Douglas V., *The Mexican War 1846–1848*, Osprey, Oxford, 2002.

Seigenthaler, John, *James K. Polk*, Henry Holt and Company, New York, 2003.

Winders, Richard Bruce, *Mr. Polk's Army: The American Military Experience in the Mexican War*, Texas A & M University Press, College Station, 1997.

FOUR—BETWEEN THE STATES

Ades, Harry, *The Little Book of the Civil War*, Barnes and Noble, New York, 2002.

Gallagher, Gary W., Stephen D. Engle, Robert K. Krick, and Joseph T. Glatthaar, *The American Civil War: This Mighty Scourge of War*, Osprey, Oxford, 2003.

Masur, Louis P., *The American Civil War: A Concise History*, Oxford University Press, Oxford, 2011.

McPherson, James M., *Battle Cry of Freedom: The Civil War Era*, Oxford University Press, New York, 1988.

McPherson, James M., *This Mighty Scourge: Perspectives on the Civil War*, Oxford University Press, New York, 2007.

McWhinney, Grady, *The Civil War: A Concise Account by a Noted Southern Historian*, McWhinney Foundation Press, Abilene, 2005.

Neillands, Robin H., *Grant: The Man Who Won the Civil War*, Cold Spring Press, Cold Spring Harbor, 2004.

Reid, Brian Holden, *The American Civil War and the Wars of the Industrial Revolution*, Cassell and Company, London, 1999.

Sears, Stephen W., *Landscape Turned Red: The Battle of Antietam*, Ticknor and Fields, New Haven and New York, 1983.

Sheehan-Dean, Aaron, editor, *Struggle for a Vast Future: The American Civil War*, Osprey, Oxford, 2006.

Sweetman, Jack, *American Naval History*, Naval Institute Press, Annapolis, 1991.

Taaffe, Stephen R., *Commanding the Army of the Potomac*, University Press of Kansas, Lawrence, 2006.

Williams, T. Harry, *Lincoln and his Generals*, Gramercy Books, New York, 1952.

FIVE—SPAIN

Bradford, James C., editor, *Crucible of Empire: The Spanish-American War & Its Aftermath*, Naval Institute Press, Annapolis, 1993.

Field, Ron, *Buffalo Soldiers 1892–1918*, Osprey, Oxford, 2005.

Goldstein, Donald M., and Katherine V. Dillon, *The Spanish-American War*, Brassey's, Washington, 1998.

Halstead, Murat, *The Full Official History of the War With Spain*, Dominion, Chicago, 1899.

Konstam, Angus, *San Juan Hill: America's Emergence as a World Power*, Osprey, Oxford, 2005.

Nofi, Albert A., *The Spanish-American War, 1898*, Combined Books, Pennsylvania, 1996.

O'Toole, G. J. A., *The Spanish War: An American Epic*, W.W. Norton and Company, New York, 1984.

Silby, David J., *A War of Frontier and Empire: The Philippine-American War, 1899–1902*, Hill and Wang, New York, 2007.

SIX—WORLD WAR I

Bowen, Ezra, *Knights of the Air*, Time-Life Books, Alexandria, 1980.

Farwell, Byron, *Over There: The United States in the Great War, 1917–1918*, W.W. Norton and Company, New York, 1999.

Franks, Norman, *American Aces of World War I*, Osprey, Oxford, 2001.

Fussell, Paul, *The Great War and Modern Memory*, Sterling, New York, 2009.

Hart, B. H. Liddell, *The Real War: 1914–1918*, Little Brown and Company, Boston, 1930.

Hindenburg, Paul von, edited by Charles Messenger, *The Great War*, Greenhill Books, London, 2006.

Hough, Richard, *The Great War at Sea: 1914–1918*, Oxford University Press, Oxford, 1983.

Keegan, John, *The First World War,* Alfred A. Knopf, New York, 1999.

Lengel, Edward G., *To Conquer Hell: The Meuse-Argonne, 1918*, Henry Holt and Company, New York, 2008.

Massie, Robert K., *Castles of Steel: Britain, Germany, and the Winning of the Great War at Sea,* Random House, New York, 2003.

Neiberg, Michael S., *Fighting the Great War: A Global History*, Harvard University Press, Cambridge, 2005.

Prior, Robin, and Trevor Wilson, *The First World War*, Cassell, London, 1999.

Strachan, Hew, *The First World War*, Viking, New York, 2003.

Terraine, John, *Douglas Haig: The Educated Soldier*, Hutchinson, London, 1963.

Terraine, John, *The U-Boat Wars: 1916–1945*, G. P. Putnam's Sons, New York, 1989.

Willmott, H. P., *World War I*, DK, New York, 2003.

Votaw, John F., *The American Expeditionary Forces in World War I*, Osprey, 2005.

SEVEN—WORLD WAR II

The War in the Pacific

Dull, Paul S., *A Battle History of the Imperial Japanese Navy (1941–1945)*, Naval Institute Press, Annapolis, 1978.

Grove, Philip D., *Midway 1942*, Brassey's, London, 2004.

Hastings, Max, *Retribution: The Battle for Japan, 1941–45*, Alfred A. Knopf, New York, 2008.

Marston, Daniel, editor, *The Pacific War Companion: From Pearl Harbor to Hiroshima*, Osprey, Oxford, 2005.

Polmar, Norman, *The Enola Gay: The B-29 That Dropped the Atomic Bomb on Hiroshima*, The Smithsonian Institution and Brassey's, Washington, 2004.

Potter, E. B., *Nimitz*, Naval Institute Press, Annapolis, 1976.

Spector, Ronald H., *Eagle Against the Sun: The American War with Japan*, The Free Press, New York, 1985.

Willmott, H. P., *Pearl Harbor*, Cassell and Company, London, 2001.

The Battle of the Atlantic

Dallies-Labourdette, Jean-Philippe, *U-Boote 1935–1945 The History of the Kriegsmarine U-Boats*, Histoire & Collections, Paris, undated.

Doenitz, Grand Admiral Karl, translated by R. H. Stevens in collaboration with David Woodward, *Memoirs: Ten Years and Twenty Days*, Naval Institute Press, Annapolis, 1959.

Edwards, Bernard, *Donitz and the Wolfpacks*, Brockingham Press, London, 1999.

Hughes, Terry, and John Costello, *The Battle of the Atlantic*, Dial Press/James Wack, New York, 1977.

Showell, Jak P., *U-Boat Command and the Battle of the Atlantic*, Vanwell Publishing, St. Catherine's, 1989.

Syrett, David, *The Defeat of the German U-boats: The Battle of the Atlantic*, University of South Carolina Press, Columbia, 1994.

Van der Vat, Dan, *The Atlantic Campaign: World War II's Great Struggle at Sea*, Harper & Row, New York, 1988.

The War in North Africa and in Europe

Atkinson, Rick, *An Army at Dawn: The War in North Africa, 1942–1943*, Henry Holt and Company, New York, 2002.

Badsey, Stephen, *Normandy, 1944: Allied Landings and Breakout*, Barnes and Noble/Osprey, 2000.

Davies, Norman, *No Simple Victory, World War II in Europe, 1939–1945*, Viking, New York, 2007.

Eisenhower, Dwight D., *Crusade in Europe*, Doubleday and Company, Garden City, 1948.

Korda, Michael, *Ike: An American Hero*, HarperCollins, New York, 2007.

Messenger, Charles, *The D-Day Atlas*, Thames and Hudson, New York, 2004.

Penrose, Jane, editor, *The D-Day Companion: Leading Historians Explore History's Greatest Amphibious Assault*, The National D-Day Museum, New Orleans, 2004.

Wilt, Alan F., *The Atlantic Wall: Rommel's Plan to Stop the Allied Invasion*, Enigma Books, New York, 2004.

The War in the Air

Carter, Ian, *Fighter Command 1939–1945*, Ian Allan, Hersham, 2002.

Cooper, Matthew, *The German Air Force 1933–1945: An Anatomy of Failure*, Jane's, London, 1981.

Copp, DeWitt S., *Forged in Fire: Strategy and Decisions in the Airwar over Europe 1940–1945*, Doubleday and Company, Garden City, 1982.

Goodson, James A., *Tumult in the Clouds*, William Kimber, London, 1983.

Hansen, Randall, *Fire and Fury: The Allied Bombing of Germany, 1942–1945*, NAL Caliber, New York, 2009.

Harvey, Maurice, *The Allied Bomber War 1939–1945*, Spellmount, Tunbridge Wells, 1992.

Hastings, Max, *Bomber Command: The Myths and Realities of the Strategic Bombing Offensive 1939–1945*, Dial Press/James Wade, New York, 1979.

Lyall, Gavin, editor, *The War in the Air: The Royal Air Force in World War II*, William Morrow and Company, New York, 1969.

McFarland, Stephen L., and Wesley Phillips Newton, *To Command the Sky: The Battle for Air Superiority over Germany, 1942–1945*, Smithsonian Institution Press, Washington, 1991.

Miller, Donald L., *Masters of the Air: America's Bomber Boys Who Fought the Air War Against Nazi Germany*, Simon and Shuster, New York, 2006.

Parton, James, *Air Force Spoken Here: General Ira Eaker and the Command of the Air*, Adler & Adler, Bethesda, 1986.

The Second World War in General

Barnett, Correlli, *Engage the Enemy More Closely: The Royal Navy in the Second World War*, W.W. Norton and Company, New York and London, 1991.

Bevor, Anthony, *The Second World War*, Little Brown and Company, New York, 2012.

Borneman, Walter R., *The Admirals: Nimitz, Halsey, Leahy, and King—The Five-Star Admirals Who Won the War at Sea*, Little Brown and Company, New York, 2012.

Burns, James MacGregor, *Roosevelt: The Soldier of Freedom*, Konecky & Konecky, New York, 1970.

Corrigan, Gordon, *The Second World War: A Military History*, Thomas Dunne Books, New York, 2010.

Hart, B. H. Liddell, *History of the Second World War*, Konecky & Konecky, Old Saybrook, 1970.

Keegan, John, *The Second World War*, Viking, New York, 1989.

Kimball, Warren F., *Forged in War: Churchill, Roosevelt, and the Second World War*, HarperCollins, London, 1997.

Roberts, Andrew, *The Storm of War: A New History of the Second World War*, HarperCollins, New York, 2011.

Roskill, S. W., *White Ensign: The British Navy at War, 1939–1945*, United States Naval Institute, Annapolis, 1960.

Ruge, Friedrich, translated by Commander M. G. Saunders, R.N., *Der Seekrieg, The German Navy's Story 1939–1945*, United States Naval Institute, Annapolis, 1957.

Sulzberger, C. L., *The American Heritage Picture History of World War Two*, American Heritage/Bonanza Books, 1966.

Willmott, H. P., *The Great Crusade: A New Complete History of the Second World War*, revised edition, Potomac Books, Washington, 2008.

EIGHT—KOREA

Crane, Conrad C., *American Airpower Strategy in Korea: 1950–1953*, University of Kansas Press, Lawrence, 2000.

Davis, Larry, *The 4th Fighter Wing in the Korean War*, Schiffer Military History, Atglen, 2001.

Fehrenbach, T. R., *This Kind of War: The Classic Korean War History*, Potomac Books, Dulles, Virginia, 2008.

Futrell, Robert F., *The United States Air Force in Korea*, U. S. Air Force, Washington, 1982.

Golstein, Donald M., and Harry J. Maihafer, *The Korean War: The Story and Photographs*, Brassey's, Washington, 2000.

Halberstam, David, *The Coldest Winter: America and the Korean War*, Hyperion, New York, 2007.

Hallion, Richard P., *The Naval Air War in Korea*, The Nautical and Aviation Publishing Company of America, Baltimore, 1986.

Hastings, Max, *The Korean War*, Simon and Schuster, New York, 1987.

Hickey, Michael, *The Korean War: The West Confronts Communism*, The Overlook Press, Woodstock and New York, 2000.

Lansdown, John R. P., *With the Carriers in Korea: The Sea and Air War in SE Asia, 1950–1953*, Crecy, Wilmslow, 1997.

Sherwood, John Darrell, *Officers in Flight Suits: The Story of American Air Force Fighter Pilots in the Korean War*, New York University Press, New York, 1996.

NINE—VIETNAM

Frankum, Ronald B. Jr., *Like Rolling Thunder: The Air War in Vietnam, 1964–1975*, Bowman and Littlefield, Lanham, 2005.

Goldstein, Donald M., Katherine V. Dillon, and J. Michael Wenger, *The Vietnam War: The Story and Photographs*, Brassey's, Herndon, 1994.

Herring, George C., *America's Longest War: The United States and Vietnam, 1950–1975*, second edition, Alfred A. Knopf, New York, 1986.

Karnow, Stanley, *Vietnam: A History*, Viking, New York, 1991.

Michel, Marshall L. III, *The 11 Days of Christmas: America's Last Vietnam Battle*, Encounter Books, San Francisco, 2002.

Murray, Aaron R., editor, *Vietnam War Battles and Leaders*, DK, New York, 2004.

Nichols, John B., and Barrett Tillman, *On Yankee Station: The Naval Air War over Vietnam*, Naval Institute Press, Annapolis, 2001.

Palmer, Bruce Jr., *25 Year War: America's Military Role in Vietnam*, University Press of Kentucky, Lexington, 1984.

Palmer, Dave Richard, *Summons of the Trumpet: U.S.-Vietnam in Perspective*, Presidio, Novato, 1982.

Rasimus, Ed, *When Thunder Rolled: An F-105 Pilot over Vietnam*, Smithsonian, Washington, 2003.

Summers, Harry G. Jr., *The Vietnam War Almanac*, Ballantine, New York, 1985.

Thompson, Wayne, *To Hanoi and Back: The United States Air Force and North Vietnam, 1966–1973*, Smithsonian, Washington, 2000.

Tucker, Spencer C., editor, *The Encyclopedia of the Vietnam War: A Political, Social and Military History*, Oxford, 1998.

Van De Mar, Brian, *Into the Quagmire: Lyndon Johnson and the Escalation of the Vietnam War*, Oxford University Press, Oxford, 1991.

Victory in Vietnam: The Official History of the People's Army of Vietnam, The Military Institute of Vietnam, translated by Merle L. Pribbenow, University Press of Kansas, Lawrence, 1994.

Willbanks, James H., *The Tet Offensive: A Concise History*, Columbia University Press, New York, 2007.

TEN—THE GULF

Clancy, Tom, with General Fred Franks Jr., *Into the Storm: A Study in Command*, G. P. Putnam's Sons, New York, 1997.

De La Billiere, General Sir Peter, *Storm Command: A Personal Account of the Gulf War*, Motivate Publishing, Dubai, 1992.

Finlan, Alastair, *The Gulf War 1991*, Osprey, Oxford 2003.

Friedrich, Otto, editor, *Desert Storm: The War in the Persian Gulf*, Time Warner, New York, 1991.

Glosson, General Buster, *War with Iraq: Critical Lessons*, Glosson Family Foundation, Charlotte, 2003.

Jaco, Charles, *The Gulf War: The Complete Idiot's Guide to*, Alpha Books, Indianapolis, 2002.

Macgregor, Douglas, *Warrior's Rage: The Great Tank Battle of 73 Easting*, Naval Institute Press, Annapolis, 2009.

Marolda, Edward J., and Robert J. Schneller Jr., *Shield and Sword: The United States Navy and the Persian Gulf War*, Naval Institute Press, Annapolis, 2001.

Rottman, Gordon L., *Armies of the Gulf War*, Osprey, Oxford, 1992.

Scales, Brigadier General Robert H. Jr., director, Desert Storm Study Project, *Certain Victory: The U. S. Army in the Gulf War*, Office of the Chief of Staff, United States Army, Washington, 1993.

Schwarzkopf, H. Norman, written with Peter Petre, *It Doesn't Take a Hero: The Autobiography* (of General H. Norman Schwarzkopf), Bantam Books, New York, 1992.

Sweetman, Jack, *American Naval History: An Illustrated Chronology of the U.S. Navy and Marine Corps, 1775–Present*, Naval Institute Press, Annapolis, 1991.

Zaloga, Steven J., *M1 Abrams Main Battle Tank 1982–92*, Osprey, Oxford, 1993.

Zaloga, Steven J., *M1 Abrams vs T-72 Ural: Operation Desert Storm 1991*, Osprey, Oxford, 2009.

ELEVEN—IRAQ

Fontenot, Gregory, E. J. Degen, and David Tohn, *On Point: The United States Army in Operation Iraqi Freedom*, Naval Institute Press edition, 2005.

Fox, Robert, *Iraq Campaign 2003: Royal Navy and Royal Marines,* Agenda Publishing, London, 2003.

Gordon, Michael R., and General Bernard E. Trainor, *Cobra II: The Inside Story of the Invasion and Occupation of Iraq*, Pantheon Books, New York, 2006.

Murray, Williamson, and Major General Robert H. Scales Jr., *The Iraq War, A Military History*, Belknap Press, Cambridge, 2003.

Purdum, Todd S., and the staff of the *New York Times, A Time of Our Choosing: America's War in Iraq*, Times Books (Henry Holt and Company), New York, 2003.

Reynolds, Colonel Nicholas E., *Basrah, Baghdad, and Beyond: The U.S. Marine Corps in the Second Iraq War*, Naval Institute Press, Annapolis, 2005.

Rumsfeld, Donald, *Known and Unknown: A Memoir*, Sentinel, New York, 2011.

Zucchino, David, *Thunder Run: The Armored Strike to Capture Baghdad*, Atlantic Monthly Press, New York, 2004.

TWELVE—AFGHANISTAN

Jones, Seth G., *In the Graveyard of Empires: America's War in Afghanistan*, W.W. Norton and Company, New York, 2009.

Maley, William, *The Afghanistan Wars*, Palgreve, New York, 2002.

Neumann, Ronald E., *The Other War: Winning and Losing in Afghanistan*, Potomac Books, Washington, D.C., 2009.

INDEX

Page numbers in *italic* indicate maps.